Italy Today

Studies in Modern European History

Frank J. Coppa
General Editor

Vol. 16

PETER LANG
New York • Washington, D.C./Baltimore • Boston
Bern • Frankfurt am Main • Berlin • Vienna • Paris

Mario B. Mignone

Italy Today

At the Crossroads
of the New Millennium

Revised Edition

PETER LANG
New York • Washington, D.C./Baltimore • Boston
Bern • Frankfurt am Main • Berlin • Vienna • Paris

Library of Congress Cataloging-in-Publication Data

Mignone, Mario B.
Italy today: at the crossroads of the new
millennium, revised edition/ Mario B. Mignone. —Rev. ed.
p. cm. — (Studies in modern European history; vol. 16)
1. Italy—Politics and government—1994– . 2. Italy—Economic conditions—1994– .
3. Italy—Social conditions—1994– . 4. Italy—Social conditions. I. Title. II. Series.
JN5451.M53   320.945'09'045—dc21   98-12025
ISBN 0-8204-4041-8
ISSN 0893-6897

Die Deutsche Bibliothek-CIP-Einheitsaufnahme

Mignone, Mario B.:
Italy today: at the crossroads of the new millennium, revised edition/
Mario B. Mignone. –New York; Washington, D.C./Baltimore; Boston; Bern;
Frankfurt am Main; Berlin; Vienna; Paris: Lang.
(Studies in modern European history; Vol. 16)
ISBN 0-8204-4041-8
NE: GT

To my wife Lois
and daughters Pamela, Cristina, and Elizabeth

Table of Contents

Preface

The second edition of *Italy Today* was written not just to update a text that had originally been written when major political events were taking place in Italy, but also to respond to requests by colleagues, friends, and students to discuss cultural manifestations that are of great importance to the understanding of contemporary Italy and that had not been previously covered. In this edition, the conventional manner of looking at Italian politics, economics, and society in a linear way, as if postwar Italian history went forward in a consistent manner under the exclusive influence of palpable dynamics, has been broadened to include cultural transformation and consumption of cultural products. In relating the purchase and use of cultural products to the social context in which they become meaningful as indicators of taste and social distinction, much can be said about the country.

The understanding of a country as reflected through its politics, economics, and society will certainly be richer if the assessment is conducted in the wider context of its culture; after all, in a complex society, culture is dynamic; it is both shaped by and shapes socioeconomic stratifications. The word culture here is meant to imply the complex whole that includes knowledge, belief, art, morals, law, custom, and any other capabilities and habits acquired by man as a member of society ("fine arts," "serious" music, philosophy as well as popular music, social rituals, popular traditions, folklore, eating habits, celebrations, and dress codes). These activities need to be understood not just in intrinsic (aesthetic, intellectual, formal) terms but also sociologically and anthropologically in terms of such things as norms of social behavior, the allocation of status and power in society, and the reproduction of values and beliefs. And the understanding of a country could be even richer if we use today's study practice of culture, which stresses heterogeneity, change, intercultural borrowing, and the way people manipulate cultural forms in pursuing diverse and often conflicting interests. Yes, the representation of a nation must also include the way its people use cultural forms as they make daily sense of their diverse, often contradictory experiences in social, political, and economic contexts that are in confusing motion.

In this kind of assessment of contemporary Italy, not only must we rely on the contribution and practice of recent cultural studies, but we must both broaden the focus of our attention and deflate old clichés and perspectives. Anyone who studies Italy comes up frequently against a series of conventional or stereotyped notions about the country, its people, its institutions, both in everyday common sense and in academic scholarship. One of the major problems with the earlier studies was the narrowness of focus. Because of the Cold War preoccupations and Italy being a key member of NATO, most studies were overly focused on politics and tended to assess Italian democracy with suspicion. Another major problem was the assumption about Mediterranean backwardness, which not only inspired the overall focus on family and politics, but also played down Italy's history and social and cultural complexity by simply considering the country as an exotic "Other" far removed from the Western reality.

We must also avoid making the mistake of many Anglo-American anthropologists who focused on small communities and tended to treat local cultural forms as homogeneous and fixed. In doing so, we must challenge the classic studies of politics, family, and gender that polarized the opposition between traditional and modern that underlies the Mediterranean perspective. Still persisting today, this perspective has been mainly set in rural or small-town and southern locales. Although the studies were carried out during years of radical social, economic, and cultural transformation, change was rarely built into their representations. Although Italy has changed more in the last thirty years than in the previous two thousand, a profound change not experienced by any other nation in such a short time, the studies of culture that were supposed to mirror such changes often treated culture in terms of rigid "codes" or syndromes. Earlier studies also made crude distinctions between elite and grass-roots ideas, failing to consider the role of culture as a means of drawing fine social distinctions in years of great socioeconomic mobility.

While questioning assessments based on the polarized oppositions of *traditional* and *modern*, it is important to see how past and present

interpenetrate, how the *traditional* may be formulated as people pursue their own interests in very *modern* circumstances. We should criti-
cally discuss the wide claim of Italy as a nation culturally split between
North and South, as a country whose inhabitants have a weak national identity and a strong inward-looking attachment to the locality
and the family. Moreover, we should identify some distinctive cultural
traits, including strong subnational (localistic and regionalistic) identities and preference for personalistic forms of political action, clientelism,
and corruption. We should see how and why local specificity is now
celebrated.

In trying to define the Italian national identity, it is very important
to identify those social problems that tend to be particularly sensitized
and important to Italy's national identity. In Italy, national identity in
no way may be seen as being reflected through its capital, as is the
case in some other European countries. In France, for example, Paris
is the seat of government—it contains the largest concentration of
population and it is the center of the French economy, academic life,
artistic culture, sports, and tourism. Italy, by comparison, seems almost centerless. Its financial and commercial capital is Milan. Its industry tends to be concentrated in the North. Florence is at the heart
of Italy's language and high culture. Tourists are as likely to be attracted by Florence as by Venice, Rome, Capri, or Taormina.

In the process of questioning old cliches, the fundamental issue of
what Italy is as a nation is raised. Is it a social fiction with no fixed
identity? Does the fact that a strong civic consciousness and a developed sense of the nation-state, said to be found in the "mature democracies," are held to be lacking in Italy, where "familism" and local
identities allegedly hold sway, justify the view that such Italian peculiarities must be turned into pathological abnormalities? The very fact
that Italy has remained uniquely plurilingual, with not only a very large
number of dialects that are still used by many speakers but also a
smaller yet still significant number of minority languages, including
Albanian, Greek, German, and Ladin, shows a profound heterogeneity of the country. However, the linguistic diversity of the peninsula
and islands, so often used as a sign of a weak national culture, is
actually the basis of a rich cultural pluralism.

This book was written under the assumption that the reader has no
knowledge of Italy or of Italian culture and history. Of course, the
reader who has some acquaintance with the history of fascism
or the development of Europe since World War II will be at an advan-

tage, as will the reader who has some grounding in economics and politics.

I have been critical of many things in Italy, but mostly in the way that a progressive minded Italian might be critical. This book tries to look at Italy from within, more from an Italian than an American point of view, and it takes for granted all that is admirable about Italian civilization. Although I have spent a good part of my adult life in the U.S., I was born in Italy and lived there until I was 20 years old. Since then, I have returned two or three times a year to teach, do research, and see friends and relatives.

A general book such as this has had to rely greatly on other people's research; the list of consulted works gives a good indication of my indebtedness. Those scholars have enabled me, through their writings, to come to a better understanding of the complexities of postwar Italy and to substantiate my own assessment. I would also like to thank those friends who have read some of the chapters and given me valuable advice; in particular Charles Franco, Mario Aste, and Paolo Possiedi for some keen suggestions; Senator Kenneth P. La Valle for his balanced views on politics and for his support and encouragement; Franco Borrelli from *America Oggi*, the American daily in the Italian language, for statistical data and specific information; my son-in-law Daniel Salzman for his informative views on mass culture and the mass media; and scores of other friends who have aided my efforts, especially the members of the Executive Council of the Center for Italian Studies at the State University of New York at Stony Brook: Anthony Marano-Ducarne, Josephine Fusco, Paul Ferrotti, Vincent Mannino, Velio Marsocci, Lou Parrillo, Devon Postiglione, Rocco Rossini, and Joseph Tursi.

State University of New York at Stony Brook
August 1997

Regional Italy since 1919 (adapted from C. Duggan, *A Concise History of Italy*, Cambridge, 1994, p. 197)

Italy and its regions with their capitals. A degree of decentralization of power to the regions was established by the new constitution (1948) but came into force only in the 1970s. Fifteen of these regions have an ordinary statute; the remaining five have a special statute which gives them greater political and administrative autonomy. These are the three border regions of Valle d'Aosta, Trentino-Alto Adige, and Friuli-Venezia Giulia and the islands of Sicily and Sardinia. Each region is further divided into provinces (95 in all), which in turn are subdivided into comuni (municipalities).

Introduction

When I begin to teach my course on modern Italy or give a lecture on the topic, I ask those present to tell me with what they associate Italy and the Italians. The spontaneous reactions do not change much from situation to situation; people's responses vary from excitement to bewilderment. "Italians! They are good singers." "Italy is a good place for a vacation; there is sun, spaghetti, and art." "Italians have fine hands; they have a real sense for beauty." Many associate the name of Italy and of the Italians with "Mafia," "pizza," "the Catholic Church," "close-knit families," "political chaos," "the Romans," "fine art," "strikes," and "gusto for life." Anyone with even little knowledge of Italy and the Italians will admit that these clichés refer to a social, political, and economic reality that only partially resembles today's Italy.

Somehow, the American view of Italy is still affected by the memories of Italian Americans whose forefathers had left crushing poverty for a land of opportunity. And although their sons and daughters are corporate heads, sit in Congress and on the Supreme Court, have risen to the top of many professions, and have been economically successful, their success has not completely erased the stereotype of their homeland as being a poor and underdeveloped country. This negative image has been reinforced by new situations: a country where the government often falls and is replaced by another with equally poor prospects, where strikes abound, where communists have been on the verge of taking power, and where people, in the 1950s and 1960s, were still pouring out of the underdeveloped South to seek work in Northern European countries or across the ocean.

The American mass media and the movie industry in particular have created and exacerbated negative stereotypes and the persistent pejorative image of Italy. The American media is more interested in Italian passion and sensational events than in representing the country as a whole. In reporting or portraying the persisting vitality of the Mafia and other forms of corruption within Italian political and social life, the American media unfairly create images of Italians that are in line with those portrayed by movies like *The Godfather* and *Wise Guys*.

The overriding American attitudes toward Italians have been molded by traditional popular stereotypes and are not uniform. The average American loves Italy's artistic treasures, despises its politics, and envies its gusto for life. Italians are generally perceived to be infatuated with nice appearance, *bella figura*, rather than the intrinsic (but often dull) qualities admired by the Anglo-Saxons. Thus, Italian cars such as Fiats and Alfa Romeos are admired for their look but are considered suspect in terms of mechanical reliability. In the world of design, the word Italian does connote flair, elegance, and passion, and car makers from Europe, America, and Japan do turn to Italian designers such as Pininfarina to design their cars.

The image of Italy has been positive when it is framed in the artistic achievements of its people. Italy has been a champion of the arts throughout the centuries. Through the works of her artists one can witness the whole spectrum of man's creativity in the last 3,000 years. Because of the high achievements in the fifteenth and sixteenth centuries, Italy has been called the "cradle of the Renaissance." Franklin D. Roosevelt once said: "If we are children of Western civilization, then Italy is our mother."

The skills and genius of Italian artists and writers, builders and thinkers—and the judgment and generosity of their patrons—were crucial to the cultural development of Western civilization. Dante, Petrarch, and Boccaccio molded an Italian literary language from their native Tuscan dialect, but their words, translated into many languages, have become part of the common store of the Western literary heritage. The universal genius of Leonardo da Vinci and Michelangelo sets them beyond the limits of category and chronology. They and Giotto, Donatello, Botticelli, and Raphael, to name just a few of the greatest artists of the Golden Period, shaped a new image of humanity in Western art. Italy has given to Western thought the ideas of the philosopher St. Thomas Aquinas and the political theorist Niccolò Machiavelli, the spiritual fervor of St. Francis of Assisi, the space revelations of Galileo Galilei, the scientific discoveries of Alessandro Volta and

Enrico Fermi, and the musical delights of Palestrina, Scarlatti, Monteverdi, Paganini, Vivaldi, Pergolesi, Donizetti, Rossini, Puccini, and Verdi.

For centuries Italy was the Mecca of the cultured. Many foreign writers and poets have sung of Italy's beauty; from Goethe to Stendhal, from Byron to Ruskin to Henry James, Italy's natural beauty and her people's creativity inspired their works. However, the foreigner going to Italy today is baffled by many conflicting impressions, for Italy is the land of dualities and paradoxes. For example, although Italy houses two thirds of the world's art—as indicated by a recent UNESCO survey—it is often difficult to appreciate it because a large number of museums and churches are open for limited hours.

"Sunny Italy" is not always all that sunny. Situated on the southern border of Europe and stretching from north to south in the Mediterranean sea for about one thousand miles, the peninsula does not have a uniform climate. Despite its geographical position at the center of the temperate zone (Rome is practically on the same parallel as Boston), Italy has rather variable climatic characteristics, but is warmer than expected. This is due to the presence of the Mediterranean, whose warm waters mitigate thermal extremes, and the Alpine arc, which forms a barrier against the cold north winds. Furthermore, Italy is subject to both wet and moderate atmospheric currents from the Atlantic Ocean and dry and cold ones from eastern Europe. The Apennines chain, confronting the wet winds from the Tyrrhenian, also causes considerable climatic differences between the opposite sides of the peninsula and creates a unique variety of climates for an area that is approximately two-thirds that of California. The Alpine arc has a generally constant rainfall in all seasons, with increased quantities in spring and autumn and much fog in the plain from late fall to the middle of spring. The rest of the peninsula has an irregular rainfall, with the most falling in the winter months. In the southern regions there is a lack of summer rainfall, and in some areas (the Tavoliere in Apulia, southern Sicily, and the Campidano in Sardinia) the scarce annual rainfall often produces serious agricultural problems.

Because of its geographical position, with its surrounding islands almost reaching the coast of Africa, Italy has a particular geopolitical function in the Mediterranean as a European country. Italy has direct contact with the main ethnic and cultural areas of the Old World (neo-Latin, Germanic, and Slav-Balkan), as well as, through the North African countries, with the world of Arab-Islamic civilization.

Consequently, while remaining firmly anchored in the world of Western or European civilization, which was the direct heir of the Greco-Roman culture that developed and flourished on this very peninsula for over a millennium, Italy seems to stretch out naturally toward the opposite shore of the Mediterranean, practically dividing its western and eastern basins. Thus Italy can be considered to be the most natural link between Europe and the peoples of Africa and Asia, bordering as they do on the same sea and sharing over many centuries both historical events and cultural influences.

It is true that all Italians, from the Alps to Sicily, love espresso coffee, want their *pasta al dente*, watch the same television programs, follow soccer with the same passion, hum the same pop songs, are equally skillful artisans, and have developed an uncommon proclivity for self-criticism. It is hard to tell northerners from southerners before they speak and reveal their accent or dialect. There are tall, blond Sicilians who look like Scandinavians (after all the Normans ruled Sicily in the twelfth century), and there are short, chubby, black-haired and dark-eyed Florentines and Mantuans, whose genes may go back to the Etruscans. But there are deep cultural differences that make sociologists question the existence of "one Italy."

One cannot lose sight of the fact that Italy is a relatively young nation. As recently as Metternich's time, Italy was just considered "a geographic expression." Roman law was the widest and strongest historic strand that interlaced the fabric of Italian national identity. However, reminiscences of the Roman Empire and the cultural heritage from the Middle Ages and the Renaissance have always made educated Italians aware, however dimly, of common bonds and common destiny.

Differences in the social and cultural character of the country persist. During the struggle for liberation from foreign rule and for national unity—the *Risorgimento*—secret societies and uprisings were organized throughout the peninsula but they did not share the same idea on how to politically mold the new nation. Moreover, the *Risorgimento* was in the main a movement of political and intellectual elites. The rest of the population, particularly the farmers, were apathetic and played almost no role in the *Risorgimento*. On the other hand, the social class leading the fight for freedom did not have a united political front either. Giuseppe Mazzini, the founder of the *Giovine Italia* (Young Italy, 1831), was an idealist and republican, and had a romantic, almost mystical vision of national unity. For him, Italy's contribution to the family of nations would flow from the resumption of its old role as teacher. His views were opposed by Vincenzo Gioberti, who favored a federation of states under the presidency of the pope. In his book, *On the Moral and Civil Primacy of the Italians,* he attacked the notion of a unitary state and prophesied the difficulties Italy would have under a single statehood. The creation of regions as administrative entities in the 1970s is in a sense the partial realization of Gioberti's plan. Italy was unified according to Cavour's political plan—as the prime minister of the kingdom of Piedmont, he wanted a unified Italy under the house of Savoy. Cavour wanted to unite only northern Italy under a monarchy; and that is what he would have done if Giuseppe Garibaldi, a well-respected general who held democratic principles, had not started his own unification from Sicily and southern Italy and forced the king of Piedmont to come down from the North and annex the rest of the peninsula.

Contrary to the myths about the *Risorgimento,* this movement for Italy's resurgence was anything but a popular groundswell; it was Italy's failed revolution. Cavour united Italy under a government guided by aristocratic oligarchs who had a great fear of populism and no intention of sharing the national government with the masses.

In 1870, Italy was a nation of approximately 25 million people. Most Italians were poor peasants who could neither read nor write. They worked long hours in the fields and lived hard, often miserable lives. Few peasants owned their own land, and the labor contracts for sharecroppers and field workers favored the landowners. None of the 20 million of them could vote. Peasants and politicians lived in two different worlds within the same nation.

The new Italy was a centralized unitary state under a monarchy with a parliamentary government. The king had large-scale powers: he could dissolve parliament, appoint and dismiss the prime minister, appoint senators, and issue proclamations with the force of law. The tradition of local government was retained, but only in appearance; the limited elected local government was presided over by prefects, administrators appointed by the king. Since everything depended upon Rome, the government was inefficient and soon was perceived as an entity far removed from the people. For most the only contacts with government were tax collection and military conscription. Because of the elitist nature of the new state, the condition of the South worsened after unification. Naples, the largest metropolis in Italy and one of the largest in Europe, lost all its political and economic power. Naples went from being the capital of the South and a very prosperous city—the Bourbons had developed a strong industrial system and prestigious university centers—to being impoverished and losing its luster. Italy had been unified, but only as a political entity. Massimo D'Azeglio, a writer and a senator of that time, said "We made Italy; now we must make the Italians." The task proved difficult.

The new Italian liberal state, a constitutional monarchy, had a very narrow electoral basis.[1] Voting eligibility, based on tax payments, restricted participation to certain classes and regions (fewer in the South because of greater poverty). In many areas, especially in the South, deputies were elected to parliament with only a dozen votes. In the years that followed, the suffrage was extended, but even by the 1909 election only 8.3% of the adult population was entitled to vote. Seventy-five percent of the population was illiterate, and the country suffered from a high mortality rate. The new state was dominated by the Piedmontese and had a system of taxation that was repressive toward the South. When the South reacted through mass insurrections, or the occasional assassination of prefects and tax collectors, it was repressed by the Piedmontese army.[2] It was clear that the South had been reluctantly accepted into the new state. The antibrigand campaign army officers and the government understood their opponent predominantly by means of a series of hierarchical binary oppositions, such as between civilization and barbarism, reason and violence, social order and crime.[3] The conceptualization of brigandage as an "Other" was set in the broader frame of an imaginative geography in which the Italian nation is constructed as the opposite of the South;[4] such a conceptualization persists up to today in the debate of North vs. South.

Italy also suffered because it had not been able to solve the "Roman Question." The pope had resisted the new state militarily; after he had been pushed into retreat in the Vatican, he condemned the occupation of Rome as an aggression, declared himself prisoner of the Italian state, and threatened to excommunicate any Italian who would take part in the political life of the country. This position had a profound impact because for many Italians the Church represented the values of authentic Italy.

The separation between the Church and the state did give to the new state the possibility of establishing liberal policies, but it decided to keep the nation divided. Only in 1929, with the Lateran Accords signed between Mussolini and the pope, was the "Roman Question" resolved. Mussolini, however, did not solve the South-North question. Cultural, economic, and social differences between North and South remained. At the end of the nineteenth century and during the first two decades of the twentieth, nationalistic politicians and intellectuals played on Italian chauvinism rather than focus on the nation's North-South tensions. And Mussolini did not improve the situation.

Mussolini, the leader of the National Fascist Party, with around thirty deputies in the chamber, took power in October 1922 with the support of the bourgeois and landed interests. The conservative system based on the systematic exclusion of the popular masses from politics was perpetuated. Italy was run by an authoritarian regime of a new type. Although fascist propaganda insisted that the National Fascist Party sought to develop a system that would be neither capitalist nor communist, it did not give any voice to the working class, it kept wages down by destroying free trade unions, and it facilitated the rationalization of Italian capitalism.[5] Unlike Marxism, fascism sought to preserve the capitalist system, neutralizing the internal class struggle by appealing to nationalism as the basis for social harmony. Since the nation was the ultimate good, it was only through the nation that the individual could fulfill his or her potential. By creating the new doctrine "everything within the state, nothing outside the state, nothing against the state," fascism neutralized class struggle and shifted the struggle elsewhere. The concept of Italy as a "proletarian nation" oppressed by the richer, more developed, capitalist nations was skillfully crafted and then embraced by most Italians.

World War II did not alleviate the split between North and South, indeed, it exacerbated the rift. For about a year and a half, the country was literally divided in two. The liberation of the country from the south by the Allies and the occupation of the rest of the peninsula (North and central Italy) by the Nazis had a tremendous impact on the evolution of the character of the nation in the democratic era that followed. In that year and half of bloodshed, North and South did not experience the struggle in the same way. The landing of the Allies in Sicily on July 10, 1943, quickly triggered strong reaction against Mussolini, who had entered the war without much support from either the politicians or the populace. In what amounted to a palace coup in Rome, the Fascist Grand Council, including foreign minister Galeazzo Ciano, Mussolini's son-in-law, forced the resignation of Mussolini on the night of July 24, 1943, and returned the power of the state to King Victor Emmanuel III. The king had the dictator arrested and appointed Marshal Badoglio prime minister. Badoglio formed an interim government that dissolved the National Fascist Party, granted amnesty to political prisoners, and entered into negotiations with the Allies for an armistice, which was concluded on September 3, 1943, to coincide with the Allies landing on the peninsula at Salerno. Fearing an invasion by Germany, Badoglio quickly (September 8, 1943) moved his government to Brindisi, far to the south on the east coast, which was then under the control of the Allies. The Germans, who already had nine divisions in Italy, reacted harshly to the news. On October 13, 1943, the Italian royal government declared war on Germany, but the disintegrating Italian army had been left without a commander. Some Italian troops joined the Germans, some the Allies. Others merged with the partisans who had started the resistance in the North. Those who resisted the Nazis with no hope of Allied assistance were massacred. In Cefalonia, south of Corfu, the Italians fought for a week. When they finally surrendered, 4,500 soldiers and officers were shot and their bodies were left in the open.

In the meantime, rescued by German commandos, Mussolini had set up a rival government—the *Italian Social Republic*—in Salò on Lake Garda in November 1943. In the new government there were the most fanatical fascist elements, who were eager to imitate the Nazis. Ciano and others who were held responsible for Mussolini's ouster were executed. The National Racial Code, unpopular in a country where anti-semitism was virtually unknown when the code was enacted in 1938 to impress the Nazis, was now enforced with terrible exactness in the occupied area. Notwithstanding strenuous efforts of many Italians, about 10,000 Italian Jews perished in Nazi concentration camps.

Because of the stiff German resistance to the allied advance, hopes for a quick occupation of Rome were disappointed. A battlefront along the *Gustav Line* during the winter of 1943-1944 engaged the Allies in a bloody standoff. Rome was finally liberated in June 1944 after the breakthrough at Cassino in May. A second German defense line in the north, the *Gothic Line*, held until the last weeks of the war. When Mussolini was caught on April 28, 1945, he was shot and his body put on public display.

In that last year and half, an important role was played by the *partisans* who fought an irregular war against the Germans and Italian fascists in the north. The Resistance Movement, started in September 1943 as a spontaneous, locally based popular uprising, by the end of the war had a following of 450,000 individuals; 55,000 of them died while about 20,000 remained handicapped from their battle wounds. The *partigiani* excluded no one: rich and poor, professionals and laborers, children, old people, communists, socialists, christian democrats, everyone had a significant role.

An especially important role was played by women. Unlike the *Risorgimento*, heroines did not simply serve as "mothers illustrious" and martyr wives. This time they took to the field, too. The women *Gruppi* worked in collaboration, not in contention, with men. The Resistance showed that men and women could pursue the same aims, but it also offered women the opportunity to prove that they were the equal of men, just as enduring, strong, brave, resourceful, and implacable.

The activities of the Resistance varied. Besides engaging several German divisions in the fighting, it provided vital information to the Allies, helped Allied prisoners to escape, engaged in sabotage, disrupted transportation, and organized strikes that slowed down production of war materials. In the last months of fighting the civil war got very brutal. It was a passionate wave of collective hysteria and private vengeance, horrible in its impact but understandable in its context.

Contrary to what happened in France or Yugoslavia, the Italian Resistance was not led by charismatic figures, but instead was organized by political parties: the Communist Party, the Socialist Party, and the Christian Democratic Party. Thus, when the war was over, the only political structures which survived were the political parties. In a popular referendum, held on June 2, 1946, the first universal suffrage, people not only voted to ban the Fascist Party, but also decided to punish the House of Savoy. The monarchy, discredited because it had given in too easily to Mussolini, was abolished and replaced by the republic. Indeed, the king was forced into exile in Portugal, and never allowed to return. His plea to see his homeland many years later, when he was about to die of cancer, was rejected without much public or political debate.

Because the South could not participate in the Resistance on which the Italian Republic was established, it once again found itself obliged after the war to celebrate and mythologize an event not part of its historic experience. The continued support for monarchism in the South and the subsequent powerful attachment to local myths and identities can perhaps be explained by the inability to identify with events and actions that could not be experienced first hand.

The result of the elections confirmed the South-North division. Almost all of the northern and central regions voted for the republic; Rome and the South, led by Naples, voted for the monarchy (79% for the king). The election of the members of the Constitutional Assembly revealed the same split: the South voted more for the Christian Democratic Party and the center-right parties, while the North and central Italy voted more for the Socialist Party and the parties of the left. During this short period, the Communist Party had gained much headway. Palmiro Togliatti played the key role in this transformation. His authority among communist cadres was immense. He was helped in this by the fact that, as the leader of the party, he could enjoy a share of the personality cult that had become established in the communist movement. Undoubtedly the prestige of the USSR played a crucial role in this, but so did the fact that the Communist Party had been the leading force of the Resistance. The Communist Party, led by its secretary Palmiro Togliatti, participated fully in the drafting of Italy's new constitution. Consequently, next to the principles of liberalism, there were also recognized new "social rights"; freedom of private enterprise was guaranteed but only "as long as it did not conflict with social utility." Since the South did not experience the civil war because it had been quickly liberated by the Allies and had remained under the monarchy, the majority of the people kept their allegiance to the king. The strong emergence of the force of the left that had been organized during the Resistance to fight Nazis and fascists created such strong fear in the South of a possible communist takeover that Sicily voiced a desire to secede from the peninsula. The political skills of the leader of the Christian Democratic Party, Alcide De Gasperi, and the American political and economic presence in the region, prevented both the secession of Sicily and the takeover of power by the left. Since no single party was strong enough to capture political power, this had to be jointly managed by the same coalition of parties that had fought in the Resistance: Christian Democratic Party (*Democrazia Cristiana*, *D.C.*) 35.1%, Socialist Party (*Partito Socialista Italiano, P.S.I.*) 20.7%, and Communist Party (*Partito Comunista Italiano, P.C.I.*) 18.9%.

Although the *D.C.* was the newest party of the young republic, it became the strongest. Its popularity was facilitated by the fact that it was the heir of the Popular Party, the largely peasant-based Catholic party which had been created in 1919 by Luigi Sturzo, a Sicilian priest, and which had already used the vast machine of Catholic social and political organizations. The *D.C.* was able to rely on the support of the Church and the mass lay organizations of the Church itself. The weakness of the old Liberal Party, the nearest equivalent to a clearly pro-capitalist party, made the Christian Democratic Party the only possible choice of industrialists. Because of the kind of base support it had mustered and its ideology, the Christian Democratic Party also became the only party that the United States came to rely on to lead Italy into the North Atlantic Alliance and the Western camp. The *D.C.* dominated the political landscape throughout the postwar period and ensured a remarkable continuity of governments, leading 49 out of 52 governments. Because it was always in government and because it tended to be a party that actively encouraged the expansion of the public sector, it had at its disposal a vast array of jobs that it could offer to those who were politically reliable. Thus, through professional and trade associations and a clientele system of patronage, the *D.C.* developed a formidable machine, especially in the South where industrial development lagged far behind that of the North. If the *D.C.* can take most of the merit for the miraculous economic recovery of Italy, it also has to take some of the painful responsibility for the ever-widening economic separation between North and South.

When the country recovered from World War II with surprising speed, foreigners voiced admiration for the *Italian miracle*. The devastating Allied air raids on industrial centers, railroad hubs, seaports, and eventually on Rome itself, were accompanied by the naval bombardment of Genoa, the loss of a major part of the Italian merchant fleet, and the disaster of the warships sunk in the harbor of Taranto. Furthermore, battles from Sicily to the Po River, with many civilian casualties and innumerable bridges blown up and buildings destroyed, atrocious Nazi reprisals for acts of sabotage and resistance, and hundreds of thousands of soldiers in prison camps, if not dead, left Italy stripped of much of its manpower and infrastructure. All this plus the restrictions imposed by the peace treaty (Paris, February 1, 1947) forced the new Italian Republic to face many problems of material and moral reconstruction.

Italy was devastated by the 1943 defeat, the agony of the ensuing civil war, and the damage to her physical resources. Paradoxically, however, these setbacks proved less destructive in their effects than the "mutilated" victory of 1918. Indeed, in Italy at the end of 1945 there was an extraordinary sense of real hope. After the many years under fascism a euphoria of freedom gripped the nation. The great event of 1945 was not so much the disappearance of dictatorship, fascism, and the monarchy, but rather the affirmation of those principles that animated the Resistance movement: the sudden awakening of the Italians from the long nightmare of war, and the rebirth of the nation and its immediate concern with the struggle for survival, the restoration of individual dignity. Many Italians saw the Resistance as a new *Risorgimento* because of its struggle against the oppressor and its principles of liberty, justice, and solidarity. It was the Resistance that restored faith in man and his ability to change his own destiny, and it gave rise to the conviction that cultural values could be saved through concrete social and political actions.

At the end of the war, with the installation of the new democratic government and the elimination of the strictest form of censorship, artists and writers also emerged with a reborn sense of civic commitment. Once the strict censorship of the fascist regime had fallen, they could turn their eyes freely to the observation of reality. The poverty, social disorder, and suffering that fascism had forbidden to be represented, and the humanity ravaged by the war, became their subject matter. The theater, the novel, and the movies became the chief means by which contemporary society was placed under investigation. In the depiction of sociopolitical situations, it was the search for truth that guided the directors and screenwriters in their first neo-realist works. Filmmakers wanted spectators to be witnesses to the ills of society in order to raise social and political consciousness. Thus, in their masterpieces, De Sica, Visconti, Zavattini, and Rossellini dealt with the themes of real life, expressing them with deep emotional involvement and consuming lyricism with a clear aim: a naturalistic slice of life and a sociopolitical perspective in which antifascism and class consciousness had to bring action. The intensity and fervor of this discovery rendered the artist inseparable from the man.

The neorealist artist generally took an instinctively populist or leftist viewpoint, espousing a more or less explicit faith both in the irresistible power of collective action and in Marxist dialectical conflict and the inevitability of historical progress—all supported by a somewhat mystical notion of Christian brotherhood. However, it did not necessarily share the doctrinaire optimism of socialist realism, with its voluntaristic faith in an ultimate, inescapable positive solution to social problems.

The process of reconstruction was complicated by the very presence of the Allies. The British favored the strengthening of the monarchy (an authoritarian democratic constitution) and penal peace settlement terms. The Americans, instead, showed a greater degree of understanding. Some Americans were surprised and appalled at the poverty and deprivation they had witnessed in the South, and were willing to give limited tacit support to relatively radical reform programs involving government aid and land distribution. The prospect of a communist takeover in such a strategically significant area for the West was also worrisome.

A policy of reconstruction and economic development was pursued by the various governments in power after 1948, the year in which the *D.C.* acquired a large parliamentary majority. Initially this took the form of severe anti-inflation measures and then a lifting of restrictions combined with public intervention through a relaunching of *IRI*, the Institute for the Industrial Reconstruction.

The establishment of the *Cassa per il Mezzogiorno* (Funds for the Development of the South) set in motion a complex series of extraordinary interventions to provide the southern regions with the necessary basic structures (roads, drainage, services, etc.) to assist in economic and, above all, agricultural development. Agrarian reform was particularly necessary in combating the centuries-old feudal structure of land estates of the South. However, because of poor planning, a new and even greater migration occurred, this time not overseas but toward the countries of northwestern Europe (Germany, France, Belgium, England, and Switzerland), where the post war industrial boom required large quantities of manpower. The movement of population was even greater toward the north of Italy (Piedmont, Lombardy, and Liguria) because of the efforts of private initiative in creating an industrialized climate whose rapid and often disorderly growth came to be known as the "economic miracle."

At the beginning of the 1960s, the highest percentage of the work force was employed in the industrial sector, while agriculture continued to diminish and the service industries began their expansion. In the international sphere, with its entry into the United Nations and participation in military alliances and economic agreements with the other western countries (European and North American), Italy began to regain the dignity and prestige that was due its geographical position and the richness of its historical cultural traditions. The Italians once again, like the phoenix, had risen from the ashes. Their innate abilities proved to be their best resource. Their multiform tactile skills and their versatility and mastery in shaping, carving, crafting, refining, drawing, styling, painting, and lettering are part of a long tradition. Today's designers of elegant car bodies and casual wear are heirs to a long tradition that embraces the pottery and tomb frescoes of the Etruscans and the anatomical and engineering drawings of Leonardo da Vinci and a host of celebrated and anonymous artists and artisans going back three thousand years.

Gradually the Italian economy changed beyond recognition and has, by and large, caught up with the rest of Europe. In terms of purchasing power and standard of living, the Italian working class has narrowed the gap with Germany and France and is at the same level as the United Kingdom. The "necessities" of the consumer society, such as remote control color television, multiprogram dishwashers, freezers, cellular telephones, etc., are as available in Italy as they are in most other Western countries. Its agricultural population has decreased constantly and so has the birthrate—two other characteristics of major economic powers.

The open market and free enterprise system have played major roles in the diffusion of consumer goods in Italian society. As in the rest of Europe, the state has had to intervene to keep costs of production lower than they would otherwise have been by taking into public ownership some basic production inputs, such as energy, and some basic segments of the infrastructure of the nation, such as transportation, and subsidizing them out of public funds. Furthermore, the state has also had to ensure that minimum standards of health, housing, education, and old age care are maintained. In other words, Italy too became a welfare state. This was achieved and maintained on the assumption that there would be a constant economic growth, which was the case for most of the 1950s and a good part of the 1960s. Problems, however, began to surface in the late 1960s and developed further in the 1970s when the economy slowed down and the manufacturing sector decreased. As a consequence of this condition, the public sector was increasingly less able to sustain a high level of employment and large areas of the private sector succumbed and had to be rescued by the state, which caused high inflation. Italy went through the same phases experienced by the developed West: development of the welfare state, state intervention, and crisis of the welfare state.

The major socioeconomic changes began with Italy's opening to the left, in early 1960, which brought the Socialist Party, previously in electoral alliance with the communists, into a governing coalition with the christian democrats, the republicans, and the social democrats. The inclusion of the socialists in government was the first concrete step in a far-reaching realignment of Italy's political forces that was aimed at isolating the largest communist party in the West and form-ing a stable governmental majority resting on a wider and solid foun-dation of popular support. The center-left governments of the 1960s may be criticized for excesses in labor legislation and wasteful public expenditures, but they were the only alternative; a center-right coali-tion with the extremely conservative liberals who depended on parlia-mentary support from the neo-fascists (*Movimento Sociale Italiano, M.S.I.*), might then have polarized Italian society.

Along with the political and economic changes, the rest of Italian life has changed radically, and most of the changes have been for the better. Compared to 1945, the average Italian is better fed, better housed, better educated, more literate, and politically more aware. The enormous gap that existed between Italians and Americans has been practically eliminated. Italians proudly say that "America is here now." That is true on many levels, as we shall see.

After some initial reticence, Italians threw themselves into the con-sumer society as eagerly as any people in Europe. Some feared that Italy was losing her soul, selling out to an ill-digested Americanization, but most people welcomed this new world of affluence and technol-ogy. They were driven by the urge to make money and enjoy the fruits of their labor; like the other losers of the war in Europe, the Germans, they rebuilt and modernized their country through a mixture of techni-cal flair, material ambition, and sheer sustained hard work at all levels, from top manager to industrial worker and farmer.

This postwar modernization has been a powerful, heroic process because it was a leap forward from a backward country to a post-industrial nation. Under the momentum of economic advance, society shifted its equilibrium. There was a massive movement of people from agriculture to industry and service, from the country to the towns. With rapid urbanization, many cities tripled in size, and many provin-cial towns became vibrant with new activity.

In private and family life, and in purely social relations, Italy has certainly evolved a great deal in the last 30 years. Women have achieved a striking new emancipation. Sexual permissiveness has developed remarkably in the past two decades. Within the family, paternal au-thority now weighs less heavily and parent/child relations are more frank and equal. In daily life, the pompous use of titles is waning, and home entertaining has become much more relaxed and casual.

Fewer people go to church on a regular basis, more use contracep-tives, and more live together without being married. Divorces and abor-tions are legal while the purchase of pornographic material and the access to risqué movies on television has no equal in the world. The strong presence of the Church and the tradition of puritanical values have not prevented the development of a lifestyle which is, by and large, an adaptation of the many negative aspects of the "American way of life."

Italians have a love-hate relationship with the state: they resent it, yet cling to it and expect it to provide endless benefits. In this, as in many other ways, Italy appears to be a country of paradoxes, especially on the political level. The game of musical chairs that cabinet ministers play, the governmental crises, past acts of terrorism in airports and train stations, high inflation, and mega-scandals, which are top news in daily newspapers, have led scholars to depict the country as a democracy headed if not to oblivion then certainly toward some mortal crises. The fact that the Italian government has been very fragile and has fallen, on the average, once a year, and that in parliament as many as 16 political parties were represented led many political experts, especially Anglo-Saxons, to suggest that the Italian political system was an anomalous democracy that did not deserve to be preserved. On the other hand, Italy has also had one of the most stable democracies in the West; it is the only country in Europe to be ruled by the same party (D.C.) for almost 50 years and has seen no change in the political elites during that same period. Governing with a multiparty system Italian-style was possible only because of the high skills Italian politicians were able to develop in the post-fascist period. Italians were able to make the business of government an art that constantly requires intuition, creativity, tolerance, endurance, and flexibility. The leading party in power, the D.C., dealt with the continuous crisis of the country by constantly changing strategies. Not only the nature of its alliance with the political forces had to change, but the nature of each of the political forces with which it had to deal changed. While the D.C. changed by leaning more toward the left, the left changed by leaning toward the center. The P.S.I. changed from being a junior supporter of the P.C.I. in the 1940s and 1950s to becoming a junior partner of the D.C. from the 1960s onward. Rejecting its traditions of a workers' party and becoming more and more a radical party of the center, the P.S.I. increasingly espoused the cause of "modernization." By being in power with the D.C., it obtained a greater share of political and economic resources, and it abused its power. In so doing, it became another party of patronage and clienteles. The P.C.I. increasingly abandoned the doctrine of Marxism-Leninism, opened its ranks to people of varying persuasions, including Catholics, accepted with increasing enthusiasm membership in the European Economic Community (EEC) and the North Atlantic Treaty Organization (NATO), disassociated itself from Soviet foreign policy, and supported a *D.C.* government for nearly three years (1976-1979). By responding to external political conditions and internal pressure and interest groups, political parties changed. Everyone has changed, but everyone has had to pay a price.

In the present era of transnational corporations, of mass international communication systems that penetrate deep into the national culture, and a powerful military system backed by superpower technology, the traditional nation-state is reduced to cosmic insignificance. The shocks of the fall of communism and the collapse of the Soviet Union certainly affected Italian politics profoundly. The disappearance of a political force seen as a threat to democratic stability allowed political parties to disentangle themselves from old alliances that created a reality that necessitated changes in the political system. As a result, in 1993, institutional reforms were enacted and a new form of democracy was instituted. The changes were bold and positive, but their success will require more than official reforms. There will also need to be a change in Italian attitudes and a new kind of civic spirit.

Especially for the South, the reform of institutions will not bring about automatic changes because the performance of institutions depends on their social, economic, and cultural surroundings. We know that if we transplant democratic institutions, they do not grow in the new setting as they did in the old because the quality of a democracy depends on the quality of its citizens. The difference between South and North has to be attributed to the difference in civic attitudes in the two areas and, therefore, the way government is regarded; however, the duality of North and South has become greater because there is a lack of serious initiatives to create jobs on the part of Italy's governing national elite. The *southern question* is an economic question as well as a political one. It is not a matter of simple modernization, or of an increase in state funds. The role of the South cannot even be understood purely in terms of the Italian North; it must be thought of anew in terms of the relations between Italy and the rest of the European Union (EU) and the Mediterranean. Its problems cannot be tackled independently from the North or the rest of Europe because Italian economic development is intrinsically connected to the South. The old solutions have done much damage to the South. For the systematic drainage of the South's sole resource, human labor, the South has been compensated by a constant stream of state funds, which have underpinned the stability of the *D.C.* regime. This money has not been directed toward "modernization" but has been channeled in a thousand directions under the supervision of all sorts of interest groups including the Mafia. Italy's future depends on its ability to make the South part of the national economic equation.

Despite the southern question and other difficulties such as high unemployment and some unresolved social injustices, I find Italy today a relatively happy and well-adjusted society, perhaps a little cynical and certainly disillusioned with politics and ideologies, but no longer daydreaming. At the beginning of the 1990s, Italians finally became aware that material progress had in itself by no means cured all the basic ills of their society. It is a society still segmented, still beset with barriers and inequalities, still attached to a number of outdated structures of which the most blatant is the overly-centralized and too pervasive machine of the state. But there is still much to be done that no government can do, for social change is a matter of habit and psychology more than of politics. As we shall see, the Italians may have changed their lifestyles, but their basic character, built around individualism, social mistrust, and desire for formalism—the desire to present a *bella figura*—remains.

Notes

1. Only 2% of the adult population had the right to vote and, of these, less than 60% actually went to the polls. Only males over twenty-five years of age who were literate and who paid a property tax of forty lire per year could vote. For the election of 1861, the electorate amounted to 1.9% of the entire population, and only about 57% of the electors voted, 240,000 of a population of approximately 25 million. Even the relatively radical reform of 1882, which lowered the age and tax requirements, produced an electorate of under 7% of the population.

2. The main factors behind peasant unrest were economic hardship, the introduction of conscription, and the accumulated discontent caused by the erosion of collective land-use rights. The Piedmontese government associated the social unrest with brigandage and severely repressed it. This aspect of the unification process was one of the darkest sides of that historical period. Without having a definite beginning or end, the war to annex the South continued for a decade, cost more lives than all the battles of unification put together, and at its peak necessitated the deployment of about two-fifths of the effective strength of the Italian army at a time when Austria was thought to be a constant danger.

3. Banditry had the entire repertoire of racist imagery deployed against it by the officers of the Italian army: bandits are black, animal, feminine, primitive, deceitful, evil, perverse, irrational. In explaining brigandage with these terms, it was placed beyond explanation in an imaginatively and emotively charged realm of monstrosity. But what is most striking is the use of images of colonialism by the northern establishment: "What barbarism! This isn't Italy! This is Africa: compared to these peasants the beduins are the flower of civilized virtues," writes a government envoy to Cavour from Teano in 1860. In Camillo Cavour, *Carteggi: La liberazione del Mezzogiorno e la formazione del Regno d'Italia*, vol. 3 (October-November 1860) (Bologna: Zanichelli, 1952); letter dated 27 October 1860, 83.

4. John Dickie, "A world at war; the Italian army and brigandage," *History Workshop Journal*, 33 (1992), 1-24.

5. Fascism did organize people in associations and enroll people in large proportions in fascist-controlled organizations, but people did not acquire an independent sense of civic responsibility. In this regard, one of the political effects of fascism was to weaken still further the already tenuous links between the individual and organized civic social activities.

Part I
Politics

Introduction

As we advance toward the end of the twentieth century, Italian politics, economics, and society once again appear far more complex than they did during the long aftermath of World War II. In the realm of politics, it seemed that Italy gradually became more moderate and began to resemble other industrialized nations in this respect. But developments since the late 1980s have pointed to a growing crisis of confidence in party politics, particularly as practiced by professional politicians, and an increased fragmentation of the party system that in some ways is reminiscent of the First Republic.

Developments in many other industrialized countries tend to confirm that touchstones so long taken for granted are now disappearing and that a new era of uncertainty is opening up before us. Politically, the postwar consensus seems now to be in ruins, with small, almost single-issue parties rising up in many Western European countries to break the post-1945 mold of domination by the center-right and center-left. Economically, neither state intervention nor market forces have been able to cure unemployment and other increasingly widespread socioeconomic problems since the early 1970s; state intervention was blamed for the lack of economic dynamism, but market-driven economics have patently failed to cure any of the ills that Keynesianism was supposed to have produced. Socially, profound inequalities, partly a result of uncaring market forces, are becoming commonplace in many countries where 40 years ago they seemed to be heading for extinction.

Italy was a country that was solidly—if sometimes reluctantly—part of the uneasy peace which the Cold War offered. But in the late 1980s and early 1990s it became abundantly clear that the postwar era was over in this respect as well. The Eastern bloc disintegrated and Germany was unified. The American President George Bush responded at the time by talking optimistically of a post-communist "New World Order," but it became increasingly clear that "disorder" was a more accurate description. The disintegration of the old Soviet bloc gave rise to a bloody civil war—the first fully fledged war in Europe since 1945—in what was previously Yugoslavia, and relations between the industrialized and less-developed countries are deteriorating rapidly as less developed countries become more defiant.

One enduring element of political, economic, and social stability since the war has been the European Community, now European Union, with Italy as a key player right from the start. But here again, it is far from clear whether the European Union can provide stability for Italy and other states in an increasingly unstable world, or whether, as it grows stronger, it will be an added source of controversy and discontent both within and between member states.

As usual, Italy is proving to be a fascinating case study in this rapidly changing world. It is a country whose uneven social, economic, political, and cultural development has meant that it is particularly sensitive to wider conflict and contradictions. Looking at Italy, as with the wider world it responds to so sensitively, we can still only guess at the shape of things in 50 years' time; will late modernization and a long-unstable political situation in the postwar years mean that it is more vulnerable to the effects of the international turmoil of the post-communist world? Or will Italy cope with uncertainty better because it experienced so much uncertainty previously?

I

Political and Social Foundations

The Molding of Political Identities and *Immobilismo*

Up to the political earthquake of 1993, Italy constantly attracted negative attention for the way it conducted political affairs; its government was always perceived as faulty and unstable. Those who follow the daily press know that Italy has had many governments, much political terrorism, and, until the fall of communism, a large Communist Party. They will know that the government is massive and omnipresent and that the Italian political parties have "colonized" Italian society. Governments do fall constantly, parliaments are dissolved frequently, and worse, every facet of Italian life is politicized. The mere act of joining a trade union or even a sporting club is inevitably a political decision in Italy. Prospective labor union members must choose whether to join the communist-socialist trade union, *Confederazione Generale Lavoratori Italiani (C.G.I.L.)*, the Catholic union, *Confederazione Italiana dei Sindacati dei Lavoratori (C.I.S.L.)*, or the socialdemocrat/ republican union, *Unione Italiana dei Lavoratori (U.I.L.)*. The whole range of cultural and social organizations, associations, and clubs is not immune to political penetration. Politics has also led to politicization of economic life, particularly in the public sector: state enterprises, banks, credit institutions, television networks, and newspapers are all politically influenced. The great majority of Italians complain about a government that does not work, about political leaders who are crooks, but even more about the related problem of *immobilismo*. Contrary to the perception of the foreign press, they usually do not complain about the constant fall of government; in fact, the complaint is that, notwithstanding the numerous governments and parliamentary elections, the same people continue to govern the country, and the political system remains *immobile*. That was true until 1993, when radical political changes were instituted.

In a country where politics is as important as the breathing of fresh air, identities are most commonly defined by political thinking and political practices. Political practices may define people as much as gender, language, religion, class, and sexuality. Political behavior is not just an activity delegated to parties and party leaders, but it is also practiced strongly by individual Italians, regardless of other factors that define their life.

Political identity is not simply defined by an individual's sympathies or hostilities toward a given set of parties and political movements; rather, as Simon Parker states, "the constitution of the polity [how it is structured socially and economically, its main regional and cultural divisions, the key historical processes that helped to shape its political institutions] creates a series of 'instances' where the vertical ordering of society [individual, family, workplace, neighborhood, locality, region, nation] interacts with horizontal cleavages [class, religion, language, race, culture] to form complex patterns of identification in which we may identify with a number of different political formations in a variety of social instances."[1] The post war period in Italy gave rise to the development of three main subcultures—Catholic, lay, and political, which were dominated by the socialist/communist subculture. The rebirth of democratic Italy after the fall of fascism offered the occasion for a reassertion of the political subcultures that had remained dormant under Mussolini's dictatorship.

The legacy of the war and the Resistance had a markedly different geographical impact on Italy, and, as we saw, this was most clearly demonstrated in the strong support for retention of the monarchy during the referendum of June 1946 in the South and the islands and the overwhelming support for a republic in the North. Thus, since its inception, the Italian Republic has been heavily segregated along geopolitical lines and citizens have displayed a strong loyalty to political parties.

Strong identification with a political party or ideology is typical of those countries where the civic culture is weak; mature democracies are composed of citizens who do not have a priori and fixed political beliefs, and are expected to make the best available choice. After the war, the strong presence of the specter of fascism and the strong position of the Left made political allegiances unbreakable and created an organic relationship of identification between citizens and political parties. The coincidence of the post-fascist and Cold War eras created a strong sense of duty and obligation and a voting behavioral ritual that did not permit many people to shift allegiance. The polarized pluralism that resulted mostly from the externally imposed polarities of the Cold War molded a society in which families and individuals were known to have a well-defined political identity, even though the casting of a vote was secret. Political polarization and political pluralism were also the result of the way Italians chose to be governed.

The Italian form of government may have been similar to that of most parliamentary democracies in structure and constitutional principles, but it functions in a fundamentally different way. The anomalies that characterize it, although subtle, complex, and deeply woven into the fabric of Italian life, are not impenetrable mysteries. If one examines the Italian constitution in its historical context by acknowledging both the important role that it gave to Parliament and the level of democratic pluralism it had desired, then the postwar Italian political history appears less Byzantine, and Italian politicians can be valued for their skills in reaching compromises and for the preservation of democracy. One will also be able to understand how the real protagonists, the political parties, developed, monopolized power, contributed to corruption, and affected the general life of the country.

One must remember that the postwar period begins with the political parties clearly in charge. They constituted the commanding forces of the Italian Resistance: the Committee of National Liberation (C.L.N.) was made up of a coalition of six parties—the partisans were organized on the basis of party affiliation.

The Constitution and Popular Sovereignty

When on June 4, 1944, the Allies entered Rome, Italy was already eager to change its form of government: the Committee of National Liberation demanded a civilian government with clear plans for immediate changes. A six party coalition government representing the political forces of the Resistance was formed. The temporary government, initially under Ivanoe Bonomi, had to cope with the disastrous economic legacy of the war and the rehabilitation of the national morale. After moving quickly to suppress the Fascist Party and its dependent organizations and by carrying out an extensive shuffling of prefects (state government representatives in the provinces), Bonomi formalized the Salerno Agreement on July 25, 1944, and established (1) election by direct universal suffrage of a Constitutional Assembly, (2) the obligation of the members of the government not to impede institutional reform which was postponed until the liberation of the country, (3) that future ministers must swear loyalty to the nation, rather than to the king, and (4) that legislative powers be attributed to the government, by way of decrees approved by the new king, who had been given the title of "Luogotenente generale del regno." A provisional decree of March 16, 1946, also established that the "institutional question," the decision to choose between monarchy and republic, had to be resolved directly by the people by referendum.

In the institutional referendum held on June 2, 1946, the electorate voted in favor of the Republic (12,718,641 or 54.26% for the Republic, 10,718,502 or 45.7% for the monarchy). Almost all of the northern and central regions voted for the Republic; Rome and the South (led by Naples, 79%) voted for the monarchy. After the results of the referendum were proclaimed, King Umberto, who had inherited the throne on the abdication of his father, Victor Emanuel III, left for permanent exile with the royal family. The elections for the constitutional assembly, held the same day, saw the clear dominance of the three popular parties (the Christian Democratic Party with 35% of the votes, the Socialist Party with 20% and the Communist Party with 19%). With this vote two objectives were achieved. First, the Italians had the final word on the institutional question that had divided the country and absorbed considerable attention on the part of the political powers, public opinion, and international bodies. Second, they opened the way for the introduction of a constitution that was to signal a new political order with the collapse of the fascist regime and the return to democracy. The new constitution was approved by secret ballot on December 22, 1947, by a vote of 453 to 62, promulgated by the provisional head of state on December 27, 1947, and put into effect on January 1, 1948.

By the standards of Italian parliamentary proceedings, or indeed by any standards, the drafting and approval of the constitution was a speedy affair. Yet the work of the Constitutional Assembly took place in an even more rapidly changing political climate. When the Assembly first met, in June 1946, the Cold War had not yet begun and the Italian Communist Party (P.C.I.) was still in the government. By the time the constitution was approved, the Left had been expelled from the government and Europe was divided into two spheres of influence. Inevitably, the political situation had an influence on the proceedings.

Christian democrats, communists, socialists, liberals, etc., worked side by side to prepare a governing chart that had to serve the people of the whole nation and that could withstand the weight of time. Since fascism had violated the fundamental rights of individual and collective liberty and had authoritatively centralized all power, the new constitution addressed these issues and emphasized the basic rights of private citizens. Heated debates were inescapable, as were the inevitable compromises. Some of the most passionate discussions centered on the make-up of parliament: the Left preferred one house rather than two. The final approval of the bicameral structure was possible only by giving both houses equal power to legislate as well as to dissolve the government. Another issue that was fiercely debated was the role of the Council of Ministers (the cabinet) and of the President of the Council of Ministers, especially whether the cabinet had to work as a collective body or be divided along internal hierarchical lines with a strong prime minister. Many issues (such as the establishment of regional administration, constitutional court, the referendum, and the freedom to strike) were not resolved and were left to subsequent decisions.

Although the framers of the constitution had used the U.S. Constitution as a model, they created something unique. In its first part, the Italian Constitution reflects the euphoria of newly acquired freedom and the determination never to lose it again. Consequently, it is rich in rhetoric, exceedingly detailed, extremely thorough, and very progressive.

The democratic character of the constitution is evident from Article 1, which states that "Italy is a Republic" and is reinforced by Article 139, which decrees that the republican form cannot be the object of constitutional change. The referendum imposed on the state the character of a republic based on parliamentary democracy. Consequently, political and civil liberties were reaffirmed; the principles of parliamentary government, abandoned under fascism, were confirmed, as was the division of power established by the eighteenth-century declaration of rights. The Republican Constitution, therefore, founded a political and social order based on a pluralistic democracy.

Of essential importance are the affirmation of the political, economic, and social rights and duties of the citizen, the recognition of the role of political parties and trade unions, institutional pluralism, political and administrative decentralization, and protection of minorities. Not only these essential principles of political democracy, but also those of economic and social democracy, are considered. The constitution also provides the mechanism by which plural democracy is achieved through political, economic, and social solidarity (Art. 2) and the fundamental equality of citizens (Art. 3).

The constitution's treatment of equality and solidarity among citizens has a double significance. On the one hand, it provides legal confirmation of the equality of the Republic's citizens both in their relations among themselves and with the institutions of the State. On the other hand, the removal of obstacles to economic and social equality by public powers is established and regarded as an actual duty. In reaction to the former preservation of social class structure, the members of the Constitutional Assembly wanted to ensure, by constitutional right, that all citizens would have real civil dignity in the social community, at work, and in education so as to allow them an active role in society.

The first article of the constitution gives clear evidence of the strong presence of certain political forces in the Constitutional Assembly. It states that "Italy is a democratic Republic founded on *lavoro*." The use of the word *lavoro* (work/labor) sparked much debate. The recognition of human labor as a fundamental value and right is further reinforced later (Art. 4): "The Republic recognizes the right of all citizens to work and shall promote such conditions as will make this right effective." Unfortunately, however, this strong constitutional right has not prevented Italy's excessively high percentage of unemployment. The constitution also recognizes that citizens have certain economic rights: to own property, to take economic initiatives within legal limits, to set aside savings and have them protected, and to work. This latter right carries with it considerable implications: representation and trade union protection of professional interests, just compensation, equality of treatment, collaboration in management, and social security. In fact, it obliges public powers to stimulate employment and safeguard it at all levels (Art. 35); and it guarantees the fundamental rights of workers concerning equal pay for equal effort, hours of work, weekly and annual paid holidays, equality between the sexes at work, minimum working age, and pension and workers' participation in management (Arts. 36, 37, 38, and 46). The constitution also provides social assistance (Art. 38) for those citizens unfit for work and without private means.

Also relevant is the way the constitution deals with the regulation of private property and wealth: its acquisition, possession, enjoyment, and circulation. Private ownership has legally recognized and guaranteed limits so as to ensure general accessibility and accountability (Art. 42). For example, private lands containing energy resources, or firms producing fuel or providing essential services, may be transferred into public ownership on the grounds of national interest with the payment of an indemnity (Arts. 42 and 43). The law can, in fact, impose limits on ownership and economic initiatives in the name of solidarity and the general social good.

It can, therefore, be said that the economic aspect of the Constitution of Italy is based on the following key elements: a mixed economy for ownership and initiatives, central planning entrusted to public authorities, private enterprise encouraged by a series of guarantees, and extensive protection for workers. All of these aspects are aimed at the creation of equally distributed public wealth.

Another clear and definitive break with fascism was the recognition and protection of ethnic and religious minorities. Provision was made both for safeguarding linguistic minorities and for the protection of religious worship. Minority rights were then reinforced by way of regional autonomy and investing the first five regions with special status, in particular, the regions of Trentino Alto Adige with its large German-speaking minority and Valle d'Aosta with its French-speaking minority.

The government of the Republic is thus formed by a system of equal constitutional elements: the president of the Republic, the Parliament, the Government (cabinet of ministers), the Judiciary, and the Constitutional Court. The conformity of the law to the constitution may be subject to verification by the Constitutional Court, which had not been provided for by the *Statuto Albertino,* the previous constitution. The base of sovereignty and, therefore, of constitutional power, rests with the people. This form of political democracy is confirmed in Art. 1, second clause, of the constitution. Consequently, the Italian people are the holders of sovereign power, which they exercise both directly through voting in elections and referenda and indirectly through institutional representation. Because of this essential principle of political democracy, the right to vote assumes a decisive constitutional significance. By means of a universal, direct, secret vote the electoral body selects political representatives who intervene directly whenever a referendum is proposed; the latter can be used for the abrogation of a law, for constitutional modification, or even for specified regional and local issues that have seen a notable expansion not always provided by the constitution. The constitution thus makes two essential provisions for the execution of popular sovereignty: first, the exercise of democratic representation in Parliament, regional assemblies, and local councils; second, participation through referenda (or direct democracy). Democratic voting and elections are the key elements of political representation and the foundation of legitimate power.

Parliamentary Organization and Political Pluralism

In dividing the Italian Parliament into two assemblies, the Senate and the Chamber of Deputies, the Constitutional Assembly was influenced by at least two factors. On the one hand, it considered it appropriate to establish political representation on a balance of power guaranteed by discussion between two assemblies, both of which derived their democratic legitimacy from direct election. On the other hand, it deemed paramount that the procedural considerations of the two chambers allow for a major reflection in the execution of their functions and imposed a need for coordination that would require at least two successive phases of debate.

The structure of the Italian Parliament has inherent problems. Constitutionally, the powers of the two chambers are equal and do not represent distinct social or geographic interests. The difference between them is so slight that it is possible to speak of an almost "perfect" double-chamber system. The major difference between them is the functional coordination of the two assemblies; in addition, the age of their members and that of their voters, as well as, until recently, the level of proportional representation, are also different.

Government *all'italiana* means that the more members the Parliament has, the better the people are served; so, Italy has more than three times as many members as the U.S. Congress, even though the American population is four times that of Italy and has a population make-up that is much more complex. Even worse, to compensate for the high number of parliamentarians, each member has a very small and usually ill-informed staff. Nothing remotely comparable to the numerous aides and well-staffed offices of U.S. senators and congressmen.

Under the Republican Constitution, the Senate is an elected body (unlike under the monarchy, when the members were appointed by the king). Until 1993, it was elected, every five years, on a regional basis by uninominal colleges or electoral bodies, with the use of regional proportional representation if no candidate succeeded in receiving the necessary 65% of valid votes. All citizens 25 years or above may vote, and citizens 40 years or above are eligible for the office of senator. To the 315 senators required by the constitution are to be added former presidents of the republic and senators, up to five, nominated by the president. These last are chosen from among those citizens who have made an outstanding social, scientific, artistic, or literary contribution to the country, a very healthy clause in a system that is heavily politicized.

Like the Senate, the Chamber is elected every five years. Until 1993, it was chosen by universal, direct, secret vote according to a proportional system of plurinominal colleges. The number of deputies, fixed at 630, is double the number of senators and is distributed in 32 electoral constituencies, each one having a number of deputies equal to the division of the entire population (based on the latest general census figures). The seats are assigned in accordance with the population of each constituency based on whole electoral quotients and the highest remainders. All citizens who are 18 or over may vote, and all those who are 25 or older may be elected to the Chamber.

Most of the work of the two assemblies is conducted at the committee level in each house, but some is also carried out through a system of interchange and coordination through double-chamber commissions. These are composed of deputies and senators in equal numbers and correspond proportionately to the size of the different parliamentary groups. Double-chamber commissions are used for inquiring into cases of criminal accusation, for directing and controlling the radio and television services, and for intervening in the problem of the *Mezzogiorno* (Southern Italy), as well as for other controls and inquiries specifically set up by Parliament.

Where the structure of Parliament is concerned, a general observation can be made that each chamber usually has a distinct function. Only in particular cases, specified by the constitution, do the two chambers unite in common session. The latter occurs for the election and swearing in of the President of the Republic, for the election of the constitutional justices (five of whom are nominated by Parliament), for the election of a third of the members of the Superior Council of the Judiciary, and for the President of the Council of Ministers (prime minister) and his ministers. When it is necessary for the two parliamentary chambers to unite, they sit together in Deputies Chamber at Palazzo Montecitorio, where the Chamber of Deputies is housed, as opposed to Palazzo Madama, the usual home of the Senate. The affinity of the two chambers and their similar functions, in addition to internal political bickering, makes the Italian Parliament a very slow-moving body. What made the system Byzantine, as we shall see, is the power that the political parties had acquired in the parliamentary structure.

The relationship between the parliamentary members and the political party from whose electoral lists they were elected is complex, and attempts at simplification can be misleading. Although the constitution confirms the classical parliamentary principle that members of the chambers represent the nation and exercise their functions without mandatory restrictions and, therefore, parliamentary members are neither the representatives of their electoral colleges nor the mandataries of the political party to which they are affiliated, political parties do exert strong control over them.

Parliament has many important functions and immense political power, primarily in its authority to legislate. Each member of Parliament can promote a legislative proposal. The right to propose laws, however, is also enjoyed by the Government (the executive branch), regional councils, the National Council for Economy and Labor (for matters involving the economy and employment), and a group of 50,000 electors. Parliament controls Government (the cabinet of ministers), that is, the executive branch, by its power to approve legislation and through the use of the vote of "confidence."

In the early 1990s, various institutional parliamentary reforms were proposed to speed up the flow of the work of Parliament, which is often dammed up by procedural obstacles. Proposals were made to introduce a single-chamber system, to drastically reduce the number of members of each assembly, to have uninominal elections, and to reduce proportional representation to only parties collecting at least 5% of the total votes. Until 1992, every attempt to reform governmental institutions found strong opposition, especially by D.C. However, in 1992, by the initiative of D.C., an attempt was made to start to correct one of the major absurdities of the Italian political system, that is, the separation between the legislative and the executive branches. In every democracy, that is the norm, but not in government all'italiana. In that year, D.C. established that the offices of Government (the cabinet of ministers) and Parliament were incompatible in the same person. Consequently, in accepting a post in government, an onorevole would have to give up his or her seat in Parliament. Aside from being freed from the potentially serious conflicts that would occur by holding positions in two branches of government, the *onorevole* could not vote in Parliament for or against his own government. Most important, the voting down of governments would not be done lightly because members of Government would not automatically return to Parliament!

As we shall see, major changes were also approved in the way Parliament is elected and political parties get their representation. The changes were so radical that political scientists have characterized them as the beginning of the second republic.

President: Head of State But Not of Government

Because the framers of the constitution were charged with creating a parliamentary republic, they had to avoid giving too much power to one individual (as is the case in the presidential republic where the president is head of state and of government). However, even though the president of the Italian republic does not enjoy the power held by his counterpart in a presidential republic, he is not a puppet. The last two presidents have given a clear indication of how powerful the president can be when the executive (Government) and legislative (Parliament) branches are weak and/or fragmented.

The president of the Italian republic is head of state but not of Government, and he represents the nation's political unity and guarantees the constitutional powers. By the power of his message, the president is able to influence political and institutional direction, both from within the institutions and in the country at large. The president has an important role as guarantor and political mediator when a government is being formed following a cabinet crisis. When he is convinced of the lack of "governability," the president is also able to dissolve the chambers early and call for new elections. The head of state in the Italian constitutional model is, therefore, charged with ensuring that the constitutional rules for the ordering of political and constitutional relations between the powers of the state are observed and with intervening to resolve any resulting institutional crises.

The head of state fulfills functions connected with all the constitutional powers of the Republic. Where parliamentary and legislative procedures are concerned, the president participates in the formation of laws by promulgation and can send laws back to the chambers for new consideration; he authorizes the presentation of proposed Government legislation and indicates political elections and referenda; he can ask for the extraordinary assembly of the chambers and, in consultation with their president, can order its dissolution; and, he nominates up to five senators. In relation to the Government and the executive function, the president of the republic is responsible for nominating the president of the council of ministers (prime minister) and, at his proposal, the ministers; he appoints, on the initiative of the Government and in those cases provided by the law, the state functionaries; he issues, after Government deliberation, decrees having the value of law (legal and legislative), as well as regulations; and he accredits and receives diplomatic representatives.

The head of state, moreover, commands the armed forces, presides over the Supreme Defense Council, and declares the state of war resolved upon by Parliament. Also very important is the formal participation by the president in the exercise of several administrative functions: the recognition of juridical appointments, dissolution of provincial and communal councils, legitimization of natural children, and decisions on recourse to extraordinary administrations and conferment of honors. In relation to the powers of justice, the head of state nominates five justices of the Constitutional Court, presides over the Supreme Council of the Judiciary, and can grant pardons and clemency.

All the acts of the president, including the exercising of his "own" powers, must be endorsed by the relevant ministers or by the president of the council so that they can assume the political responsibility. Furthermore, the president of the republic cannot be removed from power on the grounds of political irresponsibility. The only political control to which he is subject is that of public opinion and not being re-elected should he choose to stand again for office. However, the force of political interest and the power of the mass media on the president should not be undervalued. The loss of political support, accompanied by unfavorable public opinion, can lead to the president's dismissal from office.

Government in a Multi-Party System

It is the cabinet of ministers (Government) that holds the executive function. According to the principles of "parliamentary government" enshrined in the Italian constitutional model, the Government assumes the power of political decision with the consent of Parliament, which is expressed by a vote of "confidence" in the government by the two chambers. The nomination process usually begins with a Government crisis and ends with the swearing in of the president of the council of ministers (prime minister) and of his ministers by the president of the Republic. The second stage is that of parliamentary confidence. It opens with the presentation of the government to Parliament, within 10 days of nomination, and closes with a formal vote of confidence by Parliament. When a cabinet crisis occurs, the president of the republic, according to a well-established constitutional practice, engages in political consultations with individual state figures (former presidents of the republic, the presidents of both chambers, and former prime ministers) and also representatives and delegations of political parties. At the end of these soundings, the head of state, having judged that the political and institutional conditions exist for forming a government capable of winning parliamentary confidence, will entrust the creation of a cabinet to the designated prime minister. Usually, the latter accepts provisionally until he has established, through consultations with the various political forces, the concrete possibility of being able to form a government that will be supported by the majority of members of Parliament. The president of the republic then nominates the president of the council of ministers and, on the latter's proposal, the individual ministers who all then take the Oath of Loyalty to the Republic. Within the ten days allowed by the constitution, the Government must present itself to the chambers who, on hearing the declaration made by the president of the council, provide a vote of confidence. The president of the council coordinates the actions of the various ministers and maintains the unity of the general political direction, which is his first responsibility . The council of ministers decides on all the general policies of the Government, with specific competence for all the decisions involving the *collective responsibility* of the executive. Individual ministers join in determining the Government's political direction, in participating in the sessions of the council of ministers, and in making the decisions for their respective ministers. Ministers have, above all, a collective political responsibility for all the Government's acts and for many of the acts of political consideration that involve the collective responsibility of the Government.

The Government is in fact the holder of some normative powers: it decides the form in which laws will be proposed to the head of state, who must then authorize their presentation to the chambers. It also approves laws by decree in cases of emergency and legislative decrees on the delegation of Parliament. These materially legislative acts are then issued by decree of the president of the republic. Finally, the Government is responsible for regulating all the executive activity of the law and the administrative organization. The responsibility can be tested in Parliament through the "no confidence" motion, whose approval obliges the Government to resign.

By creating a governmental body that had collective responsibility and by giving it a leader who potentially could not assume too much power, the framers of the constitution have spared Italy from the abuses of an authoritative government or leader, but they also gave the country the structure for a political system which, as a consequence of this unique kind of proportional representation system, proved to be very unstable and would require skillful maneuvering and compromising in order to survive. As the coalition of various political forces, the Italian government has been increasingly fragmented and fragile. In the approximately first 52 years of the Republic, Italy has had about 54 governments; on the average, one government per year, instead of one for every five years, if it coincided with the normal five-year term of Parliament. Since the great majority of governments were coalitions of many parties allied to the Christian Democratic Party (*D.C.*), which was itself fractioned, a spirit of potential conflict and hostility forced a cabinet to fall on the slightest pretext of the leaders of even the smallest parties. The coalition formulas were dictated by possibilities for achieving the required majority in Parliament. The christian democrats and socialists, who constituted the core of the coalition until 1993, did not form an alliance based on mutual trust, parity, or programmatic accord. Their cooperation was driven by suspicion, personal rivalry, and eternal jockeying for position. Overall, the leaders of both parties were more able strategists for their parties than for the country.

The enduring but rather unproductive *D.C./P.S.I.* alliance had blocked the Italian political system in *immobilismo* and corruption. Unfortunately for Italy, until the fall of communism, there were no credible alternatives.

Multi-Party System, Pluralistic Democracy, and Chaotic Proportional Representation

The long morass of the Italian political system was partially caused by the overly idealistic aspirations of the fathers of the Italian constitution. In envisioning the role of the political parties in government and society, the framers of the Italian constitution were not only too optimistic, but were also too attached to the theoretical plan.

They rightfully assumed that one of the essential presuppositions to the concept of political democracy was allowing direct political participation to the citizen. To offer a real pluralistic democracy, the juridical channels of consultation, direction, and decision should be many and diverse. A real democratic state is, in fact, based on both fundamental juridical guarantees and an efficient interchange between public powers and civil society.

For a country where the specters of fascism were still very much present and the fear of the advent of communism was overwhelming—from the very beginning of the Cold War, Italy was at the frontier of the free world—the presence of a strong political party was scary. Proportional representation, without a minimum needed to achieve representation, was intended to foster minority parties and discourage monolithic groups like the communists or the disbanded fascists to take control.

Both the virtues and the problems on which Italian democracy was founded lay in its proportional representation system, which was one of the most representative in the world: the more an electoral system is proportional the greater the tendency for all political forces to be represented. Thus, from the very beginning a fairly wide array of political forces was represented, and it seems that voters responded enthusiastically to this wide spectrum of political choices. Although voting was not mandatory, there was a high level of electoral participation even in local elections and referenda. In fact, the proportion of eligible voters going to the polls in Italy has been the highest in Europe.

However, the system created an unworkable fragmentation of political parliamentary parties: a representation that oscillated between 12 and 16 parties. Moreover, the system did not create among Italians great faith in government. In fact, there is a curious paradox in Italy: a high percentage of voters and a high level of mistrust of government and political institutions. Italy has the lowest index of public satisfaction of any Western European industrial state. Surveys taken in the 1980s showed the level of trust in the political parties to be only around 10%. In comparison with the turnover rate of members of parliament in other democracies (France, Germany, England, USA), Italy's had been constantly higher: until 1993, each new Parliament was approximately one-third new members.[2]

In politics all'italiana, until 1993, although political parties were at the core of the system, personalities did play a role. For the house of deputies especially, even though many voters simply voted for the party and did not bother to indicate a candidate, voters could express the preference vote. They could favor three or more candidates, according to the size of the electoral district. The personal votes were counted and the candidates of each party were ranked accordingly. If a party won, say, six seats in a particular district, these would have been given to the six candidates with the most preference votes. Candidates could run for election in more than one district (and many leaders did!) and, if they won in more than one, could decide which district to represent. In this case the first of the nonelected obtained the seat that was not filled. The first of the nonelected could also "succeed" a deceased deputy or one who retired during the life of a parliament.

The preference vote system was exploited by the Italian political parties to pull in as many votes as possible. Not only did political parties allow the same very popular individuals to be candidates in more than one district, but they presented lists of candidates that were much more numerous than seats available. Even though some of the names put on the list did not have any chance of winning, they were given a spot for the simple fact that they could attract a certain number of votes for the party. In preparation for the 1987 parliamentary elections, leaders of the Radical Party had the idea of including Ilona Anna Staller, better known as Cicciolina, a hard-core porno star on their roster of candidates. The intention was to increase interest in the party, which pledged to fight for human rights, including the rights of homosexuals and prostitutes. To show the absurdity of the system, nearly 20,000 voters of the Rome-Viterbo-Latina-Frosinone district chose Cicciolina and she became a legislator. A prostitute became the *onorevole* Cicciolina, member of the house of deputies!

Parties handsomely rewarded those who pulled in votes. There was a constant link between elections, governments, and ministerial appointments. The proportional system was, in a sense, applied to the distribution of government positions and these, in turn, depended to a large extent on the preference system. The preference vote, when sufficiently high, opened the door to the continuous holding of ministerial power. Moreover, as the preference vote was the main avenue for political promotion and, given the clientele nature of the system—more votes were translated into more power of patronage, which returned more votes next time around—campaigns for election did acquire a personal flavor. This system created a high degree of stability: a good *preference vote* opened the door to a ministerial position, a ministerial position enabled the holder to exercise patronage, and this in turn increased the size of his personal vote. When sufficiently high, the preference vote opened the door to continuous holding of ministerial power, and the system got locked-up in *immobilismo*.

The method used for the Senate elections was less proportional than the one used for the chamber of deputies election and was more favorable to the two largest parties (*D.C.* and *P.C.I.*). For the senate, each party presented only one candidate, and the election was carried on regional representation.

Italy's electoral system was geared to a country emerging from fascism into the Cold War. However, even though proportional representation was intended to foster minority parties and discourage monolithic groups like the communists or disbanded fascists, and though it provided a high level of democratic representation, *proportional representation Italian style* produced several problems. It created 54 unstable coalition governments and an unworkable fragmentation of parliamentary parties—with no fewer than 16 being represented in the early 1990s. It made decision making more difficult and did not offer the electorate a clear-cut alternative between potential governments. In that kind of system, the Italian electorate could only influence a possible coalition by strengthening a particular party's parliamentary representation; it did not vote for a future government.

Although political power remained concentrated in the political parties, and members of the Italian Parliament were elected on the basis of party representation, the latter could act independently of the party because they could use a secret ballot through which they were able to avoid party discipline. And many times it was through such independence that governments fell and political crises became more difficult to solve.

In the 1980s and early 1990s, proportional representation *all'italiana* encouraged the proliferation of protest movements, local and one-issue groups which, in the 1992 April national elections, fielded more than 500 slates of candidates. Altogether, a record 16 parties achieved representation in the national parliament, even though only six of them polled more than 5% of the total vote. Italian political leaders bickered about reforms for many years with little progress. The small parties were strongly opposed to both the German and French models. In Germany, a party cannot win seats in the national parliament unless it polls at least 5% of the total vote; in France, the major parties benefit heavily from a system keyed to a single constituency, only partly corrected by recourse to a second round of balloting if no candidate wins out on the first. In Italy, the *D.C.* would have been the main beneficiary under either model, but all, or most of its traditional allies (republicans, liberals, social democrats) would have been wiped out. As we shall see later, because of the fall of communism and the uncovering of political mega-scandals, the will of political leaders was not enough to maintain the status quo.

Partitocracy and the Spoils System

However, one of the major problems of the Italian democracy has been the fact that it is a party-dominated system, sometimes referred to as a partitocracy, *partitocrazia*. In essence, it means that the formal democratic institutions of government and elections play only secondary roles. Parochial interests of the parties were so strong that they determined the creation and the fall of cabinets. It was the strength or weakness of political parties that determined the nature of the coalitions. However, the size of popular support and political influence were not necessarily correlated. To a large extent, the changes in the governing coalition were primarily the result of party politics rather than popular decisions through elections. This could certainly be illustrated by the fact that the Republican Party, with only a popular support of around 5%, shaped many government coalitions, headed many ministries and directed, under its leader, Giovanni Spadolini, the first non Christian Democratic government.

Partitocracy degenerated into a system of abuses and an uncontrollable patronage system. Americans are well acquainted with the "spoils system" (President Andrew Jackson once said "to the victor belongs the spoils"), which enables a newly elected president (governor, mayor, or even county executive, etc.) to replace the appointees of the previous administration with his own handpicked loyalists. The spoils system, Italian style, is inspired by the same principle, but, by force of circumstances, it is far more complex and has a much wider impact on the country.

Until 1994, political appointments were made in every sector of the Italian economy, from senior diplomatic posts to positions in education, to opera houses, to the sanitation department, to the health service at the local supermarket. In many cases, political appointments started at the top of the management ladder and continued, less officially, to the bottom. For example, most singers at La Scala were connected with the Socialist Party, because that was the leading party in Milan in the 1980s. The party with the most votes got to dish out the most jobs and favors. The patronage system, called *lottizzazione*, worked just like that.

The political parties claimed that their civil servants, managers, bankers, etc., were qualified and efficient. However, we know that such a system, because of its very nature, does not reward quality and easily suffers from excessive abuse. For example, a Milan politician from the Socialist Party who was caught accepting bribes did not even bother to hide his computer lists of job candidates recommended by his electorate. The lists, which included names of family members, favors granted, and political sponsors, was not proof of illegal behavior because it was not illegal to exchange favors for votes. Regularly, lists of political appointments appeared in local newspapers. At the end of the 1980s, in Milan, a christian democrat was named to head the local garbage disposal authority, while a socialist got the management of the airports, and a social democrat the city's drugstores. The national health service, the state-owned television networks, and banks were among the *lottizzazione* monster's favorite lairs. So, too, was government-controlled industry, grouped under three enormous holding companies. The largest, *Istituto per la Ricostruzione Industriale (IRI)*, was headed by a member of the Christian Democratic Party. The other two, *Ente Nazionale Idrocarburi (ENI)*—the state hydrocarbon company—and *(EFIM)*—manufacturing enterprises—were headed by socialist appointees and had christian democratic vice chairmen.

The patronage system is a patriarchal monster that won't die easily. The Italian public sector—excluding the massive state holding companies—employed 19% of the work force at the beginning of the 1990s. With unemployment at 11% (about 20% in the South), the monster will have plenty of breathing space even with the reforms being instituted.

To correct the problem, some economists and politicians put pressure on government to reduce the public sector through privatization. That is exactly what Italy has been doing in the past few years after much political infighting. It has been a heroic decision because the parties wanted to hang on to their quotas of management jobs, known in Italy as *poltrone*, armchairs. With public-sector businesses and banks accounting for nearly half of the fifty largest Italian companies in terms of revenue, there were plenty of armchairs at stake! To their credit, it must be said that, in spite of the corruption, political parties do not operate in a vacuum. Budgetary problems, the impending union with the rest of Europe, and popular discontent brought them to the realization that changes were in the best interest of both the nation and the parties.

Indeed, the results of the spring 1992 general elections convinced politicians that the people wanted radical changes. Protest votes hurt the parties most closely associated with the spoils system: the long-time ruling coalition of christian democrats, socialists, liberals, and social democrats. Parties such as the federalist-minded League in the North, *La Lega*, and the anti christian democrat *La Rete* (Network Party) in the South picked up votes from Italians weary of government mismanagement. The biggest changes, however, came as a result of the end of the Communist Party.

Dilemmas of a Revolutionary Party

Italians have not just been weary of government mismanagement, they have also been weary of most traditional political parties. Indeed, they have grown weary of the *classe politica*, the political class. During the long years of the Cold War they expressed their disappointment by voting communist. This means that many Italians voted communist in those years not because they firmly believed in communism, but because they disliked the other parties. This political behavior had positive, not negative, implications for democratic stability. It gave Italy a political balance and produced profound social reform, most likely unattainable without the presence of a strong Communist Party.

It should be reiterated that the Italian Communist Party was almost unique in its brand of communist ideology. It was in a position quite different from the Eastern-Bloc communist parties that were ousted from power at the beginning of the 1990s. It had deep, emotional roots in Italy as a workers' and anti-fascist movement before, during, and after WWII, and in the 1970s it was the leader in the Euro-Communist movement, breaking with Moscow on many policy issues and trying to project Marxism as a valid choice within a democratic society.

By rejecting Moscow's direction, Euro-communism was to be understood as an evolution within Western culture rather than as a revolutionary disruption of it. Resonating in Euro-communism was Antonio Gramsci's faith that, within Western culture, the Italian branch of communism was already peculiarly fitted for a humanism of technology and work.

Communists like Antonio Gramsci and Enrico Berlinguer are major historical figures and are even regarded as heroes; many of Italy's top intellectuals, artists, writers, and performers have been communists, and the party generally had the reputation of being more socially active and less corrupt than other major parties.

The Communist Party, too, like other political manifestations, embraced many paradoxes. As the largest, strongest, and in many ways, the most able of communist parties found among democracies, the party not only refrained from any subversive or revolutionary assaults on democratic institutions and processes, at critical moments it even acted unambiguously to support and reinforce them. Despite the Vatican anti-communist crusade, the Communist Party was supported by many practicing catholics and, contrary to all expectations, it was strongest in some of the wealthiest regions of the peninsula and often weakest in the poorest regions.

Though it regularly claimed one-quarter to one-third of the electorate and had considerable power in local governments, the *Partito Comunista Italiano (P.C.I.),* was never able to lead a national government. This was due, in part, to an unwritten U.S. veto of a Communist Party rule in a country that was a key NATO member. Without the possibility of being part of a coalition government, the *P.C.I.* remained cut off from Italy's other left-wing parties, such as the socialists and social democrats, both of which were allied with the *Democrazia Cristiana, (D.C.),* to form most coalition governments until the early 1990s. However, as we shall see later, the Communist Party was the most important cultural presence in postwar Italian society, even more important than the *D.C.*

The party used a strategy that involved the working-class movement, putting itself at the head of an alliance of social forces that was against monopoly capitalism and the political remnants of fascism and was advancing toward socialism through a combination of legal mass agitations and protests, a full use of the parliamentary and electoral machinery, and a constant effort of ideological penetration and struggle. The strategy was designed progressively to disarm the forces of monopoly and reaction and shift the balance of economic and political power democratically toward the working class and its allies.

The party's postwar strategy was also centered on a cultural policy of the masses. First, it sought to manage its own sector of popular culture by building its own capillary networks of cultural apparatuses (a party press, publishing houses, libraries, and sites of popular recreation) and thereby penetrate "civil society" at all levels right down to the smallest local area. For the postwar Communist Party, popular culture came to mean largely both autochthonous "folk" and class-based traditions. It should also be added that in the *P.C.I.* these meanings became distinctively associated with others: "popular culture" was connected with positive notions of popular community, solidarity, and tradition; working-class education was connected to a project of popular enlightenment and acculturation which, in turn, was closely linked with the party's long-term political project of working-class hegemony. Second, it sought to win over and mobilize intellectuals, whether "great intellectuals" (leading cultural figures) or middle strata intellectuals engaged in cultural work—teachers, journalists, and workers in the theater, film, publishing, or broadcasting industries. This meant building a party presence in existing cultural organizations by recruiting new members or attracting fellow travelers. Third, the party sought to project a particular set of cultural values and to promote an aesthetic and a morality that were social and collective rather than individualist or private, "progressive" rather than "decadent," outward-looking rather than introspective, and centered upon public civic participation rather than upon private activity and consumption.

While the party created a wide appeal through its cultural programs, it never became convincing enough through its ideology to win over enough voters to become the leading party and take over the government. Certainly, the winds of change that were transforming the communist states of Eastern Europe into democracies had a determining effect on the fate of the *P.C.I.* In 1992 it changed its name, calling itself the *Partito Democratico della Sinistra (P.D.S.)*, the Democratic Party of the Left, and reemerged as a new, non-communist entity that hoped to integrate with Europe's social democratic Left and, eventually, come to power. The hammer and sickle that it had held aloft for 69 years was retained, but in a reduced form, submerged beneath the roots of a large, leafy tree that became the dominant emblem. The action was not meant to be a "self-dissolution" of the party, or a cutting of the roots; rather, it attempted to give the roots new sap that would lead to a new political formation of the Italian Left that would group communists, left-wing catholics, greens, radicals, and other reformists and progressive forces.

Old-guard traditionalists, however, felt that Italian communism was not a worn-out relic but still a proud symbol of resistance to fascism and the construction of a postwar democracy in Italy. Therefore, they claimed, changing the party so radically and ridding it of its communist identity would dishonor the Party's past. Representing about one-third of the Party's membership and including key elder statesmen, these people wanted restructuring, but only within a communist framework. They founded the *Partito di Rifondazione Comunista* (Party of Communist Refoundation). They were relics of a political apparatus that had influenced obliquely the course of postwar Italian history and had contributed to the paradoxical "stability within instability" of the Italian political system.

Stability Within Instability and Democratic Dictatorship

Italy's legendary "instability" was an artful illusion in the power game. Despite the air of *opera buffa*, Italian politicians were able, through shrewd maneuverings, to mold one of the most stable democracies in the Western world. Foreigners may have talked about instability, but Italians complained of the total immobility, *immobilismo*, of their political system. What Italy did not have was the alternation in power between different political parties common to other Western countries. This is perhaps the most peculiar aspect of the Italian system until 1994.

In fact, there was a hidden stability in the Italian political system. Italy actually held two political records. In addition to having had the highest number of governments in the postwar period, Italy is also the only Western democracy in which one political party dominated the government for about 50 years. Italy and Japan were, in fact, the only two industrial democracies in which the same party governed uninterrupted for about 50 years. Alliances and strategies changed, but the Christian Democratic Party remained at the head of 49 of the 52 governments and held the highest number of cabinet posts in all of them.

Stability also came from a second source. The many changes in governments were rarely caused by serious political crises. Much more common in Italy was the "crisis" that was really a disagreement among political leaders or a clash of personalities. This kind of political dispute was fairly easy to resolve. The heads of political parties most often patched up their differences and formed a new government, sometimes in a matter of a few days. Occasionally, the "new" governments were exact replicas of the earlier ones. The Italians called these "photocopy governments." In fact, the recycling of the same people in government after government was another stabilizing element in Italian democracy.

However, the long longevity in power of many politicians, while it provided stability, also instituted a kind of dictatorship in a very democratic system. A case in point is the government crisis that occurred in the spring of 1991. Because of disagreements among the parties in the government coalition, Prime Minister Giulio Andreotti resigned. A few weeks later, he was replaced by none other than Prime Minister Giulio Andreotti, initiating his seventh term as the nation's leader. More than any other politician, Andreotti had become the symbol of christian democratic permanent power. Andreotti served in the first postwar cabinet in 1946 and remained at the center of power until 1993. Besides being prime minister seven times, he was also minister of defense, minister of the interior, and minister of foreign affairs. Nor is he a unique case; there are several other christian democrat notables who had careers of equal longevity.

How did politicians like Andreotti survive so long? Andreotti belonged to a world of compromise, flexibility, pragmatism, shrewd political maneuverings, and ruthless Realpolitik. As Andreotti himself observed with characteristic wit: "I am typically Italian, typically Roman and therefore untranslatable and unexportable." In the 1960s he was a leader of the christian democratic right wing, opposing the entrance of the socialists into the government. Then, in the mid-1970s, he headed the first Italian government supported by the Italian Communist Party. He established his reputation as ardently pro-NATO, but began flirting with the Soviet Union long before Gorbachev arrived on the scene. As foreign minister during the *Achille Lauro* hijacking, he allowed the alleged terrorists to slip from Italian custody, presumably because of his design for Italian policy in the Mideast. "In Italy we have the idea that politics is like the tailor's art. If you have to make a suit for a hunchback, the suit will be crooked," a friend of mine told me.

Compromise and flexibility were almost a necessity in the first decades of the postwar period. Italy was violently split, with threats from the extreme right and left, and the center divided. An American approach of frontal confrontation would have led to civil war in Italy. The D.C. deserves credit for lifting Italy out of chronic poverty and for maintaining democracy. However, the D.C. should be criticized for what it did in the 1980s. It continued to maintain itself through the patronage system and allowed a thin line of demarcation between patronage and Mafia in many areas. Fortunately, with the Cold War over and the dissolution of the Italian Communist Party, part of the rationale for the christian democratic power system vanished. It was no longer necessary to tolerate corruption and Mafia influence to assure the triumph of light over darkness, so the calls for serious, systemic change had become deafening in 1992. Even the ex-president of the republic, Francesco Cossiga, a christian democrat, sounded the alarm, talking about scrapping the Italian constitution and writing a new one. "The Mafia has taken effective control over the southern third of the country," said the president, "and Italy's system of coalition democracy has become unmanageable." The revelations of political corruption brought to light through "operation clean hands," as we will see in chapter III, created such vehemence against the political system by the Italians that political parties could not squabble anymore. Most political leaders had to accept the hard reality that Italy needed to become a "normal" democracy of alternating governments with clear electoral mandates. However, it was not easy to find a credible alternative to the *D.C.*

The Italian political system was unquestionably full of paradoxes when it is compared to other democracies. But comparison of one democracy with another can easily lead to misleading evaluations. In doing that, we would be inclined to believe that American or some other brand of democracy is a "template that can be stenciled onto almost any other country and produce similar effects there. We forget the spectacular failures that followed past efforts to export the American-British constitutional formula to Latin American, Asian, and African countries."[3] Moreover, no democratic country will look entirely reassuring when measured against some abstract, idealized conception of a democratic state. But the Italian system did need some profound tuning. In engaging in radical institutional reform to prepare for the "second republic," it is important for Italy not to work in absolute abstraction, even though it has the right because of its history of always being a great inventor in the field of politics. The experience throughout the centuries—from the days of the Roman Empire to the period of the Renaissance city-states, through unification and finally even during the fascist dictatorship—as a laboratory for the political experiments of all Western civilization should not be detached from the learning experience that other modern democracies may offer.

Notes

1. Simon Parker, "Political Identities," in David Forgacs and Robert Lumley, eds., *Italian Cultural Studies* (Oxford: Oxford U. P., 1996), 108.

2. Nothing can be compared to the failings of the American system. Presidents and the large majority of legislators are usually elected with the votes of less than 30% of the people eligible to vote. And that cannot be called a mandate. Moreover, of those who do vote, hundreds of thousands of citizens have no real choice of legislative candidates because they live in one of the dozens of districts where the incumbent runs unopposed or faces an opponent so underfinanced that he has no real chance to bring his case before the public.

   The fairness of the American elections has been compromised by the enormous advantages incumbents have over challengers in terms of campaign fund raising, access to the ballot, legislative mailing privileges, control of the redistricting process, and ability to dole out "member-item" funds (given to legislators for pet projects in their districts). The increasing ability of incumbents to use the perquisites of power to underwrite their reelection campaigns explains why the incumbent reelection rate for New York State legislators reached 98% during the 1980s.

   Italy not only meets the conditions of poliarchy; it manages to do so under a range of existential factors that, in many other places, would make democratic poliarchy highly improbable, or place it in jeopardy.

3. Joseph La Palombara, *Democracy Italian Style* (New Haven: Yale U. P., 1987), 6.

Italians love public demonstrations because they love to perform life. However, by dramatizing public concerns, "particularism" and "familism" are supplanted by passionate interest in the common good and high ideals. The fight for a global ban of nuclear power is as passionate as the struggle to lessen the hunger in the world. Printed by courtesy of *America Oggi*.

II

Decisive Turning Points and Constitutional Transformation

Ouster of the Communists

As has been stated, the Italian political system can be seen as either very chaotic or so stable as to be characterized *as immobile* or stagnant. Regardless of the perception, we must realize that the Italian democracy has gone through an evolution culminating in some profound constitutional changes. Although the process has been continuous, one can identify five decisive turning points: the early ouster of the communists from government, the "opening to the left," the unrealized "historic compromise" with the communists, the "fall of communism," and the "Second Republic."

The expulsion of the communists from government in the immediate postwar period, with American assistance, was probably the most important turning point in modern Italian history. In 1947 the Left was in a strong position as a result of its role in the antifascist partisan movement, as we have seen. With this momentum behind it, there were striking indications that it could take over Italy in a very few years unless some decisive political actions were taken. Most *P.S.I.* (Socialist Party) leaders, prompted by the myth of "working class unity" and by the expectation that the Soviet army would soon become the dominant force throughout Europe, chose to play a secondary role to the *P.C.I.* rather than position their party as a third force between the christian democrats and the communists. It was America's intervention and intelligent maneuverings by some Italian politicians that saved Italy from communism and stopped the advance of communism into the rest of western Europe.

The objective was reached by splitting the Socialist Party. With encouragement and financial support from U.S. unions and skillful CIA work, many *P.S.I.* representatives and about one-third of the socialist voters split away to form a Social Democratic Party (*P.S.D.I.*) under the leadership of Giuseppe Saragat.[1] The split, finalized early in 1947, a few days after *D.C.* premier Alcide De Gasperi's return from a visit to Washington, divided the "working class unity" and paved the way to the "unloading" of the communists from government. The action had also drawn the battle lines for the following general election in the spring of 1948: communists and socialists ran on a joint ticket under the label of "People's Bloc," while the christian democrats led a centrist coalition that included social democrats, liberals, and republicans.

The results of the election went better than expected for the *D.C.* and its alliance. They came close to polling an absolute majority of the votes, scoring an oversized victory. Millions of Italians, who under normal circumstances would have voted either for some rightist party or for some moderate left-of-center faction, cast their ballots for De Gasperi's *D.C.* party as the only available alternative to communism. The new Social Democratic Party got 7% of the votes. Despite the rather poor performance of the republicans (*P.R.I.*) and the liberals (*P.L.I.*) who ran under the label of National Bloc, the centrist governmental coalition won the support of 62% of the electorate, twice as much as the communist-led Popular Front. The feeling that De Gasperi and the U.S. had saved Italy from communism was widespread even among the representatives of social groups and economic interests that had not voted for the *D.C.* or had done so with great reluctance.

However, the role played by the Church cannot be underestimated. The Catholic Church had become heavily involved in electoral politics through the actions of the clergy and those of Church-sponsored lay organizations like the civic committees. The main priority was to consolidate support for the christian democrats as a block against the force of the left. Catholic unity became a key term in this political discourse, where "Catholic" increasingly came to mean not a general religious identity that was shared by the vast majority of Italians, but a specific political commitment to *D.C.* In the polarized environment of the Cold War, both sides defined themselves in opposition to each other, and the ideological connections made between Catholicism and anti-communism are particularly striking. The battle was fought out using all the media: sermons, rallies, radio, cinema, newspapers, and, most strikingly, wall posters. The Catholic Church became both the creator and the defender of the family, and this became a key theme in the ideological battle of the period. More attention was given to the threat posed by communism to the family than to any other aspect, real or imagined, of the Left's political program. Family life and values became the crucial ideological terrain on which the opposition between Catholicism and communism was established.[2]

However, the weakened Left still worried the U.S. government because it enjoyed the support of a strong labor union. There was deep conviction that unless workers were snatched away from the leftist labor union through labor issues, the Left could have easily regained influence. This led U.S. representatives to press hard for an immediate confluence into a new national union of all workers who were no longer willing to accept the communist-socialist leadership of *C.G.I.L.*, the single, all-embracing labor organization revived during the last year of the war. In the summer of 1948 a new national labor union, *C.I.S.L.*, was founded to attract Catholic union members. These political events were a major setback for communism in Italy from which the party never regained the power to enter government again.

Notwithstanding the changes, the new government, free of the presence of socialists and communists, was unable to make the radical changes the new democratic society needed. De Gasperi's task in tackling a full spectrum of reforms was difficult because his centrist coalition included both the non-communist Left and the moderate Right, whose views on social and economic issues are notoriously far apart. The country needed to implement long overdue tax and land reforms as well as a thorough overhauling of the bureaucratic apparatus and of the economic system itself in order to improve the lot of the most destitute and forgotten groups: farm laborers especially in the South, defenseless against the onslaught of inflation; small industries that had been allowed to wither and die; and labor's stepchildren, the unskilled workers. There was little awareness of the danger that in Italy political stability might turn into stagnation or that the reconstruction drive itself would result in a substantial restoration of old economic and social structures.

For the next decade, labor remained Italy's cheapest commodity—to the fortune of the few who had the money to hire and to the misfortune of the many who had only their labor to offer for hire. For millions of peasants who toiled in the fields, the only hope for change remained emigration. The country continued to be good for the rich and bad for the poor. Economic and political power continued to be vested in few hands: mostly landowners in the South, big business and industrialists in the North. A professional class of politicians, drawn mostly from the swollen ranks of lawyers and university professors, provided a parliamentary veneer. The Catholic Church continued to extend its power in every aspect of life.

Notwithstanding the "economic miracle," by 1961 Italy presented a great discrepancy in the rates of material and civic progress. The country unquestionably had all the ingredients for a successful democracy, but neither its social and institutional structure nor its administrative practices had been brought in line with those of the modern Western democracies by the 1960s. The country still lacked an equitable tax system, a farsighted approach to land tenure and agricultural problems, antitrust legislation, efficient regulatory agencies in the fields of power, trade, labor relations, etc., and a modern educational system. Under mounting conservative pressure within the coalition, it was determined that too little progress had been made. Even the great economic expansion of those years, unattended by adequate social progress and institutional modernization, failed to produce political dividends for the government coalition. The only way to have corrected this situation would have been to strike out on a bold course of social and economic reforms designed to appeal to the bulk of the communist and socialist voters.

A transitional government leaning toward a more stable political solution, approved in Parliament with the backing of the neo-fascists, had been greeted by the worst postwar threat to the state and indicated the limitations of political choices in a government the Italian people would accept. The danger to Italian democracy posed by this situation became manifest with the bloody riots that swept many parts of the country in July 1960, taking a toll of 11 dead and more than 1,000 injured. This government, headed by Fernando Tambroni, which survived only two months, remains the sole "attempt" in postwar Italy of a government supported by the neo-fascist party.

Opening to the Left and Profound Social Change

From the time of the "economic miracle" in the late 1950s, Italian society had been undergoing a profound and sustained process of modernization and secularization, and it was not a coincidence that the first center-left government of 1963 saw the socialists join the executive branch at a time when organized labor had found its voice again after a long period of relative inactivity. This also means that polarized political pluralism had become less polarized and increasingly consensus-driven.

The opening to the left in the early 1960s, which brought the Socialist Party of Italy (*P.S.I.*), previously in electoral alliance with the Communist Party (*P.C.I.*), into a governing coalition with the christian democrats, republicans, and social democrats, offered the opportunity for broadening and consolidating popular support for Italy's democratic institutions as well as for her secure anchorage to the West. By 1962 such an opening appeared possible and desirable to the majority of *D.C.* leaders. Along with an internal evolution, two things happened outside of the Party to render the move to the left possible. First, the accession, as we shall see later, of Angelo Roncalli to the papacy in 1958 had boxed-off right-wing clerics in the Vatican. Second, Pietro Nenni's Socialist Party found itself weakened by its de facto alliance with the communists. Whereas the *P.C.I.* continued steadily to construct its own separate realm, the socialists, behaving as a traditional party, lost followers to the *P.C.I.* while winning none from the right. With some new *D.C.* leaders insisting that some of the gains of the economic miracle be applied to such problems as welfare, health, old-age pensions, and education, a reformist majority within the *P.S.I.*, willing to give the *D.C.* a chance to cut its links to political corruption, clerical reaction, and economic injustice, sealed the bargain. Fortunately, John F. Kennedy understood that the U.S. would hurt its own interests if it continued to oppose an opening to the socialists—it would have also contributed to pushing them back into the arms of the communists. The "opening" turned out to be the first concrete step in a far-reaching realignment of Italy's political forces aimed at isolating the largest communist party in the West and forming a stable governmental majority resting on a wider and more solid foundation of popular support.

The center-left government of the 1960s and 1970s may be criticized for many excesses in labor legislation and wasteful public expenditures, but it increased democratization in every area of the life of the country. A center-right coalition with the then extremely conservative liberals, and depending on parliamentary support from the neo-fascist *M.S.I.*, might have polarized Italian society and blocked needed social and economic reforms. In fact, the "opening to the Left" was achieved only after a disastrous attempt to seek support from the Right.

American foreign policy, shortsighted most of the time, acted wisely in recognizing these realities and giving the green light to the center-left in 1961-1963, reversing the futile policies of Ambassador Clare Booth Luce, who wanted a Christian Democratic alliance with the monarchists, and of Deputy Chief of Mission Outerbridge Horsey, who, a few years later, was so hostile to the socialists that he considered a government dependent on the support of the neo-fascists a better means of protecting U.S. interests.

After fifteen years of government, the failings and shortcomings of the center-left coalitions were so strong that they inadvertently helped the communists not only to keep their role as the main opposition force but to increase their share of the popular vote from just over 20% in the late 1940s to almost 35% in the mid-1970s.

Flirting with the Historic Compromise

The loss of public support by the center-left coalition and the strong gain by the communists forced the christian democrats to make another turn in their political fight to hold on to power by seeking a *historic compromise* government, which would include the Communist Party. This turning point seemed almost inevitable because the communists were gaining more popular support because of an increasing electoral fragmentation. In the election of 1976, during the last months of the Ford administration, the communists achieved their all-time high in an Italian election, 34.4% of the vote. They were extending their hegemony in every important area of Italian life—the schools, the press, the judiciary, the trade unions, and regional and local governments. The possible *historic compromise* coalition of communists with the christian democrats was perceived as possibly compromising both Italian freedom and the country's support of the Western Alliance.

In this atmosphere of crisis, the Carter administration was pressured with bad advice from two extremes of the U.S. political spectrum. From the right came demands for the U.S. to take a direct role in stopping the communist threat, through covert operations if necessary. The other bit of bad advice came from the other end of the political spectrum, which argued that the *P.C.I.*'s accession to power was both inevitable and desirable. Both groups stood on solid ground in making their argument. The Carter administration gave serious consideration to the counterproductive effects of past covert operations. The communists were extraordinary experts in giving wide publicity to leaks on covert financing operations by Americans and had been very successful in gaining popular support as the defender of the country's sovereignty against "American domination." In addition, incautious statements made by U.S. officials during this period that appeared to threaten Italy with reprisals if it gave the communist party a governing role. During the Nixon-Ford years, the P.C.I. had gained in two national elections, raising its vote share from 26.9% to 34.4% while steadily extending its influence in key sectors of national life.

The Carter administration shared with the previous administration the opposition to any formula involving the communist party's entry into the government in Italy and the determination to do everything possible to avoid such a development. But there was a clear difference over the strategy to be followed. Ford and Kissinger's strategy was keyed to the concept of *trench warfare*: hammer away rigidly on American hostility to *P.C.I.*'s participation in the government by means of warnings about the consequences in the international field. Carter's strategy, instead, was built on the concept of *mobile warfare*: avoid head-on clashes, resort to a more flexible and indirect outflanking maneuver. This had very positive effects in this critical moment in Italian postwar history. The fundamental result of Prime Minister Andreotti's trip to Washington (July 1977) brought about, through an operation quite typical of Andreotti, the apparent reconciliation of two opposed purposes. The premier went back to Rome after having won Washington's green light for a political formula that involved communist cooperation, after having persuaded the Americans that he and his party were intransigently anti-communist. The Americans bet on Andreotti's consummate skills as a politician and his ability to manage to keep the communists out of government while governing with their assent.

However, acts of terrorism raised some fears of possible, uncontrollable radical political turns. Even though Italian society had shown itself to be tough and remarkably shock-resistant, the terrorists were trying to demonstrate that it was falling apart. The continued high level of street violence unquestionably carried sinister implications for the future. The wave of riots and terrorism was viewed by the great law-abiding majority of Italians as further evidence of their government's inability to govern, and it was making the communists look increasingly like a party of law and order. The situation was such that the U.S. had to be more explicit on the "communist issue" in Italy, that is, make greater efforts to underline its "preference" for political formulas aimed at keeping the communists out of government. Carter, therefore, made public statements that while the U.S. was committed to noninterference in the domestic affairs of any country in Western Europe, it did not want the communist parties to have an influential or dominant role in the governments of those countries. The best way to help assure that communist parties did not come to power in Western

European countries was for democratic parties to meet the aspirations of their people for more effective, more just, and more compassionate government. The Carter administration used every means available to present its position but it was being distorted by a large sector of the Italian mass media. Under the pretext of making a nonpolitical trip to Italy, Joseph Califano, U.S. secretary for Health, Education, and Welfare, and the representative of Italian Americans in the Carter administration, stated that "the Americans of Italian origin are increasingly aware of the situation in Italy and overwhelmingly want Italy to be free, strong, and non-communist."

It is hard to gauge the impact the U.S. move had on the future course of events. It was certainly a shot in the arm for many D.C.s, socialists, social democrats, republicans, and liberals who looked with dismay at a communist participation in the national government, and it gave pause to the political factions in the democratic camp as well as to the economic groups that favored or were ready to underwrite such a participation. The results of this well-planned position, very democratic in nature, were strengthened by the effects of an incident that was part of a revolutionary campaign against the state. As it has been many times before, history may have been changed in its course by events that had the opposite effect than was planned. The kidnapping and assassination of Italian Premier Aldo Moro by the Red Brigade (*Brigate Rosse*) was the beginning of the end of any possible historical compromise between the communists and the democratic forces of Italy. The outrage touched the heart and soul of the Italian people, and the elections of that year reflected the outrage.

By the end of 1978, communist leaders, including Enrico Berlinguer, the top advocate of the historic compromise, decided to cut their losses by taking the party back into the opposition. This precipitated new general elections that were held in June 1979, two years ahead of schedule. The communist share of the popular vote dropped from more than 34% to just over 30%. The myth of the *P.C.I.*'s inexorable, irreversible advance was shattered. In the next several years, the overall communist performance at the polls showed a marked downtrend: by 1988, the Party's vote was cut by almost one-third from its 1976 peak.

The 1979 elections paved the way for a new phase of Italian politics that featured a revival of the center-left coalition. Compared with the government formed after the opening to the *P.S.I.* back in the early 1960s, the reconstituted coalition reflected some significant changes in the political landscape. It included not only a strengthened Republican Party and a Social Democratic Party overshadowed by the newly reorganized *P.S.I.*, but also the liberals who were freed from the conservative approach and leadership that over 20 years earlier had set them on a course of strenuous opposition to the center-left policies. Even more important was the trend toward a more balanced relationship between the *D.C.* and their lay partners, the socialists first of all. This trend was fueled by the *D.C.* losses at the polls, which, however, were balanced by the growth of the *P.S.I.* vote, which powered the Party's ambition to win a top role in running national affairs by overtaking the fading communists, developing a more and more "competitive" collaboration with the weakened christian democrats, and eventually replacing them as the leading partner in a revamped government coalition. In the 1980s, under Bettino Craxi's leadership, the Socialist Party put an end to the *D.C.* hegemony over the government and to the communist hegemony over the Italian Left. The collapse of the historic compromise gave the socialists a new opportunity to perform as the kingpin of Italian politics. Craxi's *P.S.I.* adopted a pragmatic approach to social and economic affairs, wholly discarding the doctrinaire Marxism that had been a strong and disastrous feature of traditional Italian socialism. Way before the collapse of the communist bloc, the *P.S.I.* party symbol was changed from the hammer and sickle to a red carnation. The power in government shared with the communists in local administration gradually came to an end. Italy could enter into a new phase of social and economic change without the specter of communism.

In the 1980s there was a change in political identities. Although party identification remained important, the "idealist basis" of popular politics seemed almost to disappear. In other words, while on the surface strong party loyalties appear to have been sustained throughout the 1970s and 1980s, the nature of this support had changed. Instead of seeing political parties as a collective reality that confers as well as reflects political identity, voters have increasingly related to parties as vehicles for representing delegated interests. The growth of the socialists in the South demonstrated that the Socialist Party had become an "exchange party" capable of negotiating with voters as effectively as their christian democratic coalition partners.

The Fall of Communism: Is There a Free Lunch?

The fall of communism in the countries of Eastern Europe brought about the most radical changes in the Italian political system. Before the fall of communism, Italian elections were as dull and predictable as the turning of the seasons. Despite the country's endless crises and revolving-door governments, every election since 1948 had produced the same result: the christian democrats came in first, followed very closely by the communists. More than any other country in western Europe, Italy was frozen into political immobility by the Cold War. Politics had become so stable or "stagnant" that shifts of two or three percentage points were regarded as major electoral changes. The fall of communism changed all this.

After the 1989 collapse of Eastern European communism, Italy began to experience a series of tremors in its political geology which by 1993 had become a full-scale earthquake. The startling changes in Eastern Europe called into question the core of the traditional politics in Italy too. The fall of the pillars on which communism had been built over several decades and the shattering of many illusions and myths called for complete reassessment of political behavior and prompted the need for a new set of myths. But the yearning for a distinctively different and better society did not generate quick new recipes, or at least no special recipes.

As in the rest of the democratic West, Italy experienced a letdown that made the Italians more aware of the costs than of the benefits of their victory in the confrontation with the communist East. Mounting frustration and resentment over the apparent failure to reap quick and bountiful peace dividends turned into a wholesale indictment of the political and economic groups that had been in control of the nation's affairs in the previous decades.

The public disillusionment with the political process that was reflected in falling electoral turnout and Party membership was symptomatic of a decline in strong political attachments. That should be surprising when one considers the diminishing importance of class as a major political cleavage and the increasing gap between those employed in regular, well-paid occupations and those who are either without work or in part-time, temporary, and low-paid employment. What has been called the "two-thirds, one-third society," with the socially and economically excluded third increasingly taking on the features of an 'underclass', has had major consequences for the appeals made by political parties and the demands made on these same parties by the electorate.[3] In particular it has made the "friend/foe" dichotomy, considered as the basis of political subjectivity, much more problematic.[4]

The end of the "frozen party system," therefore, and the surge of nontraditional political groups, did not come as a consequence of the emergence of a new ideology, rather they are the results of the complete collapse of *an* ideology and the change in class structure. Consequently, new political attitudes will have looser political ties to parties and weaker partisan identification. In turn, this means that more Italians are effectively "in the market," shopping around at election time and available to experiment with new alternatives. The consequent broken political system could mean that relatively minor squabbles could provoke the making and remaking of cabinets with minor adjustments and realignments designed mostly to suit factional interests and personal ambitions rather than to reflect policy priorities.

All things considered, the potential for a restructuring of the party system became unavoidable. But the illusion, apparent in many quarters and propagated by the media, that institutional reforms by themselves will cure all the ills of the society is worrisome. If the history of past reform efforts in Italy is a reliable guide, the redefinition of the traits of the political system will be a long, drawn-out, painstaking process. At the end of the tunnel, it will be discovered that political engineering is no panacea; it can solve some problems but is not a cure-all medicine. All political arrangements have costs. In politics, too, "there is no such thing as a free lunch."

Aged System: Change or Collapse?

It is important to point out that the erosion of loyalty to the traditional political parties, which shook up the system in the early 1990s, had already been slowly developing with other social and economic changes. The rapid decline of the agricultural sector, the secularization of life and growing liberalism, the occupational and geographical mobility, and the higher education level of most of the population had already affected the way society responded to politics, as is reflected in an increased distrust for the traditional political parties. Although the *D.C.* and the *P.C.I.* had remained the most important parties until 1991, their percentage of votes had been declining. Their combined vote had dropped from 73.1% in 1976 to 62.8% in 1983. The Party that had been gaining the most was the *P.S.I.*

The fall of communism may have been the catalyst that coalesced all the distrust that had been increasingly developing through the years. In fact, the political earthquake recorded in the election of Spring 1992 was mostly the result of exacerbated anger at the christian democrats–led government, long held in check by the fear of communism.

The Cold War had caused a political immobility. The *D.C.* and the *P.C.I.*, although adversaries, had reinforced one another: fear of the communists kept the christian democrats in power, and intense dissatisfaction with the government kept the communists strong. There was little room in the middle for the smaller parties, which became satellites of the two big ones. With the collapse of communism, however, the situation became fluid. According to a 1993 poll, at least 20% of the vote was suddenly up for grabs. Some feared that the new climate of political despair might set the stage for a sharp swing to the authoritarian right. Italy's neo-fascist party, *Movimento Sociale Italiano* (*M.S.I.*), adopted Cossiga's pick-axe as its party symbol and embraced his calls for a presidential republic. There was also an outbreak of neo-Nazi violence, with its worst manifestations against illegal immigrants. However, most Italians are more interested in integration with the rest of Europe than in the revival of nationalism. Nevertheless, the new elections did make more chaotic the political landscape. The vacuum of political leadership was filled by a proliferation of special-interest and anti-system parties. There were two different environmental parties, numerous regional parties, even a hunters' party and a pensioners' party. The real novelty was something called the Party of Love, started by porn star Moana Pozzi, who wanted to follow her friend and colleague Cicciolina into Parliament. It could have been very possible in an electoral system that gives representation in Parliament even to a party collecting only 1% of the votes. Governing Italy was difficult enough with 12 parties represented in parliament; it is unimaginable to think what would happen with a 20-party representation.

The results of the spring 1992 elections provided clear evidence that the old Italian political system could not survive. There were 531 Party lists for the chamber of deputies throughout Italy's 32 electoral districts, and 9,742 candidates, an increase of about 20 and 13% respectively over the previous elections of 1987. In addition, as David Caputo's analysis showed:[5]

1. The four-party ruling coalition maintained its parliamentary majority, but saw it reduced to a mere 16 seat majority.
2. Despite retaining its parliamentary majority, the coalition parties captured only 48.8% of the total vote.
3. The christian democrats had their worst showing since the war, winning only 29.7% of the vote and 206 seats in the chamber of deputies.
4. The new Democratic Party of the Left (*P.D.S.*) and the former *P.C.I.* (Communist) lost strength when compared with prior

results. In 1987, the *P.C.I.* received over 26% of the vote for the chamber of deputies while in 1992, the two new parties combined only received around 22% of the total vote cast.

5. The Lombard League improved its standing dramatically, receiving 55 seats in the chamber of deputies, compared to only one seat in 1987.

It was the anti-party, the Lombard League, that made the strongest showing. Many voted for the League not to approve a set of doctrines or a political program, but to demonstrate deep discontent with the traditional political parties and their continuing tenure. The regionally based "leagues" of northern Italy which are grouped collectively under the title Lega Nord, the most important of which is the Lega Lombarda (Lombard League) led by Umberto Bossi, have maintained an extreme position and have called for the secession of northern Italy from what they saw as the corrupt and Mafia-riddled Roman nation-state. Bossi subsequently invoked federalism. It has been difficult to assess if there is distinctive Lega identity in the sense there was one for the communists and one for the Catholics. It has been difficult to define what is a *leghista*.

It should also be said that perhaps the most serious movement for reform came from within the ranks of the ruling christian democrats. Mario Segni, a leader of the Party's left wing, championed a national referendum on electoral reform and he built a broad coalition, dubbed "the party that isn't there," that included some christian democrats and even former communists. The pressure on Parliament to approve electoral reform greatly intensified when the constitutional court approved 10 of the 13 referenda proposed by Segni to be allowed to come up for a vote. Since none of the parties had yet made it clear whether they preferred a majority vote based on a British-style single round or the French system of a second-round run-off when a majority has not been obtained the first time, various measures were submitted to referenda. These included one dealing with the majority-type electoral system that would largely dismantle the proportional system and allow voters to elect their mayors and city administrators directly, wrenching local government from the hands of national party bosses. In the spring of 1993, voters approved by a large margin the eight referenda that were finally put on the ballot: this event certainly marked the end of the First Republic.

Toward the Second Republic: Difficult Transition

The new political environment freed the judicial branch from all the political constraints and welcomed a cleaner political system. The consequences were immediate and had profound impact. The widespread revulsion over the mega-corruption of leading politicians that was uncovered by Italian magistrates in *Operazione Mani Pulite* (Operation Clean Hands) and the broader, mounting resentment over the mismanagement of domestic affairs by the mainstream parties, not only rocked the political and economic establishments but forced significant changes in the rules of the political game itself.

In a referendum held on April 18-19, 1993, over 82% of the 35 million voters endorsed a shift from proportional representation to a majority system for the election of three quarters of the 315 members of the Senate. The switch to a majority system was backed by large margins throughout the country. The only exceptions were registered in Sicily, notably in some districts of Palermo. Several other referenda likewise showed very large majorities supporting curbs on the powers and privileges of politicians. Public financing of parties is now out, for instance; and three government departments were voted to be dismantled, notably the Ministry for State Holdings, which represented a larger share of the national economy than elsewhere in the West and had become a major source of patronage, abuses, and corruption.

The new government formed after the April referendum embodied several new departures clearly in line with the message from the polls. For the first time since the end of World War II, the premier was not a politician: Carlo Azeglio Ciampi had been for 14 years governor of Italy's central bank. With full backing from President of the Republic Oscar Luigi Scalfaro, Ciampi chose the members of his cabinet without going through the customary, lengthy bargaining process with leaders of the parties making up the ruling coalition. One third of the new ministers had no party affiliation.

Upon taking office, Prime Minister Ciampi stated that if Parliament did not enact electoral reform along the lines laid down by the April referendum before the summer recess, the government would submit its own bill and ask for a vote of confidence on it. In the summer of 1993 the Parliament approved a new electoral system. The reform reflects an earnest effort to reconcile the main benefits of the majority system with some protection on the minor parties' vital interests. It provides for three quarters of the House members (472 out of a total of 630) to be elected on a "first past the post" basis; i.e., along the British and U.S. models. The other 158 seats would be allotted on a proportional basis among all parties polling at least 4% of the nation-wide vote. The votes polled by the winners under the majority system would be excluded from the total available to the same parties' candidates to the seats allotted under the proportional system.

It was a courageous act because with that vote members of Parliament not only put on death row some of the small parties that flourished under the old system, but also signed their own death warrant since few of those in office were likely to be reelected under the new system.

A democratic revolution took place in Italy even though it is too early to assess its consequences. The aroused public opinion, which acted as the main engine of change and reform and brought about early general elections in spring 1994, completely changed the political landscape. The right wing alliance, led by the media magnate Silvio Berlusconi, won a majority in the lower house of Parliament and a plurality in the Senate. The election was a three-way contest involving the Freedom Pole, made up of *Forza Italia*, the separatist Northern League, and the neo-fascist National Alliance; the Center Pole, including the *Pact for Italy* and the Popular Party made up of former christian democrats; and the left-wing Progressive Pole, composed of the Democratic Party of the Left, the hard-line Communist Refoundation, the Greens, and the anti-Mafia *La Rete*. Official overall election results showed the right-wing coalition with 366 seats (155 to *Forza Italia*, 106 to *Northern League*, 105 to *National Alliance*) in the 630-seat lower house, an absolute majority, leaving its leftist adversaries a poor second with 213 and Italy's formerly all-powerful centrists with only 46. Five seats went to representatives of smaller parties. In the Senate, the right wing fared less well, winning 155 of the 315 seats. The rejection of the old political structure was so strong that *Forza Italia*, whose name is the soccer chant "Go Italy!" and was founded only three months before the election, was the biggest vote-getter of the coalition. The neo-fascists, who for years hovered on the fringes of Italian politics, securing a steady 5 or 6% of the vote but no significant representation, emerged with 12% of the votes and 105 seats in the lower house.

The new political stage has very soft ground because the right wing coalition did not cement together political forces having a lot in common. *Forza Italia* of Mr. Berlusconi favored tax cuts and a push to sell off Italy's bloated state-owned industrial sector; the *Northern League*, led by Umberto Bossi, wanted to distance the affluent North from the central government in Rome; and the neo-fascists, led by Gianfranco Fini, wanted a strong central authority and have vaguely pressed a claim to territory in the former Yugoslavia.

It should be said that Italian democracy is also experiencing the same situation as many other democracies: established political parties are in deep trouble, their legitimacy suspect, and their leader susceptible to attack by populists who preach simple, emotional answers to the complicated questions of the post–Cold War age. With so much cynicism about conventional politics and politicians around, and with the traditional Left largely discredited after the collapse of communism in 1989, it is hardly surprising that outsiders—many of them self-made businessmen with enough money of their own to run campaigns that defy the long-dominant party machine—are popping up. It is going to take some time for the new political forces to clarify their positions.

The success of Berlusconi's *Forza Italia* in the first parliamentary elections to be held under a predominantly majority electoral system suggests that these new political identities are far from solid. The election showed that while there are voters who strongly identify with a particular political formation, there has been the emergence of a large electorate whose sense of political belonging is not a central, important, and conscious feature of their lives. Public disillusionment with the political process as reflected in falling electoral turnout and party membership was symptomatic of a decline in strong political attachments and could be observed throughout the Western democracies in this period. For many, politics as a vocation became politics as spectacle. For the great majority, politics is experienced as an essentially passive activity that is almost dependent on media representations of political monologues or interviews between politicians and journalists.

A more independent approach to politics by the voters became evident very soon. Berlusconi quickly lost public support and, consequently, parliamentary backing when he was not able to deliver on the promises made during his electoral campaign. Not only was he forced to resign, but he was forced to sustain big losses at the elections held in the next two years (regional in 1995 and national in 1996). The general elections in April 1996 saw the Lega Nord lose some votes; it received 10% of the national vote. The new center-left captured the majority and formed a new government led by Romano Prodi with the participation of the *P.D.S.* Can Berlusconi stage a comeback? My impression is that the elites have lost faith in him but that many Italians perceive him as a leader brought down by politicians of a lower stature. Would he govern in the same way the next time around? Which way will the Catholics turn? Will *P.D.S.* succeed in holding the new electorate? It seems that a democracy with clear alternatives is emerging. The trade-off may be the creation of a politically volatile electorate.

The Political Marketplace

The new electorate has a new basic attitude not only toward politics but also toward the state. For one thing, the welfare state is dead in Italy, as is "liberal fundamentalism." Next to the anti-traditional party attitude there is a *new pluralism,* which seems to emphasize voluntarism rather than dependency on the state. The rise of a large number of interest groups and self-help associations, new in modern Italian society, indicates that traditional parties are no longer regarded as adequate in defining and satisfying individual needs. Many of these organizations do not have ideological ties or commitments to political institutions and their members wish to make more "privatized" demands on the political system. For example, the aged are interested in pensions irrespective of their individual political affiliation; the same is true of the handicapped, single-parent families, women, alcoholics and drug addicts, consumer advocates, environmentalists, and many others who are strongly involved in issues and problems of their immediate interest.

Although groups have emerged because of the anger and frustration people share over the failure of the state to deal adequately with problems of health, drug addiction, etc., and therefore should signal a greater predisposition toward self-help as opposed to waiting around for the state to solve problems, the formation of such organizations implies, in the Italian politicized climate, the creation of new political forces. In fact, on closer analysis, what may emerge as the underlying issue may not be an ineffective party system, but rather a populace still too dependent upon government action. It often turns out that most of these groups really want governmental authorities to do more, not less. Notwithstanding the apparent lack of confidence in government, government is still expected to solve for society an astounding variety of problems. Italians' anti-government attitude is very complex: when citizen anger is tested on very important issues, the reaction is always pro-government!

In fact, when Italians have been called to vote in a referendum, a formal mechanism provided to the people by the constitution for expressing their judgment on legislative actions by Parliament, they have *always* voted in favor of the actions approved by Parliament. Italians have never overturned a law enacted by Parliament. It seems that Italians are fundamentally content in the specific sense that they are reluctant to reverse at the polls what their representatives have ironed-out through the law-making process. It should also be pointed out that Italians have demonstrated a remarkable capacity to resist using the referendum for narrow self-interest. No better demonstration of this is offered than the 1985 vote on a law that had modified the *scala mobile* (cost-of-living increases based on inflation) to the disadvantage of wage-rated workers. To the surprise of many political experts, especially the communists who had campaigned against the measure, and who had anticipated that the electorate would "vote its pocketbook" as opposed to the "general welfare," the Italians demonstrated a high level of civic and political maturity by refusing to annul the new law. It seems that their dissatisfaction with the system had to do more with the natural attitude of people toward the "other," the abstract institutions, than with a deep-seated political lack of confidence.

However, political practices have changed. Italian politics has become more of a *spettacolo*, of a show. But the Italian political show always had a script. Even during the most chaotic years, Machiavelli was very much alive; political science has always been practiced with the flavor of an art. Political chaos has been avoided because the *spettacolo politico*, the political show, always has a script with a well-established conclusion.

Italian politics becomes more "spectacular" during election time. Public policy often becomes paralyzed, giving way to campaign pontificating and made-for-TV symbolism. Politics *spettacolo* style, fitting very nicely with the Italian character, has become more "spectacular" with the use, misuse, and abuse of television. Indeed, because of the way TV use is manipulated, political discourse has become even more than before like a "show," a spectacle. In the world of "sound bite," where political discourse becomes more uniform, it is difficult for politicians to articulate an ideology to the wider public. Television has created difficulty not only for the parties in power but also for the force of opposition, whose entire outlook on communication had been based on the development of "alternative" information.

Yet, in Italy, the language of politics is still very intense because Italians are still passionately intense in conveying their messages. In the process of changing their political structures, Italians should not copy other forms of democracies. Democracies have to be assessed in their own terms, within their particular social, economic, and historical contexts. A people's history and culture, its economic conditions and social norms, its aspirations and its work-ways, its "national character," will affect the style and structure of its government. Democracy, by its nature, does not have a fixed form; within the same country, it has to be given the freedom to change. Italian democracy is changing; let us hope that it changes for the better.

Labor Unions: Crisis of Representation

Even Italy's labor unions, once powerful enough to paralyze the country and make governments fall, have gone through profound changes and are today suffering from lack of public support. A foreign visitor to a major Italian city, seeing streets often filled with demonstrating workers carrying banners with explosive language, might conclude that the unions are still powerful and poised on the brink of insurrection. He would be wrong. These protest marches tend to be little more than remnants of an old ritual, a way of showing the flag and making up for the unions' inability to carry out more effective action. Unions are still strong in public service, but have become quite weak in industry and commerce. In the past the organized working class had a strong sense of "them and us," but the decline in trade union membership and the greater importance of nonunionized small firms in the labor market has meant that the workplace solidarity of the 1960s and 1970s has been all but lost. The southern migrant workers no longer form a separate and potentially militant subclass within the industrial cities of the North, and persistently high levels of unemployment, as elsewhere in Europe, have discouraged trade unions from taking industrial action that might result in redundancies or plant closures.

The service sector, by contrast, has seen a major expansion throughout the postwar Republic, but the structure of tertiary employment is very different from the manufacturing industry. White-collar jobs are increasingly dominated by women, few of whom are unionized or in secure full-time employment. The nature of white-collar employment almost invariably requires a face-to-face relationship with managers and employers, and this inevitably results in a greater degree of control over the employees. White-collar workers (in Italy are *impiegati* rather than *lavoratori*) persistently identify with parties of the Center and Right rather than with the Left, and their values are highly aspirational: they do not want to overthrow the boss, they want to become the boss.

During the years of profound social change, labor unions played a major role because like the trade unions in most European countries, and unlike those of the U.S., they have always been deeply politicized. Political motivation and ideological tradition have been more important than economic structure in determining union membership in Italy— as a result, union membership has greater civic significance in Italy than it might elsewhere.[6] Since the early postwar years, the two major labor confederations, C.G.I.L. (*Confederazione Generale Italiana Lavoratori*) and C.I.S.L. (*Confederazione Italiana Sindacati Lavoratori*), became deeply enmeshed in the struggle between the communists and the christian democrats. In 1950, when the two unions were regarded as not offering enough choice, in the spirit of Italian democratic pluralism some of their leaders and workers left and formed a national union of their own, U.I.L. (*Unione Italiana dei Lavoratori*), which made a point of stressing its independence not only from C.G.I.L. but from C.I.S.L. as well.

By the early 1960s, the three unions had become a very strong political force in the nation and had been able to achieve some important social reforms. Later, in the "hot autumn" of 1968, during a long and bitter confrontation which involved labor, management, and the politicians as well, the unions won sizable wage increases, improvements in working conditions, and promises of concrete progress in availability of decent low cost housing, better schools, hospitals, and public transportation.

By 1969 the unions had forced through the legislature the *Workers' Statute*, one of the most advanced and, as it was interpreted, radical industrial relations policies ever enacted in the West. Even before this piece of legislation was passed, Italy provided exceptional levels of unemployment benefits and highly attractive compensation at the point of work severance. The statute came close to making the worker untouchable inside the workplace or, for that matter, outside of it. With the help of politically radicalized judges, laborers could be absent from work with impunity and still claim their pay. Job transfers or reclassification simply could not occur without the consent of the party involved. The slightest infraction on the part of management was an almost certain invitation to a work stoppage. Side by side with these guarantees went improvements in fringe benefits that were as costly to employers as they were instrumental in changing the workers' standard of living. In those years, workers came to believe that a steep upward climb in their condition had become a birthright and that even dismissal from one's job for cause was nothing more than a quaint relic of bygone capitalism.[7] Union demands and ideology of those years were based on the assumption that the institutions of government had to assure the equality of outcome rather than equality of opportunity. As Joseph La Palombara indicated, although Italians tend to doubt that all men are created equal, they tend to believe that the state can go a long way to assure equality of results, regardless of the structure of opportunity.[8]

Much additional bitterness and strife developed when the national labor contracts concluded at the end of 1969 and the new legislature had to be implemented at the local plant level. The major labor organizations found it increasingly difficult to deal with the wildcat strikes and the sabotage of production lines carried out by small numbers of workers inspired by radical left-wing groups.

In the early 1970s, many Italian businessmen thought that the only way to conduct business was to arrange deals with organized labor, which had emerged with a vengeance from an all-too-long condition of weakness in a labor market traditionally marked by chronic unemployment and underemployment. Several of those businessmen engaged in dialogues with communist leaders because the party, which was gaining ground at the polls, maintained a strong hold on the biggest labor confederation, *C.G.I.L.* An accord was negotiated in 1975 by Giovanni Agnelli, president of FIAT and of *Confindustria*, and Luciano Lama, the communist leader of *C.G.I.L.* A key clause introduced in contracts was the "rigid and pervasive wage indexation system." Big industrialists tolerated runaway inflation as long as the bill for its magnified impact could be passed on to their customers and to the taxpayers in general.

Labor had achieved such supremacy that in the 1975 agreement between organized labor and organized business it was established that the cost of living would be reviewed on a quarterly basis and wages adjusted upward to keep pace with inflation. The technical basis for making these adjustments, however, was such that, whereas the highest wage earners would just barely stay even with inflation, the lowest wage earners would realize wage improvements slightly above the inflation rate. Something very positive came out of the process without fully anticipating such an outcome: the parties to this agreement put in motion a policy that over time brought about an unprecedented redistribution of income.

By 1980, even before President Reagan showed how to break unions in America, Italian national labor unions were suffering from a self-inflicted mortal wound. In early fall of that year, FIAT management decided to dismiss some 14,000 workers as part of its strategy to cope with a crisis that affected the automobile industry all over the world, but which had been exacerbated by recent developments in the national labor field. The unions called a strike that lasted five weeks and was openly backed by the *P.C.I.* Berlinguer himself (the leader of the Communist Party) addressed the strikers in Turin, FIAT's headquarters, pledging his Party's support if they occupied the plants. But the unions' opposition to any compromise collapsed when an estimated 40,000 workers, foremen, and employees marched through Turin shouting "Freedom to work!"

Organized labor had overreached itself and had failed to realize that the tide had turned. Many big and medium-sized industries felt encouraged enough to follow FIAT's example and start restructuring their plants along lines calling for sizable payroll cuts. Absenteeism dropped significantly, while production rose. A major move away from the rigid indexation system was undertaken by the Craxi government in February 1984. The operation of the indexation mechanism was cooled-off temporarily by an executive decree. The move was backed by the unions representing catholic, social democratic, and republican workers as well as by the socialist wing of *C.G.I.L.* But the *P.C.I.* went on the warpath.

It should be pointed out that union membership is much more common in the more civic regions. In fact, union membership is roughly twice as high in those regions. By contrast, union membership is unrelated to education, age, and urbanization, and the differences by social class are less than one might expect. The civic context is almost as important as socioeconomic status in accounting for union membership in Italy. In the civic regions, solidarity in the workplace is part of a larger syndrome of social solidarity.[9]

Today the trade unions are in decline, the victims of recent transformations in the West that caught labor organizations defenseless. In the space of a decade, the trade union movement went from a condition of unimagined power to one of precipitous decomposition. Like unions in other Western countries, those in Italy do not know how to adapt to the economic and social transformations that have occurred during the so-called second industrial revolution. The unions also ran afoul of developments that go beyond recession or economic and social change. Their earlier, heady successes contributed to their undoing. The conquests in favor of the working class did not produce a sense of gratitude to the labor confederations that engineered them. In addition, the use of robots operated by engineers in white smocks eliminated thousands of blue-collar workers. Moreover, the decline of the steel and shipbuilding industries and the fall in employment in publicly owned industries, also in trouble, are principal reasons for the erosion in labor's strength. Large-scale industry in general has also declined. Today over half of all workers are found in firms of under 20 employees, and such places are notoriously difficult to unionize.

Protests have become fragmented, with sectional interests prevailing. Instead of long strikes, the unions tend to organize one-day token stoppages, which make them appear strong and militant but they achieve little; they are a safety-valve for discontent. The old saying "their bark is worse than their bite" well characterizes the labor unions of today. Trade unions have seen their authority increasingly threatened by the rank-and-file organization of separate categories of workers and the strength of the local groups. The COBAS (comitati di base) have mobilized different groups of workers and of the ceti medi (middle class) with notable militancy, but without the ability to achieve, or indeed even to seek a unifying strategy. The rise of unemployment in traditional labor-intensive industries that once were union bastions and the anti-system mood of the country that has changed the political structure have also affected the once very strong politicized labor unions.

The unions have not been able to suggest acceptable solutions to unemployment, which is one of the most crucial problems of the nation. The claims of some conservatives that the unemployed have little incentive to look for another job quickly because high benefits are breeding laziness, and that many people were earning more on the dole than others in jobs, are certainly unfair. Most recognize, however, that the unemployment crisis is not caused solely by outside economic factors; it is also structural, linked to changes in technology. The Italians, like others in highly advanced technological nations, will have to learn to live with a high level of unemployment if some social adjustments are not made. The burden can be shared more evenly by a shortened work week so that more jobs are available. As it is now, rising unemployment has led to less job security and elimination of redundancies.

Notes

1. In the fight against a communist threat in Italy, an important role was played by the Pope family in the U.S. In the immediate postwar period, mainly through the *Progresso Italo-Americano* (the major American daily in the Italian language) and the radio station *WHOM*, the Pope family carried on a passionate campaign against a communist takeover of Italy. The *Progresso* organized a letter-to-Italy campaign among its readers and printed a series of alarming articles about the consequences of a possible communist takeover. This resulted in the dispatch of thousands of letters from Americans of Italian origin to relatives and friends in Italy, urging them to reject Russian blandishments.

2. Posters from the Cold War period vary a good deal stylistically, from the scatological to the eschatological. The majority contain a very dramatic content, to the effect that Italy must choose between the forces of good and evil in this moment of apocalyptic crisis. This is achieved partly by drawing on images from the Book of Revelation, which deal with the final separation of good and evil.

3. J. K. Galbraight, *The Culture of Contentment* (London: 1992); and G. Therborn, *Why Some Peoples Are More Unemployed than Others* (London: 1986).

4. C. Schmitt, *The Concept of the Political* (New Brunswick, N.J.: Rutgers U. P., 1976).

5. David A. Caputo, "Italy's Parliamentary Elections: New Directions or Only Minor Deviations from the Past?" *Italian Journal*, 6, nos. 2 & 3 (1992): 3.

6. Salvatore Coi, "Sindacati in Italia: iscritti, apparato, finanziamento," *Il Mulino* 28 (1987): 201-42, quotation from p. 206.

7. For an overview of the labor union achievements of those years, see Tiziano Treu, ed., *L'uso politico dello statuto dei lavoratori* (Bologna: Il Mulino, 1975).

8. La Palombara, 55.

9. Putnam, 107.

III

Dangers to the State:
Whose Law? Whose Order?

Plots and Terrorism: A State Under Siege

The Italian democratic state has been fragile and continually under a cloud of danger not so much for the kind of democratic system it is governed by, as for the kind of people that have been in government and for the presence of organizations that are corroding its social, political, and economic fiber.

Given the fragility of government and the openness of the political system, Italy became fertile ground for terrorist activity and for political forces from extreme sides of the political spectrum. Contrary to the almost exclusive attention given to ultra-left activities by media in the U.S., elements of ultra-conservative groups have been no less a threat to the Italian state from the beginning of the 1960s to the end of the 1980s.

The political terrorism began with the weakening of the political parties that had been forming the government coalition up to the beginning of the 1960s and continued through the inclusion of new political forces. With the admission of the socialists into the government in December 1963 and the consequent beginning of a new era of social reforms, which caused vast sums of capital to leave the country in an artificially created atmosphere of panic, elements of the political forces of the Right planned measures to counteract these changes; some were definitely unconstitutional.

Probably the most clamorous publicized attempt by the Right to overthrow the government was made by General Giovanni di Lorenzo,

commander of the *Carabinieri* corps, and a former chief of military
counterespionage *SIFAR*. He had made provision for the arbitrary
arrest and deportation of numerous political personalities whose names
were given to a select group of Carabinieri officers. The officers had
been told to stand-by for the order to proceed and had been given to
understand that the general was acting on personal instructions from
the president of the republic and without the knowledge of the ministers of defense and the interior. The plan would have remained a secret if the magazine *L'Espresso* had not published the details. This
was somewhat surprising since plots and terrorist acts by the Right
had enjoyed a high degree of impunity in Italy. In the case of General
di Lorenzo, a parliamentary inquiry into the misuse of *SIFAR* funds
and dossiers for political espionage and blackmail was ordered only
after a great deal of hedging by the government behind the screen of
national security. If the affair had not come to light during the military
coup d'état in Athens in 1967, it might have remained a secret. Although most Italians discounted the possibility of a similar takeover in
Italy, they were shocked to realize that, if the political will for such
action were forthcoming, the cooperation of the police and the military would not be hard to obtain.

The military would never have been able to earn any support because the crisis created by the panic of the entrance of the socialists in
government in December 1963 faded quickly because of their bland
and moderate demands. For the duration of the fourth Parliament
(1963-1968) not a single one of the so-called structural reforms touching regional government, the universities, the magistracy, the penal
and civil codes, the health services, pensions, and so forth made any
appreciable progress, and the program announced by the center-left
parties in December 1963 and retained in July 1964 was still unfinished when the coalition pulled itself together again for a third attempt
in December 1968.

By the late 1960s, domestic order was challenged on several fronts.
As long as the Communist Party had a monopoly of Marxist culture,
the state had not had any problems in maintaining civil order. But
things changed in the late 1960s when that monopoly was seriously
challenged and eventually fractured by the student revolt. Extremist
groups of the Left accused the *P.C.I.* of being revisionist and reformist, authoritarian and bureaucratic in a bourgeois way. The 1968 and
1969 student revolts worsened the situation: anarchist and radical-left
terrorist organizations fomented disorder at several universities and

openly clashed on the streets with neo-fascist and far-right groups.
This was taking place in a dangerous climate of declining economic
conditions and national political stalemate, while various labor unions
were engaged in strikes and disorders. The "hot autumn of 1969"
occurred at a time when the whole Italian society seemed to be in
upheaval. The student movement was not mere anarchy but represented a set of political demands that had to be answered by all Italian
political parties. It was not just a protest against the alienating character of the capitalist-consumer society but a specific protest against the
authoritarian, paternalistic, hierarchical structure of Italian society and
of Italian universities, which students took to be mirrors and instruments of the system. The movement became a major political phenomenon and shaped, either directly or indirectly, the crisis of Italian
society: from terrorism to the women's movement, from dissent within
the Church to the birth of a host of small left-wing parties, and to the
radicalization of large groups of intellectuals and middle-class radicals.

The student movement had profound influence. The uprisings in
southern Italy, the prison revolts, and the demonstrations and strikes
in the North all owe something to the new spirit of criticism that came
out of the universities and the *licei*. The pressures on government
were so strong that many of the reforms the students demanded were
granted even before the bill itself was passed. Something radical had
happened: once so respectful of authority, so anxious to get ahead
with the help of protection and recommendations in a society where
influence was all, youth was now questioning the structure of that
society. Some of the unionists formed anarchist and radical-leftist groups
similar to those of the students, and these labor extremist groups also
engaged the neo-fascists in street battles.

By the mid-1970s many small revolutionary organizations that had
emerged from the youth movement entered into a period of crisis.
Organizations such as *Avanguardia Operaia* (The Workers' Vanguard),
Potere Operaio (Workers' Power), and *Lotta Continua* (The Struggle
Goes On) had not been able to establish a significant presence in the
labor movement. The crisis of these organizations was in large part
caused by the fact that they had unsuccessfully tried to subvert the
system by using traditional instruments, the political parties. All this
was happening while the Communist Party (*P.C.I.*) was anticipating
an entrance into government. The intended move was a democratic
one: to provide the country with a radical reforming government without pushing a large section of middle-class groups and other social

forces into positions of overt hostility. In order to achieve a political majority it was necessary to forge an alliance with the Catholic masses and enter into some form of compromise with the D.C. The P.C.I. realized that a mere electoral or mathematical majority was not sufficient for a national legitimization and that it needed to offer some international guarantee that its presence in government would not signify a shift in the balance of forces between East and West to the disadvantage of the West. The flirtation was working well; in July 1976, for the first time since the break-up of the tripartite coalition of 1947 (the first historic compromise), a D.C. prime minister, Giulio Andreotti, appealed to the P.C.I. to support his government in Parliament. At the local level, cooperation between communists and christian democrats was becoming commonplace, and by June 1977 a wide-ranging government program had been agreed to between the D.C., the P.C.I., and the other parties.

While engaging in a work of compromise with the D.C., the P.C.I. had to react to the students' unrest. Although the initial response was hostile to the student movement, and even though one of its leaders, Giorgio Amendola, asserted that it was necessary to fight on two fronts, i.e., against the government and against the students, the party leader, Luigi Longo, was much more flexible.[1] Longo recognized that it was also the P.C.I.'s fault if there was such a wide gulf between the Party and the students, that the Party had become too sectarian and too bureaucratic, and that the importance and political autonomy of the student movement had to be recognized. This strategy implied two objectives: on the one hand, the Party was trying to fragment the student movement paradoxically by showing sympathy for the student cause; on the other hand, it was sending the message that the only source of legitimate power in Italy was to be found in political parties.

Though not in the government, the P.C.I. seemed to have become a party of the government and, in the eyes of the extreme left, a partner of the established power. For the militant groups, the P.C.I. had become a progressive force by betraying its basic revolutionary principles; not only had it sold out by compromising with the D.C., but it had also entered a policy of complete subordination.

For the ultra-left, therefore, the P.C.I. had become another enemy of the people, and it was their duty to assume the role of defenders of the oppressed. On the other side of the political aisle it was clear that the D.C. had a strategy, not understood by the American government, to transform the P.C.I. into a harmless movement for reform that would bring its supporters and the masses it inspired under the political hegemony of a new governing coalition led by the *D.C.*

The radical Left perhaps saw what was happening and acted to prevent it. From December 1969 to the mid-1980s, politically motivated bombings, murders, and kidnappings became a recurring feature of Italian life. Observers estimated that over 14,000 terrorist acts were committed between 1969 and 1985. Hundreds of Italians were kidnapped, "kneecapped," wounded, or killed. Most affected were those who represented the establishment: university professors, judges, generals, industrialists, and politicians.

All terrorist groups of the ideological Left shared the same goal—the overthrow of the bourgeois, capitalist, imperialist state and the establishment of the dictatorship of the proletariat. They also tried to bring the *P.C.I.* back into the fold of revolutionary ideology. This was to be accomplished not only through the dissemination of Marxist-Leninist propaganda but also through attacks on the property of industrialists, as well as kidnapping and assassinations.

The Red Brigades (*B.R.*) was the best known of the left-wing terrorist groups to operate in those years. To demonstrate their contempt for the democratic state, on March 16, 1978, the *Brigate Rosse* kidnapped Aldo Moro, the party secretary of the *D.C.* and promoter of the "historical compromise" and, therefore, supporter of communist participation in government. The terrorist groups considered Moro nothing more than a tool of the imperialistic American multinationals. The Red Brigades act was clearly a declaration of war against the state; the state was under siege. As in other critical moments, Italian politicians, through skillful maneuvering, preserved the democracy and defended the state. After intense discussions on how to respond, the government refused to negotiate with the terrorists.

Unfortunately, however, the mass media became deeply involved in this unfortunate event. As in many other instances the mass media played a key role as a vehicle for the gathering and diffusion of information, but in this case it also acted as a first-person protagonist who managed to instrumentalize the tragedy to its own purpose. The public and the state learned through the mass media, which likes to play on the emotions of people, all the developments of the case. Because of this the Moro case became a memorable example of politics as spectacle. The killing of the five bodyguards in the ambush and the eventual murder of Moro himself, after 40 long days of tension, shook the nation. Certainly, one should not underestimate the cultural dimension: Italians are less prepared than Americans to expect that their president or political leaders may be assassinated.

The explosion of terrorism led the *P.C.I.* to defend the state by refusing to negotiate with the Red Brigades over the Moro kidnapping and by accepting new anti-terrorist legislation. Even though the intention was to uphold the democratic principles of the state and of the constitution, the *P.C.I.* could not avoid appearing to the extremist groups as the defender of the entire edifice of the Italian state with its corruption, degeneration, and bigotry. It was accused by many on the Left of espousing anti-libertarian causes purely in order to become part of the government.

Paradoxically, rather than solidify the *P.C.I.* position, the Moro killing put an end to the historic compromise, for the Red Brigades had destroyed the key man who could have paved the way for the entry of the *P.C.I.* into the government. In the wake of the Moro killing, as well as other *B.R.* murders, 63 members of the *B.R.* were eventually arrested and put on trial. The Moro experience brought together the political, juridical, and military forces of the nation in a solid bloc, which in skillful cooperation mustered one of the most sophisticated anti-terrorist systems in the world.

The first proof that Italy was able to deal with terrorism came in December 1981. The kidnapping of General Dozier, then deputy chief of staff for logistics and administration at NATO Allied Land Forces Southern Europe, with headquarters in Verona, was foiled when the state police arrested the captors and freed the general in a counter-terrorism blitz that received praise from the international community, including and above all from the U.S. By this time the Italian government had created a special force, "the skin head," to deal with terrorism.

However, other incidents shook up the country before the nation could start to relax. In broad daylight on the campus of the University of Rome, two members of the *B.R.*'s Roman Column gunned down Ezio Tarantelli, a professor of economics. Tarantelli was an obvious target because he was the author of modifications in the *scala mobile* that the Craxi government eventually adopted as official policy. The "freeze" that Tarantelli's plan placed on wage increases was easily perceived by the *B.R.* as an act against the working class. Similarly, Gen. Licio Giorgieri, assassinated in March 1987, was singled out because of his responsibilities in NATO and the space defense program. The victims were individuals who could be associated with the established power structure or its defenders.

The state had also to face the threats posed by neo-fascist, right-wing terrorist groups. These groups were more difficult to deal with because they lacked organizational sophistication and murdered indiscriminately. Since their objective was to show the weakness of the state in handling violent political crime and social chaos, and their objective was to create the maximum possible fear, intimidation, and panic, they placed bombs in piazzas, on trains or aircraft, or in railroad stations, without making claims for their actions.

Typical of the right-wing terrorist groups was the Armed Revolutionary Nuclei (*Nuclei Armati Rivoluzionari—N.A.R.*), a neo-fascist organization that authorities have held responsible for major bomb explosions and for the killing of its political opponents. The most terrible tragedy was the carnage caused by a bomb that exploded in Bologna's railroad station on August 2, 1980, killing 85 people. This was the peak of the cycle of right-wing terrorism, although not the end to violence. Another neo-fascist group, New Order/Black Order (*Ordine Nuovo/Ordine Nero*), claimed responsibility for a bomb attack on the Milan-Naples express train on December 23, 1984, which killed several people.

Because of its strategic position in the Mediterranean, Italy also became the stage for acts of international terrorism. The most heinous act was the attempted assassination of Pope John Paul II on May 13, 1981. Efforts to establish the motivation for the plot were inconclusive, but some evidence suggested an attempt by the Bulgarian secret police, presumably acting on behalf of the KGB, to stifle the resurgence of the Roman Catholic Church in eastern Europe.

Another incident that attracted international attention was the fall 1985 hijacking of the Italian cruiseship *Achille Lauro*, while it was sailing the Mediterranean, and the killing of one of its Jewish American passengers. The incident created a major governmental and international crisis because the hijackers, who were a pro-Palestinian group, were allowed to escape after having been caught through the United States' role in forcing an Egyptian plane carrying the terrorists to land at a NATO base at Sigonella, Sicily. The incident also sparked a series of government crises. Indeed, for the first time, an Italian government fell largely as the result of an international exigency. The moderately independent stand vis-à-vis the United States adopted by Craxi and the christian democratic foreign minister, Andreotti, antagonized the republican defense minister, Spadolini, who adopted a pro-American and anti-Palestine Liberation Organization (PLO) position during the affair. Spadolini also felt he had not been adequately consulted before a PLO official, Abu Abbas (described by American officials as masterminding the hijacking), had been hastily released from Italian custody.

International terrorism struck again a few months later, in December 1985, when a pro-Palestinian group fired on a crowd of passengers in the Rome airport terminal, killing 13 people. More recently, a well-balanced international policy in the Mediterranean, especially toward the Middle East, has helped in establishing a relaxed atmosphere and a cessation of terrorist violence.

Italy has not been immune to planned attempts to overthrow the state by those in charge of protecting it, either. In 1981, the existence of a subversive Masonic lodge, the *P2*, which stands for *Propaganda Due*, was discovered. Its members included prominent figures in the armed forces, in business, and in politics. The precise objectives of the lodge have remained obscure, but there is little doubt that its head, Lucio Gelli, an affable businessman from Tuscany, was seeking to construct an anti-communist network within the highest echelons of the Italian state. His name had remained unknown to the Italian public until the mid-1970s, when the first hints of his role as a power broker appeared in the press. Eventually the media started mentioning him in connection with the sensational insolvency cases of two bankers, Michele Sindona and Roberto Calvi, both of whom died under mysterious circumstances.

To millions of Italians the world of Lodge *P2* was not of as much concern as were the terrorists, even though by 1985 terrorist organizations in Italy could be described as having failed to meet their objective of the radical overthrow of state institutions. Their propaganda and tactics had proved to be ill-suited to bring about any sort of political change. Because of increased popular revulsion and increasingly effective counterterrorist legislation and activity by the police, terrorist organizations of all ideologies had suffered major setbacks through 1984, and terrorist activity had diminished to barely noticeable levels.

The state won the battle against terrorism. In more ways than Italians themselves may have anticipated, terrorism brutally tested the proposition that Italy's democracy, at the bottom, is a strong, healthy institution. Because the preservation of high level democracy in a pluralistic society may require special security measures, Italians have adapted to a new style of living. Whether stoically enduring long lines outside security entrances to state offices, banks, etc., or voluntarily lavishing money on private security systems, Italians have quickly responded that freedom, whatever the price, has to be preserved.

Ordinary Crime: Too Ordinary

While Italians are justifiably proud of this victory over terrorism, they appear to be losing the war against ordinary crime, which has been on the rise since 1969. Before 1969, kidnapping for ransom and armed robbery tended to occur infrequently, except in Sardinia, Sicily, and Calabria; but by the mid-1970s it was a serious problem throughout the country and became a major concern for the Italian public. In 1977, for example, over sixty kidnappings occurred that involved members of wealthy families and political figures. In fact, some of the moneyed class people moved away from Italy for fear of kidnapping, while others increased personal security through bodyguards and armored vehicles.

The easy availability of heroin from the Mafia network was viewed as a major reason for the upsurge of crime. The Italian narcotics epidemic had become more virulent than in most other European countries. In Rome, considered to be Italy's drug capital, heroin, marijuana, and hashish can be purchased openly in many streets and piazzas all over the city, and any streetwise teenager knows what the going price is for any illegal drug. Used syringes can be found any day in most parks, often jabbed into the trees, and along the banks of the Tiber.

People die every month from overdoses and the authorities seize hundreds of pounds of heroin and other substances. In 1988 no fewer than 758 people in Italy died of drug overdoses, almost three times as many as in 1986. Although precise figures on the total number of addicts are hard to come by, it has been established that as many as 200,000 Italians are hooked on heroin and cocaine, while several hundred thousand others frequently smoke hashish and marijuana. Italy, with a population one-fourth that of the United States, has an estimated half as many confirmed drug users; that most of these users are under 30 makes the situation all the more alarming. The situation had become so critical that in January 1993 the government decriminalized the personal use of drugs to cope with the failure of its tough drug laws, which filled prisons with addicts and did little to reduce consumption. Instead of prison terms, this law imposes administrative

sanctions—including loss of driver's license, gun permits, and passports—for drug users.

Organized Crime:
Weak State and Lack of Civic Consciousness

According to police and senior magistrates, in 1984 organized crime
in Italy, as embodied in the *Mafia* of Sicily, the *Camorra* of Naples,
and the *'Ndrangheta* in Calabria, represented a greater threat to the
internal security of Italy than did political violence. These organizations are not inventions of Mario Puzo, Hollywood, or the mass media. The title of the article "What Happened to Heroes is a Crime,"
that appeared in the *New York Times Book Review* of October 14,
1990, is significant: for lack of positive heroes, we create bad ones.
Mobsters do not need mythification. Organized crime wields economic
and social, as well as political power, which has a destructive effect on
people and their institutions.

Mussolini had almost eradicated the Mafia by using draconian police methods such as torture and summary execution. However, in a
belief that its power could be used in the struggle against the Nazis, it
was reinstated in Sicily during World War II by the American Mafia in
alliance with the U.S. Armed Forces and regained its influence not
only through the collection of "protection money" for guarding property, irrigation systems, and fishing fleets, but also through greater
involvement in urban economic affairs. Until the 1970s the Mafia pros-
pered within the D.C. system of power in the South; and, in turn, it
was at the service of politicians. It delivered votes and financed political campaigns. In exchange it obtained local contracts and was allowed to develop protection rackets.[2]

The explosion of the social conflict in the late 1960s and early-
1970s had an effect on the Mafia's behavior. Since the state was engaged in the control of these conflicts and showed signs of weakness,
the Mafia seized the opportunity to become an independent economic
force and its own master. Old techniques were resurrected in order to
finance modern economic activities. Using force, it operated as a para-
sitic middleman between owners and workers, between producers and
consumers, between citizens and the state. Not only did the Mafia
gain control of the wholesale market for vegetables, meat, and fish
and engage in cigarette smuggling as well as real estate speculation,
but it also attempted to acquire a share of the vast resources the state

was sending to the South for economic development in its attempt to face the social conflicts and the wave of terrorism.

However, the decisive factor in the spread of the Mafia was the drug trade, of which it was the primary operator. By the mid-1970s the Mafia had assumed international dimensions because of its involvement in the worldwide narcotics market. Heroin traffic had become an enterprise of authentic multinational dimensions: it involves the importation of opium from Pakistan, Afghanistan, and Iran; it is transformed into morphine in the Middle East and into heroin in Sicily; and it is eventually transported to the U.S. and other advanced industrial countries. Italy itself, especially wealthy northern cities such as Milan, Turin, Verona, and Genoa also became a lucrative end market for hard drugs. The enormous profits in successful drug deals provided the Sicilian mafiosi and their allies with huge funds and tremendous influence. The Mafia drug tycoons used their money to buy flashy cars, build sumptuous villas, and enter legal businesses and industries. Many credit institutions in Italy and Switzerland as well as offshore fiscal havens appeared only too happy to handle all that cash, thereby becoming instrumental in money-laundering schemes. The expansion of the Sicilian banking system was also linked to Mafia involvement in narcotics. According to most estimates, by the late 1980s, the Italian Mafia earned enough money to have covered Italy's $125 billion debt.[3]

The vast sums of money at stake and the greed of the mafiosi brought about a new level of violence. In the old times, a local "honored man" did not very often have to order one of his hitmen to fire the *lupara* at some landowner who would not pay protection money, or to eliminate some traitor who had started carrying out robberies on his own. Until a few decades ago the Mafia could secure compliance with its orders through a simple warning by a go-between or a more tangible form of intimidation. The organization traditionally preferred cooperation with local officials rather than opposing them openly or having them killed. Until the late 1960s, attacks on journalists, parliamentarians, police, judges, attorneys, and other representatives of public institutions were unthinkable. In the past, rival Mafia clans fought one another, with whole families being wiped out in the process. A kind of Darwinian process regulated their existence. Today's Mafia, however, is different from that of years past.

The change came about with the Mafia's entry into the heroin business, and with streams of billions of liras that the Italian government had been channeling to the southern regions as financial aid. The attempts to industrialize southern Italy through large state projects has provided both a gold mine for the Mafia and an opportunity for local officials to get heavy bribes. With the sudden influx of wealth, power structures were reorganized, the rules of the game were revised, and the lifestyles of the mafiosi changed. The Mafia has abandoned its peasant roots. Today the successful Mafia boss has the power of a politician, with stable and powerful ties to Rome.

Because of the Mafia, drug use has become a bigger problem than terrorism ever was. Solutions are not easy to find because of serious social problems. Increasingly, teenagers become both foot soldiers and casualties in the Mafia's battles. At one time, women and children were off-limits to the Mafia, but that no longer is the case. Juvenile crime has exploded in recent years, coinciding with organized crime's recruitment of youth from local gangs. Some are as young as 10. Possibly to blame is a penal code enacted in 1989 that rules out jail time for any minor who commits a crime that would normally carry less than a 12-year sentence. With unemployment at 20% in the South, many teens either move north or turn to crime. Drug couriers are often paid in heroin, with the consequence that many become addicts and remain slaves of their newly-found "work." It is also impossible for poor teens, once they are recruited and have tasted the glamour and money of organized crime, to free themselves of such servitude.

The Italian court system has had mixed results in responding to the legal challenges posed by the spread of terrorism and organized crime in Italy. On the one hand, even though judges and public prosecutors have often been the targets of terrorist and criminal abuse, they have nevertheless managed to help the government withstand and largely defeat the threat that the Red Brigades and other groups have posed to Italian democracy since the 1970s. On the other hand, the people who make up the judicial corps have themselves occasionally been tainted because some of them were involved in major scandals, leading to well-publicized resignations and even trials. Many officials of the judiciary were implicated in the "P-2 affair" and had to resign, while connections with organized crime plagued local courts and even the Court of Cassation, equivalent to America's Supreme Court.

Sicilian violence did not cease. A new wave of assassinations started; during a brief two-week period in the fall of 1988, 18 people, including a judge, were murdered by Mafia gunmen. Sicily, Calabria, and Campania now account for 66% of the homicides in Italy although they makeup only about 25% of Italy's population. As rival gangs in Sicily, Calabria, and the Naples area started an unending series of murders in their drug-related turf wars, they also killed several magistrates, police officers, and politicians. After each spectacular assassination, high-ranking officials of the state government, including the president of the republic and the prime minister, flew to Sicily to attend the victim's funeral and use the occasion to deliver the usual political homilies pledging that the fight against the Mafia would be stepped up. Outraged citizens occasionally responded with explosive catcalls and boos. The assassinations of Giovanni Falcone and Paolo Borsellino in 1992, the two leading anti-mafia special prosecutors who were making an impact by jailing hundreds of mafiosi, outraged the nation.

In response to these brutal attacks, in which powerful bombs were used to murder the judges and many of their bodyguards, the Italian government took strong measures, including the dispatch of seven elite battalions of troops to assist Sicilian officials and local law enforcement officers. The troops were assigned to protect officials and vital installations, but they were not expected to participate in investigative procedures conducted by traditional police agencies. Most importantly, the government has at last committed itself to the creation of a national investigative force, along the lines of the United States' Federal Bureau of Investigation, to fight the Mafia. Known by its Italian initials as the *DIA*, this force will eventually grow to a strength of 3,000 crime agents.

The government has taken other actions as well. Since the members of *Cosa Nostra*, besides being drug traffickers and racketeers, are also legitimate businessmen and farmers, and therefore, are interested in public-works contracts sponsored by local governments, the state has dissolved dozens of these local town councils accused of dealing with the Mafia.

Most Italians are upset with the presence of the Mafia in Italy and are horrified whenever television and the newspapers report the latest savagery in gory detail. They frequently organize massive demonstrations to show their outrage. Yet the Mafia continued to flourish until the early 1990s. The major problem was that the Mafia lived within the walls of government. Its success had to be attributed to the fact that it infiltrated or actually controlled the nerve center of the regional government. Its collaboration was considered indispensable at election time, and some candidates, the more successful ones, did anything to secure it. In early 1984, officials of the Sicilian regional government were forced to resign and were arrested on charges of corruption. In 1991, 27 municipal administrations were dissolved because members were found to be connected with the Mafia or *Camorra*.

Serious attempts have been made by individual citizens to create a civic consciousness of the evil of the Mafia. The two most prominent names are two writers, Danilo Dolci and Leonardo Sciascia, both deceased. For many years Dolci campaigned in the slums of Palermo and the little Mafia towns of western Sicily. For a long time he seemed to be making no headway at all and though his name was widely known abroad, few people inside Italy had heard of him. Again and again, by hunger strikes and other forms of peaceful demonstration, he drew the attention of the outside world to the abuse of the Mafia and the connivance of the Sicilian and the Italian establishment. The task he had set himself was Herculean, nothing less than persuading Italians that things can change simply because enough people—ordinary people without special power and influence—want them to be different. But to do that he had to destroy the ingrained conviction of Italians, northerners and southerners alike, that the only way to get things done is by pulling strings.

The biggest hope, however, has to be found in the collective efforts of southern society, which is showing signs of civic maturity. The structure of the Mafia being classically based on vertical relations of authority and dependence, with little or no horizontal solidarity among equals, can be demolished only by establishing a pattern of horizontal trust and the elimination of the vertical "exploitation-dependence" that has characterized southern culture and social structures for at least a millennium.

The wind of radical political change, meanwhile, is having an effect also on the Mafia. In response to the massive popular outrage, in the summer of 1992, the Amato government enacted tougher measures against the Mafia and other criminal organizations, most notably the *Camorra* and *'Ndrangheta*. Thanks to the new legislation and to better coordination between law-enforcing agencies, several hundred mobsters have been arrested (including top leaders of the major criminal organizations). Mafia assets totaling over $2.5 billion have been seized.

White-Collar Crime and the Italian Social System

White-collar crime in Italy attracts attention in the press and in academic studies not only because it is important in itself, but also because of what it seems to tell us about Italian society in general. Widespread corruption has often been seen as confirming a series of related theoretical frameworks that portray Italians as particularly prone to "favoritism" and "familism," perennially subject to pressures to favor friends and relatives, and concomitantly incapable of adhering to the impersonal rules that are said to characterize a modern state. In assessing corruption, it is difficult to make comparisons of rate of corruption between countries because a whole different set of rules governs the social structures and cultures of countries. In addition, Michael Eve rightly points out that before proceeding to some basic exploration of differences in the social relations involved in "corruption" in Italy and elsewhere, it is useful to examine the issue of how we come to know about corruption in the first place, how it becomes "visible."[4]

The social visibility of an issue often varies greatly between countries because the information we have about a social phenomenon in two different countries is not just naturally given, but is socially constructed. Because "any social phenomenon, whether rape, child abuse, unemployment, fraud, or corruption, is raised to the status of a 'social problem' only when there are specialists who collect data, classify cases, and interpret evidence, fitting it into patterns," corruption comes to light through the mediation of the law, judges, the police, colleagues, companies who complain, journalists, and so on.[5] All these institutions and professions operate differently in different countries. Genuinely comparative research needs to be carried out. The search for causes can only be really satisfactory if we are clear as to what it is that is being explained. It is not just "more" corruption that marks out Italy, but the different context in which it takes place. Yet this does not mean that the special prominence of corruption in Italy is an illusion, merely the result of greater Italian sensitivity to the issue. Again, it is only under certain conditions—fostered partly by the awareness created by newspapers, academics, and political polemicists, by changes in the conceptions of how far it is acceptable for an investigator to go in probing suspicions—that many forms of corruption are brought to light and are successfully prosecuted.[6]

It should be said that the principal factor behind national differences in the prominence of corruption is not simply due to the number of hidden cases, but to the nature of the rules themselves. Therefore, it is possible that certain actions or decisions may be perfectly legal in a certain country and not in another, or be legal or illegal in the same country if the rules change. To what extent are political

contributions by companies and lobbying groups perfectly legal? Are
not political contributions by companies perfectly legal, and even tax
deductible, in many nations? But is it or should it be illegal for the
president of the United States to allow to sleep in the Lincoln bed-
room of the White House those who contributed at least $100,000 to
the Democratic Party national campaign? And should it be legal or
culturally acceptable that corporations give any contributions to any
candidate or political party? Money does not flow to the politicians
simply for an ideal; it is handed over for a contract, for bending a
regulation, for a desired piece of legislation. Even in the culture of
gifts there is a problem: although there is no immediate reward, in the
long term reciprocity is expected. The differences at issue are differences in the type of social relationships that link firms and politicians.
It is certainly noteworthy that relationships between local and national
politicians and businesses may sometimes be more intimate in Britain
or the U.S. than in Italy.[7] These relationships may have oligopolistic
consequences. In order to explain why corruption has been such a
problem in Italy, it is necessary to grasp the bases of these social
relationships, rather than simply distinguishing between corruption
on the one hand and respect for the law on the other. Sometimes,
however, a system of *tangenti* (kickbacks) is used in a country. That is
where Italy went astray and a number of crucial differences had developed between practices in Italy and those in the U.S. or in Britain.

   White-collar crimes and political scandals have become very visible
in the last few years because of changes in the political climate. A
week rarely went by at the end of the 1980s and in the early 1990s
without the public learning that an officeholder, politician, banker,
industrialist, military officer, television personality, or even a magistrate had been brought to court, and they occasionally ended up in
jail. Bribery and corruption infected almost every aspect of Italian life.
When a developer who built prisons was discovered to have handed
out millions of dollars in bribes to everyone, including the minister of
labor, it was called the "golden prisons" scandal. Since then there has
been the "golden sheets" scandal, involving lucrative contracts to supply linen for sleeper cars from the Italian railroad. In Rome there was
the "golden bedpans" scandal, in which hospital workers hired to empty
bedpans were mysteriously promoted into high-paying administrative
positions for which they had no qualifications, and finally, the mega-
scandal of bribes to political parties. The political scandals reached
such proportion as to challenge credulity. Although no party has re-

mained immune, the two parties with the most power at that time, the *D.C.* and the *P.S.I.*, have been shown to be the most corrupt.

Many times corruption was more subtle because the relationship between the private sector and the politicians was closer and more symbiotic. The relationship between Fininvest, the group headed by Berlusconi and whose interests range from television and publishing to urban development and supermarkets, and politicians, especially of the Socialist Party, was so close that reciprocal favors did not seem to have normally flowed down the channel of direct monetary exchange. The Socialist Party seems to have defended Fininvest's interests by shielding it from effective anti-monopoly legislation in the media industry. In return, Fininvest media gave plenty of interviews with *P.S.I.* spokesmen, appeared on popular entertainment or chat shows, gave prominent coverage of issues championed by the Party, or reduced rates for election advertising. In 1994 the formation of a government headed by Berlusconi and containing three former executives of Fininvest as ministers or secretaries of state raised even more intriguing questions regarding relationships between government and a particular set of companies.

Some of the estimates indicate that politicians in Italy routinely stole anywhere from $6 billion to $12 billion a year. Elections have become so expensive not because running for office costs much more than in France or Germany but because the candidates pocketed a lot of money each time the voters went to the polls. One wonders if the frequent fall of governments and the consequent new elections are not connected to the political scam. This, of course, must be the reason why so few politicians complain about having to campaign so often. It had become a custom that parties paid their general costs with contract kickbacks and "contributions," while candidates paid for their own campaigns with kickbacks from the families that depended directly on them for jobs.

Bribery had been always connected with southern Italy, and even to some extent with central Italy. The northern part of the country had always been viewed as immune to such corruption. The Sicilians talked about kickbacks by using the word *pizzo* (an old Sicilian word for a bird's beak, by allusion, when it's being dipped in food or water). The Neapolitans say *mazzetta*, which means a small bundle (of money). In the North, Milanese, Venetians, and other peoples did not have a word. Not until recently, that is, when the massive bribery scandal that shook Italy to its core started to unfold in Milan in early 1992. It not only demonstrated that the North is not ethically different from the rest of the country, but it also showed that the Italian party-dominated system that has run the country since World War II was at the core of the corruption.

The investigation, known as *Operazione Mani Pulite* (Operation Clean Hands), showed bribe collection to be one of the most efficient and organized arms of the Italian government. Officials had routinely skimmed from 2 to 14% off government contracts made by the industries of the public sector and for every public service, from airports and hospitals to theaters and orphanages. Politicians had immense power because the government controlled, as we shall see later, vast sectors of the economy, from commercial banking, steel, telecommunications, and energy industries all the way down to ice cream plants, grocery stores, and vineyards. For Italian political parties, such activities were giant spoils machines. Much of the private sector, too—from FIAT to small construction outfits—had no choice but to come to terms with *partitocrazia*, rule by the political parties.

By acting as legitimate democratic intermediaries between the individual citizen and the state, and being essentially vote-getting entities, the political parties had spawned an oligarchy of professional politicians, a *classe politica* (political class) to conduct illegal activities in an almost legal way. The political class for years had relied on graft, *tangente* (even in this area the Italians try to use some sophistication; they use a neat geometrical term for a kickback).

The scandal of *tangenti* spread rapidly to dozens of other northern cities and brought public disgrace and even jail terms to many top politicians. "Operation Clean Hands hit Italian politics like a cyclone," wrote Giuseppe Turato and Cinzia Sasso in *The Looters*, a recent book about the scandal. "After this, nothing will ever be the same."[8]

The political system was immensely damaging not only because it involved enormous waste but also because it virtually abolished normal politics, as the latter became less and less a question of competition between interest groups and different programs and more and more a struggle for control of a slice of the spoils system.

It is no accident that the scandal came to light in 1992. As we have seen, during the Cold War many Italian voters considered corruption a lesser evil than a government headed by the Communist Party. A majority of Italian voters supported a coalition of parties led by the anti-communist christian democrats and the socialists. But the collapse of communism opened a Pandora's-box of pent-up frustration and disgust with the Italian political system; voters started to desert the traditional corruption-ridden parties in droves.

The new political climate and the increased European and global competition in the economic system also changed the relation of the Italian business and industrial system with politics. The system of collusion between government and business that had worked well enough in a relatively closed, protected market, could not continue after 1992 because the onerous tax on businesses made it difficult for business to compete freely with European and other rivals. The clean-up that followed was most welcomed. Since most Italians dislike politicians, it was easy for the judges who arrested hundreds of Milanese bureaucrats, businessmen, and politicians, including deputies to the Italian Parliament, to become heroes. Indeed, the public response was euphoric. The judge-prosecutor who started the investigation, Antonio Di Pietro, an Abruzzese by birth, suddenly became a national hero, and his picture appeared on the cover of most major news magazines. Graffiti writers scrawled *Grazie Di Pietro* (Thanks, Di Pietro) across walls in Milan, and Di Pietro T-shirts became the most popular items for teenagers.

In the process, over 3,000 people were arrested or notified that they were under investigation for corruption and/or illegal acts connected with the financing of political parties. About half of them were economic operators, including top managers of Italy's biggest private corporations (FIAT, Olivetti, MontEdison) and state holdings (IRI and ENI). About as many were politicians, including over 150 members of Parliament, 4 former premiers, and a score of former cabinet ministers. By mid-summer 1993, the breakdown by party affiliation showed that every political party was touched: 465 *D.C.*'s, 288 socialists, 71 representatives of the *P.C.I.* (now renamed *P.D.S.*—Democratic Party of the Left), 39 social-democrats, 31 republicans, 20 liberals, 5 representatives of *Rifondazione Comunista* (the splinter group of the die-hard left-wingers who refused to join the *P.D.S.* and vowed to "remain communist") and 4 members of the neo-fascist *M.S.I.* Estimates put at over 80,000 billion lire (about $53 billion) or one-half the budget deficit, the grand total of the payoffs over the last 10 years.

However, corruption among national politicians is symptomatic of an entire system with very little resistance to corruption. The central question is why a sense of public morality and respect for the law has been so weak in Italy. The root cause of the problem lies in the absence or weakness of the tradition of the state and also of the community.

The general point at issue is that comparison of the extent of corruption in different countries cannot be analyzed independently of the laws that make particular forms of behavior illegal.

What Does it All Mean?

Judging by the mega-scandals and the wide reach of the Mafia over the entire territory of the nation and the power that it exercises on Italian institutions, even governmental ones, are we to conclude that Italy has failed as a democratic nation? Should we conclude that Italians don't know how to behave in a democratic system? That civic consciousness is weak in Italian society? Some political experts do think that Italy falls short on many measures we use to gauge the health and stability of democratic societies and governments. "Phenomena as various as a proclivity to go through red traffic lights, tax evasion, or the forging of documents to obtain a disability pension on false pretenses may all be cited as examples of weak internalization of the rules imposed by the national community and a disrespect for the law"(M. Eve, p. 44).

It is important to note in this context that corruption in Italy does not seem to be unambiguously associated with those features we might expect of a "weak" or even "absent" state. Well, one of the most persistent paradoxes of Italian society is the coexistence of exceptionally rigorous and detailed laws and administrative regulation designed to prevent the interference of individual interests in public interests. Italian bureaucracy imposes a high number of requirements on those demanding a service or asking for a contract in an attempt to ensure that those not entitled to the service, not best qualified to receive the contract, will not get it. Unfortunately, while all this inflexible regulation certainly does eliminate some forms of corruption, it often generates new opportunities for it. In Italy, in contrast to the U.S. or Britain, much less freedom is given to officials either by written rules or by conventional working practices covering the implementation of the rules; hence the kind of minor negotiation that is often possible in other countries is not allowed, and is classified in the realm of illicit behavior. In fact, the presence of the state is very strong in the economy of the country, and we may say that the Italian insistence on universal criteria that place all firms on an equal footing in the competition for a contract places large areas of behavior out of bounds. Italian legislation attempts to regulate the granting of public contracts with very elaborate measures to prevent one firm gaining an unfair advantage. It is expected that public officials and contractors are two completely separate parties who will act quite independently of each other. In the U.S. and Britain, expectations are clearly lower.

But in the larger spectrum, lack of loyalty to the national community is caused by another loyalty. In the Italian social system, loyalties to family and friends, or to the entourage of some influential leader, squeeze out loyalties to the state and the wider community. Hence, when an opportunity arises to favor a friend at the expense of strangers, a high proportion of Italians will sacrifice the interests of those who are not personally close. The problem is a deep-seated cultural and ethical attitude in individuals that springs from a particular historical experience. The supposedly late formation of Italy as a unified nation is often cited as the background to this weak sense of identification with the national community. An implicit comparison with a type of society that is not particularistic and familistic and where the sense of the state is more deeply rooted in national consciousness will show Italy as being civilly backward.

It should be pointed out that the very democratic form of government combined with a very "liberal" judicial system makes it very difficult for the nation to deal with political opponents of the Republic and those who threaten the stability of the nation. However, we should examine closely how Italy fares in comparison with other Western countries. On the governmental level, Italy can only draw respect. If the Italians change prime ministers more often than do the British, or than Americans change presidents, this really does not mean that Italian democracy is more unstable than the others. If 85 to 90% of the Italians vote in national elections, as compared with just over half that number in American presidential elections, is it really the case that the Italian and not the American pattern is pathological? As Joseph La Palombara has made us reflect, "which is a more serious weakness for democracy: the Italian government's apparent inability to bring the Mafia to heel in Sicily, or the failure of other democracies to deal with large-scale crime in their major cities? And which kind of corruption is more insidious: the headline-making scandals that fill Italy's daily newspapers, or the extensive 'white-collar' crime in the United States, that rarely gets any public notice at all."[9]

In talking about Italian crime, scholars and journalists generally use an unexamined and idealized vision that they wish the country would live up to. The assessment is done by transferring into the conceptual

framework all the elements of stereotype attached to the Italian society but without taking into consideration the nature of the "particularistic" and "familistic" fibers of the Italian social system. In the American system, which tends to be universalistic, those characteristics are
certainly not appealing.

So although frameworks that relate particularism to a weak sense
of the state are in many ways crucial for the understanding of contemporary Italy, they can be deepened considerably if comparison is made
not with a stereotyped and sociologically unrealistic model but rather
with the real structures of authority, responsibility, solidarity, and power.

Despite crime (though Italy is certainly not at the top of the list of
crime-plagued nations) and despite unemployment and heavy taxes, it
seems that life is still good in Italy. In 1989 polls conducted in the
French-speaking Valle d'Aosta and the German-speaking Alto Adige,
which was ceded to Italy by Austria after World War I, revealed that
although these regions desire greater administrative autonomy, in no
way do they wish to secede from Italy. The winds of total autonomy
and separatism that are sweeping through Europe are not affecting
Italian unity.

Another big challenge that the country will face is the upsurge of
regional administrative autonomy that the wealthy northern regions
are going to demand. According to the constitution, regions may have
their own administration and chart their own destiny. The christian
democratic governments, or governments of coalitions dominated by
christian democrats, had, after 1948, refused to implement regionalism because they rightly feared that it would lead to communist regional governments. But it steadily became clear that weak local governments and excessive centralization were leading to corruption and
incompetence. In the years 1968-1970, plans were drawn up for fifteen regions, not only on the periphery of the peninsula—like Sicily,
Sardinia, the Alto Adige, and the Valle d'Aosta, where regional governments already existed—but in the heartlands of the country as well.
The regional councils of these new, large areas were elected in June
1970. By 1980 the regions were spending 18% of the entire national
expenditure, and at that time the communists were in control of three
regions: Emilia-Romagna (centered in Bologna), Tuscany, and Umbria.
Communists and socialists together ran Piedmont, Liguria (centered in
Genoa), and Latium. The christian democrats, on the other hand,
controlled only two, both in the South, but shared power in eleven
others. The regions exercise wide powers, in fields like welfare and

education, and control the expenditure of considerable sums of money. Some of these powers have simply been taken over from the old municipalities, but some, certainly, come from central government. Regionalism has encouraged the growth of grassroots groups—trade unions and local businesses—but, unfortunately, in the South it has sometimes made life easier for criminal organizations like the Mafia and the Camorra. The communist-controlled regions in the North have earned a reputation for being efficient and free from corruption, yet they have not found it difficult to work with big business or the multinationals. Bologna, under communist control, had become a symbol of prosperity, efficiency, and civility: it was one of the most prosperous cities in Europe, it was immune from political corruption, and it escaped the destruction of its ancient beauty.

As the national government continues to be shaken by accusations of corruption, these regional governments, with their inherently closer ties to their constituents, may increase in importance and offer Italy new hope in its quests to combat threats to the nation and maintain its place in the forefront of Western democracies.

Notes

1. G. Amendola, "I comunisti e il movimento studentesco, necessità della lotta su due fronti," *Rinascita*, June 7, 1968; L. Longo, "Il movimento studentesco nella lotta anti-capitalista," *Rinascita*, May 3, 1968.

2. See R. Chinnici, "Magistratura e mafia," *Democrazia e Diritto* 22, no. 4 (July-August 1982), 81. Rocco Chinnici, an investigative magistrate, was killed by the Mafia in the summer of 1983. Other important anti-Mafia personalities had been murdered the year before. On April 25, 1982, the Sicilian communist leader Pio La Torre, who had been in the forefront of the anti-Mafia campaign, was killed with his driver by the Mafia. Later that year, on September 3, the former counter-terrorism chief and then prefect of Sicily (with special responsibilities for the fight against the Mafia), Dalla Chiesa, was killed with his wife openly in the streets of Palermo.

3. For a penetrating assessment of the working of the Mafia see R. Catanzaro, "Mafia, economia e sistema politico, in U. Ascoli e R. Catanzaro, *La società italiana degli anni ottanta* (Bari: Laterza, 1987), 255-79.

4. "Comparing Italy: The Case of Corruption," in David Forgacs and Robert Lumley, eds., *Italian Cultural Studies* (Oxford: Oxford U. P., 1996), 36.

5. D. Forgacs and R. Lumley, eds., 83.

6. There are certainly large international differences in the powers and the expertise of investigating authorities. In Britain and the U.S., where it is the police who have the responsibility for collecting evidence and preparing a prosecution case, resources devoted to fraud and white-collar crime in general, including, therefore, corruption, have traditionally been very limited. Because of the volume of work that fraud squads are expected to undertake, police have remained largely reactive rather than proactive

7. A good example, Michael Eve says, is provided by local development agencies such as those organizing urban renewal. In Britain and the U.S., where the idea of private-public partnership in local development has been influential, it has been common to include directors of local companies in publicly funded bodies that have access to substantial government funds and wide powers to decide how development should proceed. Representatives of building companies may thus sit on local development agencies that decide the shape of a local town plan, infrastructures, industrial development, and even allocate individual contracts. Ibid., p. 42.

8. G. Turato and C. Sasso, *I saccheggiatori* (Milan: Sperling & Kupfer, 1992).

9. La Palombara, 6-7.

IV

U.S.-Italian Relations and the American Presence

Italy: Dependent Ally or Independent Partner?

There is no question that America played a major role in the political and cultural postwar evolution of Italy. We have already pointed out that Italian internal political affairs have been deeply affected by the strange relationship between Italy and the U.S. The peculiar character of these relations is not based on the existence of any special amicability or feeling of kinship; on the contrary. The singular nature of the relationship is due to the profound and patent American involvement in Italy's domestic affairs. This meant that for much of the postwar period Italy was a dependent ally of the United States.

U.S.-Italian relations for most of the last 45 years have been dominated by questions arising from domestic politics rather than international affairs, as is the case with France, Germany, and other Western allies. The critical element in American/Italian relations was the existence, up until 1991, of a Communist Party that was potentially strong enough to share power or even lead the Italian government. From Washington's point of view, such an eventuality would have created both a political embarrassment for an American president and a risk that Italy might have left NATO or reduced its alliance commitments. The overriding American aim was always to forestall any form or degree of communist participation in the Italian government.

When President Carter was elected in November 1976, Italy was considered the greatest potential political problem the U.S. had in Europe. In the final months of the Ford administration, the communists had achieved their all-time high in an Italian election, 34.4% of the vote. They were extending their control in every important area of Italian life—schools, press, judiciary, trade unions, and regional and local governments. It seemed almost inevitable that they would enter the government in a historic compromise coalition with the christian democrats, eventually hindering the country's support of the Western Alliance.

The American Right was putting pressure on the president to stop the threat of communism through covert operations if necessary. But Carter wisely rejected that option and decided against the financing of Italian political parties, the manipulation of Italian political events, and the attempt to tell the Italians how they should vote. In making such a decision, the president was influenced by the counterproductive effects of such efforts in the past. As Richard N. Gardner, Carter's ambassador to Italy, pointed out, "early in the Nixon years large sums of money were given by the U.S. Embassy in Rome to the right-wing general who subsequently ran for Parliament on the neo-fascist ticket. Wide publicity was also given in Italy to reports that another covert financing operation was discussed and then aborted in the Ford Administration. Both of these episodes helped the Communist Party to gain support as defender of the country's sovereignty against 'American domination.'"[1]

Italy's political moves had been closely monitored by the U.S. since the war's end. During the first months of 1948, Italy was already seen as the hottest battleground of the Cold War against Communism. In their conflict with the Soviets, American governments felt free to intervene at every level of Italian domestic affairs.

Much of the intervention went on behind the scenes through covert operations. In the early postwar period the American government had provided encouragement and funding for the establishment of a political party—the social democrats—and two trade unions—the *U.I.L.* and the *C.I.S.L.* Subsequently it dispensed funds to a variety of individuals, groups, and parties, most especially the *D.C.* and a Catholic national labor union (*C.I.S.L.*). The American policy did not consider the danger that such moves could turn political stability into stagnation or that the reconstruction drive itself would result in a substantial restoration of old economic and social structures. In seeking their own self-centered aims, the Americans missed an opportunity to broaden the foundations of Italy's democratic institution. Economic and political power had always been in the hands of the few: mostly landowners in the South, big business and industrialists in the North. The predictable results of American intervention were to further strengthen the trend toward stalemate and *immobilismo*.

In the 1950s America saw Italy as "an ally in distress" and even wondered whether the country was about to become a "lost ally." During the Eisenhower years, the American ambassador to Rome, Clare Boothe Luce, based her assessment on the danger that the *P.C.I.* might "take over" in the near future or at least gain enough additional votes to "overtake" the *D.C.* and become the number one political force in the nation. The fear was so great that U.S. officials in Rome announced that aid might be discontinued if the leftist and/or rightist opposition parties gained ground in the 1954 election. In later statements America let it be known that contracts would be denied to factories where communist-dominated unions continued to poll a majority of the workers' votes. The whole program of economic assistance in Italy became controversial, especially when the spotlight fell on the U.S. intention to use economic aid not only to strengthen Italy's international commitments but to condition domestic developments. Top representatives of the U.S. administration felt that the Italian government did not display all the desirable vigor in the battle against Italian communism. They suggested, for instance, that the municipal Council of Bologna (the biggest Red stronghold in Italy) be disbanded.

Unfortunately, America was not concerned with the fact that, in 1954, despite a remarkable postwar recovery, Italy was a country where 50 million people were governed by 5,000 in the interest of 500. Mrs. Luce was still toying with the idea that the Right could make a useful and possibly decisive contribution to solving Italian problems. She was terribly worried about Giovanni Gronchi's ascendancy to the presidency and his reported inclinations toward neutralism in foreign affairs and "socialistic openings" in domestic politics, even though he had clearly voiced his support for the Atlantic Alliance and for Western cooperation and solidarity. Gronchi let it be known that he was not happy with the way Italy was being treated in the Atlantic Alliance; he felt that his country was entitled to a more equal standing in an alliance that was practically run by the U.S., Great Britain, and France.[2]

This U.S. slight toward Italy was not caused simply by fear of a possible communist takeover, but also by certain international economic policies with which Italians were having significant success. At this time, the U.S. also had a bitter aversion to Enrico Mattei's initiatives at instigating cooperation with the oil rich countries of the Third World and to Italy's sharing in the economic development of the underdeveloped countries. With the coming to power of a Republican administration in America, many key positions were entrusted to people close to the big oil corporations. Traditional ties to powerful private groups and strong hostility to public intervention in economic affairs prompted large sectors of the U.S. media to sharply attack Mattei and the Italian state oil and gas agency, *ENI*. Mattei was smeared as pro-communist, a typical charge brought against anyone with whom one disagreed in the 1950s. The situation was exacerbated by his ability to achieve significant success in Egypt and other Third World countries, including Iran, thanks to an approach keyed to partnership with local governments. In October 1957, President Gronchi protested to the American ambassador in Rome:

> quite often the actions of your oil concerns are backed by American diplomatic representatives. We feel that the behavior of these corporations does a great disservice to the United States. Just when the British and French "imperialism" has come to an end in this sector, the "imperialism" of the North American corporations is getting under way.[3]

During the same time the Italian government was trying not to be subservient to the U.S. in foreign policy and was complaining to the U.S. about its failure to consult with Italy in European and, especially, Mediterranean policy. The U.S. conferred almost exclusively with France and Great Britain, even on the Mediterranean, where the two former colonial powers had lost their clout. Italy, on the other hand, had left a good bridge with her ex-colonies and enjoyed a good relationship with most of the Arab world; she felt that the U.S. should have supported her pursuit of political prestige and economic expansion in that part of the world. The Italian government was telling Washington that there was nothing wrong, or that it was perfectly possible, for a Mediterranean country like Italy to pursue a policy of friendship toward the Arab world while continuing to cooperate with her partners in the Atlantic Alliance. In 1957, during the Eisenhower administration, the U.S. started to reassess its relationship with Italy. Vice President Nixon, on his trip to Italy in the spring of 1957, stated that it would be useful if in the Middle East the U.S. could act in closer cooperation with Italy and with other major countries more directly concerned. However, it was not easy to change American government attitudes toward Italian internal politics. Arthur Schlesinger Jr., who was to become a high-ranking adviser to President Kennedy, wrote that U.S. policies toward Italy required a thorough updating. In subsequent years, he became more and more convinced that the U.S. would greatly benefit, directly and indirectly, from the coming to power in Italy of a coalition based on collaboration between christian democrats and socialists. However, many key posts, notably in the State Department, continued to be held or controlled by officials whose ideas about Italy were cemented in the early postwar years. When the shortcomings of the center governments became unsolvable, they tended to look to the Right rather than to the moderate Left.

The U.S. was loath to allow the socialists in government because their leader, Pietro Nenni had not dropped his requests for the withdrawal of U.S. forces from Europe and for a neutralist Italian position, even though he had criticized Stalinism and the Soviet behavior in Hungary and had stated that the U.S., having been called upon twice to save European liberties, first from German militarism and then from Nazi fascism, had acquired a historical title and vested interest in European freedom and security, and had spoken against the Italian Communist Party. Despite America's opposition, Aldo Moro spared no effort to make sure that the dialogue between the *D.C.* and the *P.S.I.* would make progress. But the center-left coalition was only possible after a short-lived government had been formed with the support of the neo-fascists, which brought the nation to the brink of a civil war. Public opinion polls supported the view that the opening to the Left would not have brought about a pro-Soviet government.

U.S. Grants Approval to the Socialists

At the end of the 1950s and early 1960s the leader of the Socialist Party, Pietro Nenni, was constantly trying to clarify the position of his party for its eventual participation in government. He emphasized that Italy's links with NATO represented an irreversible position and that Italy's approach to European integration had to be closer to that of President Kennedy, which was founded on democratic and supranational principles rather than on a confederation of nationalistic countries as was advocated by the regime of French premier Charles de Gaulle. Nenni repeatedly stated that his Party's objectives were to bring Italy's social and institutional framework in line with the high rate of industrialization and the increase in production.

The possible participation of socialists in government was not opposed by the Vatican, even though some Italian cardinals did express reservations. Ever since the election of Pope John XXIII, the Vatican had adopted a policy of less direct involvement in Italian politics and viewed with benevolent neutrality the flirtation of the *D.C.* with the *P.S.I.* The Church's position was in line with its new emphasis on the social aspects of its traditional doctrines, as reflected in such papal pronouncements as the encyclical *Mater et Magistra* (*Mother and Teacher*).

The gap between Italian political reality and its perception by the U.S. diplomatic corps was narrowed during the first year of the Kennedy administration. As pointed out by Arthur Schlesinger in his book, *A Thousand Days*, Secretary of State Averill Harriman played a key role in turning around U.S. diplomacy by persuading those U.S. officials who had opposed socialist participation in the Italian government to change their point of view.[4] Schlesinger felt that the opening to the socialists provided a good opportunity for both Italian and U.S. interests and, therefore, deserved to be strongly supported by Washington; Italy had to proceed with its plan of social and economic reforms. The American administration's support for the center-left paid dividends during the crisis over the deployment of Soviet missiles in Cuba. Nenni did not share the pro-Soviet and anti-American views expressed by the Communist Party and the pro-communist wing of his own. The course followed by the center-left coalition in international affairs became even more of an asset for the Kennedy administration because of the sharpening differences with Gaullist France over its opposition to the entrance of Great Britain to the European Community (E.C.) and its concept of European unity. American support for the center-left strengthened the resolve of the Italian government to oppose the Italian conservative forces, in which many U.S. diplomats had long put their faith.

The position taken by the American administration was not followed by most of the American media, which kept repeating old charges and prejudices. Editorials and articles published in the spring of 1962 were a clear reminder of how ill-informed and biased the American press was. The slanted reporting of some sectors of the U.S. news media and their inability to understand Italy and Italian politics emerged most flagrantly when the conflicts within the socialist camp led to the failure of Moro's first attempt to form a new center-left government. The gains scored by the communists at the general elections in spring 1963 were quickly interpreted as a rejection of the coalition political forces by the electorate. The American press did not realize that the communist gains at the polls had to be interpreted in the context of spreading protests fed by practical rather than by ideological factors and circumstances. Echoing Italian conservative fears as seen in rightist papers, the American press prophesied Italy's near abandonment of solidarity with the West, of a free economy, and of an open democratic society.

This biased coverage of the Italian political scene has been criticized by politicians from the full spectrum of Italian political life. Except for occasional references, the American media did not make real efforts in those years to address the political and economic life of Italy and assess its presence as a modern industrial society. Very rarely did American journalistic reports include some sort of insight or analysis of Italy's political, economic, or social conditions and prospects.

Many in the U.S. media, for instance, also failed to understand or badly underrated the significance of the student movement, which in early 1968 was already surfacing as a new and important component of Italian society. A challenge to the entire Italian establishment was naively presented as a simple resentment of an antiquated university system. The *New York Times* (February 12 and March 12, 1968), for instance, stated that the groups involved did not represent any significant percentage of the electorate.

Because there was a complete American media panic on the outcome of the Italian elections of May 19-20, 1968, when the communists scored a big gain, there was a positive overreaction when the *P.C.I.* criticized the Soviet invasion of Czechoslovakia in the same year. The gains scored by the *M.S.I.* in the local elections held in mid-June 1971 unleashed another wave of alarm in the U.S. media. *Newsweek* (June 28, 1971) went so far as to establish a parallel between the social conditions that spurred Mussolini's rise to power and the chaotic state of present-day Italy! Predictions of civil war, impending communist takeover, and/or rightist coups were often bandied about in the headlines. When *P.C.I.* leaders bid for a deal with the christian democrats and probed U.S. reactions in the mid-1970s, the American media reached an advanced stage of reactionary paranoia. Unusual attention was devoted to Italy by the major U.S. media in 1975-1976, which reflected their fears for the *P.C.I.*'s growing electoral strength and prospects.

American interference in Italian domestic politics was used by the *D.C.* to justify their politics. The Christian Democratic Party attributed its policy of slow modernization of the country to the fact that the Party did not have complete freedom. The tendency to use the U.S. as a justification for a whole range of internal political decisions was useful to the *D.C.*, but it conveyed the perception that Italy was an American satellite.

Writers and other artists criticized the U.S. The leftist actor-play-wright, Dario Fo who would be awarded the Nobel Prize for literature in 1997, staged a play entitled *The Lady Is Fit to Be Thrown Away*, in which the "lady" America becomes the metaphor for a monstrous machination organized for the glorification of a system dominated by an obsession for money and by the overwhelming power of capital. Like much of the intelligentsia of the Left, as well as radical and leftist journalists, Fo sought to make real the idea that Italy had been, and still was, a "province," a most compliant and exploited province of the "American empire."

The covert funding of many activities certainly did not help the American image in Italy. For instance, in 1972 the U.S. provided $10 million to certain political parties to help them in the national election that year. Ambassador Graham Martin gave $800,000 to General Vito Miceli, the extreme-rightist head of Italian military intelligence, without conditions on the money's use. He later became a candidate in the Neo-Fascist Party. A 1976 report of the U.S. House of Representatives stated that the CIA had disbursed over $75 million to Italian parties and candidates during the preceding three decades.

All this should not suggest that most Italians, or even a majority of them, have become anti-American. Most Italian officials and the majority of the Italian public have tolerated such interference with remarkably little resentment. However, respect and admiration for America, which is still more prevalent in Italy than in any other European nation, has dwindled; scars caused by past mistreatment remain deep.

All in all, therefore, the relationship between the two countries is not based on mutual trust and respect. Americans do not take Italy seriously, and Italians respect the U.S. for its power, not for any wisdom in its handling of international affairs.

The Film Industry and American Cultural Domination

Even more than in political and military circles, America has come to be a dominant force on the Italian cultural scene, especially through film. The presence of American film on the Italian peninsula has al-

ways been strong.[5] By 1925 some four-fifths of the market was held
by American films. Why? The causes were predominantly economic
(Hollywood's search for export markets in Europe; Italian exhibitors'
demand for popular films), attitudinal (a change in public taste in Italy),
and political (inadequate import controls by the Italian government
and the American government's drive to promote a certain set of values through the medium of film). The fascist government did very little
to combat American domination, either culturally or commercially,
presumably because Hollywood was not sending out movies that could
be interpreted as critical of the fascist ideology. But the popularity of
American films has to be found also in the wealth and organizational
maturity of the American film industry—vertically integrated, geared
to making exportable films. The United States was a vast country with
many movie houses. A successful American film would recoup its production costs on its first run at home before being exported. This
meant that it could be offered to distributors and exhibitors abroad at
a lower price than films produced in their own home countries, where
they still had to make up their costs.

There was a significant contradiction in the fascist period between
official attempts to construct a national culture and the fact that much
cultural consumption—both of high culture and popular culture—was
of non-national products. The massive preponderance of American
films in Italian movie theaters continued until 1939, when more effective protectionist measures were introduced, and for the first time during
fascist rule the number of Italian films in circulation exceeded that of
American films. The "Americanization" of the cinema in the 1920s
and 1930s in turn influenced Italian production because it imposed a
commercially popular style that Italian filmmakers were pressured into
adopting if they wanted to have a chance of competing at the box
office. Effective restrictions designed to limit the amount of foreign
material came only during the last years of the fascist regime.

How should the presence under fascism of a large quantity of light
entertainment material, much of it foreign, be interpreted? It served a
political purpose: it provided a form of escapism. The regime promoted it, or was happy to let it circulate, because it fit into a "bread
and circuses" policy of keeping the masses happy.

When the Allies landed in Italy in 1943, they brought a backlog of
American films and took over film distribution in the occupied territories. In 1945 they forced Italy to abrogate all the measures that protected Italian films against competition on the domestic market, and

"dumped" at low prices on the Italian market over 2,000 American films, while Cinecittà (Italy's Hollywood, located in the outskirts of Rome) was used to house refugees. After 1945, the movement known as neo-realism attempted to redefine the function of Italian cinema, to introduce to popular audiences a different sort of engagement with reality. The emphasis in neo-realism was on the hidden underside— poverty, unemployment, illiteracy, the legacy of fascist neglect, and the difficulties of postwar reconstruction. But American films continued to be overwhelmingly popular. In the late forties and early fifties, a strong marketing push by American film distributors was abetted by a hostile attitude toward neo-realist films by the center-right government, by much of the press, and by Italian promoters eager to get their hands on commercially viable films and make a lot of money. These situations made it very difficult indeed for native filmmakers to get their work financed and shown.

The American supremacy was also a result of advantageous terms the Americans were able to negotiate during the time of Rome's liberation. Italy was inundated by a huge quantity not just of new productions but also of old films and reruns because the wall of protectionism came down as a result of assiduous work by the United States government and film industry to assist its commercial interests. Ellis Arnall, president of the Society of Independent Motion Picture Producers, reported on a visit to President Truman in 1949:

> The president readily agreed that our government has a responsibility to see to it that American-produced motion pictures be utilized to the fullest in carrying the message of Americanism and Democracy to the rest of the world. He expressed these views to the Secretary of State, Mr. Acheson, and requested Mr. Acheson to take such steps as feasible to the end that foreign countries would not discriminate against American-produced pictures and would maintain no unreasonable quotas or unfair restrictions against them.[6]

There was a period in the early 1960s when it looked as if the tide had turned because RAI, the Italian state-run radio and television network, was protectionist, and in the cinema the share of Italian box office obtained by American films plummeted to less than a third. Italian national production, supported by that of other European Economic Community (E.E.C.) countries, seemed sufficient to satisfy public demand. It looked as if European culture could counterbalance the avalanche of American culture. This proved to be an illusion, for while European co-production made economic sense in the cinema, the cultural character of the co-produced films could rarely be described as "distinctively" European. From the 1970s on, Hollywood dominated Italian screens, especially those of TV. The shows have been for the most part cheap to acquire and undemanding to watch.

The American Myth in Literature

The success of American films in Italy is also the result of a general Italian fascination for America. The average Italian always had a fascination for America, even more so when the only way to reach America was through fantasy. The Italians perceived America from the time of its first discovery, as a Eden, a recovery of innocence. The Europeans had to believe that somewhere there was a land free from the plagues and famines, the dynasties and social classes, the hypocrisies and cynicism of the Old World.

Most Italians, unable to visit or emigrate to the U.S., had to be content with an imaginary journey made possible through the accounts and letters of relative and friends. For them, America was a strange, mythical land, whose extraordinary wealth and generosity were often the subject of animated conversation. America was the great land of opportunity, as fictionalized in the short story "Aunt Bess, In Memoriam" by Giuseppe Berto (1914-1972), and thus an alluring haven for the hundreds of thousands of emigrants who, during the latter part of the nineteenth century, began leaving en masse for the United States in search of a better life.

The literary experience of the Italians illustrates poignantly the position America enjoyed in the aspirations of those who emigrated to America. Indeed, the Italians, like many other groups who came to this hemisphere, built a kind of mythology that remains alive even today; the more ignorant, illiterate, and poor they were, the more they were likely to maintain this dream. The peasant, especially from the South, dreamed of America not because he necessarily hoped to be here, but precisely because America represented something fabulous, and, for that reason, consoling. In Italy the myth of America was also nourished by the lack of work and land to sustain its population. The land that does not have products to export, exports its own children, or makes their minds fantasize about other lands; the people who do not find in their own country their fulfillment will search for it across the ocean among other peoples. Poverty, or relative deprivation, does not by itself create a sufficient or even necessary "push" to go elsewhere. If poverty is combined with personal goals and expectations that are perceived as not attainable at home, and if a place to relocate becomes available where such hopes appear to have a great chance of realization, the desire to emigrate may become irresistible.

The myth of America in Italian literature is strongly founded in rich popular fantasy. Probably, *Fontamara* (1930), by Ignazio Silone (1900-1978), provides one of the best stereotypes of America—as the "Eden of the poor." The central characters are a group of peasants in the Abruzzi mountain town of "Fontamara" whose water rights are stolen by the local fascist landowners in league with the local capitalists. To these peasants, among the most poverty-stricken and exploited in Italy, the word "America" has the power of a fetish: it stands simply for the opposite of hunger and deprivation. It is part of their private vocabulary of values and has nothing to do with the real United States. Some of the Fontamaresi, the luckier ones, have made the voyage across the Atlantic and after years of dogged work in America come back with a little money, which they soon lose cultivating the dry and sterile earth. Their only mistake was to come back. After a while, they fall back into the old lethargy, "holding like a memory of lost paradise the image of life glimpsed across the sea." This novel provided the sense of desperation that pushed many southern Italians to emigrate.

Cristo si è fermato ad Eboli, (*Christ Stopped at Eboli*, 1945) by Carlo Levi (1902-1975) gives a more balanced view of America. On the one hand, it portrays the positive views of America held by southern Italian villagers; on the other hand, it suggests the high price of emigration. Influenced by his own experience as an exiled in Gagliano in the 1930s, Levi gives a compassionate view of peasants' desire to emigrate, and even a sympathetic view of America as a symbol of prosperity and material progress. A journalist, he records without rancor and almost with a kind of ironic sympathy the fact that Gagliano, in the Basilicata region, had become a cultural colony of America; when he went there in 1935, it had 1,200 inhabitants, and there were 2,000 emigrants from Gagliano in America. However, he treats his material, which is factual, in a novelistic style, and he has a novelist's insight and flair for character. He thus manages to be both objective and personally involved in his material at the same time. He concludes that emigration is not a permanent answer to any problem, either personal or social. Life in America is good, but the price—to be uprooted from your native soil and to lose the source of strength one drew from the earth—is high.

A work by Mario Soldati (1906-) provided the first real confrontation between Italian and American, culture because he was among the first to combine his intellectual interest with an actual visit to the United

States. For Soldati, America was a barbaric country without culture, a fact he particularly noticed in daily American life. His *America primo amore* (*America First Love*, 1935), the first detailed account of daily life in America, adds new and strikingly different images and interpretations of the New World. It is a novelist's kind of travel book: impressionistic, vivid, and highly personal. The title makes clear from the outset that the author offered the book not as a sociological or political study, but simply as a story of a personal encounter. First loves are ecstatic experiences, but they are also emotional and unrealistic and they frequently end in disenchantment. Throughout the book Soldati's emotional relation to America is obvious; he writes about America the way any sensitive novelist would write about the girl he was in love with when he was 20 and with whom he then became disenchanted. The mood is disillusioned, often ironic, but rigidly honest and never totally hostile.

An interesting dimension can be found in Livia De Stefani's *Passione di Rosa* (*Passion of Rosa*, 1958) because as a woman writer who spent two years in the U.S., she addresses directly the theme of dislocation to another culture. Her novel communicates the experience of being a Sicilian and a woman in an America free of the male-oriented norms that dominate Sicily. Her book captures the flavor of America as it seems to an Italian in a way few other books do. In addition to her feminist point of view, the other pole of the novel is her birthplace, Sicily. Part of the interest of *Passione di Rosa* relates to the geographical resemblance of Sicily and California; the two regions are physically alike and yet their people and customs are totally different. This difference in the two societies and the effect it has on a young Sicilian immigrant is the focus. of the novel. America is presented as in a dream, and as a dream it lasts only as long as it remains a dream; at the first contact with reality it dies. For many immigrants America became a shattered dream because it had been too much idealized.

Part of the fantasy, and also because of intellectual curiosity, is the continuing desire on the part of Italians to encounter America and Americans through writings. This phenomenon happened almost accidentally. The vogue of American literature in the thirties was assisted by a quite incidental fact: that the younger generation of Italian writers, their own creativity discouraged by the fascist regime, turned to reviewing and translation for economic support. A high proportion of these young translators went on to become important novelists and critics. One was Cesare Pavese (1908-1950), who translated Melville, Lewis, Sherwood Anderson, Dos Pasos, and Faulkner. His successful translation of *Moby Dick* became for the young Italians of Pavese's generation, more than any other book, what America stood for.

Although Pavese never came to America and never even seems to have entertained the idea, in many ways emigration would have been the logical solution to his personal problems. He felt alienated and restless in Italian culture, and from the time of his first poems, portrayed America as representing a new start, a return to the primitive and genuine. But even if he never considered it as a personal possibility, the idea of emigration always lies just beneath the surface of his writings. Indeed, his first poem of *Lavorare stanca* (*Working is Tiring*, 1931) is about the myth of emigration. The protagonist emigrant, who really existed, is metamorphosed into myth; upon his return, after 20 years of wandering over the world, he tells stories to match those in the *Odyssey*. The emigration theme is further developed in Pavese's *La luna e i falò* (*The Moon and the Bonfires*, 1949), considered one of the best postwar Italian novels, in which the emigrant, a peasant, returns with two contradictory images of America: the traditional emigrant legend of a land of opportunity and easy riches, and the other, of an America he had discovered in his books—the America of the *Pensive Barbarians*, the mythic soil of Whitman, Sherwood Anderson, and *Spoon River Anthology*. It was the example of these writers that led Pavese to search his own native soil for meaning. The protagonist comes to the realization that Americans, like Italians, do not know each other and suffer from private loneliness.

Nevertheless, the desire to encounter America is not always felt with the same intensity. Because of changes in the economic condition of the country, of political propaganda of America as a world political and military power, and the perception that America puts money ahead of moral values, Italian interpretations of America have not been uniformly positive.

Therefore, the image of America as the home of the violent and the land of the gun has also become a popular and enduring one in the minds of the average Italian. For years moviegoers have watched massacres of white settlers by vicious savages and the slaughter of unarmed Indians by blood-crazed cavalrymen. They have seen shootouts at the OK Corral and gang warfare on the streets of Chicago. And most prominently they have witnessed American fighting men from John Wayne to Rambo as they mowed down hundreds of Nazis or Japanese or Vietnamese or some other "enemy." The glittering image of America is also tarnished by American images that reflect profound social differences in the American society. In fact, aside from the images of mass mayhem, Italians have also watched visions of skyscrapers, the landing on the moon, the manicured and well-equipped American college campuses, and mansions of billionaires, as well as the poverty of the South Bronx, Harlem, and Watts, the kinds of images that reflect the worlds of both the very rich and the very poor.

American Cultural Penetrations:
Language and Consumerism

The strong presence of America on Italian screens has not simply colored the Italian image of America, it has had a profound impact on Italian life. In fact, the 1950s saw the introduction in Italy of American supermarkets, frozen food, electric appliances, jukeboxes, pinball machines, pony tails, and pleated shirts. The American presence was so strong that some film directors felt it as a real cultural colonization and conveyed their message in some of their movies (Federico Fellini in *Vitelloni*, 1953, and *The White Sheik*, 1952). A number of films of the 1950s with the comic actor Alberto Sordi (e.g., *An American in Rome*, 1955) simultaneously encapsulated and parodied some of these cultural transitions. By the 1960s the model of social behavior and the consumption habits described in American situation comedies were something that was no longer seen as the image of a distant society characterized by great wealth, but as one that could be attained by many Italians through the expansion of their market.

In fact, the American way of living penetrated especially the Italian working-class house. During the years of the "Economic Miracle"(1958-1963) Italy turned into a consumer society along American lines. Italians sought consumer durables—cars, refrigerators, washing machines, dishwashers, etc.—first as luxuries or providers of social status, but then quickly as necessities. The 1950s saw the expansion in Italy of those industries that could supply these goods, while mass market, American-style "women's" and "home" magazines extolled the virtues of the custom-built kitchen and the labor-saving advantage of the electrical appliances, which the Italians called *elettrodomestici*. The ideal home of these years contained a version of the American "dream kitchen" as seen in Hollywood films and American soap operas.

America served as a model of behavior for the younger generation through a specific youth market based on cultural forms such as clothing and music. The profound influence that America had in this area cannot be underestimated. Exports by the U.S. to the rest of the world included not only the technical infrastructure for the construction of a youth culture but also the main cultural forms themselves—cheap records, casual clothes, and the know-how to produce them, including the system to transmit via radio and television the new music and the new modes of speech. The formation of this youth culture occurred in the 1960s as television became universal in Italy and as small transistor radios became available at a low price to virtually everyone. In the course of the 1960s in Italy, more than anywhere else, the U.S. cultural form of the youth generation—music, clothes, etc.—was partly integrated by highly politicized forms of protest. This remarkable politicization was more deep-rooted and had a longer lasting effect than the French 1968 movement, the only other comparable phenomenon in the rest of Europe.

America also had a strong influence on the use of media by politicians. Since the late 1960s, politicians have adapted and packaged their political discourse through various media techniques.[7] Italian politics was already delivered with a high dose of theatricality; television and American influence made the political discourse even more like a show, a spectacle. By becoming more "Americanized," the political discourse became more uniform: all politicians were subject to the same rule.

English has become the *lingua franca* all over the world; in Italy it is practically the second language. From the schools to the business office, in both scientific and social worlds, Italians are becoming anglophone. This new passion is not so much reflective of a new love as much as of the necessities imposed by new economic and industrial world realities. The passion has spilled over and has affected the Italian language. English linguistic penetration or "intimate borrowing" abounds. There has been a more permanent incursion of English terms into the everyday vocabulary of Italian business and technology, where words like marketing, cash-flow, pipeline, design, and fast food have become common currency simply because no one has invented adequate Italian equivalents. The Italian government did not become alarmed at this trend, as did the Ghiscard Government in France, which in 1977 adopted a bill that made virtually illegal the use of foreign words where French alternatives can be found in advertisements, official documents, and even on radio and television.

The two languages, as is well known, have a resemblance in a base vocabulary. Words containing a Latin or, more generally, a romance language base, abound in the technical, intellectual, and philosophical discourse in English. Such words most often give rise to loans. Aside from the remarkable number of phonographs (idea, trombone, opera, propaganda, piano, zero, piccolo, chiaroscuro, panorama, etc.) and the quasi-phonographs (umbrella, volcano, tobacco, pantaloons, etc.) to ancient Latinisms and Italianisms, there are also a number of word pairs that differ only in their respective endings (letter-*lettera*, animal-*animale*, second-*secondo*, stories-*storie*, horoscope-*oroscopo*, allergy-*allergia,* solidarity-*solidarietà*, problem-*problema*, govern-*governo,* state-*stato*, comic-*comico*, television-*televisione*, list-*lista*, infinite-*infinito*, deposit-*deposito*, violent-*violento*, brutal-*brutale*, concert-concerto) or in the suffixes (-ion and -*ione*, -ty and -*tà*, -ent and -*ente*), which are responsible for the phenomenon of the so-called false friends.[8] Expressions such as public relations, *relazioni pubbliche*; new frontier, *nuova frontiera*; and the rest is silence, *il resto è silenzio* can be translated almost automatically and are directly responsible for the formation of loan shift. In other cases the "transparency" is such as to make translation unnecessary. For instance, the reference to "palmolive oil" in the American noun *palmolive* works in such a way that palmolive is rarely felt to be a foreign word. In fact, even well-educated Italians think of palmolive as an Italian word and palmolive soap an indigenous product. Such lexical likeness points to the fact that the influence of English in Italian takes place between two languages that have a large common base to begin with.

English words by the hundreds have entered in common speech. It is not unusual to hear in daily conversation words such as OK, babysitter, picnic, bar-be-que, hamburger, popcorn, fun, rock, tester, shopping, basket, management, manager, business, leader, bus, taxi, shock, show, wham, wow, yippie, and weekend. Business, computer, marketing and advertising, sports, tourism, fashion and cosmetics, and news are the fields in which the use of English abounds. In the business world, the presence of English is so strong that quick reference dictionaries have been created specifically for greater understanding of English terminology widely used in companies (*The Influence of the English Language in Italian Companies, in Finance, in Marketing*). The prevailing reasoning in this area seems to be that why not make the means your own if it is indispensable for your survival?

This ability of the Italian business world to adapt to changing trends highlights the fact that this aspect of life probably represents the best of Italy. No society seems better attuned to the free-enterprise system than that of the Italians; private initiative in many fields has been indeed the secret of the "Italian miracle." Italian cabinet ministers must attend conferences around the world trailed by a score of interpreters because Italian politicians notoriously speak no language other than their own. Italian businessmen, on the contrary, are proud of their versatility in international communication. Not only do they attempt to minimize the linguistic barriers, but they also try to maximize their understanding of others by getting to know their culture.

Notes

1. In "Foreword" to Leo J. Wollemborg, *Stars, Stripes, and Italian Tricolor* (New York: Praeger, 1990), xv.

2. L. J. Wollemborg, 23.

3. Ibid., 40.

4. A. Schlesinger, *A Thousand Days* (Boston: Houghton Mifflin, 1965), 879.

5. Although Italian movie theaters have been dominated by Hollywood imports for much of their history, Italy's film industry has a history of its own. In the period up to 1915, Italy was one of the world's major exporters of films. Italy became known as a producer of spectacular films on historical themes, and these films were exported partially because of their exotic value. With the First World War, and the rapid growth and organization of the U.S. film industry, Italian production went bankrupt and collapsed. Whereas in 1915 Italy produced 562 films, by 1930 that number had dropped to 12. The fascist government set about reorganizing the industry along more efficient and less wasteful lines, eventually finding itself owning studios, distribution companies, and a chain of cinemas. The Cinecittà studios were built with state money and were taken over by the state; the *Centro Sperimentale di Cinematografia*, a university-level film school, was established; and the Venice Film Festival was launched as an international showcase for Italian films. In 1938 the state took over the distribution of foreign films in Italy, and in retaliation the eight major Hollywood distributors withdrew from the Italian market. The result was that by 1942 Italy was producing over 100 films a year.

6. Quoted in Thomas Guback, "Shaping the Film Business in Postwar Germany: The Role of the U.S. Film Industry and the U.S. State," in Paul Kerr, ed., *The Hollywood Film Industry: A Reader* (London and New York: Routledge and Kegan Paul, 1986), 250.

7. Giovanni Cesareo, "Il 'politico' nell'alba del quaternario," *Problemi del Socialismo*, 22, no. 22 (1981): 28-29.

8. For a comprehensive study see M. Cortellazo and V. Cardinale, *Dizionario di parole nuove: 1964-1984* (Turin: Einaudi, 1985).

Part II
Economy

Introduction

The production and exchange of goods and services, which constitute the basis of economic life, have been evolving since World War II through periods of growth and periods of recession, which in Italy have broadly followed the same patterns as in other industrialized economies in Europe. However, at a more substantive level, the Italian production system has evolved at its own rhythm. Thus we shall first describe the main stages in the evolution of the Italian production system since World War II, and then go on to analyze the changes in the labor force and in the structure of firms.

In Italy, in a way that is more marked than in other European countries, the development of production in terms of volume, value, or structure has taken place in two distinct periods, which have radically different characteristics. The first extends from immediately after World War II (the Reconstruction period) up to 1974. During that time Italy experienced unprecedented growth, comparable to that of Japan and West Germany. The strength of this trend caused by the accumulation of factors such as the considerable increase in technological developments and productive investments by firms, the rebuilding of the infrastructure and the growth of housing stock, as well as the increase in the size and qualifications of the workforce, but also by the organizing, coordinating, and regulating functions and practices of the public sector and government.

A superficial view will easily give conflicting and somewhat contradictory descriptions of the Italian economy. On the one hand, Italy's supermarkets still display rich varieties of high quality foods while millions of households are hooked up to electronic communications networks through the interactive *Minitel* system. On the other hand, the main Italian economic indicators—unemployment, prices, foreign trade—seem somewhat contradictory. For example, in the mid-1990s Italy had one of the highest rates of unemployment in Europe, but at the same time, it was achieving one of the highest rates of growth in Europe and a low inflation rate. Another surprising feature is that during the 1980s income differentials increased, thus reversing the trend of three previous decades toward a narrowing of income differentials and more social equality. Despite this, the 1980s were a period of relative social peace, with the lowest number of working days lost through strikes since World War II, again contradicting the received idea that Italian people are especially prone to protests.

The dominant theme in studies of the economy has been that of Italy's dualism, which has three closely interrelated contrasts: first, between one part of the economy that is technologically advanced, with high levels of productivity, and a more traditional part of the economy that is more labor intensive and with low levels of productivity; second, between a part of the economy that comprises very large firms and a part that comprises thousands of very small firms, with the absence of much medium-sized enterprise in between; third, between a rapidly developing North and a backward and underdeveloped South.

Of the three aspects of Italy's dualism, the territorial divide (between North and South) was for a long time the main focus of academic study. Indeed, *la questione meridionale* (the southern question) has been studied since the beginning of the century, and has generated a vast literature spanning various disciplines because the problem has not been perceived in purely economic terms. The 1980s and 1990s saw the emergence of a revisionist approach to the southern question among historians who argue that the southern question is, to a large extent, artificial. Its origin can be traced to the politics of the late nineteenth century rather than to economic reality, and its continued existence is maintained largely by comparing the South to a level of development normally expected in advanced European democracies. Consequently, all research on the South has been distorted because it has started from these premises. The revisionists' quest is to analyze the South without meridionalization.

How can these different facets of the Italian economy be reconciled? Is it possible to find a common thread uniting the conflicting trends at work in the Italian economy and the conflicting impressions given by the current situation? Three phases describe the manner and pace of the development of the economy of Italy during the half century since World War II:

1. The process of modernizing the economy has been conducted so rapidly that a number of tensions, contradictions, and problems of adaptation have arisen in a socioeconomic structure that had previously been remarkably slow to emerge from its rural habits.
2. The process of modernizing the production and trade systems was made possible through the emergence of a relative economic and social consensus regulated by the state. However, this model of economic regulation, which was never fully developed, started to present signs of strain in the 1970s.
3. The process of modernization was also accompanied by the opening up of the Italian economy to the rest of the world. Italy after World War II was still a nation living in relative economic isolation, mostly trading within its small colonial area. The opening up of the economy after the war and the participation in the creation of the European Economic Community meant that Italian industries and services had to operate in a wider and more competitive market environment.

There are many ways of describing the changes that have affected the Italian economy since the early 1970s: modernization, growth in a free market system integrated into the world economy, movement toward an "advanced" or "post-industrial" open economy, development of activities based on "services" or "information production," shift toward "post-Fordist" production and regulation systems. However these changes are described, the roots of many of them are to be found in the production of goods and services.

These changes have drastically affected the daily lives of Italian people over two generations. This obviously concerns their working lives in the first instance. At the end of the 1940s, Italy was still basically an agricultural country with an agrarian society. Now, the great majority is employed in services, and the overwhelming importance of services such as education, commerce, transport, finance, health and communications, in employment and production, is mirrored by changes in the way people consume and the way they organize their lives outside of work. Today around three-quarters of the population live in urban areas and six out of seven are wage-earners, as opposed to self-employed workers.

However, these changes cannot be seen entirely as positive or painless. Since the 1980s, unemployment in Italy has never dropped below 10% of the working population. Long-term unemployment is a form of permanent exclusion that has created a new category of poor people and families. Many large companies as well as smaller ones continue to reduce their workforces in the name of international competitiveness, and many Italian households either feel excluded from prosperity or experience deep anxiety about an economically uncertain future.

One of the most crucial challenges in the construction of some form of new, post-crisis consensus is posed by the need to reduce the social cost of economic efficiency—especially unemployment, which represents a massive waste. The second challenge is to find a way to reduce the economic gap between the North and the South. The third challenge is to find an equilibrium within the open European market. Will the Italian economy retain its specific characteristics that have made the "Made in Italy" popular in the world or will these disappear in a homogeneous European economy? A fourth matter for reflection concerns the future role of the public sector and public authorities within the European Union and the liberalized world economy which is still dominated by very severe inequalities and dependencies, as exemplified by North-South economic relations.

V

The Economic Recovery

From Ashes to World Economic Power

There is no other country in Europe that has changed so enormously and rapidly in the postwar period. In fact, Italy has changed more in the last 40 years than during the previous two thousand. Compared to 1950, the average Italian is much better fed, housed, educated, and also receives better health care. The enormous gap that once existed between Italians and Americans has been considerably reduced. Indeed, many Italians are proud to openly claim that "America is here now."[1]

The British have viewed all this with a mixture of envy and admiration. How have those damned Italians managed it? If it is not wealth in natural resources it must be the result of some deep renewal of national ambition and the will to work hard, allied to the dynamism of a new breed of entrepreneurs for whom the state bureaucracy is less a help than a hindrance. Of course, Italy was starting from a much lower level than Britain and France, and the late industrialization partly explains the high growth rate. But the so-called "economic miracle," in its Italian context, was one of the most remarkable in the world, for it was achieved in the face of Italy's fundamental shortcomings.

Economic development in the postwar era has been extraordinary, exceeded only by that of Germany and Japan. As in the case of those two countries, the very scale of the destruction suffered in the war was a blessing in disguise: it brought a chance to make a new start on modern lines. The British, who had the "misfortune" never to be defeated, lacked the same impetus.

In 1945, Italy, or a large portion of it, was one of the poorest countries in the West. A land bereft of natural resources, with only a quarter of its land suitable for farming, the country had suffered more from the war than any other Western nation but Germany. In 1947, as a loser of the war, Italy was obliged to pay within seven years $100 million to the Soviet Union, $125 million to Yugoslavia, and $105 million to Albania, besides having to mourn the loss of half a million of its citizens, care for several million wounded, face the destruction of many factories, the annihilation of the merchant marine, and the loss of one quarter of its railways, 35% of its roads, and thousands of bridges. At the end of hostilities, destitution was widespread, with the population suffering the classic earmarks of poverty: high illiteracy and infant mortality, poor diet, and limited education. Most housing lacked baths and much of it even running water. Unemployment and underemployment were high; inflation was rampant and taxation regressive. Banditry and black-marketeering had flourished. At Tombolo, deserters from the U.S. army had set up a robbers' republic. Panic seized the middle classes, and class hatred or class fear begat hostility to the national environment. A late industrial developer, Italy had only a modest manufacturing sector, which was centered in a narrow area of the northwest and depended heavily on tariffs and state assistance. Merely a third of the labor force was employed in industry; more than half was engaged in small-scale agriculture. In 1945 industrial production was only about 25% of what it had been in 1938, and agricultural production was reduced by about 40%. Per capita income was lower than at any time since unification and half what it had been in 1938.

However, by 1962 Italy was experiencing one of the fastest growing economies in the world. Economists labeled this progress as the "economic miracle." It was a miracle because of the pace with which Italy recovered from a destructive war while lacking natural resources and having a topography that does not favor productive agriculture. By 1970 Italy had become the world's seventh-ranking industrial state (member of the G7), was a leading international exporter, and held some of the most substantial gold and foreign-exchange reserves in Europe. In the 1980s she had passed England and contended with France for the fourth-ranking world industrial position. Whole new industries, such as steel, chemical, and oil refining, had been established with the most advanced technology and were able to compete with the best in Europe. Old private firms, like FIAT, Pirelli, and Olivetti, had revived to become European leaders in their fields. Unemployment had dropped from over 10% to half that figure. In about 30 years, more than five million agricultural workers had moved into industry, and the farm population had been reduced to about 11% of the total workforce. Italy had passed from an essentially peasant society to a largely urban one.

For some time now Italy has been numbered among the top five industrialized countries in the world. Leaving behind the troubled 1970s, where economic mismanagement and social disorder jeopardized its future, Italy was also named the economic miracle of the 1980s. Today, measured by almost every index of well-being, Italians are better off than most of them ever imagined possible. Fewer of their babies die in infancy, most adults live longer, and everyone eats better. In the crasser terms of consumer goods—telephones, cars, washing machines, television sets—Italian ownership matches, and on certain goods, even exceeds the western European average. True, the well-being is not evenly distributed—for the South still lags far behind the North—but things have improved everywhere beyond all recognition.

Progress has been achieved through an economy that is dualistic in character: rich North vs. poor South, private vs. public enterprise, multinational companies vs. small family-owned firms. A study of the relation and change in these areas gives a clear view of how Italy changed in the last 30 years. The amazing growth can best be appreciated when it is related to the low level of available natural resources in the country.

Inadequate Natural Resources

For a country of 57.7 million people, Italy is only modestly provided with agricultural resources and is considerably worse off with respect to other kinds of natural resources. With a few exceptions the geological characteristics of Italian territory do not comprise high deposits of industrially useful mineral resources, and only four regions (Sardinia, Tuscany, Sicily, and Trentino-Alto Adige) have a mineral content of any interest. A considerable part of the world's mercury is mined just north of Siena; quantities of sulfur are found in Sicily and near Naples. The only fuel found in any quantity, particularly in the Po Valley, is natural gas (methane), though there is consistent exploitation of geothermal resources. Small quantities of crude oil were discovered at Maloss, near Milan, and some oil was found near Gela, Sicily. There is widespread extraction of lithoid and incohesive sediments (clay, gravel, and sand) from alluvial plains; numerous quarries are scattered throughout the country, frequently responsible for ruining the landscape and disturbing the stability of sloping ground. The lack of fossil coal had already forced the country to build a number of hydroelectric power stations in the last century, mainly in the Alpine valleys, though also in several sites in the Apennines.

After the war, however, industrial expansion had to utilize power generated by coal or hydrocarbon power stations. At present a quarter of the electricity produced is obtained from water resources and three quarters from thermal sources. Italy has to import 82% of the sources of energy supply.

In spite of the variety of topographical conditions and the extent of mountainous terrain (80% of the country's area is mountainous or hilly), only 12% of Italian territory (buildings, roads, wasteland, waters, etc.) is actually unproductive. Apart from forests (about 21%), abandoned and rough ground and service areas (about 9%), the surface effectively destined for annual or stable permanent cultivation amounts to little more than 58% of the entire national territory.

Referring to the organization of agriculture, the last general census of agriculture also indicates that of a total relative surface cultivated by more than 3 million farmers (about 78% of national territory), little more than half (about 53%) was effectively utilized. Most of this land is owner-farmed (94%) and less than 2% is under the sharecropping system, once common throughout most of the country (especially in Veneto and the central regions).

Peasants' conservatism has also been a hindrance to solving the problem of land parcelization. Fly over many parts of Italy and you will see a crazy quilt of thin strips; quite a modest farmer may have several tiny fields, not next to each other but scattered over miles. This is mostly the result of the equal-inheritance laws, as farms were split up between sons with each new inheritance. Sentimental values remain very strong: how can a farmer give up a field where his father taught him to plough, or leave the cherry orchard his grandfather planted? In a nation with so strong a rural tradition, *la terra* can still rouse powerful emotions.

The land continues to be split up among a very large number of small farmers and many of the farms are not big enough to support a family. Three-quarters of the farm holdings are less than five hectares and almost one-third are less than one hectare. Italy has the smallest average (7.2 hectares) in the E.U., with the exception of Greece. Since 35% of arable land belongs to large farms (over 100 hectares), which in themselves fail to account for 1.1% of the total number of farms, Italian agriculture presumably consists of medium-sized farms (5-100 hectares, 23.5%) covering practically half (48%) of all arable land. However, the situation is changing. The period between the last two agricultural censuses (1970-1982) showed a drop in the numbers of small farms and the increase of medium to large holdings (20 hectares and more). This trend has been accompanied by fairly limited changes in land ownership and, in the case of small-holders, by abandonment of the land for the town in order to emigrate or, in any case, take non-agricultural employment.

Between 1970 and 1982 the total number of farms dropped by 10% and the cultivated area by 6%. The drop in the number of farms of all kinds and in the land area they cover may be attributed to a number of socioeconomic phenomena acting in different degrees on soil usage according to the country's various regions. A part of the cause is to be found in the persistent decrease in the population of the mountain areas, with a consequent increase in building construction; other causes are tied to the structural changes going on now in the farm sector. For example: the massive exodus of labor from farming, which has encouraged the formation of farms of greater land area; the changes that have taken place in the legal nature of farm contracts (especially as regards sharecropping and colony forms of farming); the different usage being made of land now, and, finally, the improved configuration of farms, especially in areas that were formerly highly fragmented.

Certainly, the variety of climatic and geomorphological conditions together with the heterogeneous nature of the soil are factors that have contributed, together with the force of tradition, to influence or determine the yield and kind of crops the country produces. Wheat and maize are the major cereal crops with barley becoming increasingly prevalent, while rice is a specialized crop exported in large quantities. Olive, citrus, and other fruit trees are the commonest and best known which, together with vineyards, make the country a leader in the Mediterranean and in Europe, though international competition is now strong. Italy is the largest producer of wine and the second largest olive-producing country in the world. The region with the highest production of olives is Apulia, followed by Calabria, Sicily, Latium, and Tuscany. Fruit is also important, particularly apples and peaches. Important also is the production of vegetables (tomatoes, lettuce, beans, cauliflower, and others that are deservedly well known throughout the world), which are grown especially in southern Italy—Campania, Calabria, Sicily, and Sardinia. The fine agricultural products combined with refined cooking skills have brought about the recent resurgent interest in Italian agricultural products and cuisine. The "Mediterranean diet"—lots of pasta, olive oil, little meat, and plenty of vegetables and fruits—has been touted by nutritionists in most economically advanced countries.

Floriculture is now expanding rapidly, favored by the mild climate and widespread greenhouse cultivation. Replacing floriculture designed for local needs only is an industrial type floriculture aimed at meeting the demands of a huge national and international market. Flowers are grown for commercial purposes mainly in Liguria, along the coastal arc reaching from the western Riviera between Ventimiglia and Albenga, and, to some extent, along the eastern Riviera. The crops are cut flowers (carnations and roses especially), bouquet flowers (bulbs, gladioli, chrysanthemums), ornamental plants, and flowers and leaves for perfume manufacture.

Of localized importance is certain tree-type crop production such as chestnut and hazelnut, utilized principally by the confectionery and bakery industries. Among other industrial crops are sugar beets and tobacco. Relatively unknown until World War II, sugar beets have become one of the important Italian agricultural products for industrial utilization. The production of tobacco is also important; the richest plantations are to be found in the Apulia, Veneto, Abruzzi, Campania, and Umbria regions.

Livestock breeding, a traditional agricultural activity, has also suffered the effects of the crisis in this sector, as is apparent from underdevelopment in the last few decades. Methods are somewhat backward except in the Po Valley, and consequently inadequate to the national demand for meat. Certain old customs, such as transhumance in the Apennines, are now dying out; however in the North, high altitude Alpine pastures are still grazed in the summer. One livestock sector of considerable importance to the Italian farm economy is bee keeping, which has made unprecedented progress over the past few years.

Agricultural Reconstruction

In the 1960s and 1970s Italian farming went through a real "revolution." In no other aspect of Italian life was change so dramatic, or the conflict between old and new so sharp. Farm mechanization changed the landscape of the countryside at every level. The process was not easy: imagine those poor farmers, accustomed to an instinctive rapport with oxen or horses, when they were suddenly confronted with a tractor.

Since the end of the war, the state has taken several measures to transform the very primitive agriculture that existed. A series of laws approved in 1950, to respond to the peasants' revolts of the late 1940s, provided that large, uncultivated, or badly cultivated, estates in huge areas of Sicily, Sardinia, and the mainland South were to be expropriated by state agencies. These agencies improved the land and then sold it to landless peasants at low cost and on long-term mortgages. The state also provided, through the *Cassa per il Mezzogiorno*, essential services (irrigation, electricity, houses, roads, livestock) at public expense. Similar kinds of state intervention in agriculture had been done during fascism (e.g., the reclamation of the Pontine Marshes); but in the 1950s land was actually expropriated and given to the people.

The land reform had major political consequences. It ended the *latifundium* after more than 2,000 years and, therefore, it broke the political power of the big landowners, who, however, remained economically powerful because they invested in the booming building industry the capital they received from the sale of their land. It also created a "client class" that was dependent on the agencies. The new peasant-owners grew what the agency told them to grow, lived where the agency told them to live (often in houses built by the agency), and sold their produce through agency-run cooperatives. They also voted for the party that ran the agency, usually the *D.C.* Altogether, about 70,000 families acquired land, but that was only 1% of the rural population.

This program had some shortcomings. Most of the new owners had been landless peasants, inexperienced in farming techniques. Their holdings were normally on poor land and were usually too small to support a family. These failings became more evident in later years with the increasing use of tractors and specialized machinery that are difficult to use on small farms, and with increased competition from the North and Common Market farming. The land reform, far from solving the "land question," simply increased the number of poor peasants who quickly became even more dependent on state subsidy.

In 1970 half the peasant landowners of Italy were not full-time farmers; they were forced to derive much of their income from other sources: industry, commerce, or welfare. Net welfare payments to small landowners rose from 50 billion lire in 1954 to 245 billion lire in

1960 to 909 billion in 1968 and to 1,412 billion lire in 1971. By this time, about one-third of the value of all agricultural production was going to welfare payments, a system that was producing votes for the Christian Democratic Party.

Still, Italian agriculture has improved considerably because of direct government intervention. At the end of World War II production was only 40% of what it had been in 1938, but by 1950 it had surpassed the 1938 figure and by 1960 was 40% above it. The increase continued steadily through the 1960s and 1970s. Food production doubled between 1950 and 1970. Yields per hectare increased sharply because of better seeds, mechanization, more fertilizers, irrigation, and technical assistance. Because of government policies and financial assistance, Italy has become the world's leading exporter of durum semolina and pasta products and the leading rice producer in Western Europe.

The agricultural successes and the overall affluence in Italy contributed to some rather surprising changes that could not have been foreseen. The "problem of wheat," so central to fascist policy, became one of overproduction and underconsumption. People ate less bread and less pasta, but consumed more dairy produce. In 1958 imports of cheese exceeded exports for the first time ever! The people also ate twice as much meat. Not only was there an increased caloric intake, but also a rising standard of dietary demands that emphasized meat and other protein products. However, the gap between meat production and consumption makes meat the most significant food-deficit item and makes Italy the world's third largest importer of meat and meat products. Italy has to import half the beef and veal it consumes. For many years, the Italian economy showed another paradox: Italy was at the same time an importer and an exporter of meat; it had to export the second cuts of imported meat because Italians ate only first cuts. Since the arrival of the American fastfood restaurants (Mc Donald's in Rome grosses the highest amount of any restaurant in the chain), Italy does not export any more meat!

The introduction of the American system of chicken raising, Perdue style, has also helped to meet the increased national consumption of chickens. At the beginning of the 1960s Italy imported chickens from the U.S., sacrificing quantity for quality; today Italy has become the second largest producer of poultry meat in the EU.

Italy is the EU's leading producer of fruits and vegetables, which significantly contributes to export earnings. By 1960 Italy was the world's largest producer of wine; it bottled about a quarter of all wine in the world and had improved its quality by putting on the market some of the most renowned wines in the world. By introducing an effective quality control, first by creating the *DOC* (Denomination of Origin Controlled) wines and later the *DOCG* (Denomination of Origin Controlled and Guaranteed) for very few exclusive wines, exports increased considerably. Not only did the wines from the more traditional areas of wine country (Chianti and Brunello da Montalcino in Tuscany; Barolo and Amarone in Piedmont; Soave and Bardolino in the Veneto) consolidate their position on the world market, but wines from the South (Taurasi and Aglianico, in Campania; Corvo from Sicily) conquered a good slice of the market reserved for prestigious wines.

However, overproduction of wine has created serious problems in the E.U. French farmers resorted to riots in the 1970s to stop the competition presented by some of the more cheaply produced and often more robust Italian wines. The issue was solved when the two nations banned all planting of new vineyards and granted new subsidies for uprooting poor vines. Many producers have now pulled up their vines and changed to other crops, with the help of special grants from Rome and the E.U.

Through acts of legislature, the government has also been trying to consolidate farm holdings: any time a farmer puts property on sale, by law, the adjacent owners must be informed and must be given preference, if interested, in the sale.

Overall, the government has succeeded in substantially improving the social conditions and status of the farmers. In the 1950s the peasants still fell into the lowest income bracket; they had the least access to modern conveniences (running water and indoor plumbing) and owned the fewest consumer items (appliances and automobiles). They had the lowest level of education, and their occupation (working the land) was accorded the lowest social prestige. Much of the peasantry's apparent resignation had in fact been a result of its long history under a static and feudal system. In the Italian tradition, culture resides in the city, in the *civitas*; life outside of the city lacked any refinement or spiritual fulfillment. Ignazio Silone, in his novel *Fontamara* (1934), discussed in chapter IV, represented with somber intensity the life of poverty and sacrifice endured by southern farmers and the scorn to which they were subjected. Farmers used to be a social class apart, afraid of progress. In the 1960s the situation started to change and there has been a radical change in the self-image of the peasants and their attitude toward the social system. Improvement in their living conditions, advances in communication (local roads, transport, availability of telephone, special TV programs dealing with agriculture issues and farm life), and awareness of the world beyond the boundaries of their own community have made farmers accepted citizens of the wider community.

Traditional peasant society, once such a strong and picturesque feature of Italy, is passing away, and the new-style farmer is more like a small businessman; he often has a beautiful car and a modern home, and his children are scarcely different from town children. Thus, although the old-style peasant, semi-literate, living little better than his animals, still exists in some areas, especially in certain areas of the South, a new generation of modern-minded young farmers, with a totally different outlook from their parents, has arisen. They have promoted a new creed, entirely novel in this individualistic milieu, a creed of technical advance, producer groups, and marketing cooperatives. Finally, the old class of *contadini* or *cafoni* (pejorative terms for farmers) has largely become integrated into society.

Unfortunately, as old problems were solved, new ones emerged. The Italian government has had to face an aging farm population and an alarming shortage of skilled agricultural workers. Many small farms are in the hands of people who are recorded as employed in manufacturing or service or as unemployed, and who use family farm plots to supplement their food supplies and their incomes. Worse yet, Italian farming is still plagued by a high degree of traditional individualism. Thus, the country has to solve major dilemmas: the old one of how to reconcile the nation's economic needs with the human demands of the family farm, and the new one, shared with the rest of the E.C., of how to reduce costly food surpluses without depressing farmers' incomes.

The Changing Face of the Industrial Sector

The most significant improvement in the Italian economy and society came through a very innovative and largely expanded industrial sector. Today, Italy has a large industrial-based economy with heavy dependence on imported energy. Manufacturing is the largest sector of the economy, comprising 35% of G.D.P. and employing 30% of the labor force.

The structure of industrial production and service industries is characterized by the prevalence of small and medium-sized companies (94%

and 5.6% respectively), employing 70% of the workforce, with 30% being monopolized by large companies (more than 100 workers) although these comprise only 0.45% of the total. This means that companies are widely dispersed over the whole country, obviously with significant location and concentration of industry, and more than half the industrial companies operate at little more than workshop level, as is seen by the small workforce in each production unit.

There are only a limited number of cooperative companies (food sector and the processing of agricultural products), while large companies tend to become multinational. The presence of companies with foreign capital monopolizing specific commodity sectors (pharmaceutical, photographic materials, electronics, cosmetics, etc.) is far from rare.

One particular kind of development may be seen in medium-sized companies. Frequently these have expanded from small family-run businesses with specialized production technology, and through management flexibility and technological innovations they have succeeded in reconverting production and increasing competitiveness. They have penetrated international markets and have contributed to the consolidation of the Italian image and presence throughout the world. It was because of the high productivity of this sector of the industry that in the mid 1980s Italy experienced the second so-called "economic miracle."

In addressing the specific industrial sectors, the country's economic revival in the immediate postwar period was essentially sustained by development and expansion of the basic industries, particularly the steel industry, itself conditioned by the importation of raw materials such as ores, scrap iron, and coal.

Membership in *ECSC* (European Community for Steel and Coal) enabled the Italian steel industry, which had installed the integral processing cycle, to attain extremely high levels of production, thus satisfying increasingly greater domestic demand, such as that of the engineering industry, as well as the export market. Although this sector is now stagnating, owing to the international economic situation dominated by strong competition from Japanese industries and plastics, leading to overproduction in the principal European countries, it gave a strong impetus to the Italian industrial structure in those years of industrial recovery.

Mechanical engineering production became extremely varied and included industries such as shipbuilding, aerospace, car building, etc., with complex work cycles, together with manufacturers of simple tools.

Component manufacturing also became well developed and closely allied to companies that produced durable goods not easily classified in any one sector (for example, non-metallic materials used in the car industry: rubber, glass, plastics, etc.)

In practice, mechanical engineering, with its diversification and multiple relationships with other industries, is still today considered the mainstay of the national production system in terms of the large workforce employed (over 2.2 million according to the 1993 census). Apart from cars and other vehicles, the most highly developed industries are tools, household appliances, electronic equipment, and precision instruments. The industrial machinery sector is particularly active with extensive overseas markets and includes components for complete process cycles.

Another very important change in the industrial sector of the Italian economy was the surge of the chemical and energy industry. The chemical industry is closely linked to mining and quarrying and uses mostly liquid (oil) and gaseous hydrocarbons (methane), from which a high range of materials is produced (rubber, plastics, synthetic resins, synthetic fibers, fertilizers, etc.) in addition to the traditional utilization of heating fuel, engine fuel, etc.

Like the steel industry, the chemical industry went through a critical period because of over-production and problems related to plant modernization. One serious additional shortcoming is the need to resort to large-scale importation of raw materials for transformation, with the consequent submission to fluctuating conditions on the international market.

In any discussion of industrial sectors that greatly spurred the Italian economy, it is important to mention the textile industry. Textiles are, in fact, the oldest Italian industry. Although widespread throughout the peninsula, they are chiefly concentrated in four regions (Lombardy, Veneto, Tuscany, and Marche) and are frequently linked to the rural community, which provides plentiful low-cost labor. In the postwar period, this sector faced a period of crisis caused primarily by the use of antiquated machinery and inefficient working methods, though also by competition from foreign producers, particularly in developing countries, which were already raw material suppliers (cotton, wool, jute, etc.). The crisis in the textile industry has deeper roots in the progressive decay of some traditional related activities, such as silkworm breeding and the cultivation of hemp and flax. The utilization of artificial fibers derived from cellulose, and later on synthetics derived from hydrocarbons, together with renewal of production plant (mainly automated) and job reorganization, has enabled far higher levels of productivity to be reached, offset by a considerable decrease in the workforce and concentration of companies in a few areas.

For its raw material supplies (synthetic fibers) and the utilization of the fabrics produced, the textile sector is closely allied (also by vertical merging of companies) to the chemical and the garment manufacturing industries. The latter, in particular, is still scattered over the country in the form of small firms.

Another sector that must be mentioned is the food industry. Development of this industry is a direct consequence of the expansion of large urban centers and progressive industrialization. Strictly allied to the primary sector (agriculture and livestock), it makes considerable use nevertheless of imports, the result of insufficient national agricultural and livestock production. A scattering of small artisan-type firms generally oriented toward meeting local demand has now been joined by a number of medium-sized companies operating at a national level, using advanced systems of processing, conservation, and packaging. The food conservation industry is in a special position, connected as it is with agriculture, livestock, and fisheries.

The diversification of Italian industry has reached the point where it becomes difficult to classify producers in specific sectors. Certain industries, some traditional, have made a highly important contribution locally or in a specific context to the country's development. One example is the building industry in general (constructions, roads, etc.), particularly the housing sector, which after the depression that affected the whole country between 1975 and 1985, appears to be in a new phase of development. Satellite activities include cement production, with Italian raw materials (lime, marl, etc.), other building materials (ceramics, bricks), and glass manufacture. The woodworking industry, a solid, generally localized industry, uses mainly imported raw materials specifically in the production of household goods and furniture. The manufacture of paper and allied materials has been traditional for centuries and is linked to the production of packaging and particularly to printing and publishing.

Industrialization and State Industries

Lacking basic natural resources to become an industrial nation, Italy had to create a transformational economy much as Japan has done.

This implied major changes and gambles because Italy became a nation dependent on raw material and a target nation for the export of manufactured goods and, therefore, vulnerable to changes in the international economy. But Italy accepted the challenge and quickly fostered a policy of open economy to stimulate international trade. The major event was the establishment of a European Common Market (Treaty of Rome, March 1957), which opened a larger market for Italian products.

The Italian industrial sector is part of a dualistic economy: private enterprise with a large public sector. Except for agriculture, there are few sectors of the economy in which the state does not operate and several in which it dominates. Not only do many companies have mixed public and private ownership, but all firms, both public and private, are subject to many legal and financial restraints and carry heavy burdens of social welfare responsibility.

Until the early 1990s, in no other country with a free economy was the government asked to play such an important role in the economy as in Italy. The Italian government was asked to restructure industry, to improve exports, to make Italy more competitive in world markets, to win it more prestige and respect in international politics, to close the amenities gap between the North and the South, to protect the lira and keep inflation within bounds, to reduce inequality, to provide cheaper energy and curb nuclear power, to take care of every special interest group, and to guarantee everyone work, adequate housing, and health care.

Today, as we shall see, governments bend to allow more freedom to free enterprise, for the view has gained credence that too much state control puts a damper on private firms' initiative, especially in a competitive free market. This may well be so now. But it does not invalidate the policy of state economic intervention or participation in the earlier postwar decades that was largely a source of strength at a time when private industry was backward or nonexistent and needed a strong lead. In fact, there seems to be no doubt that during that period dynamic state leadership was able to do much for economic development. Governments were able to plan bold new ventures and build up certain key industries.

At the beginning of the 1990s, the government's involvement in the economy was still extensive, especially through state-owned industries. Indeed, the basis for public intervention in the economy was the system of state holdings—regulated by the ministry bearing that name, established in 1956—which represented a necessary tool by means of which the state could exercise control over, and act directly in, the country's development, causing it to attain those results dictated by state economic policy.

Initially concentrated in the vicinity of large cities, busy ports, or sources of energy and raw materials, with the declining importance of agriculture, industry moved nearer smaller centers with adequate infrastructures before spreading into the countryside, competing with agriculture for land and changing the face of the country. Nevertheless, in both the North and South the most highly industrialized and urbanized areas are mainly in the densely populated regions.

The traditional industrial triangle (Lombardy-Liguria-Piedmont) has now widened to include practically the whole Po Valley, with the highest concentrations along the foot of the pre-Alps, pre-Apennines, and the Adriatic Coast, as well as the large Alpine valleys. Industry in Tuscany and Umbria is concentrated on the plains and in hollows near the Arno and Tiber river basins; in the Marches it spreads over the whole region, scattered throughout the network of valleys. Industry in Latium and Abruzzo is concentrated in the intermontane hollows and along the coasts as well as around the larger cities.

The distribution of industry in southern Italy, however, follows an irregular pattern, with excessive concentration in certain coastal zones (such as the Caserta-Naples-Salerno belt) or in a number of geographically favorable positions (the Bari-Taranto-Brindisi triangle). Industrial areas on the islands are generally peripheral to port cities.

Three state holdings played a very important role in the Italian economic recovery: *IRI* (Institute for Industrial Reconstruction), *ENI* (National Hydrocarbons Agency), and *EFIM* (Agency for Holdings and Financing of Manufacturing Industry). Until the beginning of the 1990s, they covered every sector of the economy, including banking.

IRI had seven sectorial holding companies.[2] Before the privatization in the early 1990s, in the banking sector *IRI* had a large majority of the share capital of such banks as the *Banca Commerciale Italiana*, the *Credito Italiano*, the *Banca di Roma*, and the *Banco di Santo Spirito*, all of these being banks that carry on their activities in the field of short-term credit. Approximately 90% of the banking activity was in the hands of public sector banks.

Besides the companies headed up by the holding companies and the banks, the group also included a number of firms that were directly controlled by *IRI*. Among these, the most important were the firms operating in the air transport sector (*Alitalia*), in the toll-expressway sector (*Autostrade*), and in the radio-television sector (RAI). In 1982, one year before the start of the "recovery schedule" recorded in 1983, *IRI* had over 535,000 employees (ranked second in the world, after General Motors, in number of employees). That year it had a turnover of 32.9 trillion lire ($26 billion) and grew to an estimated 47.6 trillion lire in 1989, ranking it fourteenth in the world and third outside the U.S. The privatization that took place in the early 1990s reduced considerably the size of *IRI*.

ENI, the National Hydrocarbons Agency (1953), is a public holding company whose purpose is to promote and carry out initiatives in the nation's interest in the hydrocarbons and natural steam fields. The group's organizational structure breaks down into four main sectors: hydrocarbons (coal, oil), chemical and nuclear, engineering and services, and manufacturing.[3] With privatization taking place, it is difficult to predict what *ENI* will look like by the end of the 1990s.

EFIM, the Agency for Holdings and Financing of Manufacturing Industry, privatized in 1992, had as its purpose, intervention in the industrial sector to aid further development. Its activities were carried on through firms controlled and coordinated by means of sectorial holding companies.[4] This job was carried out not just through financing but through the performance of services and functions as well, which made it possible for even average-sized firms to get into foreign markets and to make use of more efficient computer and management systems and more effective applied research.

In the 1980s, these state industries became too inefficient and were even considered a liability. Under the new world trade conditions of open frontiers and multinational groupings, the Italian economy can prosper only if it becomes more market-oriented and firms cease to rely so much on the state. Even more detrimental to the national economy was the fact that the big state projects have too often been directed with an eye to political kudos rather than economic usefulness. The public sector has been ruled more by political needs than market demands, and this situation has to change if Italy is to compete in the open markets of the future.

The Economic Phoenix

Italy's economic development has evolved in several phases and has followed a tortuous road. Economists are in broad agreement that the basis of the launching pad for the economic growth was provided in the immediate postwar period by Luigi Einaudi's harsh deflation policy, with its tight credit and cuts in government spending that brought inflation under control, stabilized the lira, and won international confidence. The internal policy was supported with aid from the Marshall Plan, which provided a massive infusion of funds to finance vital imports; the discovery of natural gas in the Po Valley, which gave Italy its first indigenous energy source; and a great reservoir of cheap and highly mobile labor. The continuing high level of unemployment was largely caused by the massive shift of population from the South to the North, from rural areas to the cities, and from agriculture into manufacturing and services. Between 1958 and 1963, the number of workers in the agriculture field had declined by 50%. The resulting low labor costs also helped to make Italian goods highly competitive in world markets. In this situation, profits were high and, reinvested in capital stock, produced rapid industrial growth.

The years between 1958 and 1963 were a time of economic growth so remarkable that it has appropriately been called an "economic miracle." During that period the gross national product rose at an annual rate of 6.6%, against a European average of 4.5%. In 1960 alone industrial production went up by 20%.

With the Italian entry into the European Economic Community in 1957, the country not only gained an expanded market but also was forced into free-market competition in which its products surprised everyone by selling extremely well. In fact, it was exports that led the economic miracle to its heights between 1958 and 1962.

In the early 1960s, many U.S. and other Western observers suddenly discovered the Italian "miracle." They extolled the unexpected developments that seemed to enable Italy to join the leading group of the major industrial nations of the West. Improvements were given additional luster and appeal by a happy season of Italian creativity in such disparate fields as interior decoration, movies, shoes, architecture, and office equipment. To label as a "miracle" Italy's performance not only represented a dangerously superficial reading of events but was also grossly unfair to many Italians. The economic "boom," as it was also labeled, happened because of the politicians who had fought successfully to replace the protectionism traditionally prevailing in Italy with a wide-ranging liberalization of the country's foreign trade. The "boom" also took place because of the industrialists, technicians, and businessmen who had risen to the challenge by making many Italian products competitive on the international markets. It also took place because of the millions of hard-working and often poorly paid Italians who had played a decisive part in the "quality jump" of the "Made in Italy" label.

The growth was due mainly to low wage rates, which were possible because of high unemployment in the South, weak trade unions, the mobility of the population, and international monetary stability. The exodus from the farms, which gave factories a steady supply of new recruits, with a peasant's readiness to work hard for low wages helped to keep down the price of Italian goods and make them competitive on the international market. Another factor that affected the growth in those years was the fact that export prices rose 3.8% per year while the cost of imported raw materials fell on the average of 2% per year. The resulting profits provided substantial capital for investments.

The rapid economic expansion soon brought problems, however, because it ameliorated some of the basic conditions which had helped to spark it—notably the low level of wages and the mass consumption that reflected, in turn, a large and chronic unemployment and under-employment. Too many Italians did not foresee that any sudden speedup in economic growth involves and sharpens tensions, imbalances, and frustrations. In the case of Italy, the costs could be very high because the benefits of the "forward jump" were mostly concentrated in the industrial sector (and did not affect all of it, either) and because the country's administrative, economic, and financial structures were far from adequate for the requirements of a modern democracy.

In 1963, when the unemployment rate reached a record low of 3.6%, unions started to press for concessions, especially in wages. Gradually these increases went above productivity growth, squeezing profit margins and reducing investments. With more money available, private consumption increased and demands became greater, which resulted in high inflation. The industrial system reacted in its tradi-tional conservative way: lower investments and more utilization of existing labor. As one may expect, the economic crisis brought about a social crisis that then exploded in the "Hot Autumn of 1969."

It is clear in retrospect that, economically, Italy was a puzzle. The country may have had all the trappings of a modern democracy, but neither its social and institutional structure nor its administrative prac-tices had been brought in line with those of the other Western democ-racies. The country still lacked the facilities to deal with its problems: an equitable and effective tax system, a foresighted approach to land tenure and agricultural problems, antitrust legislation, efficient regula-tory agencies in the fields of power, trade, and labor relations, and a modern educational system. At the same time, the tremendous development of television and other communications, although state-controlled, was bringing home to more and more Italians the great gap between the formal ideology that was supposed to guide the country's affairs and their daily experience of the way those affairs actually were conducted.

The Communist Party did not miss the opportunity to exploit this situation, and increasingly strengthened its position as champion of social and economic reforms, and fighter against arbitrary authority, public graft, mismanagement, and attempts to hush up scandals and abuses.

The 1960s were years of workers' struggles and political changes. During the recession in 1964, the Socialist Party joined the christian democrats in order to form a government based on a program of economic development. This coalition attempted to make the economic system more dynamic by *nationalizing* certain corporations in the electrical and chemical sectors, including many public services, and started a program for far-reaching reforms and modernization of Italian administrative, fiscal, and financial structures. This economic program was supposed to contain the tools necessary to carry out the reforms required to do away with the chronic geographic and social imbalances and to insure, at the same time, a steady growth. This program was also supposed to render the communist opposition, already weakened by its decision to engage only in parliamentary struggle, completely ineffective.

Social Transformation and Resourceful Italians

By early 1967, it was clear that very little progress had been made in implementing the center-left's program that was agreed on in 1962-1963. The paramount need to avoid an economic slump, following the disorderly boom of the early years, led to the delaying or watering-down of the other social reforms originally pledged by the alliance. This had suited most christian democrats, who sought to gain votes from the fading parties of the Right. But most socialists, fearful of losing ground on their left, were pressing again for more vigorous action.

The Italian people, for the most part, had become restless. Unprecedented protests and rebellion by university students represented the most significant challenge to the political establishment and were the most evident symptom of the problems besetting a country that had become one of the seven leading industrial and trading nations but still retained many institutions and administrative practices that had changed little since the turn of the century (this topic will be treated in greater depth in chapter IX). The student population, which was less than 60,000 in 1935, had now reached almost 450,000. Despite some progress, physical facilities had expanded at a much slower pace and the number of professors had risen to only 8,000, in comparison to 2,700 in 1935. Moreover, many professors were too busy in politics or business to show up for classes, let alone to devote sufficient attention to their students. University power was (and still is) concentrated in a small and self-perpetuating group of deans and full professors. Students demanded a complete revision of the system and wanted their own representatives, as well as those professors of junior rank, to have a voice in running university affairs. Under the leadership of a small group of activists, sometimes self-labeled as "Maoists," "Castroites," or "anarchists," students started a vague but loud and even violent revolt against society. Such a development was taking place just when the center-left governmental coalition had finally presented a reform bill intended to correct at least the most outdated features of the university system.

Similar dissatisfaction was behind industrial and civil servants' strikes and recurrent unrest over such issues as reorganization of the bureaucratic apparatus, modernization of the social security system, and hospital reforms. In those and other fields, the center-left coalition had achieved more than previous governments, but less than it had pledged or had been thought possible.

A turning point came in the fall of 1969, when workers set in motion a revolution in industrial relations. The delayed effects of the prolonged series of strikes in the industrial sector during the "Hot Autumn of 1969"—which continued well into early 1970 and resulted in sharply higher labor costs and lower productivity—were eventually felt throughout the economy beginning in the late 1970s.

In 1969 the trade unions changed tactics. They became more militant; not only were they asking for better wages and job protection, but they also demanded better working and living conditions. The newly urbanized migrants from the rural South were increasingly dissatisfied with living conditions in the fast growing cities in the North and demanded better housing, schools, shops, transportation, and health care. The demands were accompanied by frequent strikes and violent demonstrations.

Italian society wanted to change and demanded legislative action. One truly startling shift had taken place in the Italians' views on such issues as divorce and birth control. In a 1967 public opinion survey, 58.6% of 12,645 Italians interviewed were in favor of introducing divorce and three out of four favored birth control. Two out of three said their views or behavior on the subject were not affected by Pope Paul's pronouncement reaffirming the Catholic Church's rigid ban on contraception. Just five years earlier, a similar survey had shown that almost seven Italians out of ten were against the introduction of divorce.

The outcome of the Italian elections of May 19-20, 1968, sent a message of concern to the government. Although the center-left coalition had slightly increased its share of the popular vote and parliamentary representation, the communists and the extreme left socialist splinter group scored sizable gains, jolting the governing coalition.

As a consequence of all these manifestations, the Italian government started to plan for radical changes. The early 1970s went down in history as the years when Italy enacted some of the world's most advanced social legislation.

Unfortunately, at the same time the quadrupling of oil prices beginning in 1973 dealt the Italian economy a tremendous blow. Having to import 85% of its energy needs, Italy was hit harder than any other Western country and had to work feverishly to avoid a complete economic collapse. The combination of wage and oil price increases badly hurt industrial profits and drastically reduced the competitiveness of many public and large private enterprises. Consequently, in 1975 Italy experienced the worst postwar recession. In the first half of the 1970s there was a significant deterioration in economic performance. In 1975, for the first time since World War II, the economy contracted. Real gross domestic product (GDP) dropped by 3.5%, industrial production fell by 9.5%, and inflation topped 17%, the highest in Europe. Most of these losses were regained in 1976 with a 5.6% increase in GDP and a 12.4% jump in industrial production, but inflation, caused mainly by the demands of militant labor unions, and unemployment remained at high levels. The Andreotti government took steps to restore the economy to steady growth without high inflation. A series of measures to check the growth of government budget deficits and labor costs were adopted, paving the way for a $250 million standby loan from the International Monetary Fund in April 1977 and another $500 million from the European Community. By 1978, these measures, plus favorable exchange rates, had given Italian exports a tremendous boost and moved Italy's current account and even its trade balance firmly into the black, despite the skyrocketing prices of imported oil.

In addition to the increasing energy costs, there were many blunders and actions that hindered company productivity more than was necessary, or possible, in order to reach the desired level of social justice. Many economists link the beginning of Italy's chronic economic troubles of the 1970s to the wage settlements that resulted from the labor unrest that characterized the autumn of 1969. Industrial wage increases averaged 25.5% in 1973 and 24.3% in 1974, while increases in the consumer price index in those years were 10.8 and 19.1% respectively. During the first five years of the 1970s, the consumer price index rose to 171, while on the same scale wages rose to 249. These developments virtually wiped out the low labor-cost advantage enjoyed by Italian industries in the late 1950s and early 1960s which was, as previously mentioned, a major contributor to the economic boom of that period. More damaging to trade performance were the strikes, absenteeism, and high labor costs that rose continuously throughout the 1970s—accounting for a 40% increase in the price of Italian manufactured goods between 1977 and 1979 alone.

However, employers were able to regain the upper hand. The FIAT strike of 1980, which ended in a large number of redundancies, was a major test of strength and a turning point. At Olivetti, Carlo De Benedetti took over an ailing firm and restored it to profitability with an aggressive anti–trade unionist stance (by the late 1980s he would be setting his sights on a takeover of Mondadori). From the end of the 1970s, a prolonged economic crisis and the rise in unemployment had weakened the bargaining power of the unions and pushed them onto the defensive. In 1983-1984 the Craxi government was able to exploit the new divisions in the union movement to push through anti-inflationary measures. Another factor was the emergence of a self-confident, new-look political center, based around Craxi and Christian Democratic Party leader Ciriaco De Mita. The latter had taken the helm as part of a move to refurbish the Party's image after the damaging scandals of the mid-1970s, culminating in the resignation in 1978 of President of the Republic Giovanni Leone, named in a scandal that involved Lockheed Aircraft.

After 1980, strikes and absenteeism dropped, productivity and capital inflows improved, and profits in many industries soared. Unemployment went from 6.4% in 1977 to 14.2% in 1985, with some three-quarters of the unemployed estimated to be persons under the age of 30.

In the mid-1980s the Italian economy presented, in short, a bewildering spectacle. It continued to be plagued by high unemployment, high interest rates, high labor costs, high inflation, vast public expenditures, and a staggering public deficit. At the same time, exports were back at an all-time record, some state industry was being restructured and modernized, large private firms were once again European leaders in their fields, the performance of small and medium-sized companies bedazzled observers, and a general sense of prosperity pervaded the country.

Nevertheless, in the early 1990s, the state enterprises still held a dominant position. The purely private-sector economy was still proportionately the smallest of major Western industrial countries, accounting for 35 to 40% of Italy's industrial production. This private sector is remarkable for its large number of small producers and its small number of large producers. At least 90% of Italy's industries employ fewer than a hundred workers. The major industries at the top of the pyramidal structure of the private sector are, and have traditionally been, concentrated in remarkably few hands—a narrow cartel of northern entrepreneurs.[5]

The Agnelli family, which owns 40% of FIAT, Italy's biggest private-sector company, remains at the center of power. The purchase of Alfa Romeo has given FIAT a virtual monopoly on the production of cars in Italy; it also owns Lancia, Ferrari, and Autobianchi. FIAT has 60% of domestic car sales—a bigger share than any other European carmaker has in its home market. FIAT remains Italy's forte today because it produces a very popular range of smaller family cars that feature low gasoline consumption, thereby maintaining its competitiveness in an oil-anxious age. But FIAT is going to have a difficult time when the Japanese are allowed more access to the Italian market. Italy is much less competitively placed than Germany to meet the Japanese challenge in other countries, for Italy does not produce the same kind of luxury high-performance cars, such as BMW, Mercedes, and Porsche, which have no Japanese equivalent—the Ferrari is completely in a league of its own. The Italian price range is similar to the Japan's.

Not limited to just automobiles, FIAT dominates many parts of the Italian economy. Cars accounted for only half of the group's turnover of 38 trillion lire (4% of GDP); the rest includes components, commercial vehicles, factory automation (robots), aviation, telecoms, and financial services. The subsidiaries of IFI, the family holding company, include Rinascente, a department-store chain; Prime, Italy's second biggest mutual fund; and stakes in banking, publishing, and television. The Agnelli family interests account for a quarter of the Milan stock market. The group also controls 24% of Italy's national daily newspaper sales: it owns *La Stampa*, a Turin-based daily, and effectively controls Italy's biggest publishing group, Rizzoli, which owns *Corriere della Sera*, Italy's most popular newspaper.

The other industrial superstars are Carlo De Benedetti, who took over *Olivetti* in 1978, and Raul Gardini, head of the *Ferruzzi-Montedison* agribusiness and chemicals group, which includes an empire that spans publishing, insurance, and retailing. The Agnelli family, De Benedetti, Leopoldo Pirelli, Carlo Bonomi, and Attilio Monti all control large holding companies with a wide array of interests.

Recently, the major firms have changed their character considerably; for one thing they have become increasingly multinational while giving the appearance of shrinking in size. Through merger, association with large foreign companies, and restructuring, they have increased international competition, improved productivity, and become financially more solid. In the process, the most striking change was the decentralization of production through subcontracting to small specialized factories and cottage firms. FIAT, for example, reduced its workforce by 24% from 1981 to 1985 while increasing productivity by 25%.

Italian business has long been dominated by a few families. In the past, the power of private business was balanced by a large public sector and strong unions. Today the trade unions, as we saw earlier, are weak and the public sector is slowly being dismantled through privatization; there is, therefore, a greater danger that the power of private business will go unchecked. Italy is the only EC country that does not have any antitrust laws, and demands for such legislation have been mounting.

Creating Capitalism: The State and Small Business

Italian economic dualism has been debated by some scholars who prefer to see the Italian economic structure in three different patterns.[6] It has been demonstrated by some studies that in the 1950s and 1960s, a pattern of differentiated economic growth existed, which had effectively created "Three Italies" each with different industrial structures and business cultures, rather than the two traditionally associated with the North-South divide: a northwestern area characterized by older, heavy industry and large-scale factory production; a central and northeastern area of small family-based firms that produced goods for export to customized rather than mass markets; and the South, which remained underdeveloped and dependent on government subsidies and employment.

The discovery of the "Third Italy" spawned a new research agenda on flexible specialization in production methods, the dynamism of small firms in advanced economies, and the socio-political and cultural underpinnings of these areas. Using Italian examples of flexible specialization, some scholars have argued that the economy of other countries may be developed along the same lines.

Flexible specialization and industrial districts emphasize the importance of informal cooperation and linkages between firms as a recipe for success. Yet, it should not be overlooked that Italy has a strong tradition in some areas (e.g., Emilia Romagna) of groups of firms organized along cooperative lines.

Notes

1. There is a large body of literature on Italy's economic development and agricultural, industrial, and business structures. The decline in the importance of agriculture in the postwar period is charted in Camillo Daneo, *Breve storia dell'agricoltura italiana 1860-1970* (Milano: Mondadori, 1980), while Russell King analyzes one of the few major reforms of the 1950s in *Land Reform: The Italian Experience* (London:Croom Helm, 1985), and Valerio Castronovo, *L'industria italiana dall'Ottocento a oggi* (Milano: Mondadori, 1980).

2. STET (Telephone Holding Company), whose task was to manage IRI holdings in the telecommunications and electronics fields; *FINMARE*, for shipping company holdings; *FINSIDER*, for steel industry holdings; *FINMECCANICA*, for machine and mechanical holdings; *FINCANTIERI*, for ship-construction company holdings; *ITALSTAT*, for the urban infrastructures and urban planning sector; and *SME*, the Southern Holding Company, for the food, paper, and automobile sectors in the south of Italy, and for the commercial distribution and promotion of various activities there. To give a broad idea of the level of its presence in the Italian economy, it suffices to say that in the services sector the telephone company *SIP* (a company belonging to *STET Group*) covers 82% of the Italian *TLC* traffic; *Alitalia*, 91% of air transportation; *FINMARE*, 21% of maritime transportation; *Autostrade* (a company belonging to the *ITALSTAT* Group), 45% of highways. In manufacturing, *FINSIDER* has 55% of total national production of steel; *FINCANTIERI*, 70% of shipbuilding; *Ansaldo*, 60% of power supply components; *Selenia* and *Aeritalia*, 55% of aerospace; *Italtel*, 50% of *TLC* switching; *SGS*, 98% of micro-electronics.

3. Operating in the hydrocarbons sector is *AGIP*, which oversees various activities from prospecting for coal and petroleum and uranium ores, to mining, and to the distribution of petroleum products. *SNAM*, too, operates in the hydrocarbons sector, carrying on the transport of hydrocarbons and the importing and distribution of natural gas. Another is the Italian Petroleum Products Industry, which operates in the refining and distribution sector. In the chemical and nuclear sector is *ANIC*, which works in the chemicals and refining industry, and *AGIP Nuclear*, heading up all activities concerned with the nuclear industry. In the engineering and services sector is *SNAM Progetti*, which oversees the study, design, and construction of gas and oil pipelines and of petroleum facilities and petrochemical plants; it also oversees scientific research activities. *SAIPEM* carries on drilling activities and the assembly and construction of pipelines and industrial plants. *TECNECO* sees to both general and detailed development planning for water resources and for developing the territory in general. In the manufacturing sector, textile weaving activities are headed up by the *TESCON* holding company, incorporated to give the management policies of the companies it holds greater coherence and to give them more strength on the financing level. The main companies under *TESCON* are *Lanerossi*, *Lebole*, *Monti*, and *MCM*.

4. The most important were the *Ernesto Breda Holding Company*, chiefly con-
    cerned in the mechanical sector, instrumentation in particular; the *Breda
    Railway Company*, operating mainly in the transport and motor sector; *SOPAL*
    (Food Holding Company), which carries on a large-scale activity in sectors
    running from procuring raw materials for the food industry to their conversion
    and to the distribution of food products in Italy and abroad. *INSUD* is a hold-
    ing company that specializes in projects in the South, promoting and carry-
    ing out initiatives there in the tourism and manufacturing industry sectors, in
    combination with Italian and foreign partners. *EFIM* supported, monitored,
    and coordinated the leader holding companies and operating companies sub-
    ject to it.

5. Six Italians were listed among *Forbes Magazine's* annual survey (1992) of the
    world's richest people. The family names of Agnelli, Benetton, Ferrero, and
    Ferruzzi, and those of Silvio Berlusconi and Salvatore Licresti, once again
    made the list of 291 billionaires. The Agnellis are first among the Italians,
    with an estimated fortune of three billion dollars.

6. Arnaldo Bagnasco, *Tre Italie: la problematica territoriale dello sviluppo
    italiano* (Bologna: Mulino, 1977); Michael J. Piore and Charles F. Sabel, *The
    Second Industrial Divide: Possibilities for Prosperity* (New York: Basic Books,
    1984); Raffaella Nanetti, *Growth and Territorial Policies. The Italian Model
    of Social Capitalism* (London: Pinter, 1988); Michael Blim, *Made in Italy:
    Small Scale Industrialization and its Consequences* (New York: Praeger,
    1990); Mark Holmstrom, *Industrial Democracy in Italy: Workers' Co-ops
    and the Self-Management Debate* (Aldershot: Averbury, 1989).

VI

Industrial Change And
Social Transformation

The Economic Boom of the 1980s

By the end of the 1980s, Italy had become one of Europe's great success stories. Suddenly was a land of upward mobility, of vital computerized industry, of bustling young business managers and slick middle-aged tycoons who had abjured their 1960s ideals in the sacred cause of profit. Even the English, long critical of Italy, at the end of the 1980s were saying that the Italians must have been doing something right, and doing it despite a political and administrative system that remains the least adapted to the requirements of modern, efficient government in western Europe.

In 1987, the year of the *sorpasso,* in which Italy actually surpassed Great Britain as an economic power, the government added an extra 18% to its estimate of Italy's national income. Italy's GDP became 10% bigger than Britain's in 1986, and its GDP per capita was 9% larger. These figures shook up the industrialized West. The average Italian was shown to be richer than the average Briton when standards of living were compared using the ownership of consumer goods. In Italy 76% of households have a car, compared with 58% in Britain; 81% have washing machines and 14% have dishwashers, compared with 77% and 3% respectively for British families.

It seems that Italy understood at the end of the 1970s what Americans have not yet grasped—*flexible production*, that is, a new, more cooperative way of organizing relations between firms; a populist sense of who has useful knowledge about how to manufacture things; a recognition that small firms with highly motivated, skilled workers can be more responsive to market changes than multibillion-dollar institutions with dozens of layers of supervision and hundreds of volumes of operating manuals. Mass production in large American industries had created a monopoly of management expertise at the top, and the polarization of corporate rewards—the top executives who make as much as Madonna, and the unskilled workers who increasingly earn little more than welfare mothers—have corroded the work ethic of the majority who are required to keep the machine working and working properly. Moreover, flexible production can respond better to consumer markets where tastes change rapidly because a premium can be put on design qualities and craft skills, on workers who can take the initiative. Flexibility enables workers to develop craft skills, to reacquire the technical knowledge monopolized by management.

In Italy, flexible production has featured the rise of "SMEs"—small and medium-sized regional enterprises. Emilia-Romagna now has over 300,000 SMEs; nearly 70,000 are industrial firms. The leading sectors are machine tools, agricultural equipment, ceramics, metalworking, mechanical engineering, garments, and textiles. A lot of the same industries that New York City planners wrote off as too small and too high-cost to compete globally fared very well in Italy. Firms in Bologna, Modena, and Forlì exploited their flexibility; they moved products from design to market very quickly. Instead of New York–style yippie networking, the Italians formed industrial networks: strategic alliances, buyer-supplier partnerships, joint ventures. In the garment industry, they went "upmarket" to escape competition with low-cost producers. These sub-giants have formed cooperative networks that compensate for the lack of large sums of capital and have been the industrial engine that brought about the resurgence of the manufacturing industry in some cities. The more successful firms have invested intelligently in new equipment, have pushed productivity up, and have given technical innovation its head. As a result, Italy has moved into the forefront of advanced technology, able to export massively both her products and her "know-how."

Some of Italy's cities, like many American cities, had experienced a big loss of blue-collar jobs in the second half of the 1970s. Third World competition, rising energy costs, high wages, and rigid union rules were the cause for the big decline of the manufacturing sector. To relieve unemployment and replenish dwindling revenues, many cities gave up on industry and looked to services, such as banking and insurance. But bold policies in some cities showed that there was no need to give up on manufacturing. The economic resurgence came about through very small, flexible enterprises organized around multiple-use, automated machinery. The tiny shops became intermediate producers, which link together in varying combinations and form networks to carry out complex manufacturing tasks for world markets. Frequent subcontracting within networks makes it easy to upgrade product specifications and even change product lines rapidly in response to market signals. Moreover, the small-scale industrial enterprises have bridged the distance between artisans and modern production methods.

Development of this system of flexible network manufacturing is encouraged by local governments across the country. City and regional governments pitched in with municipal land, credit, child care, public transport, and advanced industrial training. Many municipalities provided affordable workspaces in converted factory buildings and mini-industrial parks. Local schools turn out well-trained apprentices and keep shop owners up-to-date through evening programs. Publicly subsidized research centers provide assistance in product innovation, technology transfer, and export marketing. The emphasis on innovation and quality means that experimentation and education are encouraged. There is continual upward movement as former apprentices open their own firms. And rigid work rules make no sense where machine operators must contribute willingly to the constant revision of processes and products if the shops are to prosper. The basic features of this Italian industrial system are very much in the American grain. It stresses entrepreneurship, self-employment, the pleasure of making things, creative challenges, and good income.

Manufacturing is the largest sector of the economy, comprising 35% of GDP and employing 30% of the labor force. However, there are signs of a lessening of Italy's industrial strength. Footwear and textiles have experienced a gradual decrease in export business. That loss must be compensated by growth in other industrial sectors such as machinery, transport equipment, and chemicals. Products from the metal-mechanical industry account for 25% of total exports; textiles, clothing, leather goods, and furs, 19.5%; metallurgy, 8.8%; and chemicals, 8.5%.

Luckily for Italy, Italians seem never to lack solutions. Look at how the country reacted to the major crisis at the end of the 1970s. What gave impetus to the second "economic miracle" was certainly the *de-*

centralization of production. The process of such decentralization was mainly caused by the sharply rising labor costs and an expanding social welfare that burdened large companies. Social security contributions and related payments to the state meant that the total cost of labor to an employer escalated to more than double the net salaries. All salaries were linked to inflation, and it was virtually impossible to lay off workers.

By the early 1980s, it had become clear that labor union demands and a strong state presence in the economy, which had created the basis for the "welfare state" in the 1960s and 1970s, were now crippling the nation. Lack of vigor in the banking world, an out-of-date fiscal system, poor liaison between pure and applied research, excessive state bureaucratic interference in private industry, all were problems that needed to be addressed. Clearly, the state and the labor unions' strong role in the economy had fulfilled their original mandates, but now their excesses needed to be corrected. Gradual political changes and visionary entrepreneurship brought about a remarkable shift and turnabout in economic direction. The remarkable success of the small and medium-sized industry was a blow to the powerful labor unions and served as a clear message to excessive presence of the state in the economy.

As part of the process, Italy started a program of *privatizzazione,* following a pragmatic approach in adopting a set of measures: transfer of activities from public sector to private through share offerings; utilization of private companies to manage services previously in the hands of state or local governments; and introduction of a "fee" for services previously offered and financed through taxes. These measures were not entirely based on the standard of what was best for Italy, however. There were some political motives involved, for the center-right wanted to build up the electoral support of a body of small-scale capitalists who benefitted from the liberalization of the market.

At first the privatization programs affected mainly large enterprises. In addition to industrial and financial restructuring, the state giant *IRI*, in its strategy for recovery, followed the path of privatization and partnership, which means "divestiture of enterprises." It considered putting up for sale three kinds of enterprise: first, marginal ones, which were not integrated with other *IRI* companies, and therefore had no "mission" to accomplish inside the IRI Group. Second, companies that were operating in the red. And, finally, enterprises, or even subholdings of *IRI*, which were or could be profitable and could even form an integrated whole, but did not appear to be consistent with the group's basic long-term objectives. Between 1983 and 1992, over 30 enterprises of different sizes, from big Alfa Romeo to small Ducati (motorcycles), from banks to washing-machine producers, have been divested. The process of divestiture slowed somewhat in 1985, but starting in July 1986, regained steam and has touched every sector of the economy, including services.

Small-Sized Firms and the Underground Economy

One of the most striking peculiarities of the Italian economy has been the remarkable strength of the export sector, which in some ways is a paradigm of Italy's economic performance. In the fashion world, Italian clothing, furniture, and textiles have emerged as world leaders, while in some industrial areas, such as machine tools and robotics, Italian products have earned an outstanding reputation for quality and have won a growing share of the world market.

Because of their exceptional ability to sense changing consumer demand and to produce attractive goods, Italian exporters have been highly agile in shifting into new markets and alternative products. The Italian export industry is remarkable for its ability not only to move quickly into new geographic areas but also to change to the production of items for which demand is on the rise.

The achievements in this area are all the more impressive because exporters have rarely received help from the government, either through assistance in penetrating world markets or through export credits. The trade policy, as a result of free-for-all agreements, greatly helped the Italian economy.

The principal question concerning the Italian economy is whether giants like the state holding companies *ENI* and *IRI* and private giants like FIAT and Olivetti will be competitive without state protectionism. Although FIAT currently maintains 15% of the European car market, its dependence on the protected Italian market makes it especially vulnerable to European competition. The same may be said about textiles, a historically vital sector of the Italian economy, accounting for 38% of the clothing imports of the EC as of 1988 and Italy's third largest industry. There is no question that the successful international performance of Benetton, Stefanel, and fashion designers such as Armani, Fendi, Krizia, and Valentino shows no signs of letting up. Benetton is recognized as a leader in the "Europreparedness" stakes, having established a vast chain of shops throughout Europe and the U.S. by the early 1980s. Similarly, the late Versace's firm is aiming to go public and thereby raise enough capital to expand its already multinational operation. However, there are serious doubts as to whether the Italian textile industry as a whole will be able to compete with the newly industrialized countries such as Taiwan, Korea, and Brazil, which are able to exploit "mature" manufacturing technology with cheap labor.

The success achieved by the medium-and-small-sized industries has proven that Italy will be able to sustain the assault that will be coming from Third World countries. In fact, this industrial sector, which was behind the economic boom of the 1980s, became the most outstanding trait of the country's current industrial structure and the most dynamic anywhere in Europe and has caused mass social changes without precedent in Italy. Originally most of these companies were set up to escape the trade union regulations that followed the "Hot Autumn of 1966," since firms with fewer than 15 employees need not be unionized or pay standard wages and social benefits. They, therefore, operated at great cost efficiency and high productivity and without risk of strikes. There was still another impetus. Firms with annual incomes below approximately $75,000 were not required to make their books available to income-tax authorities. The astonishing consequence of this has been that starting in 1984, fully 95% of Italian firms declared incomes of less than that figure!

Since the production of these small firms escapes official records, the country's real GDP and export statistics are appreciably higher than official accounts would indicate. It is estimated that the "underground economy" employs anywhere from 2 to 4 million persons and helps the economy produce fully 20 to 30% over the official GDP.

This small-business sector has changed the industrial map of Italy. No longer does the Italian economy entirely hinge on the old industrial triangle of Milan-Turin-Genoa. The new firms are not in large cities but in provincial towns in former agrarian areas. And they have spread from Emilia-Romagna, the Veneto, and Tuscany into the Marches and on to Umbria, Abruzzi, Apulia, and the area south of Rome. They produce clothing, leather products, shoes, furniture, textiles, machine tools, agricultural machinery, toys, car parts, and jewelry. The manufacturing sectors are regionalized: in the Northwest there is a large modern group of industries; in the Northeast there are small enterprises of low technology but high craftsmanship; in the Center and

South, the two forms exist side by side. Thanks to the low price and high quality of their innovative products, these firms are remarkably resistant to the ups and downs of the international economy.

Among the distinguishing features of these decentralized, but integrated industrial districts is a seemingly contradictory combination of competition and cooperation. Firms compete vigorously for innovation in style and efficiency while cooperating in administrative services, raw material purchases, financing, and research. "A rich network of private economic associations and political organizations have constructed an environment in which markets prosper by promoting cooperative behavior and by providing small firms with the infrastructural needs that they could not afford alone."[1] These networks of small firms combine low vertical integration and high horizontal integration through extensive subcontracting and the "putting out" of extra business to temporarily underemployed competitors. Active industrial associations provide administrative and even financial aid, while local government plays an active role in providing the necessary social infrastructure and services, such as professional training, information on export markets, and so on. The result is a technologically advanced and highly flexible economic structure, which proved precisely the right recipe for competing in the fast-moving economic world of the 1980s and 1990s.[2] The degree of success of these firms is higher in the Emilia-Romagna region because of the higher level of civic traditions, of contemporary civic community, and of high-performance regional government. Most observers have demonstrated that what is crucial about these small-firm industrial districts is mutual trust, social cooperation, and a well-developed sense of civic duty in short, the hallmarks of the civic community.[3]

Public Indebtedness and Democracy

The success of medium-and-small-sized industries has had a positive impact also on the private heavy industry sector, because the industrial giants, by subcontracting to the smaller industries, were able to overcome certain labor demands and, consequently, produce goods more cheaply. However, occasionally big industry has chosen to expand abroad rather than at home. Industrialists like Carlo De Benedetti of Olivetti have been leading the way.

Situations like this could signal very serious problems for the average Italian worker, but in the Italian scene it is always difficult to assess just how changes will influence workers' rights. In economic, as in social reforms, Italians have gone from one extreme to another, and they are still struggling to find a happy equilibrium. They find salvation in the fact that they are great lovers of drama; whether in opera, politics, or soccer, they swing from the depths of depression one moment to excessive optimism the next. Italians have long proved their ingenuity in the face of apparently insurmountable obstacles.

Italy has long been famed for its hidden economy—that mysterious underworld of tax dodging, illegal employment of foreign workers and students, and civil servants who moonlight in the afternoons when their offices close. Rigid labor laws, high taxes, social security contributions, and a general willingness to break the law are the reasons for the largest underground economy in the industrial world.

Italian wage-earners are the ones who have to carry the national fiscal burden. Statistical data indicate that the total "tax burden" for the average Italian reaches only 22.7% of his or her income, a rate lower than the average for citizens of the European Union. Worldwide, Italy places ahead of Switzerland (21.8 %), U.S. (20.6 %), Japan (19.5 %), and Spain (16.9 %), but well behind the northern European countries where taxation is heaviest: Denmark (47.4 %), Sweden (38%), and Norway (37.9 %). Because Italians prefer to grandstand, tax cheating, too, either for its blatancy or its pervasiveness, frequently makes big headlines. Italian movie stars get in the news because they claim to make less than the sanitation employee; industrial magnates report little more than some of their clerks and secretaries; doctors, lawyers, dentists, architects, and accountants are shown to be reporting, on average, less income than is paid to skilled industrial workers. The owners of well-known restaurants and cafes regularly report less income than they pay to their chefs, waiters, and dishwashers. Much of this collusion is based on the implicit assumption that the fiscal laws are not fair, that they are not rigorously enforced against everyone, and that the state, in its imperious way, has so defrauded the ordinary taxpayer that it is entirely natural and acceptable that the latter should return the favor in kind. In a nation where the overwhelming majority of the population regards its democratically elected political leaders as a bunch of *ladri* (thieves), anyone cheating the government may be sure of general benevolence. "None of my money for that rotten system," most of the tax dodgers say. There is something fundamentally democratic about tax evasion; one way or another, the practice extends to a very large proportion of the adult population. It is true, of course, that those on fixed wages and salaries cannot evade, but this applies only to one's first—not second or third—job. Those who are working in the second, and unreported economy, include hundreds of thousands of blue-collar workers or members of their families, as well as professionals. The practice of auto mechanics, plumbers, carpenters, physicians, dentists, and lawyers wanting payment in cash and their willingness to be prompt and accommodating when told the customer doesn't need a receipt, is commonplace in Italy as it is in America.

In 1992, the Italian Finance Ministry published a list of about half a million alleged tax dodgers in an attempt to shame evaders into paying. The "Red Book" report included well-known actors, businessmen, and journalists. The total amount of unpaid taxes was 33 trillion lire ($25 billion), which would have covered about 25% of Italy's budget deficit. The government has passed stiff laws to combat tax dodging. Customers by law have to walk out with a *ricevuta fiscale* (register receipt) from any premise where goods were bought or services were rendered (from the purchase of a cappuccino to a hair cut). But, even though fines are heavy and are enforced rigorously, Italians enjoy the thrill and the satisfaction of tax evasion.

In the official economy, the Italian worker is well rewarded with high wages, good benefits, and many paid holidays. In 1992, the average employee in the industrial and service sectors worked about 40 hours per week, 1,622 hours per year (compared to 1,847 in the U.S.) and received 40.5 paid holidays and vacation days (compared to 23 in the U.S. and 31 in Britain). The cost of each hour of manufacturing labor, including benefits, was $19.49 (compared to $13.70 in Britain and $15.39 in the U.S.).[4] All this places Italy on the high side as far as growth in unit labor costs, even though the country ranks toward the top among leading nations as far as growth in labor productivity.

The question, again, is how come the state does not collapse? Some convincing reasons were given by the respected weekly of London, *The Economist*. The first reason is that unlike governments in America, Belgium, and Denmark, which have financed a large chunk of their borrowing abroad, only 3% of Italy's public debt is owed to foreigners. Second, Italian households are among the thriftiest in the world. They save some 23% of their disposable income, even more than the Japanese, and thus provide a large pool of cash from which the government can finance its deficit. In contrast, America's budget deficit has caused such problems because American households save less than

4% of their income. Unlike Americans and Britons who happily mortgage themselves up to the hilt to buy a house, the two-thirds of Italians who own their homes save up much of the money first. The old
tradition of parental support is also still very much alive. In Italy there
is a strong family tradition not to fall into debt—learning how to save
rather than how to spend is taught from childhood. But savings cannot be relied upon forever; consumers are starting to overcome their
aversion to debt and are being wooed by new financial intermediaries.
The third reason is that the Bank of Italy remains staunchly independent and highly respected. The central bank has, thereby, helped to
maintain investors' confidence. Governors of the bank are appointed
for life and so are free from political interference.

Nevertheless, the government's huge budget deficit, which is almost as big as America's, even though America's economy is seven
times larger, has brought Italy to the verge of collapse. Historic ineffi-
ciency and waste in the public sector, huge welfare costs, especially on
the health provisions, and corruption of politicians and government
officials at every administrative level have forced the country to a rude
awakening. Because of the need to coordinate national tax systems
and because of the limits on public deficits and debt contained in the
Maastricht treaty, solving the problem is not just a national priority
but a European Union requirement.

Other Serious Problems

In the early 1990s, public services represented the most dismal feature of the Italian economy because they reflected and compounded,
more than other sectors, the still unsolved, or only partially solved,
problems of a traditionally poor and underdeveloped country, as well
as the new problems besetting a nation which, only recently and very
hastily, has become affluent and demanding. Public services in such
key areas as health care and railroads, social security, the mail, justice,
schools, and airports needed profound changes. By and large, these
services are more expensive than in many other Western countries
and they often operate at a loss while their performance is generally
well below the standards required by a modern democracy.

Although Italy has a marvelous highway system, its rail system is in
dire need of modernization. This situation may not be important for
passenger transportation because Italians love their *macchina* (car),
but it spells trouble for the effective transportation of goods. The state
railroads' freight service is so unsatisfactory that today less than one-

eighth of all goods moving in Italy are shipped by rail. Trucking in Italy costs three times as much as shipping by freight train, but farmers and manufacturers usually put up with this higher expense for the sake of speed and reliability. One striking example is that southern fruit and vegetables cannot be sent by rail to northern markets because the trip may take three weeks instead of one day!

Mail service, notwithstanding recent improvements, is still a serious problem. It may take half an hour to buy stamps at the postal office, or it may take a week to send a letter across Rome. These difficulties persist despite a slackening demand brought about by the increasing appeal of fax machines.

Moreover, in the early 1990s, welfare was still one of the most problem-plagued sectors of Italian social policy. One factor is the early retirement age, for men 60, for women 55. In most countries men retire at age 65 and women at 62, when they do not follow the same age limit as men. The only country that has a lower retirement age than Italy is Turkey, where men retire at 55 and women at 50. Yet in Turkey the average longevity is at least ten years lower than Italy. Among industrialized nations only Japan has the same retirement age eligibility as Italy. However, Japanese pensions are calculated on the earnings average of one's entire career, whereas in Italy the average is based on the last five years of work. Italy's generosity in its pension system needs fine tuning. In the years 1985 to 1990, social security expenditures went from 182,975 to 308,493 billion lire and revenues went from 192,161 to 323,839 billion lire, with an increase, as compared to GDP, respectively, from 22.6 to 23.6% and from 23.7 to 24.8%.

The large population of "invalids" also has to be reexamined. Toward the end of each month, one out of every ten Italians runs to the post office to collect the pension that the state pays its army of invalids. With 5.5 million certified *invalidi* (including about 700,000 people officially wounded or who suffered some bodily harm during World War II), Italy would seem to be one of the world's most hazardous countries. Yet Italians on average live longer than do Britons, French, or Germans.

Few of the 5.5 million supposedly handicapped Italians are incapacitated. The overwhelming majority of those who receive monthly disability pensions are well-nourished and are fit to work. By far the major part of the spurious infirm live in the South. Since southerners have a hard time finding jobs, to be pronounced officially invalid guarantees them a state pension that is equivalent to earning minimum wage or unemployment compensation. Abuses persist: for years, candidates for elective office have been busy obtaining disability status and pensions for reputedly disabled constituents.

Social security absorbs 42% of public expenditure, while at least three quarters of the deficit is due to the social welfare programs of the state. Moreover, the system of social security contribution for public employees, which differs from the private one, legitimatizes unequal treatment.

In 1992 the country's balance sheet was horrendous. The budget deficit had risen to 11% of GDP, above the 10% average of the previous two decades. The public sector debt (including both the central government's and localities') had ballooned to 106% of GDP. (To give some relative terms, in the U.S., the public debt is about 37% of the country's GNP.) Just to service this 1,469,831 billion lire debt, equivalent to over $1.2 trillion, the government spent an amount equivalent to 10.2% of the GDP.

Hard Choices Ahead

The Maastricht Treaty, in an attempt to establish a monetary union in Europe, imposed unequivocal rules. Italy did not have any choice if she wanted to continue to belong to the European Union. The European linkage, first of all, meant a commitment to a sound economic system that is in tune with the E.U. and the international market. To meet Italy's commitment and to ensure the country's continued participation in the E.U.'s economic unification program, and the monetary union in particular, the government had to reduce the budget deficit to 3% of GDP, and the national debt to under 60% of the gross domestic product. These were difficult goals to achieve because accomplishing them would create hundreds of thousands of additional jobless workers, on top of an already high 11% unemployment rate.

Italy is one of the countries furthest from meeting the conditions for participation in the final phase of the EMU (the European Monetary Union). For years Italy was unable to eliminate an inflation differential caused entirely by domestic factors, or to resolve the imbalance in the public finances. The consequence was the loss of competitiveness, an astronomical deficit, and the growing tendency for production to be transferred abroad.

To respond to the gravity of the situation, the Italian parliament supported for prime minister Giuliano Amato, a socialist and a graduate of Columbia University law school, a man of integrity, intelligence, and character. He had to head the first Italian government after the collapse of communism and had the thankless job of steering an economic course for the country that would enable it to comply with E.U. requirements for continued full membership after the single European market was established on January 1, 1993. Premier Amato's task was to form a government that promised less to its citizens and at the same time asked more from them. Amato was seen as a Gorbachev-like figure, an innovator, though still attached to the old system. The guidelines approved by his Council of Ministers in July 1992 were intended to begin to plug the enormous shortfalls of the budget; they were intended to be the beginning of a plan to return to a rational and responsible financial system.

The government engaged in a policy that would wage war against tax evasion and the growth of public debt, while attempting to hold inflation to a level close to the rates prevailing in the most stable European economies. It also made recommendations on how to improve the efficiency and productivity of public services. The package of economic measures consisted of three separate areas. The first, dealing with fiscal policy, outlined ways to raise $26 billion through tax and excise increases and the imposition of 0.6% levy on all monies held in bank deposits and on residential real estate. The second set of measures was destined to save the Treasury tens of billions of dollars in future years by raising the retirement age for workers covered by the nationwide pension plan operated by the government to 65 years for both men and women (as pointed out earlier, under current laws, women can retire at 55 with full pension benefits, and men at 60). At the same time, the Treasury's support of Italy's universal health care system was also cut. Third, the government would speed up the privatization of two of Italy's public sector companies, IRI and ENI (they were estimated to account for some 40% of the country's GDP and were the foundation of the nation's powerful patronage system) through consolidation of all major groups of government-owned business into two giant holding companies. It was decided to dismantle EFIM, the other state holding, rather than privatize it, because of its precarious financial situation (it owed its bankers about $8 billion, including about $3 billion in principal and interest to foreign lenders). This action would reduce the relative size of the country's government-owned industry to 10-12% of the GDP. The government proposed also to privatize the *Istituto Mobiliare Italiano*, the country's oldest and most powerful merchant bank, as well as *Banca Nazionale del Lavoro*, a commercial bank.

Between EU and the Regions

Since Europe does not want to remain the offshore battleground of the consumer superpowers of Japan and the U.S., it is forging a single consuming and producing entity that can offer the world a third alternative. In this struggle Italy has to raise itself to a level that will enable it to play a primary role. The success or failure of the challenge is like life and death.

However, the road to European integration is full of obstacles. One of the principal impediments is the fact that, within the borders of the 15 EU member countries and their non-EU neighbors, seethe hundreds of years of social, cultural, and moral differences. Some, such as language, are profound; others, such as ritual lunch hours, can be downright amazing.

Geographically, two countries, the United Kingdom and Greece, do not even touch any other EU member's borders, although the UK has connected with France via the Channel Tunnel. One nonmember country, Switzerland, drives a geographical wedge into the EU between Germany to the north and Italy to the south. The 15 countries speak 11 languages, though they would claim 16. The UK and Ireland, alone among the EU states, drive on the left-hand side of the road. Work habits also differ sharply. The Germans arrive early, take a short break for lunch at noon, and leave the office at 4:00. By contrast, in many parts of Italy, most stores close for the midday meal from 1:00 to 4:00 p.m. and do not shut their doors until 8:00 in the evening. Public offices in Italy operate in an even less efficient way: most of them close for good at 2:00 p.m.!

The EU has to break down centuries of physical and cultural barriers. Besides the hard obstacles—which include the different and, at times, conflicting laws, procedures, and administrative practices that dominate each individual country—the EU also has to solve soft obstacles, which encompass the cultural and social methods, morals, and mores that have kept Europe a patchwork of separate states since the decline of the Roman Empire. Interestingly, the EU finds the soft issues the hardest to address.

The unification implies the elimination of tariffs among EU members and, therefore, profound adjustments. For instance, because of tariffs, a BMW priced at $25,000 in Germany retails at over $40,000 in Italy. Obviously, the Italian government wants to limit the numbers of BMWs its citizens buy so as to encourage the purchase of its own

high-priced cars—tariffs have traditionally aimed at protecting indigenous industries from cheaper or more attractive foreign competitors.
Nevertheless, unification is going to take place and it will eventually
be beneficial to Italy, and will have a profound effect throughout the
world.

Not less important, certainly, is how Italy, a very centralized nation,
continues to delegate power and authority to the regions. The process
of administrative reform and renewal is taking a long time because the
christian democrats were opposed to the decentralization of power.
Even though the constitution called for the immediate formation of
regional governments, the D.C. governments, or governments of coalitions, dominated by the D.C., refused to implement regionalism because they feared that it would make it easier for communist regional
control. When regional governments were finally approved in 1970,
the fears proved to be unfounded. By 1980, out of twenty regions, the
communists were in control of only three—Emilia-Romagna (centered
in Bologna), Tuscany, and Umbria.

By the beginning of the 1990s, the new governments, barely two
decades old, were spending nearly a tenth of Italy's gross domestic
product (only slightly below the figure for American states).[5] Total funds
available to the regions had grown rapidly—from roughly $1 billion in
1973 to roughly $9 billion in 1976 to roughly $65 billion in 1989. All
regional governments had gained responsibility for such fields as urban affairs, housing, agriculture, public works, hospitals and health
services, vocational education, and economic development. On
paper, the 20 regional governments are virtually identical and potentially powerful. However, the social, economic, political, and cultural
contexts into which the new institutions were implanted differ dramatically.

Some regional governments have been consistently more successful than others—more efficient in their internal operations, more creative in their policy initiatives, and more effective in implementing
those initiatives. The regions in the South have been less effective.
We agree with Robert D. Putnam that the main reason for the lower
level of effectiveness must be found in the lower level of civic virtues
in southern society.[6] The fact that southern Italians, argues Putnam,
tend to pursue personal interests and to be less civic minded, make
the South less successful in its quest for socioeconomic modernity.
The same attitude makes it easier for criminal organizations, the *Mafia* and *Camorra*, to enter the government.

Nevertheless, the Italian South has to find new energy and resources in the new wave of regionalism. Of course there are dangers in the process of regionalism. The individualistic character of the Italians could certainly create parochialism and entrenched local autocracy. The regions are now competing more vigorously with each other—not just by lobbying for favors from Rome, as in the old days, but by seeking their own solutions. The new system can in time produce a new and dynamic generation of younger local leaders and could provide a lively new focus for local loyalties and energies. While this seems to be a positive factor, there is a danger that more force will be expended on local issues than on the larger, national scene. Another problem is that poor regions may fall further beyond. It will be up to the state to provide them with good roads, telecommunications, research centers, and so on—and then hope that the new industries will develop of their own accord.

Overall, the process is positive, for it releases new local energies and may allow Italy to capitalize on the richness of its diversity. The drawback is that the competition could lead to some waste and duplication of effort and that it could accentuate the disparity between the rich dynamic regions and the poorer ones. The decentralization has created new vitality and self-awareness in many towns and their regions. The cultural revival of many towns has been striking: new theaters, concerts, and art galleries help to make life more exciting, and the influx of new populations has created a more open and varied society.

Thus, economically and socially, Italy has gone through a profound change. The percentage of those employed in industry and agriculture in Italy has decreased, while the tertiary sector has grown to include half the working population. The numerical importance of the working class is in diminution, and Italy is fast becoming a "post-industrial" society like other advanced Western countries. However, in Italy there remains the issue of an astronomical deficit, a very corrupt political class, and the problems associated with full participation in the E.U. Underneath all of these difficulties lies an even more serious obstacle to Italy's future success. It is an issue that differentiates Italy from every other European nation and we will deal with it in the following chapter.

Notes

1. Mark H. Lazerson, "Organizational Growth of Small Firms: An Outcome of Markets and Hierarchies?" *American Sociological Review* 53 (June 1988): 331.

2. Patrizio Bianchi and Giuseppina Gualtieri, "Emilia-Romagna and its Industrial Districts: The Evolution of a Model," in Robert Leonardi and Raffaella Y. Nanetti, eds., *The Regions and European Integration: The Case of Emilia-Romagna* (New York: Pinter, 1990), 83-108. See also Robert N. Putnam, *Making Democracy Work* (Princeton: Princeton U.P.), 159-162.

3. See especially Pyke, Becattini, and Sengenberger, eds., *Industrial Districts and Inter-firm Co-operation in Italy* (Geneva: International Institute for Labor Studies of the International Labor Organization, 1990).

4. "High Pay for a Short Week in Seven Industrialized Countries," *Italian Journal*, 6 no. 4 (1992): 57.

5. The establishment of the regions did not make the Italian system of government fully federal, for the constitutional and political status of the Italian regions is less autonomous than, for example, the American states or the German Lander.

6. Putnam, *Making Democracy Work*, 86-91.

Italians are masters in preserving antiquity while embracing modernity. Naples, for example, is experiencing a renaissance after years of decay. While new attractive buildings are being erected, old parts of the city, neglected for years, are being claimed as important cultural areas. Scores of neglected churches, museums, and palaces in dilapidated districts have been reopened and are attracting large numbers of visitors. The cultural renaissance not only has given Neapolitans the opportunity to rediscover their identity, but it has also made Naples one of the most attractive Italian cities again. Printed by courtesy of *America Oggi*.

VII

The Two Italies and the Southern Question

The South and its Representation as "Other"

The recent debate on the role of the South in the development of the Italian state and Italian society has tended to draw heavily, and indeed rhetorically, on a series of well-worn stereotypes that equate the South with forms of social and economic backwardness, delinquency, organized crime, and political corruption. The old resentments of the prosperous North toward the less developed South have acquired such dimensions as to generate concerns. Many northerners would like to think of themselves as being closer to the continent than to the peninsula: to France, which has had much influence in Piedmont; to Germany, through the old ties to the Austro-Hungarian Empire, which provided efficient administration for so long; and to Switzerland, to which many of those on the borders commute. They feel that the Southerners have ruined their dream of being the richest country in Europe. There is good reason to reflect, therefore, on the historical accuracy of these images, and indeed to look more closely at the assumptions that have equated the history of southern Italy over the last century with the southern problem.

We should start by asking what is meant by the South. The answer becomes problematic because the South cannot be easily defined in economic terms because there are no fixed boundaries. The boundaries of Bossi's North have shifted over time and include an area that has no historical precedent as a political entity. They include an imagined area that extends as far as wealth and supposedly perfect government extends, or where rising crime, Mafia, clientelism, and a disfunctioning state begin. Such a representation has found expression in wall graffiti slogans and journalistic and academic discourse, besides in heated political debates. Today's political and scholarly views of the South as a "problem," as if it were a colonial or underdeveloped country and was interpreted in terms of "backwardness" and "resistance" to modernization, have their roots in views that were first articulated at the birth of the nation.

In a very interesting and persuasive article entitled "A Word at War: The Italian Army and Brigandage 1860-1870," John Dickie claims that the South was transformed into an "Otherness" against which the new Italian state and society sought to define itself.[1] The "question of brigandage" in southern Italy during the most critical years of Italy's unification was identified with a "Southern Problem."

The brigand war lasted for about a decade, cost more lives than all the battles of unification put together, and at its peak required the deployment of about two-fifths of the effective strength of the Italian army. But some historians have raised a fundamental issue on the process of unification.

Was the South "liberated" or "annexed" and "subjugated"? In 1860, the lands belonging to the Kingdom of the Two Sicilies, which became part of the new united nation, were in a weak position and were obliged to measure themselves against cultural and economic models based on profoundly different societies. The South's identity was in fact based on negation, on what it lacked in relation to the ideal model as it was represented by the Kingdom of Piedmont. The ruling class of the North showed a total lack of understanding of the culture and institutions of the South in establishing its hegemony on the rest of the peninsula; any resistence was met with force. John Dickie claims, with a convincing argument, that the Piedmontese establishment was able to mold a very negative image of the South to consolidate its authority without conceding any social change.

We know that the main factors behind peasant unrest were economic hardship, the introduction of conscription, and the accumulated discontent caused by the erosion of collective land-use rights. In the period 1860-1864, large bands, often numbering in the hundreds and with varying degrees of legitimate support and motivation, attempted to spark popular uprising. In 1860-1861, particularly, some towns were briefly taken over by troops and national guard units. As the brutally repressive military measures to combat banditry took hold, there followed what has been seen as a slow but certain descent into simple crime, perpetrated by smaller groups, with at most only the trappings of political affiliation.

Many modern historians, in representing brigand and brigandage, mask or misrepresent peasant unrest and the strong element of social protest, but focus their attention on the criminality that tends to reflect the authorities' view of the phenomenon. The authorities certainly did not see the peasant revolts and the support given by the so-called bandits as a form of class mobilization, "the extreme, armed manifestation of a movement of revenge and protest which reaches the level of crude forms of class struggle."[2]

It should be remembered that the first historians of the conflict were almost all army officers who had fought in it. In the anti-brigand campaign, army officers and the government understood their opponent predominantly in the form of a series of hierarchical binary oppositions, such as between civilization and barbarism, reason and violence, social order and crime. A young officer writes to his father in November 1861: "The brigands are like the Arab Phoenix; everyone says they exist, no one knows where they are; and I am beginning to believe that their existence is only the product of the over-active imaginations of these people." Ethnocentric keywords such as "barbaric," "primitive," "irrational," and "violent" repeatedly color the perceptions of elites of the immediate post-unification period at moments when aspects of Southern society do not fit with the nation they projected.

Banditry had the entire repertoire of racist imagery used against it by the officers of the Italian army: bandits are black, animal, primitive, evil, perverse, irrational. In defining it this way, the Piedmontese establishment placed it beyond explanation in an imaginatively and emotively charged realm of monstrosity. The conceptualization of brigandage as an "Other" is set in the broader frame of an imaginative geography in which the Italian nation is constructed as the opposite of its South.

In the general process of nation-building, the South was postulated as an "Other"; it was used as a negative term of comparison, i.e., as representing those cultural and ethical traits—much nearer to the Arab than northern European countries. The more general perception of the region was as a foreign and barbaric land that the young nation should strive *not* to imitate. The South was a cauldron of images of the Mafia and Camorra; brigandage and feudalism; indolence, illiteracy, superstition, and magic; cannibalism and corruption; dirt and disease coupled with pastoral beauty and tranquility.

Perhaps the most frequently employed of the many ethnocentric parallels for Italy and the ex-Kingdom of the Two Sicilies is the familiar spatial and cultural opposition between Europe and Africa or the East. A government envoy writes to Cavour from Teano in 1860: "What barbarism! This isn't Italy! This is Africa: compared to these peasants the beduins are the flower of civilized virtues."[3] Nino Bixio, writing to his wife while working with the parliamentary commission of enquiry into brigandage, exclaims, "in short, this is a country that should be destroyed or at least depopulated and its inhabitants sent to Africa to get themselves civilized!"[4] Even Francesco Crispi, a national political figure by any standard, did not escape being compared to an Arab.

If banditry was constructed as the very antithesis of law, civilization, and reason, and as 'occult, invisible, secret,' and if it extended throughout the social fabric and even into the "instinct of the people," then to combat it the army must have an unrestricted mode of operation. The use of unconstitutional measures to combat it becomes not only justifiable but ethically imperative. And that is exactly the way the government allowed it to operate. Because of the social and political unrest, large parts of the South spent the first five years after incorporation into the new state under different forms of what was essentially a military regime. The use of summary execution and collective punishment began with the first entry of Piedmontese troops and the first signs of peasant unrest. A "state of siege," which was declared when Garibaldi landed in Calabria in August 1862, officially suspended constitutional guarantees and allowed the use of summary execution, detention without trial, collective punishment, special tribunals, and the widespread use of the death penalty.

In fighting brigandage, as an invisible "monstrosity," as an "Otherness," the government could go as far as to establish (through the approval of appropriate laws) that any band of three or more people caught in the countryside with arms of any kind (including agricultural tools) could be accused of brigandage. If one now tries just to visualize or imagine the kind of agrarian society that existed at that time, it is easy to understand how easy it was to accuse people of brigandage, and, therefore, to crush any social unrest. In this way, the social features of banditry could be intentionally wiped out. Thus the construction of the South, *Mezzogiorno*, as "Other" within an imagined nation, was the way it was incorporated into the Italian state.

In this context, it must also be said that at the time of unification, Italy was a mosaic of local communities, each surrounded by a symbolic boundary; however, whereas in the process of nation-building some community boundaries were de-emphasized, others were "forced" into becoming strong and discrete markers.

The issue of brigandage and the way it was treated by the political establishment sheds some new light on the understanding of how the "Questione del Mezzogiorno" came into being and how the South has been perceived almost exclusively in social and economic terms and as a problem. If everything in this reified South is related to brigandage, then brigandage becomes the key to understanding the South as a whole. Just as the army represents and embodies Italy, so brigandage is seen to embody the *Mezzogiorno*: brigandage comes to typify the *South*, becomes a metonym of it.

At the superficial level of the kind of images evoked, one can find the same ethnocentric themes across a century of Italian history. There is a relation between past and present moments of pervasive ethnocentrism toward the South. Today's perception of the South has its roots in the construction of the "Otherness" defined at the dawn of the nation. Indeed, references to the South are defined mostly as an Italian problem, a problem that emerges through the construction of the "Other." Even the rise of the Northern League and the League's attitudes toward the South are built on the concept of "Other." The League has managed to get people to think that national political and social problems are territorial, that is, coming from some "Other" place.

The wastefulness and degeneration of the Italian State can be selectively blamed on the presence of southern workers in state jobs, and on *assistenzialismo* and clientelism in the South, all of which are seen to contrast with the image of a widespread self-reliance in the North. Vague aspirations to a European identity can be seen simultaneously as a move away from "Africa"; as Bossi commented just after the general election of 1992: "The North has chosen federalism and Europe, the South has chosen Fascism and Africa." The ethnocentrism of *leghismo* is tied into an exclusive, centrifugal regionalism; it is a function of the construction of a regional political identity.

However, the Lega's technique of thinking of political problems in geographical and ethnic terms not only is not new, but it is not uniquely Italian. Stereotyping can tell us about regional and national identities, and about the anxieties, fears, and desires that are released into Italian culture when those identities seem uncertain. It could inform the models of the "collective psyche" which underlay political thinking; or provide an imaginative encapsulation of more articulated ideas; or merely give a polemical edge to an argument. There is also a theoretical necessity to the way we are bound to that which defines us through contrast: the more we loathe an "Other," the more we need that loathing. Therefore, for political geographic areas that would like to shape for themselves a new identity, the construction of a negative "Other," from which they want to separate, is very appealing. The South has been used as a powerfully charged emblem of threats and problems; rising crime, social decay, and the drug trade can be thought of as entirely the product of the Mafia.

In the same way, culture has been responsible for presenting the South as "Other," and has given political expression to ethnocentrism. In fact, it is important to note that southern intellectuals themselves appeared to accept and indeed concur in shaping those images of diversity. Thus, at a time when the process of nation-building was being defined in antithesis to social and cultural traits attributed to the South *en bloc*, Neapolitan culture was busy retreating into mythical and self-contained worlds, constructing its own positive stereotypes. One of the problems has been the difficulty of writers in rethinking Naples outside of its traditional image. This is a problem because it can only be through culture that the South can be freed of the endless images of abnormality and diversity under which it suffocates. The cultural concepts of *napoletanità* and *sicilianità*, and the concept of *meridionalismo,* which have supported for so long the myth of diversity, find their sustainment in this broad social and political base.

The representation of the South as a *national*, not a regional failure could help in the understanding of national problems. (Rosi's cinema used the South as a metaphor for problems in Italian society as a whole in *Salvatore Giuliano*; even Lampedusa, author of *The Leopard*, suggests that the *questione meridionale* is associated with the whole country).

But the risk is that the metaphor can be turned into a scapegoat—in other words, from the South as a symbol of social and political ills that characterize Italian society as a whole, to the South as a geographical area where such ills originate and are to be found. This degeneration of the South from metaphor of the nation to scapegoat for the nation parallels the degeneration of the South as "Other," which, from being seen as an integral part of the process of nation building, becomes the sick limb that needs to be cut off from the still healthy body. Paradoxically, the South is being demonized at a time when the South-as-metaphor is increasingly applicable to the North—when the myth of Milan as moral capital of Italy has been irrevocably destroyed, and systematic corruption and moral degeneration have been exposed as national rather than regional phenomena.

The images that identified the South with backwardness, barbarism, primitiveness, crime, and violence amount to no more than ill-informed and prejudiced northern perceptions, which in the last ten years have been a central target of a lively revisionist historiography. Some sociologists have focused on social constraints on growth. Carlo Triglia, for example, has recently reexamined Gramsci's insistence on the "disaggregation" of society in the South, to argue that the failure to develop forms of horizontal social mobilization comparable to the trade union and cooperative movements in northern Italy have been central barriers to economic growth and social change in the South. In the absence of alternative forms of collective organization, primary social institutions retained their primacy in ways that inhibited the emergence of small-scale entrepreneurship and encouraged the persistence of clientelist politics.[5]

The southern issue was taking shape also within the context of American aid to the war-torn economies of Europe. In Italy, U.S. influence was of considerable importance in the development of state intervention in the South. It operated at a theoretical level through the example of Roosevelt's "Development-areas" and in practice through the consultancy of American experts, on loan first to SVIMEZ (*Associazione per lo Sviluppo dell'Industria nel Mezzogiorno*) and then to the *Cassa per il Mezzogiorno*. We should point out that the South-North dualism was also reinforced especially by American scholars. Edward C. Banfield had a profound impact with his study in which he confirmed one of the many stereotypes about the *Mezzogiorno*: that of its immobility and exclusion from history. For Banfield, who spent several months in a small village of Basilicata in 1955, the backwardness of the South was explained by a "traditional" ethos, which he called "amoral familism."[6]

The term "amoral familism" designates a form of behavior directed solely toward the pursuit of the good of the family. It implies, therefore, an endemic inability to act for the common good—what is popularly called a lack of civic consciousness. It is often associated with centralized and authoritarian states that discourage the growth of intermediate institutions of government between state and citizens. In

Banfield's view, "amoral familism" was stripped of its descriptive and scientific content, and it came to mean simply the tendency of southerners to favor the family group; as such it was identified as one of the major causes of clientelism or patronage. In this way, the strength of the family was linked to the persistence of "tradition," and tradition, in turn, to the extended patriarchal and patrilinear families, which are dominated by the blood tie. In this reworking of Banfield's concept, southern society, already considered backward and traditional according to one powerful stereotype, now also becomes patriarchal. At the same time, this stereotyped perception has coincided with another, which is closer to Banfield's original idea: that of a fragmented South, lacking valid principles of social organization, dominated by extreme individualism, riven by the war of "all against all," incapable of creating permanent group identities—the South of the Mafia and competition over limited resources.

The history of the concept of amoral familism illustrates well the processes by which the image of the *Mezzogiorno* has been constructed. Both within the South and outside, the image of backwardness has been adopted. The falsity of the concept may be quickly detected when an identical phenomenon, the patriarchal family —commonly associated with underdevelopment—goes unnoticed if it relates to a society in the North. Thus the representation of patriarchal families in the Veneto or Tuscany are neutral facts not worthy of mention, while similar images referring to the South make a powerful impression on public opinion and confirm the mental model. It must also be underlined that the patriarchal family practically does not exist there; women have a "traditional" power there, which is unquestionably greater than that of other Italian women—division of wealth between the sexes according to an equitable method, careful protection of the dowry throughout a woman's life and its direct inheritance by the children, enormous moral and contractual power within the family, and so forth.

In the discussion of the conflict between North and South, it should also be pointed out that there is a considerable integration between the two areas: one need only consider all the intermarriage between northerners and southerners, the assimilation into the northern cities of several millions of southern migrants in the 1950s and 1960s, and the high number of southerners among the Italian ruling class (in Milan and Turin, for example, there is a substantial group of company directors who were born in the South and graduated there).

By switching the focus back to the internal as opposed to the external obstacles to development, the debate on the "social constraints" revives the earlier contrasts between endogenous and exogenous obstacles around which earlier debates on the southern problem revolved without reaching any clear conclusion. Banfield's less than happy concept of amoral familism has found a new energy, while recently the American political scientist Robert Putnam has revived the old argument that the divergence between North and South is rooted in the absence of a civic tradition in the South and has tried the breathe new life into a thesis of cultural determinism that extends from the Middle Ages to the present.[7]

While we demonstrated how the prejudices toward the South were first created, an attempt should also be made to explain some of the faulty ground on which the structural dualisms are built. The contrasts pay little attention to the positive models against which the South is generally depicted as a negative. Although the systematic study of Italian entrepreneurship has been relatively recent, some works have revealed the presence in Lombardy, Emilia Romagna, and the Veneto in the late nineteenth and early twentieth centuries of forms of entrepreneurship and economic innovation that bore little resemblance to the models of balanced social and economic growth against which the South is deemed to have failed. A steadily growing body of research provides examples that suggest that capitalist development and "modernization" in many parts of northern Italy was as 'unregulated' or "self-regulated" as in the South, and that neither the state nor collective social mobilization were significant intermediaries. Precisely those features that are often deemed peculiar to the South—the weakness of the state, the predominance of private over public power, the persistence of forms of paternalist social and economic organization, the juxtaposition of modern economic activity and "traditional" social structures—can be found in those parts of Lombardy, Emilia Romagna, and the Veneto that were leading Italy into the twentieth century. This is not to argue, of course, that there were no differences between North and South or that forms of social development were identical. It is rather to warn against easy generalization and to emphasize the need to take more careful account of the historic specificities of each case.

One of the major issues is that the South has consistently and repeatedly left itself exposed to exploitation. It seems that the southern elites failed to establish greater autonomy for their region and that made a difference. In fact, the contrast with the North is more strik-ing, and in comparison with the aggressively autonomous entrepre-neurs of Emilia Romagna and the Veneto their southern counterparts remained more closely dependent on the state and public administra-tion.[8] The explanation is that the vulnerability of the southern econo-mies made them more dependent on state intervention and that the bureaucratic state was an older historical reality in the South, whose importance grew in the nineteenth and twentieth centuries in direct proportion to the failure to develop more robust and spontaneous forms of economic growth. Very often the debate on the Southern Problem has hinged around the premise that the state was in some sense ab-sent in the *Mezzogiorno*. In reality, the case could probably be made much better for many parts of northern Italy. What distinguished the South was not an accident of geography or physical terrain, foreign occupation, or any other reason, but the historical evolution of the state in forms quite different from those of central and northern Italy. The reasons for this do not lie in the nature of the dynastic state in the South, which evolved with much greater difficulty toward a centralized bureaucratic state in the eighteenth and nineteenth centuries than its Piedmontese and Austrian counterparts, nor in any supposed lack of civic tradition. They are to be found in the precocious collapse of paternalism and deference in the South. It was the social tensions and conflicts that reached greater levels of intensity in the mainland South and in Sicily in the first half of the nineteenth century that drove the propertied classes to seek the protection of the state, and wherever possible to bring public authority into the sphere of private power. Although the League has argued for various forms of political separa-tion from the South, it still needs the South in the sense that it is dependent on the Otherness it projects onto the South to mobilize its supporters.

The Historical Division

The southern question has been exacerbated by the combined effects of the deep recession of the early 1990s and the liberalization of the Italian economy. Liberalization and privatization have resulted in the gradual termination of subsidies to state industry in the South, a drive to reform a welfare state that used disability pensions in the South to disguise long-term unemployment, and the winding up of the Fund for the South. Connected to these effects are increasing threats posed by organized crime in Naples (the *Camorra*), Calabria (*'Ndrangheta*),

Apulia (*Sacra Corona Unita*), and Sicily (*Mafia* and *Cosa Nostra*). The fact that the South is lagging so far behind the North needs additional explanation.

What is the South (*Sud, Mezzogiorno, Meridione*) in geographic terms anyhow? It is difficult to define because, as we have seen, it is much more than a geographical area; usually it is a metaphor that refers to an imaginary and mythical entity, associated with both hell and paradise. Since it is usually defined or molded through a comparison with the North by scientific paradigms and preexisting stereotypes, the boundaries that separate the two areas depend on how northerly one's vantage point may be.[9] The South cannot even be defined easily in economic terms because, as recent studies show, the area is not economically uniform or undifferentiated. If one accepts the well-established geographic division of Italy into three parts (North, Center, and South), the South includes the southern regions of the peninsula (Molise, Campania, Apulia, Basilicata, and Calabria) and the surrounding islands, including the two major islands (Sicily and Sardinia).

The South has a history markedly different from the North and the Center. It is a history not only of high culture and prosperity, but also of exploitation and poverty. It is often hard to realize how southern Italy was virtually part of Greece for hundreds of years before the Roman conquest. It was called *Magna Graecia,* and many Greek legends actually had their setting in southern Italy. Greek settlers built large urban centers and religious shrines and established a brilliant civilization. City states like Taras (now Taranto), Syracuse (Siracusa), and Akragas (now Agrigento) flourished. Many place names are of Greek origin, including Naples, derived from *Neapolis*, a Greek word literally meaning new city, and Gallipoli in southern Apulia. Pythagoras, Herodotus, Aeschylus, Euripides, and Plato visited at various times what is now called the *Mezzogiorno* in much the same way world artists visit Central Italy today. The philosopher Empedocles belonged to the ruling clan of Akragas. Archimedes, the greatest mathematician of antiquity, was a native of Syracuse. Some of the most splendid remains of Greek temples in the Mediterranean are in southern Italy: at Paestum, near Salerno; and at Agrigento, Syracuse, and Segesta, in Sicily. In Bova, a village in Calabria, the inhabitants speak a dialect based directly on ancient Greek.

In ancient times the South was the most prosperous part of the peninsula. Under Roman rule it became an expanse of enormous farming estates, the *latifundia*, where a slave population worked the soil, enabling the absentee landlords to regale themselves in Rome. Then came raids and invasions by Germanic tribes and centuries of domination by Byzantines and Arabs, and by Norman, German, French, and Spanish rule.

It was during the domination of the Normans, at the court of Frederick II, that the first Italian literary school, *La Scuola Siciliana* (the Sicilian School), started to produce a literature with a national character. The *Scuola Siciliana* preceded the well-recognized Tuscan school, *Il Dolce Stil Novo* (the Sweet New Style), by about half a century.

Refugees from other Mediterranean areas have also played a part in the southern culture. There are 26 Albanian villages that originated from Mehemet II's invasion of Albania after he had taken Constantinople in 1453.

Between the fifteenth century and the *Risorgimento* of the nineteenth century, the South was subjected to foreign rule and exploitation numerous times. Colonialism imposed a strong tradition of strict class structure that was reinforced by the presence of a powerful and oppressive feudal organization, which was abolished much later than those of other European countries, creating certain sociocultural barriers to development.

With the unification of Italy things did not improve. Count Camillo Benso di Cavour, the diplomatic architect of Italy's unification, was not interested in liberating the South or making it part of Italy. Since Garibaldi's march from the South made this an accomplished fact, Cavour did not have a choice in the matter. However, as prime minister of the Kingdom of Piedmont, Cavour never even bothered to visit the South.

Consequently, southerners quickly gained the feeling that they were not citizens of a new Italian state with the same rights and opportunities as the northerner, but instead had become subjects in a colony. The new institutions, laws, and economic policies were generally alien to the customs and contrary to the interests of the South. Taxes became ruinous, and the area's economic base was undermined, while the industrialization of the North perpetuated and even deepened the division. Some southern intellectuals did react persuasively to the damage that was being inflicted on the South.[10] The strongest defense of Southern interests came from Francesco Saverio Nitti. His theory was that Italian unification had been created at the South's expense, by squandering its immense financial resources and thus preventing it from developing independently through its own energies. He was convinced that the state had to intervene strongly with an industrial policy in order to compensate for the imbalance that had been created. Nothing happened. Economic conditions were so hard that in the 50 years before World War I, roughly half of the southern population—5 million people—emigrated.

The fascist regime contributed not only to halting political and economic development, but also to remodeling the image of the South on old stereotypes. In fact, despite some spotty reforms, under fascism the South was still regarded as a "no man's land" and it continued to lag behind. The fascist regime carried through some of the land reclamation projects they had devised, but instead of using them for a radical transformation of the South's industrial infrastructure, the land reclamation for the generation of energy and industrialization was transformed into land reclamation for ruralization. Whereas in the North the fascist regime played a modernizing role, in the South the message was populist and ruralist. During the economic crisis of the late 1920s, as had happened before in the history of the South, capital flowed back to the North, along with control of the economic system. The South's dependence on the North increased.

More evidence of how Mussolini regarded the South as a "no man's land" may be found in the fact that when fascist authorities wanted to dispose of "dangerous" individuals, they would exile them to the South. And it is from one of these experiences that while in Basilicata, writer Carlo Levi, wrote the stunning book, *Christ Stopped at Eboli* (1945), in which he represented the primitive society and pattern of life he found in a land that he felt Jesus had never touched. Another stunning representation of the precarious conditions of the southern peasants was given by Ignazio Silone in his novel *Fontamara* (1949):

> The same earth, the same rain, wind, the same feast days, the same food, the same poverty—a poverty inherited from our fathers, who had received it from their grandfathers, and against which honest work was of no avail. The life of men and beasts, and of the land itself, revolved in a closed circle. . . There has never been a way out. At that time, a man could perhaps save twenty or thirty *soldi* a month, and in summer perhaps even a hundred, so that by the autumn he had thirty *lire*. They disappeared at once—in interest on some loan, or to the doctor, the pharmacist or the priest. And so one began again, the next day. Twenty *soldi*, a hundred *soldi*.[11]

In the same book, Silone gave an ironic picture of the hierarchy of a region still pervaded by strong feudalism:

At the head of everything there's God, the master of Heaven.
That everyone knows.
    Then comes Prince Torlonia, the master of the land.
Then come the Prince's dogs.
Then come the Prince's guards.
Then nothing.
Then, still nothing.
Then come the *cafoni* (the peasants).
And that's about all. (p. 29)

Fontamara eloquently represents the hopeless world of the south-ern *cafoni. Cafone*, explained the author, means "flesh accustomed to suffer"(p. 43). Silone was well aware that the name *cafone*, in Italy, was an insult. "But I use it in this book in the certainty that when in my country suffering is no longer something to be ashamed of, it will become a title of respect, perhaps also of honor" (p. 6).

Works such as those above started to have a profound impact and started to generate debate on the theme of economic backwardness. Economists and sociologists were brought in to define the economic features of the South. The debate was about how to trigger development in a society that was considered to be still at zero. The South was once again a land without history, in a state of nature. Writings by Carlo Levi, Ernesto De Martino, and Rocco Scotellaro, although very different from one another, had in common the desire to interpret the popular culture of the South. The peasants of the South became a uniform category and were made into a symbol of a universal category of pain, suffering, and oppression. However, those studies were important attempts to understand a culture from within and restore a measure of dignity to it.

Some of postwar Italy's leading writers—Domenico Rea, Leonardo Sciascia, Saverio Strat—were also publishing eloquent novels on the plight of the South. These authors understood better, felt more deeply, and conveyed more powerfully than the politicians and anthropologists what life there was really like. In the mid-1950s, the national mood was ripe for change and the government had no choice but to act. The new republic undertook one of the largest and most ambitious regional development programs in western Europe to solve the southern question. It followed three courses of action: land reform, infrastructure development, and industrialization. The single most important institution to become involved in this process was the Fund for the South (*Cassa per il Mezzogiorno*), founded in 1950. Its main source of funding was state revenue, but it also drew on foreign loans.

Initially, the fund concentrated on infrastructure projects in agriculture, sanitation, and transportation; in 1957 the focus shifted to an effort to industrialize the South. That year the government approved legislation obliging state holding companies to locate a substantial share of new investment in the South and providing one of the most generous investment incentive packages in Western Europe.

State Intervention _To Help South

It is clear that images that identified the South with backwardness, barbarism, primitiveness, crime, and violence amounted to more than ill-informed and prejudiced northern perceptions. The negative stereotype has marked the divisive political and economic arguments of all the postwar period; the state developed its regional policy accepting the broad view generated by these faulty conceptions. However, the state has also solved many serious problems. By the early 1990s the state had poured into the *Mezzogiorno* an estimated $150 billion of public funds. Approximately two-fifths of this expenditure went to public works, the remainder being allocated primarily to investments in agriculture, industry, and tourism. As a result, thousands of miles of new streets and hundreds of bridges, many new schools, universities, and hospitals, and a network of modern hotels, restaurants, and service stations were built. Running water, electricity, and telephone service were brought to even the smallest hamlet; and a few large, new industries, like the Taranto steel mills and the petrochemical complexes at Brindisi and on Sicily's east coast, were built. Infant mortality declined by three-quarters, and illiteracy among youngsters has been practically eradicated as well, and while the overall character of the South has remained rural, its principal cities have greatly expanded. Their historic cores are now surrounded by vast belts of condominiums and new housing projects. The countryside is also full of elegant new housing.

Surprisingly, however, the economic gap between the *Mezzogiorno* and prosperous northern and central Italy continued to widen. By the early 1990s the South—an area the size of Greece, with 40% of Italy's land area and 30% of its population—accounted for only 20% of its GDP, and has an official unemployment rate of nearly 20% of the labor force, against 5% in the North. The per capita income in southern Italy was still barely 60% of the average in the rest of Italy, while the per capita income was more than 80% in the North.[12]

Modernization Without Economic Growth

No one denies that the southern development, despite a number of isolated successes, fell short of all its original expectations and goals. Economists and political scientists have given many possible reasons:

1. Physical disadvantages of the South, including distance from markets, unfavorable terrain, and lack of natural resources;
2. Misguided government policies;
3. A culture of patron-clientelism.[13]
4. Lack of civic traditions.

It would be safe to say that throughout the 1950s the South was not conceived of as a center of industrialization and that the new government had planned to continue the same policy of the prewar governments, that is, to keep the South agricultural.

The first attempt to institute reforms came as a consequence of the 1949 southern peasants' takeover of some of the *latifondi*, or large estates. At that time over half the population of the South—compared to a third in the rest of Italy—earned its livelihood from the soil as small holders, tenant farmers, or day laborers. These peasants barely made a subsistence living. In the face of the spreading discontent, the government enacted a modest land reform program in 1950 to buy-out some large estates and sell the land to the peasants. During the first dozen years, from 1950 on, the government, through the *Cassa per il Mezzogiorno,* concentrated its efforts and roughly 78% of its money on agriculture, with most of the remainder going to related infrastructure. Land reclamation, construction of dams, irrigation, aqueducts, and a vast extension of the road network gradually changed the face of the South. Technical experts introduced new farming and marketing methods. Malaria, which had afflicted the fertile lowlands in many parts of the South, was finally eradicated. State intervention contributed to the end of the *latifundia* system and the birth of a new small-scale peasantry.

However, when the program was largely completed in 1962, a mere 1.5 million acres had been transferred to some 85,000 peasants. For many, especially in the mountainous areas, the redistribution amounted to no more than a small plot of poor soil, insufficient to maintain a family. In the South as a whole, land holdings—half the average size of those in other Common Market countries—were too small to achieve fully modern and low-cost production. The real income of the average farmer did not increase much. As a consequence, in the course of the postwar years the share of those employed in agriculture in the South declined from 57 to 27% of the workforce. Soon enough it became clear that efforts to improve agriculture had not reduced unemployment, raised incomes, or narrowed the overall gap between the South and the rest of Italy. So the flight from the land intensified. Tens of thousands continued to leave the farms and poured into the labor market in the cities both in the South and the North. As in the previous hundred years, state intervention in the South was subordinated to the interest of the industrial economic groups.

In fact, the massive migration from the South, which could supply cheap labor for the North, was not the result of "natural" causes, but it was politically determined. Angelo Costa, President of the Italian Employers' Confederation (the *Confindustria*), in the course of an investigation conducted by the government explained that he thought that the adoption of policies for the localization of industry along the UK model would be detrimental to the Italian economy. He asserted that it would be preferable to "move people" rather than things.[14] In other words, Costa was in favor of internal migration rather than the location of industry in the South. This implied that the role of the South in postwar reconstruction would have to be that of providing the northern industries with a necessary supply of low-cost labor. The development of the North was thus financed by the systematic drainage of the South's sole resource: human labor. In exchange, the South was given a constant stream of state funds. This policy was spearheaded by the *D.C.* because, through the process, it could establish a strong patronage system and would have underpinned the stability of its regime. The christian democrats followed the plan outlined by Costa, who accepted the need for public works programs in the South provided that the wages in the southern public-sector programs would be less than wages in the industrial northern sector in order not to compete for labor with private industry. Thus, there was a conscious political decision to intervene where private industry is reluctant to intervene and to do so on the basis of a low-wage policy.

Costa's plan of assuring cheap southern labor for the North was sustained by a consciousness that the southern Italians, unlike workers in other underdeveloped countries, had a cultural level, however low it might appear to some, already structured by the ethics and the mentality of the technological world. It is this cultural aspect that permitted the transformation of the southern peasant into a high-productivity, assembly-line proletarian in a couple of weeks, whereas such a transformation is unthinkable in a similar space of time in the majority of underdeveloped countries.[15] Thus government policy protected a section of the southern population and more or less forced the rest to seek a life away from the land.

The agrarian reform and the creation of the *Cassa per il Mezzogiorno*, while intended to restrict the numbers of absentee landlords, created a large class of small land-owning peasants and united them in a political bloc that stopped the communist advance in the South. However, it would be difficult to demonstrate that the nonindustrialization of the South was part of a political design to keep the conservative land-owning peasants from becoming progressive urban proletarians—the great majority of southerners who became northern factory workers became communists.

When the agrarian reform began to be criticized for its failures, the *Cassa* embarked on large-scale projects to create infrastructures. The strategy of public works programs, which was in the hands of the *Cassa* and other state agencies, was meant to consolidate the infrastructures, strengthen the agricultural sector, and develop tourism. State intervention could be accepted by the North because it developed a market in the South for northern produce without increasing the competitiveness of southern industry. It obtained the favor of southern political and business leaders because it helped to expand the building industry, sustained a vast network of small peasant properties, and created a sector of dependent public employees. In fact, through the development of the state sector, a large class of white-collar workers was also created, which with time became a clientele system for the leading party of government, the *D.C.*[16] However, in reality, government action in the South helped the North more than it did the South: first, by increasing southerners' income through a public works program, it expanded the market for northern industry; second, the monies spent on the infrastructure, e.g., highways, helped northern industries both directly and indirectly.[17] Moreover, in the process, the *Cassa* programs also created a sector of marginalized workers who were marginally trained. Those who had left their land to work in one of the *Cassa* projects could not return to it when the project was terminated; they, too, had to move farther North. The massive decrease in employment in agriculture was partly caused by the change in emphasis in the direction of state intervention in the agricultural sector. This became clearer with the second *Green Plan* (1966): small farmers were discouraged and public intervention went increasingly toward electrification and irrigation projects that were meant to favor existing entrepreneurs in rural areas rather than the marginal farmer.[18]

Many experts had insisted all along that only rapid industrial development would create the jobs and prosperity needed to break the vicious cycle of unemployment and poverty. Put simply, industry was to be moved to the area of surplus labor rather than labor's moving to the area of industrial activity. The shift of state investment funds from agriculture to industry would have paved the way for a serious attempt at industrialization of the South.

The *Cassa*'s spending on infrastructure was therefore cut from 42% in 1957 to 13% in 1965, while assistance to industrial enterprises was stepped up from 48% to 82%. To encourage private investment, the government offered generous credits and tax incentives. It also required the state holding companies *IRI* and *ENI* to invest increasing amounts of capital in the South. *IRI*, the major investor, injected over $20 billion into the South between 1963 and 1978.

The industrial policy for the South had two political motivations: first, to enable local entrepreneurs to become full-fledged industrialists instead of remaining craftsmen or farmers; second, to attract northern investment. The state intervened with large public projects through its enterprises: *Istituto per la Ricostruzione Industriale* (*IRI*) established giant steelworks near Taranto while *Ente Nazionale Idrocarburi* (*ENI*) located large petroleum refineries in Sicily. In this way a steel industry (at one time the most modern in Europe) at Taranto, an Alfa Romeo plant near Naples, and giant petrochemical factories in Sicily and Sardinia were created. The volume of industrial development in the South during this period was remarkable.

However, even though some of these investments were productive and profitable, the all-out heavy industrialization program did not turn out to be the magic solution to the South's problems. The new industries were not labor intensive and created relatively few jobs. The managerial and technical personnel were recruited from the North and later returned there, leaving the South without an indigenous managerial and technical class. And the industries themselves were subsidiaries of northern companies that never developed links to the local economy. These large-scale, technologically advanced plants had no connection with the rest of the southern economy. They were a sort of colonial enclave with little if any contact with the small local firms. They did not generate ancillary small and medium-sized enterprises in their areas; on the contrary, they maintained a direct connection with the North. Moreover, the *Cassa* began to finance basic large-scale enterprises, both private and public: electricity, steel, paper, chemical, gas—all industries that are fairly capital intensive but which contribute little to employment.[19] Italians speak of the solitary industrial giants in the South as their *cathedrals in the desert*. Some factories in the South were apparently built only to collect the state subsidies for economic development in the region. Furthermore, many firms from the North were able to obtain considerable funds from the state in the form of subsidies, low-interest or interest-free loans, as well as direct grants as a part of invested capital. Consequently, the cost of the *Cassa* often went back to the North. Northern firms got subsidies for starting-up factories in the South and then went bankrupt and re-exported their machinery to the North. One example southerners frequently cite is the Taranto steelworks, where all the overalls used were imported from the North and paid for by government subsidies which should have gone to the South. Or the firm that went down to Maratea, in the Calabria region, bringing its old machinery, and then starting a new factory in the North by purchasing new equipment with its government subsidies.

Often these new southern industries could not compete in the international market or withstand changes in economic trends. The steel plants at Taranto and Naples-Bagnoli were dragged down by the decline of the entire European steel industry in the 1970s. The huge petrochemical plants on the coasts of Sicily and Sardinia were based on cheap petroleum supplies; after the price increase in 1973, they, too, failed.

Overall, by 1980, the old South had changed. About 2,400 new factories employing over 305,000 persons had settled in designated industrial estates. However, new industrial jobs were concentrated in a limited number of sectors; 73% of southern factory employment in 1980 was in the chemical, mechanical, or metallurgical industries. Most of the firms in these sectors were large, state-controlled, capital-intensive units. In 1982, *IRI* accounted for 52.5% of employment in southern manufacturing plants having over 1,000 workers. Other state holding companies represented another 11.5% of employment compared with 36% for the private sector.

However, at the beginning of the 1980s a continuing problem was the fact that industrial development in the South was confined to specific geographic regions as well. The bulk of development was concentrated in three main areas: Naples and its neighboring provinces, the Bari-Brindisi-Taranto triangle, and the Syracuse-Augusta axis of eastern Sicily. Eighty percent of the funding of the *Cassa* went to only four regions—Apulia, Sardinia, Sicily, and Campania. Spending was also extremely concentrated within the regions. For example, two-thirds of the Apulia investments were directed to Taranto.

The government had enacted laws in 1971 and 1976 requiring the *Cassa* to concentrate on a new range of intersectorial and interregional projects. These included the further development of industrial infrastructure, the exploitation of natural resources, social projects in metropolitan areas, water-reclamation projects, cleaning the Gulf of Naples, extending the road network into remote mountainous areas, reforestation, and promotion of citrus fruit production. Many of these programs had to be scaled down or scrapped as a result of the economic crisis following the oil price increase after 1973. Some of them were gigantic fiascos.

Emphasis then shifted to the selective encouragement of small and medium-sized firms, which in the early 1980s accounted for over 90% of the projects and 85% of the investment of the *Cassa*. Unfortunately, this has met with limited success. Only Abruzzi and Apulia have witnessed the growth of a dynamic sector of small firms similar to those that have developed in northeastern and central Italy.

As a result, the private investment that was to follow the development initiated by the state never came. Private investors had to cope with the so-called southern Italian risk, that is, worker absenteeism, low productivity, labor unrest, and low labor mobility. A concrete example of such "risk" was the Alfa Romeo plant constructed near Naples in 1972. It was so afflicted by labor strife and absenteeism that it ran up losses of $700 million, which had to be covered by the parent company in the North. For many years, every "Alfa Sud" car on the road was sold at less than its production cost.

Potential investors, Italian and foreign, consequently often decided that the South was too great a hazard, and in fact, in the late 1970s and 1980s there was a net decline in foreign companies investing in the South. Even the investment that did occur in the South did not do much to reduce unemployment because industrialization and employment were not entirely compatible goals. This problem was typically faced through the expansion of the bureaucracy and of the public purse.

Development had been the victim of bad planning, bad economics, and above all, bad politics. The emphasis shifted from agriculture to infrastructure development, to large industry, to small and medium-sized industry, and back to agriculture. The whole development process went ahead, Gianni Agnelli, president of FIAT, remarked at a conference of southern experts in 1980, either in "the good faith of error" or in "the bad faith of political 'necessity.'"

By becoming an employer even in the industrial sector, the government entered into a compromise with the social groups by establishing clientele relations. Through the development of the state sector, a large class of white-collar workers was also created. This class owed its existence to the *D.C.,* but did not—as in other countries—appear to be the natural consequence of economic development.

The diminution of employment on the land and the relative failure to industrialize the South brought about a considerable expansion of a protected sector in the economy of the South: a sector where the state played the leading role through direct use of public spending. This was achieved through a kind of welfare assistance: pension and disability policy and again through the expansion of the bureaucracy. Disablement pensions increased at a phenomenal rate in the mid 1960s. Unlike old-age pensions, disablement pensions depend on "subjective" factors, such as a certificate from a compliant doctor who is employed by the pension fund that is controlled by the small farmers and is funded by the state. By 1974 the pension funds paid disability pensions to nearly 1.5 million small farmers as compared to 625,000 for old-age pensions. Fifteen to seventeen million welfare benefits and pensions, in a population of 57 million, were paid out mainly to southerners.

The South did not derive any particular benefit from the effects of the decentralization of production toward the hidden sector, which permitted Italy to achieve a growth rate higher than most industrial nations in the early 1980s. The small and medium-sized firms of the hidden sector were located, on the whole, in the Center and in the North, with very few in the South. Therefore, when the larger firms, both public and private, decreased the rate of growth of their investments, the South was hit harder. The state resources that could have been used otherwise had to be directed toward enabling existing firms to pay their debts or reorganize existing plants.

The distinction of the South from the North must be found in the historical evolution of the state. The social tensions and conflicts that reached greater levels of intensity in the mainland South and Sicily in the first half of the nineteenth century and drove the propertied classes to seek protection from the state, and wherever possible to bring public authority into the sphere of private power, had a lasting impact. The social unrest of the 1860s reconsolidated the view of the need for strong government control that persisted into the twentieth century.

But the South suffers mainly because of its own faults. The southern elites have failed to establish greater autonomy. Because of the vulnerability of the southern economies, the South remained more dependent on state intervention. In contrast to northern and central Italy, the bureaucratic state was an older historical reality in the South, whose importance grew in direct proportion to the failure to develop more robust and spontaneous forms of economic growth. In the *Mezzogiorno*, the observation made by Pasquale Villari in 1883—"One feels too much the 'I' and too little the 'we'"—is still valid.[20] Civic traditions and civic engagement alone do not account for the big difference between North and South, but their weak presence in the South has made a profound difference. Civic traditions help explain why the North has been able to respond to the challenges and opportunities of the twentieth century so much more effectively than the South.[21] The most relevant distinction is not even between the presence and absence of social bonds, but rather between horizontal bonds of mutual solidarity and vertical bonds of dependency and exploitation. The southerner has sought refuge in vertical bonds of patronage and clientelism, employed for both economic and political ends.

Let's not Despair

The future of the South lies in its ability to become a mature civic society and in the prospect of seeing the young generation fully integrated into a productive Italy and Europe. The Italian government has finally undertaken a serious effort in this direction without placing politics as the first item on the agenda. In order to create entrepreneurs in the new generation of the South, under a 1986 law, the government established the *Committee for the Development of Young Entrepreneurs in the* Mezzogiorno. The financial assistance provided for under the law is aimed only at residents of the *Mezzogiorno* under age 29, which also happen to be the largest unemployed age group. In spite of limited financial and human resources, the Committee has shown that it is possible for a state agency to help train skilled, young entrepreneurs even in the *Mezzogiorno*. The task of the Committee is to assist young people with good ideas and imagination who do not have the necessary capital and structures to back them up.

The Committee has won its gamble on creating young entrepreneurs in the South thanks in part to the support systems, which are tailor-made for each of the new enterprises. The new business is accompanied during its first year of activity by another company, a tutor (Isvor-Fiat, Hewlett Packard, Ferrero, Elea-Olivetti, Enidata, to name a few), which helps it to overcome the thousands of obstacles a novice may otherwise stumble over. The relationship between the Committee and the tutor is formalized only after this teacher-company has presented a valid plan of action. This plan must mainly diagnose what is needed to launch and then nurture the new venture. The tutor pays for the study out of its own pocket, and in some cases it does not bear fruit if the Committee judges the proposals inadequate. If the tutor's plan is accepted, the tutor goes to work and is bound by contract to make a report every three months on the work accomplished. To the recipients of the Committee's financial aid, the term "advance payment" is unknown. They receive the state's money only after the person in charge of the project has demonstrated to have truly done what was stated in the project. However, once the go-ahead is given, they receive the financing in a short time, approximately 76 days.

Over $40 million were approved for this training. By mid 1991, the project had funded over $15 million in investments and created 13,000 jobs. There are already over 350 companies open for business, 650 projects have been approved, and another 450 are presently under evaluation. The experiment shows that young entrepreneurs can actually be created in the *Mezzogiorno* and that the suspicions about the lack of professional training available and the impossibility of overcoming obstacles with initiatives funded through state agencies are not necessarily true.

Southern Italians have demonstrated their competence in many fields throughout the history of modern Italy. They make shrewd lawyers, able administrators, sharp police investigators, and consummate diplomats; they excel in philosophical speculations or mathematical theory. The plays and novels of Luigi Pirandello, Nobel Prize–winner for literature (1934), provide penetrating psychological insights into the South.

Beyond any doubt the South has been transformed and the social changes are very striking. The *Mezzogiorno* is no longer isolated;

southerners have gradually gone through a process of "Americaniza-tion" or modernization. Their outlook and mores—the secularization, the standards of consumer society, with all its defects, and the social values—have come close to those of the northerners. The South is now linked to the rest of Italy not only through radio and television, but also through one of the most advanced networks of roads and highways in Europe and a web of economic relationships.

Thus, in the 1990s, the southern question is not a matter of simple modernization, or of an increase of state funds. It cannot be addressed by pointing fingers at southern shame or northern guilt. The "prob-lem of the South" cannot even be understood purely in terms of the Italian North, but must be thought of anew in terms of the relations between Italy and the rest of the EU and the Mediterranean.

So, we are left with two final questions: (a) whether it is possible to free the South of all metaphors of evil and Otherness, from the ste-reotypes, both positive and negative, endogenous and exogenous, which are contributing to its increasing isolation; and (b) what, if any, is the real identity of the South and who should carry out such a complex cultural and ethical project.

Notes

1. John Dickie, "A World at War: The Italian Army and Brigandage 1860-1870," *History Workshop Journal* 33 (1992): 1-24.

2. Franco Molfese, *Storia del brigantaggio dopo l'Unità* (Milan: Feltrinelli, 1964), 342.

3. In Camillo Cavour, *Carteggi: La liberazione del Mezzogiorno e la formazione del Regno d'Italia*, vol. 3 (Oct.-Nov. 1860) (Bologna: Zanichelli, 1952); letter from Farini dated 27 October 1860, p. 208.

4. *Epistolario di Nino Bixio*, vol. II (1861-1865) (Rome: Vittoriano, 1942); letter dated 18 February 1863, p. 143.

5. Carlo Triglia, *Sviluppo senza autonomia* (Bologna: Il Mulino, 1992).

6. Edward C. Banfield, *The Moral Basis of a Backward Society* (Glencoe, Ill.: The Free Press, 1958).

7. Robert D. Putnam, *Making Democracy Work. Civic Traditions in Modern Italy* (Princeton, N.J.: Princeton U.P., 1993).

8. F. Barbagallo, "Il Mezzogiorno come problema attuale," *Studi Storici* 31 (1990): 587-89.

9. Some of the Lega representatives have sought to explain what the North is by reference to ancient invasion by northern peoples or to a mixture of historical and ethnic traits that produce a "non-Mediterranean" mentality. It is, however, a well-accepted fact that the most politically significant aspect of the imagined North is the hostile forces seen to lie beyond it.

10. A few southern economists dissented from the northerners' view of the South and put forward alternative interpretations and solutions. Napoleone Colajanni, for example, argued that it was precisely the supremacy of the bureaucracy, an uncontrolled power, that generated corruption. He criticized what he defined as "fiscal inequality," and claimed it was caused by the state, which "because of its absurdly centralized organization, acts on the periphery like a suction pump, which only returns a tiny part of what it absorbs." *In Sicilia* (Rome, 1894), 42. Gaetano Salvemini (a federalist) and Guido Dorso (an autonomist) were both convinced that the South could only reassert itself by being autonomous from central government, and it was the duty of political activists to make sure that the southern upper and middle classes would push for progress. These classes had the extremely important historical task of completing the "unfinished revolution of the Risorgimento" and thus of bringing about a real unification of the country, one which involved the mass of the people.

11.   *Fontamara* (Milan: Mondadori, 1974), 7-8.

12.   In a European contest, if the average GDP in the European Union in 1991 equaled 100, the GDP of northern and central Italy was 122, that of the South, 68.9. Indeed, northern and central Italy had a higher per capita GDP than Germany (113.8), France (108.9), and the UK (106.3). In the same year, if the South received 53% of the capital transfers from the Italian state, it only paid 20% of the national direct tax revenue, 29% of all indirect revenue, and 16% of national social security contributions.

13.   Robert N. Putnam, *Making Democracy Work*, 158-159. For a good assessment also read Gianni Toniolo, *An Economic History of Liberal Italy: 1850-1918*, trans. Maria Rees (New York: Routledge, 1990); Vera Zamagni, *Industrializzazione e squilibri regionali in Italia: Bilancio dell'età giolittiana* (Bologna: Il Mulino, 1978).

14.   In L. Villari, ed., *Il capitalismo italiano del Novecento*, vol. 2 (Bari: Laterza, 1975), 486-87.

15.   Marcello De Cecco, "Lo sviluppo dell'economia italiana e la sua collo cazione internazionale," *Rivista Internazionale di Scienze Economiche e Commerciali*, October 1971, 982.

16.   Mariano D'Antonio, *Sviluppo e crisi del capitalismo italiano 1951-1972* (Bari: De Donato, 1973), 236.

17.   Guido Fabiani, "Agricoltura e Mezzogiorno," in *AA. VV. Lezioni di economia. Aspetti e problemi dello sviluppo economico italiano e dell'attuale crisi internazionale* (Milan: Feltrinelli, 1977), 158.

18.   Giuliano Amato, *Economia, politica e istituzioni in Italia* (Bologna: Il Mulino 1976), 52.

19.   Vittorio Valli, *L'economia e la politica economica italiana* (Milan: Etas Libri, 1979), 107.

20.   Cited in Tullio Altan, *La nostra Italia*, 13.

21.   For a convincing argument see Robert N. Putnam, *Making Democracy Work*, especially chapters 5 and 6.

Italy is facing a brand new problem: immigration. A flood of over a million immigrants in the last decade is producing radical tensions that Italy never knew. In March of 1991, nearly 24,000 Albanians arrived at the port of Brindisi in the southern region of Apulia. Many Italians fear that the thousands coming from Albania, Morocco, Algeria, Somalia, and the former Yugoslavia may be just the forerunners of waves of wildcat immigration from less prosperous nations. Printed by courtesy of *America Oggi.*

VIII

Emigration, Migration, Immigration, and Social Transformation

In Search of a Better Life

A complete knowledge of the development of postwar Italy is not possible without an understanding of the significant demographic changes that have occurred through emigration, internal migration, return migration, and immigration into the country.

Because Italy in the mid 1950s was still, in many respects, an underdeveloped country, Italians, mainly from the South, were still emigrating by the thousands in search of a better life. Emigration was still a way of life for many, just as it had been for the previous three or four generations. Naturally this had a profound impact on the economy of large areas of the country, on family life and structure, and caused the socio-transformation of many villages and small towns.

Migration has been massive and it has not been unidirectional. The currents have flowed overseas, within Europe, from southern to northern Italy, from poorer rural areas to richer rural areas and/or to cities, and back home from abroad. But the primary motives for migration have always been economic and social: poverty, unemployment, and the quest for land.

The invention of the steamship certainly gave impetus to the movement across the ocean and made emigration a big business. Agents acting on behalf of steamship companies or foreign employers were eager to enlist laborers because they were getting a cut per head. Moreover, the small-town "political class" had a vested interest in emigration because it was an important unofficial source of income.

Lawyers, teachers, politicians, and travel agents were all involved in arranging for passports, booking the passages, lending the money for the fares (often at usurious rates), and finally selling off the peasants' land and houses. Such "businessmen" were often not much more than venal speculators and traffickers in human flesh. By the 1890s, the southern middle class was busy enrolling peasants, hiring ships, and making money on those whom it had previously been exploiting the most. Sometimes it even managed to export its social dominance across the Atlantic, to reappear in America as "bossism."

For millions of Italians, especially from the South, America, as a dream land, offered hope for a better future. The Italians who immigrated into America took pick-and-shovel jobs, entered the building trades, provided manpower for the waterfronts, and worked for municipal sanitation departments. Some managed to scrape together enough money to open small restaurants or groceries. The women became seamstresses in the sweatshops and factories of the garment industry.

Many who had left their families behind dreamed of going back to the old village one day to buy a piece of land that would give them independence. Quite a few did go back, sometimes 20 or more years later, when the children they had last seen as infants were adults. Most, however, changed their minds and had their wives and children join them. Although the bulk of them were originally from rural areas, in the U.S. they tended to cluster in cities and suburbs, forming "little Italies"; this kind of relocation, of course, caused problems for those who did attempt to reestablish their roots back in Italy.

Many of the immigrants from the South were virtually illiterate, and the country's cultural heritage had no meaning for them. In a sense, many of them had left Italy before becoming Italians. If this situation was contributing to a negative impression of Italians, it did not really matter to the United States because the growing country needed large numbers of sturdy laborers for the heavy construction work. And the southern Italians played a key role in building America, for they dug the ditches, toiled in the mines, laid the rails, and carried the bricks and mortar. They tacitly gave their sweat and blood in laying the material foundations of America.

Those Italians who stayed home generally welcomed the exodus because it was seen as a remedy to social problems. In the 1890s, Prime Minister Francesco Nitti described emigration as a "powerful safety-valve against class hatred." Sidney Sonnino, another prime minister of the exodus period, maintained that to prevent emigration would be a clear attack on the poor. Nevertheless, emigration was controlled in some areas of the South where the big landowners controlled local government and wanted to preserve the system of exploitation. There were others who were opposed to emigration because of the way emigrants were being treated abroad or because of the impact that emigration was having on family structure. Edmondo De Amicis (1846-1908), a socialist, aroused much indignation by representing emigration as shameful in the account he gave in a very moving book, *Sull'oceano* (*On the Ocean*, 1889). The Catholic Church was also not supportive of emigration because of the effect it had on family life (families were split for many years and very often were never reunited) and on religious belief (thousands of emigrants to America became Protestants, often Pentacostalists). In fact, Protestant groups actively conducted missions in an effort to convert Italians. At one time there were almost 300 Italian Protestant missionaries engaged in full-time work. Prominent figures like Leonard Covello, Fiorello La Guardia, Ferdinand Pecora, and Charles Poletti were Protestants.

Nationalists were also opposed to emigration because they worried that Italy was losing too many of her potential soldiers; they believed that southern overpopulation should have been remedied by colonies in Africa, not through emigration to America. Thus, after 1907 the debate on emigration gradually changed and was combined with imperialistic ideas. In the 1930s, stories about America in the depths of the Depression certainly weren't favorable to emigration, and the fascist regime also did its best to keep people at home by making emigration regulations more bureaucratic. Mussolini wanted to build up the male population to fight his wars and had to increase the overall population to justify his colonial expansion and his imperialistic dreams. The "great safety valve" had suddenly been shut. Not only was emigration discouraged, but during the Depression Mussolini was sending ships to New York to pick up any Italian who wanted to return to Italy. Depressing accounts of those Italians who came back thinking to escape the American Depression are given in novels mentioned earlier, *Cristo si è fermato ad Eboli* (*Christ stopped at Eboli*, 1945) by Carlo Levi and *Fontamara*, 1933, by Ignazio Silone.

Postwar Rural Exodus

After World War II the exodus resumed, especially from the South. And it was again a consequence of deep disillusionment, and this time probably also of impatience.

In the 1951 census, agriculture was still by far the largest single sector of employment; it accounted for 42.2% of the working population nationwide, including 56.9% for the South. But the agriculture was still rudimentary and the livelihood it provided, especially in the South, was still very poor: in 1950 the income per capita was about 60% that of 1924! Emigration was again an escape from the crushing poverty; however, now it took different forms; people left the countryside by the thousands but most of them remained in Europe.

Between 1951 and 1961, about 1.75 million people left the South; this increased to 2.3 million in the following 10 years. These are net figures and do not include seasonal workers. The figures of total emigrants that include those who returned to the home areas are understandably much higher: 7.5 million emigrated from 1946 to 1976 (net emigration of 3.5 million).

Because of the full awareness of their social situation and the prospect of better conditions in the urban industrial world, farmers flooded the cities of their own country. Those who were more adventurous and could not be absorbed by the expanding Italian economy went abroad. One shocking statistic is that Italy is the only country of the advanced industrial world that suffered massive emigration while sustaining rapid economic growth.

The most dramatic form of emigration was overseas, to the Americas and Australia. Between 1946 and 1957 the numbers of those leaving Italy for the New World exceeded by 1,100,000 the number of those returning: 380,000 had remained in Argentina, 166,500 in Canada, 166,000 in the U.S., 138,000 in Australia, and 128,000 in Venezuela. They were for the most part artisans and peasant proprietors rather than landless laborers; nearly 70% were from the South.

Initially (1946-1954) there was a certain balance between emigration toward other European countries and that directed toward other continents, but after 1955 Italian emigration was essentially European.

Emigration to Western Europe

In a silent mass migration that made no headlines either at home or abroad, six million southern Italians—nearly one-third of the population of the *Mezzogiorno*— moved northward. Between 1946 and 1957 the numbers heading to northern Europe exceeded by 840,000 the numbers of those who came back: France took in 381,000, followed by Switzerland with 202,000, and Belgium with 159,000. The emigrants to these countries tended to go for short periods, six-month or one-year contracts, and regarded work abroad as a temporary rather than a permanent solution to their problems.

After 1955, emigration from the rural South was directed both toward countries of Western Europe and to urban areas of northern Italy, which by now had taken their place among the world's advanced industrial centers. The movement became easier in 1968, when citizens of the EC were given the right to free movement within EC boundaries; however, migration to Europe had already peaked in 1961. In northern Europe, the emigrants provided manpower for large and small industries, went down into coal mines, worked as ditch-diggers and bricklayers, as hotel maids and waiters, as cooks and dishwashers. Many made good quickly and became foremen in factories and construction firms, or opened their own pizzerias or restaurants.

This export of labor continued until 1973. In that year, for the first time in the history of modern Italy, more Italians returned home than left: between 1973 and 1978 the "balance of labor" showed a gain of nearly 68,000 people.[1] In fact, starting in the early 1970s and until 1981, repatriation was proceeding at a higher level than emigration. The return of Italian emigrants was mainly due to the international economic crisis that hit construction and manufacturing, particularly assembly-line work in the car sector. This led countries such as West Germany to "unload" some of its surplus laborers by sending them back.[2]

The emigration to Western Europe is notable for some peculiar features. Not only were emigrants disposed of like any other surplus goods, but the host countries had saved all the expense of educating the imported workers and providing social assistance for their families. Since many came when they were young and able-bodied and without their families, they saved the host country expenses associated with schooling, pensions, health services, etc. In other words, foreign workers were putting into the economy far more than they were getting out of it in terms of social services.[3]

Migration and Regional Identities

During the period of the "economic miracle," many southerners migrated to the north of Italy. This internal Italian migration acquired, from the very beginning, a form of permanent migration. This was a new phenomenon because until the mid 1960s migration was still illegal because the fascist laws had not yet been repealed, and officially the migrants needed a job to get housing and housing to get a job. It had been the fascist way to preserve the social stratification. But with the new laws, Italian citizens could move freely both geographically and between categories of work. The workers who left the countryside for the northern industrial triangle of Milan-Turin-Genoa had citizenship rights equal to those of the local people. Unlike those emigrating abroad, they could not be discriminated against politically or isolated by language barriers or risk being expelled.

However, the problems of adjustment and integration were not less severe. Many southerners met the same unfriendliness, slights, and hostility in the North as did those who emigrated abroad and, as we shall see later, suffered some form of racist prejudice. In Italy's North, the standard disparaging nickname for any native of the *Mezzogiorno* became—and still is— *terrone*, a word derived from terra (soil). *Terrone* suggests less a yokel than an uncivilized but cunning fellow, an individual who is clannish and anti-social. For northern Italians, the *terroni* are the causes of all Italy's ills. Northerners' antipathy for southerners has found increasingly less subtle expression, especially in the northern news media. Newspapers in Turin, Milan, Venice, and Bologna often make a point of noting that an arrested robbery, burglary, or murder suspect was born in Palermo or some other place in the South. Northerners do not hesitate to openly accuse the bureaucrats of the nation's capital and the southerners of stealing and squandering the tax money that they contribute out of what they earn through their efficiency and hard work. However, official estimates show that many more millions are lost through the tax dodgers in the North than through waste in the South; moreover, the scandal of the *tangenti* has shown that northerners, especially politicians, public officials, and industrialists, are no better than southerners when it comes to compromising morals or civic values.

The adjustment to the northern environment has been difficult for southerners of every age group. Even for the youngster, for whom social and cultural adjustment was easy, integration was difficult. A very perceptive representation of that condition has been given by many artists in their films and literature. *Rocco e i suoi fratelli* (*Rocco and His Brothers*), by Luchino Visconti, a movie released in 1960, focuses upon the migration of southern Italians to northern industrial areas and the struggle to survive in an environment that demands profound adjustments. Visconti concentrates on the dramatic clash of differing value systems—that of the traditional southern peasant family and its archaic code of honor and family loyalty on the one hand, and a more individualistic and contemporary morality that reflects industrial society, on the other. Although *Rocco* omits much of what a historian or a sociologist would consider essential to a discussion of urban migration in Milan—unions, strikes, racism, crime, and so forth— he does give a penetrating picture of the effects of rapid cultural change upon the ancient values of traditional southern Italian families.[4]

For southern Italians, the absence of collective festivals, of the piazza as a meeting place, of street-living and inter-family visits had a profound impact. On the one hand, families suffered in the stifling atmosphere of a shanty-town; on the other hand, each nuclear family unit tended to be more closed in and less open to community life or to forms of inter-family solidarity. The problems and inadequacies that emerged from these environmental and familial shortcomings were not to be underestimated.[5] Certainly, the younger members of the family found greater opportunity for social pleasures in the new urban settings. Bars, dance halls, soccer matches, etc., did offer new freedoms and pastimes. Moreover, authority structures within the family became less rigid, as did paternal control over family finances.

Unlike the emigrants to Germany and Switzerland, the southerners who emigrated to northern Italy brought along their families, their demands, their right of influencing political organizations and trade unions, and, in 1969, they could be in the forefront of the events leading to the "hot autumn." With emigration, the southern question was not solved; indeed, it became more complex. Its reserve army of labor fed the Italian "economic miracle" and when this came to an end the tension remained, grew, and exploded.

However, in a sense, migration worked. Besides relieving rural over-crowding, the prosperity of immigrants and repatriated emigrants and the substantial remittances received from relatives who had emigrated had a strong impact on the economy. Within the local social system, the remittances of emigrants have been responsible for the rapid rise in the standard of living of many. It could be said that both, those who have migrated and those who have stayed behind, have been affected positively. Indeed, it could also be said that the most visible changes in the South came through emigration. At last, the poor became upwardly mobile, unfortunately, while becoming outwardly mobile. Despite the often appalling conditions of emigrants' life and work, it was better than staying at home. Moreover, migration served to expose more and more Italians to life beyond the village. Returned migrants brought back new ideas and new ways of looking at the world. Those who remained were not forced to unacceptable terms of sharecropping. The huge disaffected rural proletariat, the *braccianti*, could find work at last and make demands.

Unexpectedly, there were also some ecological benefits. The abandoned hills began reverting to pasture and forest, just what Italy needed. After years of deforestation and reclamation, mountains and hills were increasingly surrendered to nature and were spared from the constant dangers of landslides and erosion.

However, emigration also had a profound negative effect on the social structure, which was more apparent in the towns than in the countryside. The cities became overcrowded. Turin, for example, had to cope with 700,000 immigrants in fifteen years, and by 1970 had more southerners than any other city except Naples. Rome, with 1.1 million inhabitants in 1936 and 1.6 million in 1951, passed the 2 million mark in 1960 and had over 3 million at the end of the 1970s. Dreary tenement housing arose everywhere in city outskirts, most of them hastily erected without benefit of planning and often without adequate roads, schools, electricity, or even sewage systems. Parks and open spaces were destroyed. The hopeless immigrants were often put into huge blocks of flats, with densities of 500 people per hectare in some parts of Rome. In short, Italian cities became "Americanized."

Since most of the immigrants to northern cities were southerners, they aroused much resentment and even racial hostility among natives. The immigrants, as usual, were blamed for crime, illiteracy, sponging off welfare, and overloading the available public services—transport, public housing, schools, hospitals, etc. Because of the new political and social awareness, the immigrants did not accept tacitly the negative reactions to their presence and responded by voting communist at the general elections.

All this was part of the cost of "making Italians." Millions of southerners were being assimilated into northern cultural values, although the process must often have seemed to be working the other way around.

The cost to the emigrant and the community that was left was higher than that incurred by those who hosted them. The cultural shock for the emigrant on entering a new way of life was considerable. Considering the fact that most emigrants were moving from an agricultural to urban setting, the adjustment process usually called for a complete change in life, from habits, to customs, to traditions, and use of language. The separation from home and family created serious psychological as well as social problems for many: the problem of identity, the price of assimilation, the pain of discrimination.

A film directed by Franco Brusati, *Pane e cioccolata* (*Bread and Chocolate*, 1973), captures these problems in poignant images. The protagonist, Giovanni Garofali, a classical southern Italian worker in Switzerland, is pathetically out of place in his "guest-country." The clean, tidy, but cold nature of Swiss culture is juxtaposed to the more exuberant and humane, although somewhat tacky Latin culture. The urban life, with its rules but also social benefits, is in marked conflict with the old habits enjoyed in the rural setting, which is more relaxed but always accompanied by deprivation and suffering. Every time Giovanni starts home toward southern Italy, the sight of singing immigrant workers on the trains turns him back to Switzerland. It is a desperate situation, one experienced not only by hundreds of thousands of Italians abroad but by millions of others in Europe as well: forced to leave their homeland and their cultural roots, these workers fail to discover anything abroad to replace their old values and attachments. Like Garofali, they are trapped between a world that forces them to leave to escape poverty and a world where prosperity is given at the cost of identity.[6]

Immigration:
A New Phenomenon of Social and Cultural Change

Because of the economic success that Italy was achieving, a strange turnabout was soon to take place in the matter of Italian emigration-immigration. By the early 1980s, Italy had ceased to be a net exporter of workers: there were an estimated 800,000 immigrants (mostly illegal, called *clandestini*) in Italy; by the early 1990s, the number had gone well over one million. They were coming from sub-Saharan Africa (Ethiopia, Somalia, Nigeria, Senegal, Cape Verde), the Middle East (Iran, Iraq), Asia (India, Sri Lanka, China, the Philippines), Latin America (Brazil, Peru, Argentina), and Eastern Europe (Poland and Yugoslavia). The total number of recent immigrants amounts to no more than 1.8% of the Italian population, a much smaller percentage than that found in Germany, France, or Britain, but their presence has caused a degree of social alarm that can only be explained by taking into account the historical circumstances in which the immigration has taken place.

Since returning Italian emigrants were not willing to take low-paying jobs, immigrants from the Third World were allowed to fill them. The immigrants were finding jobs in the informal labor market—picking tomatoes for the southern canning industry, working as domestic servants for Italian families, and taking on jobs in dangerous and polluted work environments such as chrome or tanning factories in the building industry. Others became street-pedlars or washed car windshields at the traffic lights as they waited for a job. Their most visible activity, dominated by the Moroccans, is the selling of poor-quality clothes, bags, and trinkets on streets and beaches up and down the peninsula. The humiliation and suffering of the Italians in northern Europe in the 1950s and 1960s are now those of the Africans in Italy.

Until recently, the word "immigrant" bore connotations of refugees from the Third World. But with the upheavals in Eastern Europe and, more particularly, in the Balkans, Italians had to face a new tide of economic refugees from across the Adriatic Sea. The flood of Albanians strained Italy's self image as a land of tolerance for immigrants and of welcome and benevolence toward the dispossessed.

The Albanian exodus started in July 1990, when about four thousand refugees landed in small boats in the port of Brindisi. In March 1991 the refugees started coming by the thousands. The Italian government responded by relocating some of them to the other regions like Friuli, Piedmont, Liguria, and Campania.

It soon became evident, however, that as the refugee total topped 28,000 with more still coming, the Italian authorities would have to find other solutions. Pressed to put an end to "the inferno of Bari"—where conflicts arose between Italian police officers and angry, disillusioned Albanians held in a soccer stadium—the government made the decision to repatriate 15,000 Albanians and to restrict more boats from landing in Italian ports, pledging to help Albania's plight by sending $70 million in food aid and other emergency needs.

This decision may have strained Italy's image as a nation of tolerant, welcoming people, but for many it remained the only solution to a problem of international dimensions. Albanians were fleeing poverty more than repression, Italian authorities felt that letting them in would have been an irresponsible invitation to other economic refugees or asylum-seekers searching for a place on a crowded continent. As of

August 1991, Albania was giving the impression of becoming a democracy. Few Albanians could convincingly argue that it was political oppression that drove them to flee to Italy rather than a search for a consumer paradise, which they were seeing on Italian television programs that reached their country. The 1997 Albanian revolution dumped several more thousands of its citizens on the Italian shores.

But the new immigrants, for the most part, come from far away and are non-European; about 50% of them are women, many come from cities, and up to half have at least a secondary school diploma. Although most immigrants are in regular work, there is no doubt that many of those without work are sucked into illegal rackets: drug-pushing, prostitution, and the managing of teams of young pedlars. In Turin it has been estimated that there are nearly one thousand Nigerian and East European prostitutes that work under threat of violence and in particularly brutal conditions. There are also large numbers of Moroccan (male) child and teenage pedlars. Half the inmates of Turin's young offenders' prison are immigrants, imprisoned for drug-peddling or petty theft. Because of this situation, immigrants are easy scapegoats for whoever wishes to avoid tackling the structural reasons for the persistence of widespread corruption and crime.

The drug traffic existed long before the arrival of the new immigrants, as the Turin prefect was quick to point out after public protests in the main Turin street market. The immigrants, he said, could not be blamed for the disorder there. They could be seen doing a hard and honest job washing down the pavements or preparing the market for the next day. Thirty years ago there were southern Italians on the pavements, now they were behind the stalls.[7]

It appears from a study on attitudes toward the immigrants in the North that southerners with an experience of emigration are no more favorable than others to the settlement of non-European immigrants. This is probably related to the fact that although many of the first-generation southern immigrants consider themselves integrated, they are still more vulnerable than other groups and occupy a lower position in the labor market.

Ethnicity, Racism, and the
Process of Industrialization

There are some very strong anti-immigrant campaigns organized, especially by the Northern League. The Northern League has often been described as a party with a racist or quasi-racist ideology, although the party has systematically rejected such accusations. Bossi himself admitted in his autobiography that the Northern League exploited anti-southern and anti-immigrant feelings in order to gain attention from the media and from the public.[8] He seemed to be saying that although the Northern League itself was not racist, quasi-racist sentiments were diffused among northern Italians and provided the stimulus for the rise of the League.

The League has espoused a very complex form of racism that arises from a specific society and economy that can be defined as tightly communitarian. It is also complex because whereas the Northern League racism can be at least partly explained by the recent wave of extra-European immigration, this explanation does not hold for the anti-southernism of the League. To a large extent anti-southernism and anti–foreign immigration can both be linked to the ethno-region-alist aspirations of the party, but this still begs the question of why a pseudo-Lombard ethnicity has achieved political prominence at a time when linguistic and cultural differences within Italy are on the wane.

The Northern League has promoted a process of auto-racialization of the Lombard people and in so doing has taken on board aspects of the "communitarian-differentialist" racism. The 1992 political program of the Northern League stated explicitly:

> Our party's strongly critical attitude toward migratory policies stems from our specific concept of mankind. A human person is not simply an economic agent: s/he is also made up of affections, cultural values, and identities which can find their best expressions in separate historical and environmental communities. Immigrations, having a purely economic value, break up this equilibrium which forms a vital part of human nature. The theorization of a "multi-racial society" as the predestined future for mankind is both vain and openly instrumental (*Lega Nord-Lega Lombarda*, 1992).

This process of racialization has a subtext: southern Italians are attributed with a very specific negatively evaluated culture (which can be subsumed under the term of *mafiosità*) whereas the other ethnic immigrants are seen as possessing potentially threatening but as yet unidentified and undefined cultural specificities. The Northern League's position is that of other right-wing extremist parties who believe that all ethnic groups should live in their natural environment. Whereas the Frenchman Le Pen discriminates on the basis of skin color (his racism is more openly based on skin color because the main target of the French National Front were the immigrants from North Africa), Bossi discriminates on the basis of cultural differences and, therefore, while he discriminates against Arab fundamentalists and Maghrebians who are two non-assimilable groups, the target for his party is also the Southern *mafiosità*.

The whole racist discourse of both Le Pen and the League is also based on the construction of myths. Le Penism treats national identity as given and thus creates a myth out of French ethnicity that is totally devoid of content, so much so that among the threats against French identity, the party program cites fast food and the Americanization of the French language. Departing from the view of the socioeconomic homogeneity of the North (nothing is more false: the North has seen countless invasions, immigrations, and occupations, and it has a highly variegated regional and linguistic culture and highly contrasting economic activities), the League has invented a Lombard ethnicity that in reality had to be created, a sense of imagined community *ex novo*. The myth of Lombard ethnicity is built around a core of fairly specific cultural characteristics: a strong work ethic, entrepreneurship and personal risk-taking, a spirit of sacrifice, a high propensity to saving, as well as trust, solidarity, and law-abidance. These civic virtues that are preferred in every society are contrasted with vices that are present in today's societies but are isolated in southern Italians and immigrants.

It is clear that the League does not accept traditional modernization theories, which argue that the process of industrialization would be accompanied by the related phenomena of urbanization, political mobilization, and cultural uniformity. According to these views, these processes would dissolve "tribal" affiliations in favor of new attachments at the national level. Urbanization would lead to a convergence of economic and social systems toward a global pattern, consisting of a comparatively small number of relatively homogeneous nation-states.[9]

But where are the roots of racism? The northern Italian economic system developed geographical concentrations of small manufacturing units operating in close-knit communities characterized by an overlapping of business and family ties, low social and political polarization, and a high degree of entrepreneurship. The socioeconomic characteristics of this system are primarily the preservation of the family as an economic unit and the protection of primary ties and localistic, community-based allegiances.[10] The process of industrialization of these regions with a strong political subculture rests on the preservation of a tightly communitarian society. In the community of small-scale industries, trust and solidarity are born out of living in the same village, speaking the same dialect, and sharing family as well as business ties. Trust and social cohesion are viewed as part of a dual process of inclusion/exclusion. Therefore, when trust and solidarity are community-based, the community becomes racialized; a sharp division exists between those who are seen as belonging to the community and those who are considered outsiders; it is *Us* against the *Other*. Northern racism is, therefore, built into the local socioeconomic structure. The League has exploited racist sentiments that are already present in the population, particularly in areas of diffused industrialization. Having taken over from the *D.C.* the representation of the interests of the local small-business, the Northern League had been able to translate the xenophobic and inward-looking culture of the Lombard communities of small firms into the myth of Lombard (and northern Italian) ethnicity.

But besides the problem caused by northern racism, there are complex general national problems. Italy has been caught totally unprepared politically, psychologically, culturally, and bureaucratically in its attitude toward immigration. Moreover, job-seeking immigrants overlap with 2 million Italian unemployed. Italians have long prided themselves on being less racist and less anti-semitic than other nationalities and are considered politically progressive and tolerant, but there are some who are falling short of civil expectations when confronting immigrants who, not being provided with proper housing and work, appear to be idlers, thieves, and a nuisance to the community. After all, 15% of Italy's prison population is made up of immigrants, of whom 52%, many of them North Africans, have been convicted of selling drugs.[11] Tolerance and open-heartedness are being put to the test.

The Left takes a positive approach and, therefore, favors immigration. They argue that immigrants—particularly illegal immigrants—accept wages and working conditions that citizens, even poor citizens, would not. The Center-Right, on the other hand, has been more cautious and has been pressing for more control. It maintains that the low-skill immigration of recent years has not helped the economy of the country; if anything, it has helped a few businesses that have profited from the supply of cheap labor, leaving the community at large to pick up the social costs. The Right also argues that what most immigrants pay in taxes, when they work legally, does not cover even a fraction of the services they receive; moreover, it claims that the downward trend in immigrant skills has been accompanied by an upward trend in their use of public assistance. Immigrants compete with citizens for drastically reduced public services. It further argues that no immigration policy can remedy the failures of other nations to meet the needs of their poor, so it is both sensible and moral to base Italy's national policy primarily on the needs of the country: generating an economic revival and raising the standard of living of the nation's poorer citizens. On the other hand there are those who argue that immigrants arrive with a high level of desire and drive, so much so that their basic contribution could be felt in the stimulation of the natives to do better. Immigrants usually live, at least in the beginning, in areas where the lesser achievers live; their presence may become a social and economic reawakening force.

Many are also genuinely concerned about the impact that the flow of immigrants will have on Italian culture—in its psychological, social, and anthropological dimensions—since the immigrant groups are characterized by ethnic, linguistic, and religious diversities that pose completely new cultural and social problems, Islam has become the second religion in Italy, and Rome is the home city of the largest mosque in Europe. Considering the large number of races, languages, and dialects that make up the people coming from the very same country (e.g., Ethiopia, Senegal, Nigeria), some Italians perceive in the immigration flux a potentially explosive mixture, especially where conflicts present in the country of origin are transplanted in Italy.

In the mid-1980s, Italy made it easier than ever for illegal immigrants to enter the country. At the very moment when other European countries were becoming more restrictive, Italy loosened up visa requirements. This action was taken totally *alla garibaldina*, that is, with cheerful audacity, little advance planning, and plenty of gambling. Many things in Italy are launched *alla garibaldina*: sometimes they succeed beyond reasonable expectations, but most of the time they end in shameful failures. The handling of immigration belongs to the second category. There was no mechanism to match the kind of jobs available with the people being allowed into the country. Until 1991, there were no funds available for counseling or housing new arrivals, no Italian-language or job-training courses. At first no government ministry was responsible for immigration. Then the newly created Ministry of Immigration had only a skeletal staff and an essentially advisory role.

The laws on immigration of 1986 (Law 943) and 1990 (Law 39, known as the *Legge Martelli*), the first since 1931, made some progress toward providing immigrants with legal status, and many employers took them on with regular contracts and social security contributions. However, all those who arrived after 1990 were unable to obtain a legal permit to stay, and so remained ineligible for all except irregular jobs and the living conditions that went with them. The government took only a few steps to meet the emergency. However, as usual, state failures are compensated for by individual inventiveness. There is a growing tendency among the public to promote a culture of acceptance. This attitude of acceptance animates the work of numerous voluntary associations that have either sprung up to offer help to immigrant workers or existed before the influx of foreigners and have subsequently changed their priorities. Among these last there are widespread national service networks, of a religious or trade union character, which operate all over Italy and involve the immigrants themselves. The most supportive organizations are the efficient Catholic charities, especially Caritas. Quite often the initiatives of Catholic charities, trade unions, or other voluntary organizations are coordinated with those of the local authorities whose decisions anticipate or go beyond those of the central government. A first wave of Catholic or municipal reception centers and services for immigrants was reinforced with the help of immigrant leaders and associations, and by a second wave of voluntary initiatives that promoted the perception of immigrants as people who, on the one hand, were being denied their civil rights, but who, on the other, were contributing something of value to Italian society. Immigrants were not just "people needing help." Now there are groups for the legal defense of immigrants, Italo-immigrant cultural associations, groups to promote multicultural education in schools, trade union offices for immigrants, and so on. It is sometimes pointed out that the effect of immigration on the economy is positive given the low Italian birth rate and the aging native population. The speed, generosity, and highly articulated nature of the voluntary effort to meet the immigrants' needs and to reduce the impact of any racist backlash has few parallels in other European countries.

As a result of Italy's generally liberal immigration policy, there is concern in many European nations that with the free movement throughout the European Community that began in January 1993, Italy will serve as a port of entry for an influx of illegal immigrants from Asia, Africa, and South America. The Italian government would prefer to see uniform European immigration laws, but it may be forced to institute visa requirements in the near future. As the overwhelming demographic and economic disparities between Europe and the developing nations grow, the movement of desperate job-seekers will certainly increase; so too, however, may the series of anti-immigrant violent acts.

Meanwhile, Italy is adopting a policy of economic aid to countries in its proximity that are in distress. One example previously mentioned was the decision to repatriate some of the Albanians in 1991; this was accompanied by a pledge equivalent to $70 million in food aid to Albania to tide it over for three months of acute shortages, in addition to other emergency help.

Italian immigration problems may be solved only with policies linked to those of the EU. One of the major steps adopted by the EU is to abolish all internal controls, and at the same time to strengthen security at the external border points. The community members are trying to put into effect a strategy that would harmonize the issuing of visas and the adoption of a "one-chance rule," under which asylum seekers can apply to only one of the countries; denial by one means denial by all. In the words of former Belgian Interior Minister Joseph Michel: "We run the risk of becoming like the Roman people—invaded by barbarian peoples such as Arabs, Moroccans, Yugoslavs, and Turks. People who come from far afield and have nothing in common with our civilization."

Many economists and most people feel that the recent influx of immigrants has helped fuel much of the economic growth during the past decade. And, while some perceive foreigners as taking jobs away from native-born Europeans, those who have studied the matter say recent immigration has had little impact on the employment opportunities of people born there. New immigrants, these experts say, tend to go into low-wage industries, where native-born groups don't usually compete for jobs.

One of the consequences of immigration has been some racist feelings, directed mainly against the immigrants of color. This has been fueled above all by rising unemployment. It is all very sad and perplexing, because the Italians always enjoyed the reputation of being less color-conscious than most western Europeans and, in another respect, a good deal less nationalistic and chauvinistic. Their legitimate patriotism has taken on a more modern flavor; except at international soccer matches, it is difficult to see Italians displaying their flag as an expression of passionate nationalism. And the sight of that flag never creates tears in the eye or vibrates strongly nationalistic heartstrings. They are less insular than the British and less chauvinistic than the

French. Italians have traditionally been less xenophobic toward other people and more open to outside influences, more aware of belonging to a wider community. Clear evidence of this may be seen in news coverage by the national media. International cultural or sporting events tend to be under-reported by the British media, while in the Italian media they get much fuller coverage. In France it is done with a strong emphasis on the French role. The Italians do seem to think of themselves in terms of a wider community, and in conversation will often talk of "we in the West" or "we in Europe," where an Englishman may still say "we in Britain."

Therefore, apart from the very few isolated incidents of antagonism against immigrants, Italians do not have discriminatory feelings. In the same vein, Italian attitudes to the Third World are rather positive. Italy today spends large sums on overseas aid, and I would say that the Italians are at least as ready as most other European nations to play their part in helping poorer nations.

Notes

1. Claudio Calvaruso, "Rientro dei migranti e condizione delle collettività italiane in Europa," *Civitas* 31, no. 1 (1980): 34.

2. In 1982 there were 296,200 Italians classified as workers and a total of 601,600 Italians in West Germany; 41,400 Italians entered West Germany, and 81,800 left that country. A favorite destination from 1950 to 1980 was Switzerland, which in 1982 had 233,100 Italian workers with annual contracts, who with their families totaled 412,000. In 1982 some 11,800 Italians entered Switzerland, and 20,200 Italians with annual permits left that country. France had attracted migrants early, and in the 1940s and early 1950s became, along with Belgium, a major target. In 1982 France had 136,800 Italian workers and 441,000 Italians, including family members. Rinn-Sup Shinn, *Italy, A Country Study* (Washington: The American University, 1985), 110.

3. Bruno Trentin, *Da sfruttati a produttori* (Bari : De Donato, 1977), xi.

4. Peter Bondanella, *Italian Cinema: From Neorealism to the Present* (New York: Ungar Publishing Co., 1983), 199.

5. For a valuable assessment of this phenomenon see: L. Balbo, *Stato di famiglia* (Milan: Mondadori, 1976).

6. The plight of emigrants has also been repeatedly represented in compelling literary works by Rocco Scotellaro, Mario La Cava, Nino Palumbo, and especially Saverio Strati.

7. B. Frandino, "Così sistemerò Porta Palazzo," *La Repubblica*, 30 April 1994.

8. Umberto Bossi (with D. Vimercati), *Vento dal Nord* (Milan: Mondadori, 1992).

9. A. H. Richmond, *Immigration and Ethnic Conflict* (London: Croon Helm, 1988).

10. A. Cento Bull and P. Corner, *From Peasant to Entrepreneur. The Survival of the Family Economy in Italy* (Oxford, Providence: Berg, 1993).

11. In 1992, one-third of Rome's criminals were said to be immigrants, with an overwhelming majority of them born outside the European Community. The foreign-born criminals, who in that year numbered about 1,000, were not spending time in jail for having committed a violent crime. Rather, of the approximately one thousand, 543 were jailed for drug-related charges, and 339 for petty theft. Most of the criminals were arrested in the city's historic center, particularly in the area surrounding the train terminal.

Part III
Society

Introduction

The years since World War II have seen deeper and more rapid social changes in Italy than any time before. In the last 50 years the rural exodus has been strong. Most Italian people now live in town and those that remain in the country have had their lives transformed by the provision of public utilities and the modernization of agricultural methods, while town and country have been brought closer together by vast improvements in the infrastructure of public transport and telecommunications. The nature of work has changed, as has the composition of the workforce; the age structure of the population has altered and, with it, people's aspirations and expectations. The social structure familiar from the prewar period, with its seemingly rigid divisions between *borghesia,* employed in the city, and the significant number of *contadini,* or people working on the land, has been profoundly altered by the disappearance of the traditional working class that was composed of male industry workers and their families, and the concomitant growth of tertiary sector employment. Mass secondary education and the mass media have undoubtedly had a homogenizing effect and the cultural specificities that attached to earlier social divisions, with distinguishably different bourgeois and working-class cultures, have almost disappeared. At the same time, other forms of cultural diversity have emerged, which are based on regional, generational, gender, and ethnic differences.

The motor of these changes has been economic and political as well as cultural. As described in Part II, the Italian economy experienced unparalleled growth during the 30 years following the war. The consumer society arrived in Italy with an impact that was rendered all the greater because of the dramatic contrast it created with the relatively low living standards of the prewar period. But in embracing consumerism and the "affluent society," Italy has also lost many of its peculiarities and has become more like other western European countries. Side by side with economic convergence has been a political *normalization*, as described in Part I, together with a sustained effort on the part of Italian leaders to promote European integration. The content of politics has become national and European, and this encourages convergence with the remainder of western Europe.

This evolutionary process has not proceeded smoothly. Two periods of social change may be noted whose separation is marked by the student unrest at the end of the 1960s. The first is a period of modernization that accompanied the high economic growth of the "economic miracle." Living standards improved dramatically and the advent of the consumer society brought with it changes in habits, lifestyles, and expectations. Physically, Italy was transformed by massive programs of building and renovation. Then came the revolt of students and workers. The strikes and demonstrations lasted for several months and affected industries, businesses, and public services. Banks, broadcasting, and transport were all affected alongside the education system and the manufacturing industry. Although the political revolution, led by workers and students, did not overthrow the government, it did have a profound social impact. Social and industrial relations changed for good: the old hierarchies and the old paternalism were replaced by the more relaxed, flexible, and nonhierarchical forms of institutional and interpersonal relations that are common today. This was evident in all kinds of ways, from the widespread use of the *tu,* "you", familiar form of address, to the clothes worn to school and in the street, to eating habits, as well as in the adoption of participatory management in industry and in public institutions such as universities.

With the start of the 1970s, Italian society ceased to be bent on unquestioned modernization. For as long as families had been inadequately fed and housed it had seemed obvious that modernization should have as its object the provision of basic amenities and a decent standard of living for all. Qualitative considerations began to replace quantitative calculations, so that the consumer society, for example, was not universally seen as a good thing. Criticism of consumerism is, of course, the luxury of affluence, but it was none the less real.

The 1970s marked the beginning of the second period of social change. The effects of the first oil crisis caused the first interruption in rapid growth since the war and led to a less rapid expansion of living standards; however, it was a great period of social reform. Virtually all the popular demands of the 1960s and early 1970s were embodied in social legislation, bringing Italy into line with other western countries. Contraception and abortion were legalized, equal opportunities legislation was enacted, and paternal authority was reduced.

But this social modernization also reflected a shift in the debate about social inequalities. Until the end of the 1960s, social policy was implicitly underpinned by a model of a society based on the division into classes. This meant that the process of social change was directed at integration—at incorporating the less privileged workers and peasants into the national community by offering them comparable living standards and the social protection to those available to the middle classes. From the middle of the 1970s onward, however, other forms of social grouping, based on factors such as sex and age, rather than class only, were recognized as significant, and legislation was directed at ensuring equal provision of benefits and amenities for such groups. Individuals rather than the family became the focus of social and economic change. Thus, women, for example, achieved equal rights but forfeited the expectation that they would be supported and cared for by father or husband.

By the 1980s, Italian society had changed profoundly because of the deep changes in education, family structure, Church and state relations, and different expectations of the individual from the state and its agencies. The pages that follow will discuss the major social changes that have taken place in Italy since World War II and will examine some of the factors of convergence and division.

IX

Democratizing the Education System

Education Only for an Elite

Like every other institution and aspect of Italian life, Italian education has drastically changed in postwar Italy and, like everything else, it had to be rebuilt in every aspect. Because of the sociopolitical changes caused by the war, in a sense, the new government faced a condition that demanded a restructuring and revamping similar to those needed after the unification of 1870.

Education under fascism and under the liberal regime that preceded it was the ideological and cultural reproduction of a narrow ruling class.[1] Not only was an elite student body taught by an elite teacher corps, but the education system was built in such a way that it preserved the established social class structure.

The destruction brought about by the war demanded and, ironically, permitted a complete reshaping of that system. Not only was it necessary to rebuild the physical infrastructure, but everything else, including the outline of the studies, curricula, syllabi, teaching methods, school management system, and the responsibilities of the administrative offices and operators at all levels had to be profoundly transformed.

At the end of the war most of the school buildings were severely damaged, if not destroyed; the classrooms that were available were very crowded, had no heat, had scarce furniture, and lacked proper sanitary conditions. In some areas of the country, especially in the South, many children could not attend school because they even lacked proper clothing. In mostly agricultural areas of the South, many parents were still keeping children on their farm to help with the daily tasks. There is a moving scene in the Taviani brothers' film *Padre Padrone*, set in the 1950s, when an authoritarian shepherd comes to school to physically remove his son from the classroom. Based on a true story, it gives a stark picture of the Sardinian families so completely dependent upon their herds that their children had to be kept home to help with the work.

As late as 1951, as many as 5 million people (about 10% of the population) were still illiterate! The new democratic government had the overwhelming task of rebuilding the infrastructure and of reorganizing the system on a democratic base; that is, giving the right to every citizen to reach the highest levels of education, even though one lacked the financial means. To achieve this democratic principle, steps had to be taken to put every citizen in a condition to acquire that common level of education deemed indispensable to participating knowledgeably in the life of the country.

These changes also involved reshaping the general attitude of teachers, who had to become more conscious of their need to keep up-to-date and of the necessity of continually improving their professional knowledge, and therefore, the progress of their schools.

Changes were possible across the country because the system was highly centralized. The Ministry of Education had, and still has, central control of curricula, syllabi, hiring and salaries of teachers, and much of the financing; even financing of buildings came from the Ministry of Public Works, as well as the Ministry of Education. By the early 1980s, the system had completely changed its character. The expansion of education not only increased the number of educated young people but also changed qualitatively, not always uniformly, the education system in Italy.

In few other areas has Italy advanced more since the war than in progressing from a poor to a relatively modern educational system under which practically everyone goes through the upper-school, and a very high percentage continues to the university. Despite these advances, much remains to be done.

Reforms and the Student Revolt

In the immediate postwar years, reforms were still conducted in a very conservative way. Although there was clearly a need for a profound change that had to span from the lowest to highest levels of education, the changes made during the first 15 years were just window dressing.

The first substantive reform came about with the establishment of compulsory secondary schooling until the age of 14 and the establishment of a single system of middle schooling. The basic reform law that triggered this transformation process, approved in 1962, abolished the old lower secondary school (*scuola media*), that was attended by students intending to continue their studies, and the secondary technical school (*avviamento*), attended by those intending to enter the job market as soon as possible. It instituted a new lower secondary school (*scuola media unica*) that was equal for everyone. It was an important reform socially and democratically, since it enacted the constitutional norm, which established a period of equal compulsory education for at least eight years for every student. It also tried to ensure that another constitutional norm was applied, whereby the most able and deserving were entitled to reach the highest levels of education by assuring that everyone enjoyed the same opportunities at the outset. The two main aspects of the new system, training and guidance, were an attempt to achieve through the reform, greater social justice.

However, reform of this very regressive structure could not be easily implemented because many middle-school teachers remained hostile to the new law because they claimed it watered down the curriculum (Latin became optional) and threatened discipline; implicitly, the teachers did not want to see the old elite middle school "destroyed." Consequently, to a certain extent, the curriculum remained archaic until the end of the 1960s, when radical change swept through the entire academic system. However, in bringing to eight the number of mandatory school years, the state made a heroic effort to make education accessible to everyone, including the children of farmers who, for economic, cultural, and social reasons had stayed away in large numbers. In the 1960s and 1970s the government spent billions of dollars in this effort; schools were built in even the most remote hamlets, sometimes serving only a few dozen children. With these new schools came all the other supportive facilitation: roads, electricity, and free transportation.

Consequently, the number of students and the make-up of the student population changed radically. For the first time in Italian history children from every social background had the same opportunity for a basic education. The impact of the changes brought about a cultural revolution. Indeed, the material bases of the explosion of protest in the Italian universities and high schools of the late 1960s are to be found in the education reforms of the early 1960s. The mandatory reforms for the middle school opened the road to demands for mass education beyond the eighth grade. The student body, whose number increased rapidly, for the first time included a high percentage of girls and children from the low, middle, and working classes. Many of them, especially from the middle classes, decided to continue their studies and go on to the university. Legislation of the 1960s made this easier: in 1961 access to science faculties was opened to students from technical institutes, and in 1965 entrance to the university by examination was abolished. By 1968 the number of university students totaled over 450,000, compared to only 268,000 in 1960. The number of female students had doubled in the same period, but in 1968 still constituted less than a third of the new students beyond the mandatory years.

This new generation of university students entered a university system that was still terribly antiquated. The expansion of infrastructure carried out in secondary schools had not been continued at the higher level. The number of universities had remained the same and all had maintained their essentially feudal structure. Worse still, many of the professors were rarely present in the university. Their obligations to the universities were limited to 52 hours of teaching per year; once their obligation had been satisfied, they could attend to their "main" profession, that of being doctors, lawyers, engineers, architects, chemists, and, above all, politicians. There were no seminars, no tutorials, and no faculty-student contact. Not surprisingly, the number of students who failed their oral exams was very high. In 1966, 81% of those with a secondary school diploma went on to university, but only 44% succeeded in graduating. In this kind of situation, the poorer students faced the highest odds of success. Even worse, most of the sons and daughters of the "new" university society who graduated, mostly from the expanding urban middle classes, suffered a series of disillusionments when trying to enter the job market. It seems that the university continued to operate a particularly subtle form of class-based selection. The Left in government had succeeded in opening up the doors of the university to everyone but had not been able to prepare the system for the new student population.

This kind of environment, nourished by ideological issues that were brewing in many parts of the world, led to the student revolt of 1967-1968. Many students of the mid-sixties were doubtful of the values that had become predominant in the Italy of the "economic miracle"—

individualism, the exaltation of the nuclear family, and consumerism. Education had made them more critical of society's failures and the need for social justice. The dream based on achieving success through talent and hard work was revealed to be just a myth for many students coming from the lower classes. Social status and connections (whom you know) seemed to remain the big factors for success. The power of social status was recognized as the major constraint to upward mobility. By finding the door of the university open, the influence of a father's or mother's occupational attainment or a son's or daughter's occupational attainment had been overcome, but the effects of social origin on academic success and occupational achievement and mobility remained significant. Students' questioning of this situation was carried out by leaning on the current Catholic social doctrine and Marxist thinking; values of solidarity, collective action, and the fight against social injustice and social division were juxtaposed to the individualism and consumerism of "neo-capitalism."

Some world events certainly had their impact on this situation in ferment. The Vietnam War changed the way a whole generation of Italians thought about America: the image of a powerful and destructive America had replaced that of an America that offered opportunity and a realizable dream in the 1950s. The Cultural Revolution in China in 1966-1967 was interpreted in Italy as being a spontaneous, antiauthoritarian mass protest movement; Mao's invitation to Chinese youth to "open fire" on headquarters was interpreted in Italy as a cultural revolution that had to be carried out from below. Finally, there were the teachings of radical South American priests who sought to reconcile social Catholic doctrine and Marxism. This should explain why the first university revolts took place in strongly Catholic institutions. The explosion that started in the autumn of 1967 (long before the French unrest) at the University of Trento, followed by those at the Catholic university at Milan and at the public university at Turin, set the stage for a cultural revolution that swept through the nation. Students questioned not only what was being taught, the "canon," and the way the mental process was put to work, but also the individualistic ways of presenting one's image. Students changed the way they dressed and looked. Men let their hair and beard grow, and abandoned jackets, ties, and somber-colored clothes in favor of jeans and other casual attire; the women abandoned make-up, dresses, and high heels in favor of jeans, pullovers, and boots. The movement reached its climax in spring 1968 but continued throughout the 1970s.

The most unfortunate aspect of the democratization process was the deterioration of quality. The open-enrollment policy aimed at eliminating the privileged situation of some schools (*licei*) was supposed to be temporary. The awaited reforms at the upper secondary school level and those undertaken in universities were supposed to bring some balance to the system. To date, however, this long-awaited reform has not yet seen the light of day. The extended period of open enrollment has had profound effects on the entire university system. The open-enrollment policy instituted in 1969 proved to be only a ploy of the Left to demonstrate another victory for the masses, without in reality providing a real gain. The *democratization* of the school system has transformed the system from a university for the elite into a university for the masses, but the transformation has taken place more to satisfy a political necessity than to prepare a society of highly educated and skilled citizens; it was done more to fulfill a political agenda than to raise the level of education of the nation.

In the mid-1970s, when the welfare state was being instituted in a most bizarre way, the education system was experiencing the same turmoil as the rest of Italian institutions. The principles at the base of the workers' statute and other social insurance laws that were aimed at bringing about considerable equality of conditions were also at the base of the democratic reforms in education. In education, too, equality of opportunity was meant to be also equality of results; in the democratic spirit, regardless of how well-prepared students were, everyone was expected to be passed and graduated. Once enrolled, students were expected to graduate as a matter of right. Thus, great pressures were placed on professors to relax the stringency of the oral examinations that prevailed throughout the system. During those chaotic years, not only did the quality of students and academic standards decline, but those who taught moved politically to make their own jobs permanent as a matter of law. Several legislative reforms had the effect of granting tenure, in one fell swoop, to thousands of academics, irrespective of their qualifications as scholars and teachers. Although not all of these got to be full professors (*professori ordinari*), they all joined the ranks of millions of other public servants in public-service jobs who had lifetime job security.

The state also responded in a very confused way in meeting the serious problems created by overcrowding. Although the state opened many more universities throughout Italy, this new generation of university students entered a system that was still grossly inadequate.

Overcrowding strained all academic facilities. In the 1991-1992 academic year, the state universities in the three largest Italian cities (Rome, Milan, Naples) enrolled over 40% of the total university population; nine university centers throughout the country are so over-crowded that each enrolls more than 40,000 students. In the mid-1980s, the University of Rome, "La Sapienza," had an enrollment of 160,000 on a campus built for about 33,000. Some professors lectured to audiences of more than a thousand students. Rome's medical school was supposed to train 23,000 students concurrently; many of them never made it to the anatomy laboratory. To secure a library seat, students had to line up early. However, most Italian students (especially in the humanities and social and behavioral sciences) did not bother to go to classes; they expected to accomplish more by studying in the comfort of the home atmosphere instead of going to a class where seats were scarce and professors frequently canceled classes. As some form of standards started to be reapplied, not surprisingly, many students failed their exams, with the complaint from the Left that the reforms had not satisfied the aspirations awakened by the social changes. Indeed, the Italian university system unintentionally started to operate a subtle form of class-based selection; while it was supposedly open to all, the odds remained heavily against poorer students earning a degree or finding a job.

Ideology and Academic Freedom

The system never found the correct balance in the democratization process. Like everything else the system became highly politicized. Politics seeps into every area of the educational system—from bottom to top, from nursery and elementary schools to the high schools and universities. Schools actually produce in some students and reinforce in others clear-cut political predispositions.

Needless to say, university student bodies are politicized as well. In the late 1960s and early 1970s, they represented the prime recruiting ground for political terrorist organizations, particularly those of the Left. Several founding members of the Red Brigades were contemporary students of sociology at the University of Trento. Even the most "normal" organizations are typically organized along the same lines that define Italy's political parties. Italian student organizations are in line with European student practice. They are vigorously active bodies with, very often, formal ties to the political parties within which many students will pursue political careers or from which they intend to seek support when they go out to look for jobs. Italians cannot conceive of student organizations American style, that is, ones having just social and cultural aims.

Unfortunately, many students become *professional students* who, supported by political parties, make a living out of being political agitators. The system is so absurd that in theory it is possible for a student to spend up to 25 years getting a degree. Not surprisingly, only one-third of all students who enroll in Italian institutions of higher learning ever graduate; the other two-thirds remain "professional students," eventually dropping out to look for some job or swell the unemployment lines. On the other hand, it could be argued that the Italian university system anticipates the time when, as in all industrial countries, further education will probably be encouraged as an alternative to unemployment. The system gives hundreds of thousands of young people a chance to educate themselves, and a sense of belonging to society. The Italian government has come to understand that it is cheaper to pay for an education that is a "parking place" than to be forced to pay for other social services, or even more detention institutions as a consequence of the lack of employment.

Besides being political and social, the problem is also ethical. Even though the prospects of finding a job with a degree in the humanities are remote, the largest percentage of students enroll in those disciplines because they are easier than the sciences. Very few enroll in physics, notwithstanding the high demand for physicists and other scientists. Physics still enjoys the reputation of being the heir to an illustrious tradition, but also produces statistics that are unattractive to students who are not highly motivated: of those who enroll, only about 30% graduate and most of them take five or six years instead of four. The enrollment in medicine is also very high in spite of the vast number of doctors scrambling for jobs. Italy has the highest ratio of doctor to inhabitants in the EU because politicians have pursued a policy of employment rather than one that assures that doctors are professionally prepared.

Since Italian life is politicized at every level, changes cannot be implemented easily and in some cases are even impossible. The answer seems to lie in a selection system for applications for enrollment, as well as in a suitable strengthening of structures and premises that should also be evenly distributed throughout the country. The state has tried to respond to the overcrowding by opening new universities.

Although between 1970 and 1990 about 30 new universities were opened, some in large urban centers already with one or two universities but most in areas never touched by academic life, the overcrowding in the old centers was not alleviated. Most students preferred to enroll in institutions with a tradition and which are associated with names of scholars and scientists who have made a long-lasting impact in many fields throughout history. No one can convince students that a degree from a new university such as that of Calabria is worth as much as that of a university with an illustrious past, such as that of the University of Bologna or Pavia. Students are also very aware that the new centers attract only the young professors who accept those first appointments as a "parking place" while they wait to move to an older university as soon as the opportunity presents itself. In a country where traditions still have meaning, it becomes even more difficult to reduce their significance when they are attached to a glorious past. Italy has the oldest university tradition in the world. Salerno was the first, founded in the ninth century by "four masters": a Jew, a Greek, a Saracen, and an Italian. In the twelfth century, before Oxford or Cambridge colleges were founded, Bologna University, which opened in 1088, had ten thousand students. The University of Padua was founded in 1222, Naples in 1224, Rome in 1303, Pisa in 1342, Turin in 1404, and Catania in 1444. Some of them are among the oldest and most distinguished in the West. Many boast centuries of humanistic and scientific achievements. Even today, despite the intrusion of politics into the system, several universities remain islands of intellectual rigor and innovation that rival similar institutions anywhere else in the world.

Today, however, the troubles of the system stem from the strong power achieved by the students and by the old autocratic faculty system. Students have become so powerful, or the government has conceded so much power to them, that reforms have been difficult to come by. When in November 1984 the prefect of Rome suggested that all universities should limit enrollment in the medical schools to 70% of the previous year's number, there was such a political uproar that no one who had been contemplating the measure was willing to support it. In 1985, in reaction to a proposal by Minister of Public Education Falcucci to increase tuition by about $100, the students of the Left organized such a general protest that the government backed off. The problem was not that Italians are overburdened with the cost of higher education (today even the poorest university student spends $100 in a weekend out for pizza) but that students assumed the position that education should be completely free. On that occasion, the lack of political maturity of students and their politicized positions became more evident than ever. No student organization leader responded to the government with a counterproposal or with a constructive critical assessment of the university system and how it should be improved if additional fees were accepted. No student group responded to the government that the extra $100 would be paid provided it would be spent in the university system, say, to improve the libraries, which at the present time are a disgrace.

When another attempt was made to reform the system in spring 1990, the system was practically shut down for almost two months. Reaction to a proposed law that would give individual campuses more autonomy to set course requirements than they now have under a highly centralized system, and which would also allow individual universities to sign contracts and start other joint projects with private companies, brought back memories of the late 1960s and mid 1970s. Students worried that big corporations may be given a free hand to reshape the country's schools to fit their own needs. While the sciences and engineering are likely to get adequate financing, they argued, the liberal arts will fall by the wayside.

In American universities, good science departments, through the grants they bring to the campuses, may also enhance the life of humanities and arts divisions. Usually, real scientists support university policies to share the "indirect costs" charged by the universities on grants with every academic area of the campus because a good comprehensive university needs humanists and artists to prepare a more "humane society," especially in a scientific age. In Italy, however, laboratory researchers joined the protests because they also felt that they would lose their independence and become tools of industry. Large companies, it was also argued, are more likely to invest in the well-developed Italian North, further widening the considerable gap with the relatively poor South. Not coincidentally, the campus protests first erupted in Palermo, where the unemployment rate is over 20%, three times that in Turin. Objections to the plan reflect widespread cynicism about the concentration of economic and political power in the hands of a few industrialist titans like Giovanni Agnelli of FIAT, Carlo De Benedetti of Olivetti, Raul Gardini of the Ferruzzi-Montedison agrobusiness group, and Silvio Berlusconi, a television magnate.

However, today's students are very different from those of the late 1960s and 1970s. Protest may flare up over specific grievances, but gone is the old political idealism. The vast majority share the current Italian disillusionment with ideologies; the few politically active ones are either on the extreme Right or extreme Left.

How Democratic Can a System Be in the Hands of *Barons*?

As we have previously mentioned, one of the major problems of the Italian university system, like the entire education system, is the high level of politicization. Professors are openly concerned with politics and are openly lined up with political parties. Despite arguments about the importance in a democratic society for intellectuals to remain relatively autonomous, either aloof from political parties or with politics kept at a distance and in perspective, so that they may be honest critics of social and political arrangements, in Italy the situation is completely the opposite. "By and large, Italian intellectuals not only shun any such effort; they thrive in political works. Far from being the critics of political parties and party factions, they are often the latter's major spokesmen. Far from seeking a modicum of space, in a politicized society that admittedly offers very little of it to anyone, they hanker after the rewards, including public offices, that the parties can distribute to the faithful."[2]

Although no academic institution can and should be immune to political fermentations, the Italian system thrives on ideological confrontations. Political parties find it prestigious to have candidates or ministers who are university professors.

What is even more damaging to the entire system is that the universities are firmly in the hands of autocratic senior professors, unfondly called *baroni*. As La Palombara underscores, the Italian "barons" are not just playing academic politics; they are intricately a part of the bigger political game as well. In the bargains, the "barons" strike; in the trade-offs, they concoct; and in the "balance," they seek to establish within the university community, political and ideological considerations that reflect the politics of the nation. The political coloration of the competing candidates weighs at least as heavily as their professional qualifications, and sometimes more (p. 72). So, despite appearances to the contrary, professors practice the same division of the spoils enjoyed by the political parties in the patronage system, which almost brought Italy to ruin. Italian professors are known as *baroni*, not only for the prestige they enjoy and the influence they exercise, but also for their authority and independence. Still today, they can choose the date of when to begin the academic year; they can delegate their work to a host of assistants; and until recently, they could freely take up another post. Efforts have been made to induce professors to devote less time to their private affairs and more to their academic duties. For instance, if a professor is elected to Parliament or receives another important public appointment, it has been established that she or he will be placed on leave of absence from the university. However, efforts to induce professors to hold one position, to reside in or close to the cities of their chair, and to teach and undertake research in their universities have been only partially successful. It is not uncommon in Italy for professors to reside two or three hundred miles away from the university where they teach!

Moreover, as in most universities throughout the world, there are no tests on the actual ability to teach or lecture. It is inconceivable that an Italian university professor would allow students to evaluate classroom experiences the way we practice it and value it in the American university system.

A law was passed in 1980 to restructure the ranking of the academic body and to create some 45,000 new positions. These would be divided into three categories—the *ricercatore*, "researcher," the lowest position, which is appointed through a *concorso*, a state competitive examination and assessment of publications, and three years teaching experience; the next stage, *professore associato*, associate professor, can lead to the last stage, full professor, *professore ordinario*, both of which are achieved through a national competition. These changes, which were meant to break the feudal system, have met with only partial success.

As in the American university system, there is an overemphasis on research and a corollary distaste for teaching. This research is "make-believe scholarship," which can be confirmed by how infrequently a researcher's work is cited by others within five years of publication. In the sciences, fewer than half the articles published were cited in that period of time. In the social sciences the "uncitedness" index rises to 74.7%, in religion to 98.2%, and in literature to 99.8%! It's not difficult to conclude that much research is self-defensive and self-indulgent.

Today there persists much controversy about what role a university should play. Should it be primarily for research or for teaching? Italian universities are certainly distinguished by the former rather than the latter. Can it still fulfill the Renaissance ideal of producing the well-rounded, cultivated individual? Or, in this age of the masses that is also an age of specialization, should it become more vocational? Should it teach for "culture" or for professional ends? There are many who believe that it can and should do both, but that its courses should distinguish more clearly than at present between these two ends, instead of blurring them. On the whole, Italian universities emphasize culture, and the classical tradition is still strong.

The most serious problem that the Italian university system faces, and one that has slowed down any reform because of its implications, is that of its independence as an institution. The question is: "should the constitutional norm, which recognizes the right of universities to be autonomous organizations, be applied in a complete way?" It is, in fact, obvious that the problem of autonomy for universities is connected with innovation and the development and programming of university studies. The very future of the university lies in finding the balance that permits accessibility and affordability while providing a sound education.

There Can be no Democratization Without High Standards

Primary and secondary schools have also been democratized while sacrificing quality education. Curricula were not only reformed because of the emergence of new fields—aeronautics, electronics, marketing, computer science, linguistics—but above all because the middle-class values of the system did not match those of many of the users. The school had to respond to the problem of how to equalize educational opportunities for all children, regardless of their socioeconomic background. The new breed of students during the militancy of the early 1970s had engaged in a sociocultural revolution. They not only asked for curriculum reforms, but also questioned the old methods of teaching based on *nozionismo,* the accumulation of knowledge without relating it to a practical context. It was also propounded that a less authoritative teacher in the classroom would make the learning process more effective. In a series of memos written after 1968, the government's education authorities directed high school teachers to take into consideration the entire personality, intellectual commitment, and mental process of a student, not his or her performance on a specific test. This was an implicit rejection of *nozionismo*, and it encouraged students to cultivate the old Italian penchant for rhetoric. The testing, mostly through oral exams throughout the whole educational system, certainly allows the teacher and pupil to cover more ground, since speaking is obviously so much faster than writing, and if the student's thinking is woolly, the teacher can question more searchingly. It should also be said that in Italy, personal communication has always been highly prized.

As a result, at the compulsory levels, a new method of assessment of students was introduced. Progress reports based on numerical markings were replaced by brief analytical reports. Moreover, in planning class activities and programs, teachers were asked to take into account not only the needs of the group but also of individuals. In this regard, it should be pointed out that special efforts have been made to integrate handicapped children into regular classes in elementary and lower secondary schools. *Special education* was seen as demeaning and negatively affecting the potential learning abilities of students; therefore, it was limited to the severely physically and mentally handicapped. Consequently, remedial teaching activities for pupils with problems, foreseen by law, were reinforced and provided through the support staff properly trained in two-year specialization courses. It must be said that the situation of these experiences is not uniform throughout the country owing to the diversified social context in Italy. While some are well advanced, others are facing difficulties and contradictions. This process of integration of the handicapped into normal classes would seem to be irreversible, and is no longer questioned. However, there is still some discussion on how to achieve this integration; that is to say, on how to plan teaching activities and how to organize all the other aspects connected with the presence of a handicapped child in the class.

The evenness of the quality of the system is guaranteed by the fact that public school teachers are considered state employees and get their jobs through state competitive exams, *concorsi*, administered by the ministry of public education. They are assigned or transferred without consideration of the exigencies of the individual schools. In Italian public schools, teachers cannot choose the schools they prefer, and no school can choose its own teachers. Contrary to the American system, which is classist (separatist) because of the close connection of real estate value with school district prestige and the internal selection of students in each school through the creation of honor sections, advanced placement (AP) courses, etc., the Italians do not use a tracking system. Italian educational authorities feel that students tend to stay in their track throughout their school years and that remedial students develop poor self-images and are alienated from schooling.

Students in a tracked-system do not learn better, and the content and quality of education offered in each track is very different. Students form self-concepts, social relationships, and aspirations that reflect the status of the track in which they are placed. In America, this problem is alarming because the racial and socioeconomic makeup of students in different tracks tends to mirror the race and social class stratification of the larger society. In Italy, on the whole, everyone from the son of the doctor to the daughter of a waiter mixes in the same classroom. Indeed, because of the reforms of the 1960s and 1970s, the social class distinction in education was wiped out. This does not imply that elitism has been completely eradicated. The most prestigious high school is still the *liceo classico* which, notwithstanding all social changes, still attracts for the most part children from an educated background. Indeed, some educationists criticize this system. However, Italy has understood that in today's high-tech world of work, countries cannot overemphasize college and demean technical training. Italian school officials help the non-college bound students to pursue a more demanding curriculum than the "general" course so many American kids choose. It spares Italian industries and businesses from spending more money on training workers, and it spares colleges from spending so much on the remediation of ill-prepared freshmen who may not belong in college at all.

The democratization of the system did not eliminate gender preferential divisions that are determined by tradition and social predeterminations. As most studies show, girls are very selective in the choice of the type of school they attend. Their number is greater than that of boys in those professional schools that lead to elementary school teaching careers (girls comprise 90% of the total enrollment in these schools), in art schools (64%), in technical schools that prepare for clerical occupations (53%), and even in those schools for children of the upper- and upper-middle classes. Girls are more numerous in the *liceo classico,* centered around literature and philosophy (53%), than in the *liceo scientifico,* based on mathematics and natural sciences (38%). The same situation can be found at the university level, where girls account for only one-fourth of the enrollment in medicine, economics, and law, one-fifth in physics and chemistry, less than 10% in engineering, but 60% in biology and 75% in literature and philosophy.

Flirtation with educational practices that skip rudiments, inflate basic concepts, and hurry to results has had detrimental effects. Secondary schools have been moving toward the American school model, where fun-and-games, talk-ins, and so-called self-expression take the place of real intellectual training. Experimental teaching methodologies aimed at finding easy ways to make learning less laborious and demanding abound, while the use of audio-visual machinery has become more desirable than subject matter. As in everything else, Italy has been looking at the U.S. for an improvement of its education system; unwittingly, it has been looking at a system that has been in search of its own easy fix!

On the positive side, when compared to other countries, Italy presents a favorable academic picture. Italy has 210 class days, compared to 180 in America. It has the lowest teacher-to-student ratio in Europe; between 1980 and 1992, the enrollment in the first eight years went down by almost one and a half million students while the number of teachers grew by about one hundred and thirty-five thousand. Parents still play a key role in the learning process of the students at home. Another important feature of the elementary school is the inclusion, among the new subjects, of foreign languages as a means of understanding and comprehension and as part of the overall framework of linguistic education.

Teachers Must Be Accountable

Many teachers and parents alike are simply left bewildered by the spate of often contradictory reforms and tinkering over the past 30 years, and are skeptical as to whether any solution will succeed. But it is clear that no new system or reform will ever work effectively without a more flexible commitment and generous attitude on the part of the teachers. In and out of class, they remain the key to the whole problem. They have certainly evolved since the late 1960s in terms of more relaxed human contact with their students. But one of their handicaps is still their lack of up-to-date training: they were taught to instill academic virtues and few of them have much knowledge of modern teaching methods, of child psychology, or of what might be called "education for civics and leisure." But the teachers' attitude remains the most serious problem. Few are the teachers who are ready to put their hearts into the kind of work usually accepted as a basic part of the job in Britain or America. It is the usual Italian problem: teachers complain about state control, but then have no idea how to use their freedom when they get it. Too many of them lack any initiative, except that of protest. No educational system can attract quality faculty if it must indiscriminately pay its teachers/professors the same regardless of talent, potential, or performance.

Like other professions, the teaching profession includes three general groups: the excellent, the good, and the bad. Since unions bargain for pay increases as if all teachers performed at peak levels, excellent teachers become consistently underpaid while poor teachers become consistently overpaid. The cost of carrying poor teachers falls on the backs of the large middle group of good teachers. If the unions supported a *merit pay* structure, as is done in the U.S., they would lose their clout overnight. Unions argue that since teaching is a subjective art that cannot be accurately measured, a merit system could not possibly work. The argument may be sound, logical, and fair, but it completely misses the point. All institutions, both public and private, in a free market system evaluate performance on subjective as well as objective bases. Politicians win elections, executives capture promotions, and consumers buy goods and services, not just because they meet strictly measurable standards, but because people vote, work, and spend their money by whim and perception as much as by fact. Periodically, the education process itself looks rather subjective from the students' point of view. Grades, test scores, and most evaluations reflect subjective criteria to some degree or another. To improve quality in a real sense, schools should be allowed (the impossible dream) to ruthlessly expel teachers who do not perform to set standards. Doing so would traumatize a system that has long protected and promoted its incompetent labor force, but in the long run, such paring of the inferior will better prepare the system, its teachers, and students to compete in the age of a global knowledge network.

The situation has been changing. On the one hand, the ministry of education has been trying to overhaul teacher training, making it less purely academic, with a new stress on modern pedagogic techniques. On the other, the education system has reacted positively, showing great reserves of vitality. There is a growing awareness at the grassroots level that billions of lire alone cannot improve the quality of a democraticized school system. High academic achievements and a relevant education are achieved through revision of course content and updating of teaching methods, which must be carried forward by the teachers themselves with the full involvement of the community and individual parents. But in the politicized Italian world, such a transformational process from the grassroots level has raised some concerns—the Left has raised the smoke of the inequalities that such initiatives may cause. That is to say, while such initiatives toward reform are developed in some areas where the situation is favorable, they may be lacking in others. Here lies perhaps the most important challenge facing the government and school administrations in the coming years. Instead of imposing new global reforms from above, the ongoing reform process should be better monitored and guided in order to infuse the system throughout the country and stimulate those weaker areas less aware of the need for such initiatives.

Student Life Today: Less Political But Not Civic-Oriented

Incidents of the last few years indicate that students are very different from those who stormed the barricades in the late 1960s. Protest may flare up over a specific grievance, but it is not the old political idealism. The vast majority share the current Italian disillusion with ideologies; the few politically active ones are usually extremists.

As individuals, Italian students are hard-working, serious, and worried about their own futures; they are not indifferent to the world's problems, but they are skeptical and have lost faith in the ability to improve even their university or school environment, let alone society. Significantly, only a tiny percentage of university students even bother to join a student union. And a severe setback to the 1969 ideal of *participation* is the fact that very few students vote in the new university elections or come forward as candidates. So students stay quietly in the background, their noses in their textbooks, obsessed by the hunt for diplomas (*laurea*) that may stave off unemployment.

Even in their leisure time many feel isolated, for Italian universities and secondary schools are not warm club-like communities, as is often the case in America. Unlike in Britain and the U.S., the tradition is that students go to their local university; therefore, the great majority live at home, where they at least have the comfort of family and a nucleus of existing friends. But others, whose homes are too far away, live in rented rooms or dormitories, and here they can be very lonely.

The paucity of clubs and organized social life has always seemed— to an American or Briton—a striking feature of Italian universities, which have no equivalent to the big American "student union" building, a focus for community. Many large universities do not even have any student drama group or orchestra; and attempts to start them have been growing ever rarer now that students are so preoccupied with work, exams, and job prospects. Consequently, students seldom show any enthusiasm for the university or school.

Whose fault is that? Not altogether the students'. The building of campuses has not helped. Until the late 1960s nearly all universities were downtown. Here the students crowded the local *caffè*, deriving some warmth from the town and adding to its liveliness in return. But, with the growth in numbers, many departments are now scattered throughout the cities or have been transferred to big new campuses on the outskirts. Some of these are quite attractive, and they have eased working conditions; but the students are now more isolated than ever. For both universities and secondary schools, the problem is still institutional. Neither local faculties nor the state ministry, since the end of the 1960s, have made much effort to turn the school or university into more of a real community—a focus for loyalty and a fun place for students to stay around when classes are over. That is not the Italian tradition. Schools, and to a large extent universities, are facilities for the transmission of knowledge and the passing of exams, and nothing more. There is nothing like the American clubs and teams life. Photography clubs, drama societies, concerts, plays, recitals, sport events, and other cultural or recreational events are unheard of in most Italian universities. The ministry pays lip-service to the need for more out-of-class activities, but in practice puts them near the bottom of its budgetary priorities. It does not even provide proper funds for libraries, which even in the best *licei* tend to be miserably small and ill-stocked.

If out-of-class activities such as clubs are so few, it's also because so few teachers are prepared to stay on afterhours to help organize them. Teachers do not see this as part of the job; in fact, most likely they belong to a union that militantly opposes this kind of unpaid overtime. The average professor/teacher regards the school as a kind of office job: one arrives, holds classes, maybe with donnish brilliance, then goes home. The students' out-of-class lives are not their business. True, this attitude is changing a little among younger teachers; but it is still widespread. School/university activities are considered marginal to the academic life. Real life for students is what they get from outside—travel, television, friends, family.

Training in democracy, leadership, and civic feeling helps American students feel part of a living community and allows them to share responsibility for it. But in Italy, the traditional thinking is that it is the family's responsibility, not the school's, to build character. Parents look on school as an academic utility that should not compete with them as a center of loyalty; and if a school were to attempt training in leadership or civic responsibility, this would be resented as an intrusion into their own sphere. From an Anglo-American point of view, this leaves a void in the youngster's full education.

In conclusion, it is easy to be impressed by Italian students' resilience and their apparent ability—helped no doubt by their *home background*—to survive the system to which they are subjected. Yet, one is equally sure that a system that would attend to the formation of a social conscience might go a long way toward healing the maladjustments in Italian society and Italian public life. This is true of secondary schools; it is even more true of the universities.

A Reform That Works

Because of needs posed by social changes, pre-schooling was instituted and gradually, as the industrialization level of the country increased, was expanded. However, nursery school, *asilo nido*, and kindergarten, *asilo infantile,* for children from 3 to 5 years of age were only optional since they serve more as preparation for the compulsory school, though both are of special social importance, providing as they do babysitting service for working parents. Since it is not mandatory, such service is not funded by state government but run either by the municipalities or by private bodies; therefore, once again, it became either available privately to those who could afford it, or publicly by only those municipalities that were financially stable. Public nursery schools are in short supply, and even those run by the local public administrations can be expensive to support. Therefore, children of mothers who have jobs are given preference. In urban centers like Milan and Rome, more than one-third of the demand is unsatisfied.

At this level, Italy has instituted some very good school reforms from which United States' educators could borrow some ideas. One such system is the pre-school program in Reggio Emilia, which has received worldwide praise. Departing from the basic concept that each child is unique and different, the school system works on the assumption that in pre-school, teachers should only be concerned with the physical, emotional, and social aspects of development and should provide children with a rich and stimulating environment that is, at the same time, warm, loving, and supportive, and create in them a solid sense of security, positive self-esteem, and a long-term enthusiasm for learning.

The program is designed to foster young children's learning, representation, and expression through exploration and mastery of many symbolic media. Reggio educators believe children have preparedness, potential curiosity, and interest in constructing their learning, in engaging in social interaction, and in negotiating with everything the environment brings them. Creativity is seen not as an exceptional occurrence or a separate mental faculty, but as a characteristic way of thinking, knowing, and making choices.[3] Children's work is not casually created, but rather is the result of a guided exploration of themes and events that are relevant to the life of the children and the larger community. Classwork is organized around themes that allow children to learn a variety of skills and help them understand their world. What looks like art, for example, is actually a science, math, and art lesson. The classroom space is utilized in a manner that encourages creativity and individual freedom.

These schools are tax-base supported; however, families with children enrolled in the childcare (*asilo nido*) pay a monthly fee of $69-$269 based on the family's ability to pay. Disabled children and single parent children are admitted automatically. Other admissions are based on interviews.

Many features of the Reggio Emilia pre-school reflect Italian values. The relationship that is created between parents and teachers is similar to the roles played by the Italian extended family. Parents, teachers, and other members of the community have worked together to produce a unique pre-school/day-care program that proves that children learn and grow in a social atmosphere outside of, and in addition to, the home. The emphasis on the arts and aesthetic insights expresses an appreciation of detail and sensitivity to design that is in the mainstream of the Italian cultural tradition of being creative. And so, amid endless debate, the struggle goes on to find solutions to the educational problems of a new age.

Notes

1. G. Vacca, *Quale democrazia?* (Bari: De Donato, 1977), 168.

2. J. LaPalombara, *Democracy Italian Style* (New Haven: Yale U. P., 1987), 68.

3. For an informative report and assessment of the Reggio Emilia preschool system see: R. S. New, "Excellent Early Education: A City in Italy Has It," *Young Children* 45, no. 6 (1990): 4-10; (N.C.), "The Ten Best Schools in the World," *Newsweek,* 2 December 1991, 50-58; P. Hinckle, "A School Must Rest on the Idea That All Children Are Different," *Newsweek*, 2 December 1991; D. Newbold, "A State Nursery School That Is Simply the Best," *Time Educational Supplement*, 14 February 1992, 15; B. Rankin, "Inviting Children's Creativity: A Story of Reggio Emilia, Italy," *Child Care Information Exchange*, vol. 85 (1992): 30-35.

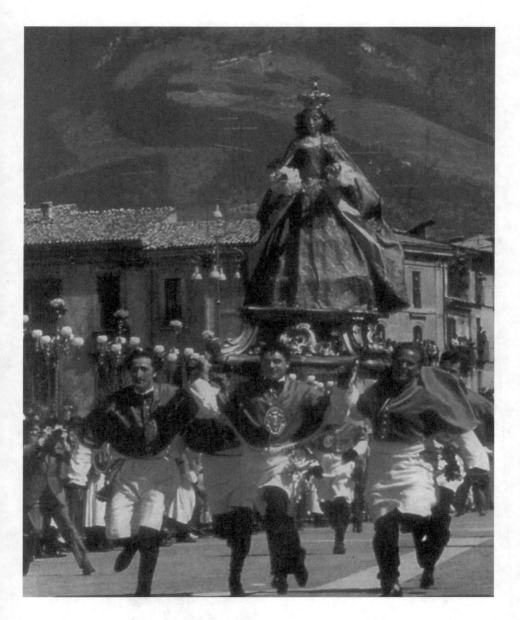

Processions carrying statues of Christ or Mary to celebrate major holidays in the liturgical calendar, or of local patron saints on their feast day, are still popular practices notwithstanding the big drop in church attendance. Printed by courtesy of *America Oggi*.

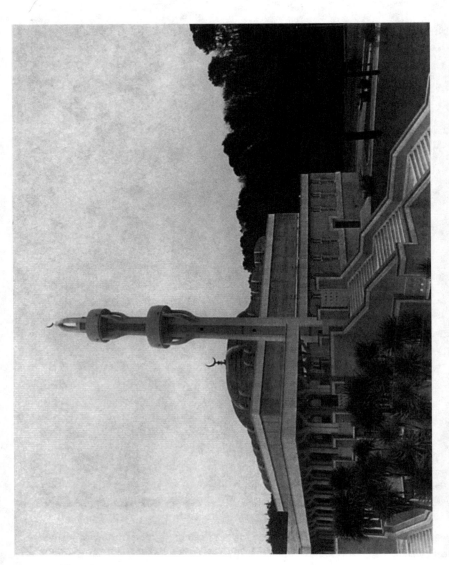

Immigration into Italy has had a profound social and cultural impact. Islam has become the second religion in Italy and Rome is the home of the largest mosque in western Europe. Printed by courtesy of *America Oggi*.

X

Secularization of State and Society

The Catholic Church:
The End of Its Hegemony Within Italian Society

One of the most radical changes that Italy has undergone in the last 25 years is the secularization of every aspect of life and the consequent change in the relationship between state and Church. Being rooted in a peasant society and culture, the profound change in Italian Catholicism was inevitable with the rise of industrialization and economic development. While the authority of the Church as an institution has diminished, a new-style, liberated spirit of religion is very much alive and takes the most diverse forms.

At the end of the 1950s, the Italians' outlook toward the Church and religion was basically that of many centuries before, reflecting primarily agricultural society. Italy was still the geographic center of the Catholic world. The Vatican was an Italian institution and the pope himself was bishop of Rome and primate of Italy. By the terms of the Italian constitution, the Church enjoyed privileges unique among democratic countries. Catholicism formed a profound and natural part of the social fabric of the nation; it permeated every aspect of Italian cultural life. Catholicism had a position of overwhelming dominance within Italy and generated an enormous variety of cultural forms. Catholic values had played, both anthropologically and culturally, a decisive role in shaping individual lives and collective behavior. For the average citizen, church ceremonies were both social and religious events, and the profession of faith was still felt with strong passion. Religion, in the form of adoration of a host of local saints in a widely diffused pagan religiosity, offered especially the peasants a sustaining refuge from the harsh realities of life.[1]

The Church's presence in the life of the citizens was strong at every level also because of its education and welfare activities. The parish priest was the center of community life—he was lawyer, adviser, teacher, psychologist, and social and spiritual healer—he had responsibility for the local nursery schools, for bible classes, oratories, the parish library, etc. Over many decades the Church had built up an impressive network of hospitals (the most popular bearing the name *Fate bene fratelli* [Do Good Brothers] and nursing and old people's homes that were staffed by various religious orders. In addition, the POA (*Pontificia Opera di Assistenza*) organized a large number of educational and recreational institutions. These varied from seaside and mountain camps to kindergartens, to *doposcuole* (afternoon activities for six-to-twelve-years olds), to *case del fanciullo* and *della fanciulla* for runaway teenagers. In the absence of state provision for old people, families turned with gratitude to Catholic welfare institutions.

In trying to present a view of how Italians live their religion(s), it is important to look at the cultural tradition and to weigh the different experiences that constitute it. This is important because although the Catholic Church endows some people with authority to assure the authentic practice of religion, people have developed particular practices and beliefs (from baptism to the invocation and veneration of saints) that show clearly that religion could be very personal and is a continual process. It is in dealing with this process that the Church constantly struggles in achieving and defending its hegemony within Italian society.

Church teaching provided many of the basic conceptions in a cosmology of ideas about human agency, natural forces, fortune, and misfortune. God's grace was invoked when the priest made the annual blessing of all the houses of his parishioners before Easter and later blessed the field of the village. A whole range of practices grew up to deal with misfortune, from the ringing of church bells to avert storms, to exorcism, or to the invocation of particular saints specializing in help with bodily illness. The celebration of the mass was no more important than the use of a religious amulet as protection against the evil eye. The blessed olive branches on Palm Sunday and other objects blessed on other occasions, together with religious formulas and imagery, were used by laity faced with misfortune, in private acts of divination and curing. In part these practices slipped out of the control of the clergy. We are in the presence of magical practices whose interpretation has generated controversy. Certainly there are parallels between these practices and those of non-Catholic peasantries; some have their roots in a pre-Christian culture that the Church has been unable to eradicate. However, far from being survivals, some of these magical practices show a fundamental continuity with central parts of Catholic theology, for example with the rite of exorcism that is part of baptism.

Being a Catholic meant also to be shaped by certain specific social practices that generated an identity. Catholics are all baptized and receive a baptismal name that is chosen from the calendar of saints, and that saint's name day (*onomastico*) is celebrated by everybody carrying that name. Catholic identity expanded to forms of identity based on territory. In many parts of Italy people have a very strong sense of pride and identification with the town or village of birth; there are names and stereotypes for these regional and local identities, and in a number of areas it was the Church that provided the focus for many of the large-scale activities that brought a village together as a collective entity. The village patron saint, with its statue, cult, and processions, provided one way in which a village collective identity was articulated.

In the 1950s Italian parishes were spilling over with activities. In 1956, 69% of adult Italians said that they were going to church on a regular basis. The great number of masses, confessions, and communions in each parish each week testified to the Church's vigorous state of health. So too did the number of organizations associated with parish life, especially Catholic Action, which represented the *civic* face of Italian Catholicism. However, Catholic Action was two or three times stronger in the civic, more association-prone regions of the North than in the less civic areas of the South. In Italy, as Robert Putnam demonstrated, organized religion was an alternative to the civic community, not part of it. Vertical bonds of authority were more characteristic of the Italian Church than horizontal bonds of fellowship.[2]

This world largely vanished in the course of two decades or so. By the mid-1970s, with the rapid secularization of Italian society and turmoil within the Church following the Second Vatican Council, the presence of the Church in society diminished rapidly and its power structure changed immensely.

The process, begun in the early 1960s, had as a most significant development the gradual transformation of the Church from a Eurocentric body, in which Italy was the leading country, to an international body whose center of interests spread far more to the rest of Europe and to the Third World, particularly Latin America. When Pius XII died in October 1958, the College of Cardinals had 55 members, of whom 36 were Europeans, half of those Italian, and Europe had the highest number of baptized Catholics. When Montini became pope (Paul VI) in 1963, 52 of the 80 cardinals were Italian. After the mid-1960s, the size of the body was expanded and the number of Italians in it declined through attrition. By 1971 there were 120 cardinals, of whom only 28 were Italian. For the first time the Italians were not a majority.

At the same time, Paul VI had reduced the importance of the Italian hierarchy in other ways. In the second half of the 1960s, the Italian dioceses were consolidated and the number of bishops reduced from 315 to 270, still a disproportionate number when compared to France's 88 and Spain's 65. This change was accompanied by an effort to place some distance between the Holy See and the Italian hierarchy. With the pope as Primate of Italy and the curia essentially Italian, the Vatican and the Italian Church had always been inseparably interconnected. In 1966, for the first time in Vatican and Italian history and about one hundred years after similar bodies had been established in other countries, an independent conference of bishops, the *Conferenza Episcopale Italiana* (*CEI*), was established. When John Paul II was elected 20 years later in October 1978, the College of Cardinals had doubled in number (110), with 56 non-European cardinals, 44 of whom came from the Third World, and Latin America had the highest percentage of Catholics (40%). Therefore, the election to pope of Karol Wojtyla, Archbishop of Cracow, the first non-Italian to ascend to the throne of Saint Peter since 1522, although somewhat dramatic, was not unexpected. The election of a Pole to pope also implied that the Church was going to play a much less important role in Italian affairs than in the past and that the time was approaching for a renegotiation of the relations between state and Church.

The Problematic Solution of the "Roman Question"

The formal basis of Church-state relations in Italy is the Lateran Treaty of February 11, 1929, signed by Mussolini and Pope Pius XI. With that accord, the Church and the Italian State brought to an end a conflict that had begun with the unification of Italy. Italy had been unified on liberal, secular principles and, in keeping with Cavour's famous principle of "a free church in a free state," most of the Church's legal privileges had been abolished. When Italian troops entered Rome in 1870, the pope ceased for the first time in centuries to be a temporal sovereign. In anger he shut himself into the Vatican as a self-proclaimed prisoner of the Italian state. The Church refused to recognize the new state, excommunicated its monarch, and forbade the faithful to hold public office or vote in national elections. In assuming such a position, the Church not only fostered a widespread popular alienation from the state but also isolated itself and its faithful from the vital forces of society.

The *Roman Question* was not settled until Mussolini saw advantage in gaining Church support and was willing to pay a high price for it. The Pacts of Lateran, which solved the Roman Question, were in three parts. One was a treaty creating an independent Vatican city-state of 108 acres and giving the Holy See possession of a number of churches and palaces in Rome; a papal summer residence at Castel Gandolfo, on the outskirts of Rome; basilicas at Padua, Loreto, and Assisi; and custody of all catacombs in Italy. The pope was recognized as juridically sovereign, and the Vatican was accorded the attributes of a sovereign state, with the authority to maintain its own police, postal system, bank, and radio enterprises. In return the pope recognized the Italian state and renounced the Holy See's claim to the former papal territories. With mutual agreement, crimes committed on Vatican soil would be tried in Italian courts and be subject to Italian legal penalties.

A second accord was a concordat that established Catholicism as "the sole religion of the state" and gave the Church sweeping privileges in civil affairs. Catholic religious instruction was compulsory in both elementary and secondary schools. Church marriages were deemed legally valid and did not have to be followed by a civil ceremony; their dissolution was solely the responsibility of ecclesiastical courts. Religious institutions were authorized to hold property and were exempted from taxes. Seminarians and priests were exempted from military service, and those expelled from the priesthood were banned from teaching, government employment, and any position that brought them into contact with the public. Priests were also banned from party membership and political activities. The state was given the right to approve the appointment of bishops.

A third accord dealt with the financial settlement that gave the Holy See more than 750 million lire, plus an additional one million lire in Italian state bonds, as compensation for the loss of the pre-1870s territories; this huge indemnity, in time, became the basis of a financial empire, first in Italy and then abroad. Moreover, in its few years in office, Mussolini's government increased clerical salaries, granted several million lire for damaged churches, restored the Crucifix in classrooms and law courts, rescued the (Catholic) Banco di Roma during the Depression, and closed down all brothels and anticlerical journals. It also set up a national examination system to enable Church school students to graduate on an equal footing with those from state schools and recognized degrees given by the new Catholic University of the Sacred Heart in Milan.

Unquestionably, Mussolini did settle the *Roman Question*, but he settled it at the expense of the separation of Church and state, which had been at the core of the *Risorgimento*. But for all the legal concessions, the fascists did circumscribe the activity of the Church in civil life, with the result that relations between the Church and the government were at times strained. For example, under fascism there was great hostility to Catholic Action because it was regarded as a vocal alternative rather than a support of the regime. Many leading christian democrats such as Aldo Moro, Amintore Fanfani, and Giulio Andreotti were closely linked with the Church and had been leading members at the time Cardinal Montini, who later became Pope Paul VI, had an influential role. With the fall of fascism, and the supremacy of the christian democrats in political affairs in the immediate postwar period, the Church became very powerful politically and established a strong grip on every aspect of Italian life. Its activities were facilitated by the fact that the Constitutional Assembly, by a vote of 350 to 149, supported the incorporation of the Lateran Pacts in the new constitution. That decision, in fact, set the stage for the subsequent course of Church-state relations: a nearly organic relationship, almost in symbiosis, between the Church and the christian democrats.

Church Strategies and Changes

Twice in the postwar period, the Church developed new strategies to conserve consent in the face of major changes. The first time it defined true Catholicism in terms of obedience to the political directives of the clergy, the second time it modernized its liturgy and priorities in relation to the secular forces within Italian society. However, both shifts did not prevent the loss of parishioners and its status as the state religion.

At the end of the 1940s, the hierarchy of the Church identified itself closely with the ruling upper-bourgeois class and protected its interests by defending the social status quo. In rural areas, priest and gentry were natural allies. Although the Church was anti-temporal, it did meddle in politics. Priests were taking an oath to devote their lives to the re-Christianization of the working class. Many Catholics, especially younger ones, felt that it was time for the Church to broaden its role and to share in building a better world; and with their ardent faith they set about this task. Strong faith, they claimed, was necessary in order to defend belief from the possible influence of satanic political doctrines.

The Cold War had a profound impact on Italian Catholicism and Church relations with its faithful and redefined the characteristics of Catholic identity. The 1948 election was fought not just for control over the state but also to determine the position Italy was to occupy within the emerging world order. The Church committed itself totally to this political contest, and its organizational and ideological support were crucial to the victory of the *D.C.* The battle was fought-out using all the media: sermons, rallies, radio, cinema, newspapers, and, most strikingly, wall-posters. The iconographic tradition representing good (the Archangel Michael or other figures of strength and purity) and evil (the Angel of Death, masked devils, demons, and monsters) had a center stage. In this ideological battle even the concept of family became a means. The Church was the creator and defender of the family, recognizing its unique and sovereign status, whereas under communism the moral and sacred ties of family life were destroyed, people's loyalty and allegiance were to the state, divorce and free love were encouraged. In representing the Cold War as part of the eternal struggle between good and evil, the Church was conducting a struggle for the soul of Italy which had to be defended from the barbarian hordes: Catholicism was a central component of Italian identity, communism was an external threat.

This evolution of Italian Catholicism had its own dynamic. Communism could be fought by creating a society consistent with Catholic doctrine, and to achieve that the Vatican, the hierarchy, and the laymen's organizations had to work together to mold Catholics into a political bloc and to tie that bloc to the Christian Democratic Party as a necessary alternative to the dreaded Communist Party. At election time, the Church, from pope down to the parish priest, stated that it was a religious duty to vote for the *D.C.* The *D.C.* was greatly helped by Catholic Action, or *Azione Cattolica (AC)*, an organization based on the parish and not on the party. It was open to members of both sexes, but women always prevailed: in 1946, AC had 151,000 men and 370,000 women; by 1969 it had 183,000 men and 459,000 women. Church and AC provided the strongest basis for women in the *D.C.*

If one looks closely at any of the grass-roots movements of postwar social reform, in nearly every case one will find that some nucleus of Catholic militants played a very important role. The new militant social Christian action took many forms, but always with the purpose "to build the Kingdom of God on earth," something the Church, it was claimed, never used to care much about. The Church had also developed a political ideology known as the *social doctrine*, a fairly vague set of principles that could be used for social and political activity and that could be constantly reinterpreted by the Church. Its central idea was class reconciliation.

Italian society was further polarized when on July 13, 1949, Pius XII issued a decree that prohibited Catholics from joining the *P.C.I.*, and from writing, reading, publishing, or distributing any communist literature. Those engaging in any of these activities could be excommunicated and would not receive any of the sacraments. Two weeks later the Vatican explained that excommunication would apply not only to those who joined or supported the Communist Party but also any of its associated organizations or allies, including the trade union *C.G.I.L.* and the Socialist Party. The position and actions of the Church legitimated a policy of excluding the Left from positions in the state, and, in the hands of the local civic committees were also designed to marginalize non-Catholics in all spheres of public life. This was an alienating message for many Italians who had been hoping for big social changes. Most of them were neither atheists nor devotees of free love. They married in Church, baptized their children, placed a high value on family life, and participated in many of the same devotional practices as other Italians. Yet now they were being defined as not true Catholics and were being asked to choose between Church and party.

All this had a deep social impact. By injecting itself into every aspect of civil life and dividing the political world into saints and devils, the Church reinforced the country's historic problem of social division. As La Palombara commented, the Church's massive political intervention had the same effect after 1945 as after 1870 by separating "loyal Catholics" from other Italians.[3] Some broke with the Church and no longer recognized its authority in any domain of life. A larger number recognized it only in a restricted domain of religion and personal morality, separate from the social and cultural domains in which the Church had once been hegemonic. This action also came to be a mistake because it did not stop the growth of the Left over the next 40 years, nor did it prevent the *rapprochement* between the *D.C.* and the *P.S.I.* in the 1960s. Indeed, the conservative position of the Church up to the end of the 1950s did not have any positive results either on the spiritual or the political level.

The election in 1958 of Angelo Roncalli, as Pope John XXIII signaled the desire of the Church to move with the times. The new pope had an acute sense of how fast the world was changing and how important it was for the Church to understand this change and adapt to it. In his brief papacy he dedicated himself to an *aggiornamento*, a modernization of the Church. Where Pius XII tried to erect barriers, John XXIII sought to open doors. As a first step he designed a strategy to revise Church relations in three areas: (a) toward Eastern Europe; (b) toward non-Catholics, including Marxists; (c) toward capitalism.

Certainly, the political changes in Eastern Europe were just as important. Historians will eventually assess the kind of direct and indirect role or influence the Church might have played in the fall of communism in Eastern Europe. The process of *détente* with Eastern Europe was initiated with a series of symbolic acts. Pope John's meeting with Khrushchev's daughter and son-in-law was symptomatic of that new mood.

While the pope himself began to look at the larger world picture, Italian political affairs were being delegated to the Italian bishops. And as a consequence of this change, the Church intervened more, not less, in Italian politics. In May 1960, in a leading article in the *Osservatore Romano*, the official Vatican daily, the Church hierarchy attempted to establish its supremacy in Italian affairs by making some "basic points":

1. The Church must guide the faithful in both ideas and practice;
2. The Church cannot be politically neutral;
3. The Church must be the judge of whether political cooperation between the faithful and the nonbelievers was permissible; and
4. The Church cannot allow believers to cooperate with Marxists.

Meanwhile, however, the pope was making some very radical pronouncements. In the encyclical letter *Mater et Magistra* (*Mother and
Teacher*, 1961), he began to question the support given by the Church
to capitalism. Concentrating on the social teaching of the Church, he
rejected the free play of market forces, emphasized the need for greater
social justice, and called for the integration of the disinherited into the
social and political order. This position coincided not only with the
debate on the modernization of the Italian economy, but also with the
debate on the constitution of a center-left government of the *D.C.* in
alliance with the *P.S.I.* The 1963 encyclical *Pacem in Terris* (*Peace
on Earth*) called for international conciliation based on the neutrality
of the Church and its refusal to accept the barriers of the Cold War.
The encyclical was addressed to "all men of good will," not just to
Catholics, and argued the need for cooperation between people of
different ideological beliefs. In addition, the encyclical stressed the need
for the betterment of the economic and social development of the
working classes, the entry of women into public life, and the justice of
anticolonialist struggles in the Third World. The possibility for a dialogue between the Catholic and Marxist worlds had been opened. The
repercussions in Italy of *Peace on Earth* were very strong, for in practice the pope had given his effective blessing to the new coalition.

The changes in the Church were also underlined by the papal decision to convene an ecumenical council (the twenty-first in the history
of the Church and the first since 1870). The Council, known as Vatican
II, was called to modernize the Church as an organization, develop
better relations with other religions, and face the problems of modern
society. In political terms, it was seen as an "opening to the left": the
campaign against communists was lifted while the support for the
D.C. continued.

Vatican II opened in October 1962 and closed under Paul VI in
December 1965. It represented a renewal of the Church, an attempt
to respond to the forces that were changing society and to reconsider
the position of the Church in an evolving international context. As a
result of the council, the position of the bishops was considerably
strengthened by instituting synods of bishops to be elected by the national churches. The distinctive contribution that the laity could make
to the Church was recognized and encouraged. But the most striking
changes came in practice and emphasis: the introduction of the vernacular, instead of Latin, into the celebration of the sacraments. For
the first time during the Mass, the priest was speaking the same lan-

guage as the laity, and this together with other changes in the form of the ritual can be seen as reducing the distance between the two. The use of deacons from the laity to read the lessons, choral singing, the offer of wine as well as the wafer to communicants, all these increased the level of participation by the faithful in the service.

Vatican II, besides reducing the distance between laity and clergy, also changed the prevalent conception of God as a remote figure. Emphasis shifted from God the judging Father to God the loving Son who makes himself available to us through the sacraments and can be approached through prayer and good deeds. This also involved a reminder of Christ's commandments to love one's neighbor and that a Christian life is lived not just through private acts of devotion and the sacraments, but in acts of love, charity, and fellowship with other human beings.[4] These shifts of emphasis to the teachings of Jesus Christ and his sacrifice, which are at the core of religious life, have been called Christocentric. In the process, there was the devaluation of the external cults that focused on the power of the mediating figures, Mary and the saints. Local clergy also began to withdraw their support from many popular forms of celebration, including the procession with a saint's statue or other religious images, which often included a great deal of locally generated ritual and symbolism.[5] There was a concern among Church leaders that parishioners were participating in the events more out of social convention and tradition than for the spiritual significance. Nevertheless, these kinds of celebrations lost much of their significance for people who migrated because the village collectivity that provided the bounded and stable community did not exist anymore. Therefore, forms of Catholicism that had permeated and shaped many social identities and that had operated through ritual acts and symbolic forms, lost their resonance and were replaced by a view of religion that was concerned essentially with the spiritual aspect. There was a general shift away from traditions, which were embedded in particular social contexts whose existence was normally unquestioned, to a more universalistic ethos based on individual conscience. These kinds of changes in religious practice also found better reception with middle-class values.

The new pope, Paul VI, continued the policy of détente with the East and vigorously pursued a policy of dialogue with the Third World. As the Vatican became more international in body, it also became less of a christian democrat support system. The important encyclical *Populorum Progressio* (*Progress of the People*) (March 26, 1967) stated that the Christian principles are incompatible with a political system that puts at the base of everything the pursuit of private profit and competition and the absolute right to private property. The encyclical also asserted that even though revolutionary insurrections can be evil they may be necessary in exceptional circumstances such as the struggle against a permanent and cruel form of despotism.[6] In the *Octogesima Adveniens* (May 14, 1971) Paul VI asserted in stronger terms his belief that no social system could be derived from the "social doctrine" of the Church. If there was no "Christian political thought" then it followed that there could be no "Christian political party." This meant that Catholics could be active in various political parties.[7]

The implications for the Italian political scene are obvious. After 1968 some clergy had already started to assume political aims; they felt that Christianity needed to be liberated from the Church, which they regarded as still a tool of the bourgeoisie. Social issues became their main focus. "Priests don't talk about God any more, they talk about the housing crisis," was an often-heard complaint of many older Catholics.

The autonomous role of the Church in political affairs was parallel to the autonomy declared by the lay Catholic organizations. Organizations such as the Association of Italian Christian Workers (*ACLI*) and Catholic Action (*AC*) officially cut their political affiliation with the *D.C.* When the *D.C.* sought to abolish the divorce law through a popular referendum, expecting the Vatican's support, the Vatican delegated to the Italian bishops the anti-divorce campaign. The attitude of the Vatican could not but encourage Catholic dissent in Italy. The youth branches of *ACLI* came out in favor of divorce; *ACLI* itself refused to take a position and so did a number of leading bishops and some important cardinals. Many Catholic intellectuals fought openly on the side of the divorce parties, and during the campaign loosened their ties with the *D.C.* For some of them the difference created such an emotional and ideological split that in the next political campaign they ran and were elected to Parliament as candidates on the *P.C.I.* or *P.S.I.* lists. In the referendum held on May 12, 1974, the opponents of divorce were able to muster only 41% of the vote.

The *D.C.* had come to rely on the formidable organization of the Church and, through it, to establish a presence in virtually all sectors of society, but by 1975-1976 the *D.C.* had lost its monopoly over Catholic representation. The Church and the *D.C.*, the two institutions that dominated postwar Italian society, had lost their power; a decisive majority of Italians had stated implicitly that religious doctrine was not to be the basis of the country's laws or social life. The 1970s were, in fact, a traumatic period for the Catholics in Italy and the world. As a result of the cultural crisis of the 1960s, the end of the *economic miracle*, the workers' unrest, the growth of political dissent, the students' movement, the birth of feminism, and the changes within the Church itself, young Catholics became attracted by new forms of internationalism and, particularly, by the *new theology*, or *liberation theology*, coming from Latin America, as well as by new anti-authoritarian forms of organization. At the base of these reactionary forces there was both an anti-establishment attitude and an inner desire to improve the world. Many of the groups were community-based and active in helping those who were at the fringes of society, like the handicapped or drug-addicts; others assumed more of an international posture and campaigned for world peace, anti-nuclear policies and economic assistance to the Third World.

The largest renewal movement in contemporary Italy is *Comunione e Liberazione*, founded in 1969 in Milan. It is an organization of devout laity that has spiritual leadership from powerful sections of the hierarchy. It emerged first on the political scene as a radical force, bringing news of the liberation struggles of Catholic peasantries in Latin America and denouncing the corruption and loss of spiritual purpose in the Italian political establishment. At the grass-roots level, *Communion and Liberation* is strongest in the North and in the cities, and especially in the universities, where it has eclipsed the Left as the major political force. For young students leaving their homes in rural areas and villages, *Communion and Liberation* offers a network of assistance and welcomes recruits into wholesome social activities, parties, outings, and music, and all are pervaded by an active Christian evangelism.

Another Catholic lay organization that assumed a very important active secular and political role is the *Movimento Popolare* (Popular Movement), founded in 1976, which represents a more militantly political Catholic element that is ready to oppose the Left, take part in demonstrations, and heckle at communist meetings. With the intent to work at the sociopolitical level, the members of the *Popular Movement* have worked to take control of student assemblies in schools and universities and have created hundreds of cultural centers. Although fervent Christians, they are an independent community.

Ambiguity, conciliation, and passivity were not the traits highly prized by the Polish John Paul II, and in the course of the 1980s a change of style and direction in the papacy became increasingly evident. From the start, the hallmark of his office was the affirmation of a monolithic, authoritarian, and aggressive church. Appalled by Western secular and materialistic values, he pursued a mission of promoting traditional—and conservatively interpreted—social and ecclesiastical values.

The pope was very critical of the Italians' religious practice: a secularized society afflicted by a "de-Christianization" of mentality and morals caused by a "practical materialism" that was abetted by atheistic ideologies. The substance and manner of John Paul's approach contrasted starkly with the conciliatory stance of the majority of the hierarchy. For the first time in modern history there were substantial differences between a pope and most Italian bishops, and it wasn't just that they did not speak the same language! The central disagreement was over the Church's political and social engagement. It is very important to make clear the difference between the Vatican as the center of the world organization and as the Italian Church. In the past, this distinction hardly seemed to exist. Although the ultimate head of the Italian Church is the pope, it is the cardinal who presides over the Italian Episcopal Council and who has the day-to-day responsibility of running the Italian Church. The new system, a quarter of a century old, originated with John XXIII and gives the Italian Church its own identity, similar to the French, Spanish, German, American, or any other national Church.

Yet the Church remained a strong presence in Italian political life with its approximately 28,000 parishes performing about 160,000 Sunday services that were attended by several million people. Its cultural apparatus is responsible for producing several hundred books every year, as well as a daily paper, *Osservatore romano*, over 50 weeklies (one of these, *Famiglia cristiana,* is the largest circulation weekly in Italy), well over 200 monthlies, and several hundreds of parish bulletins.[8]

Secularization Within a Strong Catholic Culture

The drastic population shifts from the land to the cities and from the South to the North destroyed the centuries-old social order. And one of the most dramatic effects that the process of urbanization and industrial development had was the secularization of society.

Migration, especially, had such a profound impact because there was a marked difference between northern and southern religiosity.

Southern migrants missed the local customs, patron saints, and feasts of their village churches and could not reconcile themselves to the somewhat barren and arid life of the northern churches. Some northerners denounced the southerners for living their religion in a totally superficial way, more as magic and bigotry than in a truly Christian manner.[9] Moreover, as the growth of the Welfare State made state and local authorities more responsible for social services, which for years had been the prerogative of the Church, the social functions of the Church contracted remarkably. Not less important, the American model of a consumer society unquestionably helped to erode Catholic values. Political parties, clubs, social circles, and sporting associations could provide outlets for a host of activities that were once primarily centered around the Church.

How extensive and how fast was the secularization process? In 1956, 69% of the population attended mass regularly; 20 years later the figure had declined to 37%, and by 1985 it had fallen to 25%. In a 1974 poll, 59% of those questioned characterized themselves as "indifferent" to the church and 11% in "opposition" to it. Only about 30% described themselves as practicing Catholics. Another indicator was the number of couples who had only civil marriages. Before 1970 there were very few of them; by 1980 the figure reached 10% and in Rome 25%. The number of abortions soared during this period. A 1980 survey by the Diocese of Rome on sexual morals, abortion, and divorce showed that even among practicing Catholics, 60% approved of divorce, 47% of abortion, and 52% of birth-control methods. More surprising were the results of a poll conducted in 1984 by the Regional Episcopal Council of Piedmont. It showed that only 9% of the Catholics in the region attended Mass every Sunday, with another 21% going to church at most once a month. Although 89% had a religious wedding and 92% had their children baptized, only 12% shared the views of the Church on sexual morals and a mere 6% opposed abortion. In step with the times, in 1970 the Constitutional Court annulled a law making adultery a crime and several months later canceled a prohibition of contraception and public dissemination of birth-control information.

The process of secularization is also evident in the rapid decrease in the number of clergy. Between 1961 and 1981, while the population increased by about 2%, the number of priests declined from 43,000 to 40,600. In 1961, 601 persons took holy orders, in 1980, the number was down to 347. Not only has it become increasingly more difficult to recruit new priests, but the diocesan clergy has become an aging body ever less able to cope with a growing and changing population. Today the priest is no longer the center of the community as he once had been; in a society in which roles were more diverse, he can easily be lonely and isolated.

The most startling indication of the changes that can occur in religious belief is the public's stand on abortion. In 1978, Parliament enacted a liberal abortion law. Despite a Catholic campaign against it, abortion became widespread. It is calculated that in the 1980s the abortion rate was 800 for every 1,000 live births. When the pope and the D.C. forced a popular referendum (May 1981) on the issue, merely 30% voted for repeal. To the surprise of everyone, women in the conservative South voted to retain abortion by roughly the same proportion as those in the North.

The old Catholic culture is very much alive today: magical curing practices, the belief that all communist women are immoral, flourishing and evolving saint cults, and lay groups devoted to charity are still present. However, for the most part, religion is no longer a matter of social convention but of real conviction, and so it is now more sincere. A young man's faith is no longer so "protected" by the environment of family and parish. It has to pass through the ordeal of contact with atheism, and if it survives, it may be more real than in the old days. While social action continues, if less widely than in the 1960s, simultaneously many people are now turning back to the true spiritual sources of Christianity, to the fundamentals of prayer and worship. In some cases this is due to a feeling that social action for its own sake had gone too far and that Christ was in danger of being forgotten. It may also be caused by the fact that in this new anxious age people feel greater need for spiritual consolation. At any rate, the trend is widespread; it does not, however, take the form of a return to traditional church services. Like some other countries, Italy has seen the rise of the so-called charismatic movement, whereby informal groups meet regularly for prayer and discussion, often in private homes. It is all vaguely revivalist, very different from old-style Catholic worship. Often no priest is present. Prayers are spontaneous, and expressed in everyday language, a complete break with the ritual rosary-type prayers of Catholic tradition.

Therefore, there has also arisen a number of religious communities of a new kind, often formed by laymen who find the traditional parish context inadequate. These are not enclosed and tightly disciplined centers like the old monasteries, but informal meeting places where lay-men can come together in their leisure time, maybe under the guid-ance of a priest, or maybe not. These groups represent a new desire of laity and priests alike for more self-expression, for finding their own ways to God and to Christ.

The hierarchy of the Church in Italy has reacted warily to the new trends. On social issues it projects, sincerely, a liberal image. At the same time, partly under the Vatican influence, it is now outwardly adopting a much tougher line on abortion, birth-control, pre-marital sex, and even divorce. Its problem, like that of the Vatican, is that its doctrines are no longer in tune with the actual behavior of the major-ity of Catholics. The Church may preach against birth-control, yet most younger Catholics practice it and do not find it inconsistent with their Christian faith. Indeed, it may not signify any waning of real Christian belief, but it does certainly have serious implications for the relationship between Church hierarchy and the laity.

Farewell to the Catholic State

This high level of secularization of Italian society indicated that the 1929 concordat had become a relic of the past and the time was ripe for a new agreement. It was signed in February 1984 by the Vatican secretary of state Agostino Casaroli and Bettino Craxi, the Italian prime minister, the first from a party of the Left. In the three most important articles—dealing with marriage law, religious instruction in public schools, and tax exemption of church organization—the Church did not retain much power. Although a religious wedding retained its validity in civil law, the act of marriage had to conform to the legal requirements set by the Italian laws. Marital annulments by ecclesiasti-cal courts were subject to approval by Italian courts. Religious instruc-tion in public schools was made purely voluntary. The issue of state salaries to priests and the taxability of church property required more time for a complete solution. The Vatican had for years claimed ex-emption from taxes both on the property of Church organizations and on the Vatican's shareholdings in Italy. When under parliamentary pressure it was forced to pay taxes, the Vatican sold off its Italian stocks; but it continued to lobby for tax-exempt status for some 50,000 ecclesiastical organizations and properties that were used at least in part for commercial purposes—such as monasteries that rent rooms to tourists. At the end it was agreed that only church properties of a strictly religious nature would retain their tax exemption. The stipend to the clergy (which amounted to $175 million in 1984), as well as funds for the construction of churches, were phased out by 1990, leaving the Church dependent on voluntary contributions, which are tax deductible as in the United States.

The most difficult problem to resolve was finding a way to control the activities of the Vatican bank, which operates as a normal commercial bank for depositors of the ecclesiastical order, and has always been very secretive about every aspect of its affairs. Not being subject to Italian banking regulations and exchange controls, the bank has operated freely. Until the end of the 1960s, the bank's investments were in a broad range of Italian industries and in vast real estate holdings. With the taxation pressure on its stock dividends from the Italian government, in 1968 the bank moved its assets into financial shareholdings outside Italy, especially in the U.S. In transferring these funds, the bank's president, Archbishop Paul Marcinkus, an American with no financial experience, depended heavily on the assistance of two Italian bankers, Michele Sindona and Roberto Calvi. The two bankers turned out to be first-rate financial swindlers who brought embarrassment and huge financial losses to the Vatican.[10]

Secularization, defection of the laity, and virtual disestablishment by the state have left the Church adrift in Italian society, more so perhaps than at any time since early in the century. In searching for a proper place for the Church in the country's rapidly changing social and political environment, most bishops have assumed a conciliatory position in political ideology. However, the bishops and the curia still have the firmest links with the *cattolici popolari,* the descendants of the old *D.C.* It is that party that the Church sees as its last best hope of finding a defender of its worldly interests. The bishops know that the *cattolici popolari* need Catholic electoral support as much as ever, but they recognize that each side can do less for the other. The Church's interest in politics and its influence on them have declined. Although remaining an important factor in national life, the Church can no longer command the allegiance of the majority of Catholics on any issue of public life. In practice, the area in which the Church and state interact has steadily diminished and is now quite small. What has evolved is a Church-State relationship of the sort Cavour originally intended back in 1870.

In the process of secularization, the number of clergy has decreased considerably, especially in the figures for male members. Nuns constitute more than three-quarters of the ordained or consecrated Church personnel. From a total of about 155,000 nuns in 1971, the figure had declined by 129,000 in 1991; meanwhile, the male clergy in 1991 had fallen to only about 25,000. In the South and the islands, there is one nun for every 300 women over the age of 20; in the Center-North the ratio is one for every 150. About two-thirds of them work in the Center-North and are engaged in hospital work, teaching, and social assistance. To fill the vacuum being created by the fall in number, some religious orders are recruiting novice nuns in Africa and Asia.

In the face of these deep social and ecclesiastical changes, the bishops have shifted their attention to pastoral matters, in particular religious renewal at the diocesan and parish levels. The conviction that the past obsession with anti-communism had led to a fundamental obfuscation of reality; that it was not Marxist materialism but the materialism of the consumer society that, in the wake of secularization, had weakened the Church's position.

A New *Modus Vivendi*: Pluralism and Cohesion

Practicing Catholics are now a minority of only 30% in Italy. In today's increasingly urban society, the struggle is between faith and apathy. There is a lack of interest in religious problems and a rejection of Christ and the Gospel because it is felt that neither the Gospel nor Christ has anything to say to a modern man. The loss of faith is partially the consequence of a cultural crisis, the result of the shattering of many successive illusions in the last two hundred years, from the eighteenth-century faith in Reason, to that in Progress, Nationalism, and Development. And the fall of Marxism, for many, is the fall of yet another god.

However, among those who do practice their religion, there has been a reexamining and sharpening of faith, and a major shift of emphasis away from old-style pious liturgy and toward social action and private prayer. Moreover, although most Italians do not go to church on a regular basis and regard Church laws as any other laws, which means, therefore, they can be broken (contraception, divorce, abortion), their spiritual adherence to Christian teaching is still very strong. They have an almost innate sense of what is right or wrong and a capacity to view everyone as people with individual souls, to feel that there may, perhaps, be a purpose in this life because it leads to another one. The Church has helped to give Italians much of their humanity, their balance between spontaneity and restraint. In every village, the Church and its bell tower, *campanile*, dominate the town square, looking down from above like a guard guaranteeing order and calm. In fact, the Italian word *campanilismo* means local patriotism, love of one's village. In times of joy, it functions as a place of welcome, crowded with celebrants of christenings and weddings; in time of sorrow, it is like a black hearse, followed by weeping relatives to the tolling of a bell.

The Church's worldly role today is mainly to help those in trouble. Instead of just providing handouts for the poor, the Italian Church and Italian Catholics are involved in many projects to assist the needy and those living on the fringe of society, such as drug addicts and homosexuals. The Church still staffs hospitals, schools, old people's homes, mental asylums, and homes for the handicapped. *ACLI* still runs universities and trade unions, while the *Movimento Popolare* finds work for its members and has centers where they sell food at a discount to poorer people. The Church involvement in Italian society still stirs an active conscience both in the individual and in society.

There are non-Catholic populations in Italy: small historic communities of Jews and Protestant Waldensians, agnostics and atheists who have broken with the Church, growing numbers of Jehovah's Witnesses, and Muslims from the Third World diaspora. In fact, Islam has become the second largest religion in Italy.

Notes

1. The various cults of the South, from the *tarantismo* ("dance of the spider") that is analyzed by the famous Italian ethnologist Ernesto De Martino to the "festivals of the poor" described by Annabella Rossi, were different expressions of an autonomous culture, separate from the structure and social doctrines of the Catholic Church. This was a world that offered the possibility of trance and release, of mass pilgrimages and miraculous cures. E. De Martino, *Sud e magia* (Milano: Mondadori, 1959), *La terra del rimorso* (Milano, Mondadori, 1961); and A. Rossi, *Le feste dei poveri* (Bari, Laterza, 1969).

2. Putnam, *Making Democracy Work*, 107.

3. La Palombara, *Democracy Italian Style*, 60-65.

4. In view of these changes, some priests took a more radical view of their society and their role: worker-priests and organizers of community initiatives amongst the deprived.

5. Processions carrying statues of Christ, Mary, and patron saints to celebrate major events in the liturgical cycle remained an important part of Italian religious practice, especially in the South. The processions clearly reveal the relationships between the human and the divine, and at the same time establish various social identities.

6. For more on this encyclical see Lucio Lombardo Radice and Luigi Pestalozza, "Intervento sulla *Populorum progressio*," *Problemi del socialismo*, 9, no. 18, (May 1967): 78-92.

7. Gianni Baget-Bozzo, *Il partito cristiano e l'apertura a sinistra. La DC di Fanfani e Moro 1954-1962* (Florence: Vallechi, 1979), 128-29.

8. Carlo Cardia, "L'area cattolica dopo il 20 giugno 1976," *Critica marxista*, 17, no. 1 (1979): 48-52.

9. Church-going plummeted, especially on the peripheries of the big cities where the new urban population was most concentrated. See A. Monelli and G. Pellicciari, "Comportamenti di voto e pratica religiosa," in G. Pellicciari, ed., *L'emigrazione nel triangolo industriale* (Milano: Mondadori, 1970), 334.

10. For an account of the financial scandal in which the Vatican was involved, see Luigi Di Fonzo, *St. Peter's Banker: Michele Sindona* (New York: Franklin Watts, 1983).

XI

Family: Tradition and Change

Crisis of the Institution

While secularization has brought about a significant revolution in the relationship between Italians and their Church, it is not uncommon to hear older Italians complain how modern times have brought sweeping changes also in the family structure and family values. The traditional picture of the Italian family as the institution where the individual finds consolation, help, advice, provisions, loans, weapons, allies, and accomplices, which remained unchanged for many centuries, has changed profoundly as a consequence of political, social, and economic factors that have undermined the social stability, effectiveness, and social values of both the extended and the nuclear family. After Italy became a welfare state, the family world described by Barzini as a closely knit community held together by emotional attachments and material interests, ever ready to form a common front against all outsiders and to take care of its own, could not avoid being affected by all the social changes.[1]

That description accurately mirrored, to a large degree, the main features of the Italian family until the early 1960s. In a nation whose other social institutions are notoriously brittle, the Italian family had indeed long been functioning as the sole unit that, rock-like, withstood all adversities. That picture is becoming a thing of the past.

There is a decline in the number of marriages, an increase in illegitimate births, and a rise in the number of legal separations. Census figures also show that there is a sharp decrease in the "extended family" (i.e., married couple with children and other relatives in the same household). There is an increase of households made up of only one person, of childless couples, and those whose children have left the home, of couples living together without being married, families with one parent, and families that have been reconstructed (second marriage after divorce). While before World War II, because of high fertility and death rates, families had, on the average, large numbers of children and tended to be rather young, today, because of the low birth rate and increasing longevity, families are older on the whole.

The most radical changes have taken place in the last 25 years not only because of industrialization and more women entering the workforce, but also because of the legalization of divorce and abortion. In 1970, the average number of children per woman was 2.42 (like the European average); 20 years later, in 1990, the average had gone down to 1.27, which is the lowest among the members of EU. However, *the* Italian family still is changing slower than that of other European nations. When one takes into consideration the number of divorces, one-parent families, and children born out of wedlock, the average Italian family remains one of the most traditional in Europe.[2] The big change is the emergence of the "prolonged family," caused by the fact that a very high percentage of adult children, mostly unemployed (and this is the main cause of the change), continue to live with their parents, even though they enjoy a high degree of independence and they have developed their own network of social relations.

Changes in the family structure are uneven. In 1951, nuclear families, composed only of husband, wife, and children, formed 55.7% of the total number of Italian families; 20 years later they formed 54.1%; today the percentage has not changed much. In the same period, extended families declined more rapidly, from 22.5% to 16.9% of the total, with percentages for the South remaining much higher. In the last 20 years, however, there has been a considerable increase in "nonfamily" households (only one person), a steady increase, even though more limited than the preceding one, in "married couple" households, a slight decrease in *nuclear* households, and a big decrease in *extended* households. From a rather general point of view, these figures confirm that the structure of the Italian family tends to be moving toward a prevalence of the conjugal or nuclear pattern. Because of industrialization and the mobility imposed on working individuals, the extended family has registered increasing numbers of breakups.

In 1971, households comprising five or more members were nearly twice that of one-person households. Between 1971 and 1981, one-person households increased by 5%. Households made up of six or more persons went down from 9.7 to 5.4% of all households. As might be expected, in the North one-person households are now twice as common as large households. In the last two decades there has been a considerable increase in the number of *non-family* households, a smaller increase in *married couple* households, a slight decrease in *nuclear* households, and a large loss of over 10 percentage points in *extended* households.

The main change since the war is that the focus of loyalty has been steadily narrowing from what sociologists call the *extended family* to the *nuclear family*: from the big multi-generation clan to the immediate home cell of parents and children. The trend varies from class to class. In the property-less lower bourgeoisie, the nuclear family has long held more importance than the clan, but now even in rural areas the big patriarchal peasant families have been losing their influence as the young drift away to the town. In the upper bourgeoisie, as property gives way to income, as family managements disappear and sons disperse to new salaried careers in other parts of Italy, the tight network of the big family gathering has become less necessary for the individual's future and security, and also less easy to maintain. Many younger couples are today likely to prefer pleasure traveling, or a weekend cottage shared with a few close friends, to the traditional big family reunions on Sundays and in the summer.

Although the structure of the Italian family has changed in the last two decades, as has the interrelation among its members, the family, as the basis of human relations, is as strong as it was 2,000 years ago. The dynamics of Italian families can easily be compared with those in most Western countries, which have been influenced by a process of progressive nuclearization of family forms over the last couple of decades. Still, in its percentage of extended families, the Italian situation markedly differs from other countries with an equal degree of economic development. For one thing, while economic development has undoubtedly contributed to modify the family unit for a considerable part of the population, it has not caused traditional structures to disappear. Moreover, the social and economic changes have not altered family values. Though clan loyalties toward more distant relatives may be waning, an adult's ties with his own parents and with *their* parents often remain remarkably close. If many younger people are today trying to lead more emotionally independent lives, it is often not without a sense of guilt or an awareness of the pain it causes their parents, who cling to a different family tradition. This may be so in any country; it is especially sharp in Italy.

"Particularism" and "Familism"

When we talk about the Italian family, we usually fall into the trap of terrible generalization and, therefore, equally terrible misrepresentations, because it is easier to deal with general characterizations. Although *the* Italian family has *never* existed, because even before the postwar anthropological revolution, the structure of Italian families differed according to geographic areas, social classes, and urban/agrarian societies, the notion of the Italian family became popular because of the book by the American anthropologist Edward Banfield in which he introduced his controversial and hotly disputed thesis of *amoral familism*.[3] Indeed, North American anthropology of Italy became almost obsessive in its focus on this debate in the period before the 1970s, to the neglect of researching other important areas.

Banfield claimed that southern peasants were relegated to poverty by a traditional ethos that made them maximize the material, short-run advantage of the nuclear family, thereby inhibiting the cooperation and solidarity basic to modern political and economic life. The term implies, therefore, an endemic inability to act for the common good—what is popularly called a lack of civic consciousness. It is related to societies where the fundamental unit is the nuclear family and more complex forms of social organization are absent. It is associated with centralized and authoritarian states that discourage the growth of intermediate institutions of government between the state and its citizens. The concept was then extended to the rest of Italy to demonstrate that because of the high degree of individualism that characterizes Italians, Italian families do not interact well with the social structures at large, and in fact, the Italian familial institution has been the cause of negative social, economic, and political development of the country. Banfield's idea of *familism* was challenged by S. Silverman, who saw southern peasants' exclusive attachment to their nuclear family as an effect, not a cause, of their poverty. Landless peasants were unable to support the large families that were to be found in areas of peasant ownership and long-term tenancy, such as central and northern Italy.[4]

Strong *familism*, whether conceived as moral or amoral, also characterizes other societies around the Mediterranean. Domineering patriarchs, clinging matriarchs, and relatives who stick together to defend and further the interests of the family or the clan can be found among Spaniards, Greeks, Turks, and Arabs.

In the case of the Italians, the causes of *familism* are mostly attributed to historical circumstances. In *Prison Notebook*, Antonio Gramsci lamented the negative effects of the exclusion of the lower classes in the *passive revolution* that brought about the unification of Italy in 1870 and the failure of the ruling elite to integrate the popular classes into the new state and to establish their own hegemony.[5] The *passive revolution*, by its exclusive nature and repressive tendencies, accentuated the antagonism of the Italian lower classes toward the state and their propensity for autonomous organization; it also made them less open to class ideologies, whether Marxist or anarcho-syndicalist.[6] It should be pointed out, however, that in the Italian lower classes, *familism* did not originate with the unified state, though it may well have been intensified by it. The origins of such attitudes should be sought in the effects of centuries of foreign domination, with the consequent destruction of any *fede pubblica* and the influence of Catholic teaching on the family, with its emphasis on the natural law that determines the preeminence of the family in civil society and its separation from the state.[7]

One can say, however, that after unification, in the absence of almost any adequate structures, apart from repressive ones, linking civil society and the state, the mass of Italians concentrated their attention on the single structure in civil society over which they could exercise some control—the family. The family became the epicenter of life, the only moral force, so much so that for some observers, like Pasquale Villari, the relationship between individual and community, between family and collectivity, seemed not to exist at all.[8] Luigi Barzini used to say that the true patriotism of the Italians is loyalty to their own families. In a nation whose other social institutions are notoriously untrustworthy, the family has indeed long been functioning as the sole unit that, rocklike, withstands all corrosive elements.

Certainly the Church played a major role in shaping the moral and social core of the Italian family. The weekly magazine *Famiglia cristiana*, which had its largest circulation in the 1950s and 1960s, was one of the best media for reaching the Italian family in preaching the sanctity of the Christian family and the primacy of the family in civil society.

The *Enciclopedia Cattolica* (1950) stated that "the precedence of the family over society is above all temporal; the family was the first form of social organization, the first school and first temple." Furthermore, in a hierarchy of values, society was subordinate to the family "since society is a means to assure to the family and through it the individual that which is indispensable for its [family] self-realization."[9] In family-state relations, the emphasis is on the need to protect the family from external control. Again the *Enciclopedia Cattolica* stated "the state must recognize the family as it has been constituted by God" (pp. 994-95). The state's duties were, therefore, to protect the family and to enable it to "accomplish its mission"; only if the family failed in this task did the state have the right to interfere. Tullio Goffi made a similar point in saying "the family enjoys a pre-eminence over civil society in an ordering of ends . . . family duties, founded on piety, love and unity, are of a superior essence, although less defined and distinct, than social duties, which emanate from justice."[10]

In the relationship between family and collectivity, the Christian family thus had many more rights than duties. The family's duties were primarily internal, not external. Such an ideology could be accused of catering to *familism*, of isolating the family from society, of stressing private rather than public virtues.

If this was the predominant view of family-society relations, it should be stated that Catholic social teaching, as we saw in the preceding chapter, balanced the picture by placing the family in a wider social context. The Catholic family had to be defended against the communist menace and the threats of modern society. It could do so only if it emerged from its isolation.

The prime mission of the family within the Church was to link with and help other Christian families: community spirit over individualism. Therefore, there was a permanent tension in the Catholic view of the family. On the one hand, there was the tendency to stress the family's internal values, its primacy over society, and the need to protect it from a hostile world. On the other hand, there was the desire to overcome the family's isolation, both with relation to the Church and society.

Family and Associational Life

The present structure of the Italian family and its role in society, as in the past, is obviously affected by economic factors. Indeed, there is a definite link between the socioeconomic characteristics of region and the living arrangements that may be found within a single area. In fact, it would be safe to say that the changes are more profound going from the agricultural to the artisan areas and small-industrial to the industrial areas. In the urban areas, which are industrially dependent, it is more common to find the permanence of relatively atypical family structures that are very similar to the pattern of the "modified extended family." Areas of small land ownership and micro-artisan and industrial enterprise display the configuration of models of family organization based on the extended (or corporate) family.

There is no question that families have determined the political and economic history of Italy. Countless small or medium-size businesses that have boosted the Italian economy are family enterprises, or started as such. The outstanding case in contemporary Italy is that of the famous clothing empire founded by Lacuna, Galena, Gilbert, and Carlo Benetton. Olivetti and Pirelli are among other family-run businesses that come readily to mind. Family bonds were essential also to the fortunes of the Ferruzzi agrobusiness empire. In 1989, the Agnelli, De Benedetti, and Ferruzzi families controlled 45% of all the shares quoted on the Milan stock exchange. Most of Italy's privately owned, large industrial companies have retained some features of a family enterprise. Outside the hefty state sector, Italy has many fewer corporate giants than do the other leading industrial nations; the largest is FIAT, and it is still, in effect, the family holding of the Agnellis of Turin. There have been places and periods when family strategies have acquired an overridingly private dimension and the collective aspect of social life has become secondary. The decline of collective values and the vigorous new emphasis on the material prosperity of the individual family unit have led to a new age of *familism*: families have become ever more concerned with their own well-being and less with the collective problems of society as a whole (trend dominant in the 1980s).

Anyone who visits Italy and has occasion to assess the workings of the Italian family and the relationship between the family and the group will return with a view that is more complex and less one-sided than that presented by Edward Banfield and Tullio Altan.[11] The family has both contributed to, and worked against, collective action; the furtherance of the family can lead both toward greater solidarity and away from it. In other words, attachment and devotion to the family do not necessarily carry the negative social connotation of *familism*. It is the historical and ideological context in which working-class families operate that to a great extent conditions the degree of nonsociability and exclusiveness of family values and actions.

The Italian family and the relationship between family and collective action have changed profoundly since the early 1940s. In the early 1940s, when Italy was still predominantly a rural and small town nation, there certainly existed in many parts of the South and the islands those social structures that Banfield found in Basilicata: nuclear families, the size of which were largely determined by the agrarian conditions, by the strips of land on which the peasants had to make a living. In these years southern and central Italian families were large and usually multiple and vertical in structure, in the sense of having more than one married couple and more than two generations living under the same roof. Hierarchies within the families were clearly established (in the Center more than the South). The male head of the household had sole control of the family's money and took all responsibility for relations between the family and the outside world. The senior female figure, usually his wife, also exercised considerable power within the domain of the household and over the other women of the family.

Here too we can find the lack of trust among the peasantry, their lack of associationism, their fatalism, and their despair. It might be expected, given these structures and the extent to which the family was a world unto itself, that Tullio Altan's Albertian family reigned supreme. This was only partly the case, however, for side by side with these attitudes, we also find the greatest mobilizations in terms of land occupations and outbreaks of dissent that the inland areas of the South had ever seen. The southern peasants displayed a strong horizontal solidarity. The habitual distrust and ingrained individualism of the South were eclipsed by those elements that prompted solidarity among the peasants.

Indeed, collective consciousness and a strong sense of community did exist in the peasant life during these years. They were based on a complex system of favors and exchanges, and on a social network that was almost exclusively confined to the neighborhood; family and collective action related in a variable and complex way, and certainly not in a simple polar opposition to each other. The core of collective consciousness, the focal point of action, was the *paese* (village) itself, with its closed concentrated formation and its *piazza* (square). The dimension of the *vicinato* (neighborhood), of face-to-face relations, had fundamental importance; it was the basic element of aggregation. Faced with the uncertainties of work, with the particular harshness of life on the plains (the miles and miles covered on foot or on bicycle, the risk of malaria, the difficult relationship with the landowners), the *paese* was the symbol of peace, of solidarity, of physical rest and recovery, of affections, of friendship. The *paese* offered *civiltà*, culture. People used to sit outside their doors, on chairs and stools, chatting away. Allegiances developed between families as well as among kinfolk. Even in the agrarian society, where farmers operated in social isolation and the family's binding internal structures would make one expect the degree of contact and cooperation between neighbors to be very limited, the Albertian concept of *familism* does not reign supreme. Italian literature gives ample testimony to this cooperation and collective work efforts—especially at crucial periods in the agricultural calendar; Giovanni Verga's narratives, for example, provide some classic examples of certain collective practices (salting of anchovies, etc.) in Sicily.

Sharecropping families had, for example, developed a rich network of exchanges and mutual aid. The exchange of labor between families at crucial moments in the agricultural calendar, such as at threshing and harvest times, and other farm seasonal work drew families together with a spirit of generosity and strong cooperation.

On a cultural level there was also the important practice of the *veglia*. During the long winter evenings, families would gather in the kitchens of the farmhouses to play cards and games, to knit and to mend, to tell stories and to listen. Participation in the *veglia* was not segregated family by family, but it involved rotating hospitality and a varied system of visiting. *Carnevale*, which culminated with mardi gras, was the time of maximum community interaction.

One cannot forget the strong Catholic tradition of collective action and solidarity, of mutual aid and cooperative societies that affected the life of every family. We cannot underplay the influence of Catholic ideology and leadership on the relationship between family and collective action, especially in the South and in the Northeast, even though Catholic teaching asserted the primacy of the family in civil society and the need to protect it from the interference of the state. On the other hand, the Church's strong emphasis on the internal morality of the family—on its indissolubility, on the responsibility of the parents to educate their children in a Christian manner—had its impact. The approach was essentially defensive and inward looking. The Christian family had more rights than duties in a hostile world from which it had to be safeguarded. However, as mentioned in chapter X, we cannot ignore the important historical experience of Catholic social activism in Italy.

On the political level, the christian democrats were concerned with the lack of social activism of Italian families, and at the first congress of the party in April 1946, Guido Gonella, the party secretary, made a strong plea to Catholics to emerge from the shell of the family:

> It is an illusion, and the women present should understand this better than the men, to try to defend the family from inside the family. The state with its wars will tear you away from your husband or your brother, and atheist education or the corruption of the streets will steal the soul of your child. The family is a fortress which cannot be defended from inside the fortress. Certainly we must build up its internal strength, but we must also issue forth and fight the enemy in open battle.[12]

Family and collective action combined in a crusading spirit, which was not to be transformative of social relations, but was to defend the Christian family from the Marxist and atheist threats.

Sociality was certainly higher in the working class of the urban areas than in the agrarian South. Italian housing, with long balconies on each floor looking over the street or inwards onto a communal courtyard, facilitated dialogue and human connection. Even in the working-class quarters on the periphery of the great cities where the housing usually took the form of flats in tenement blocks, isolated from the rest of the city, a strong sense of community developed, as did solidarity between families. They were based on a complex network of favors and exchanges, on a sociality that was almost exclusively confined to neighborhood, and on the powerful political culture of socialism.[13]

Modernization and New Family-Based Communities

Looking at Italy as a whole in the 1940s, there is a danger of idealizing the relationships that existed between family and collective life at that time. In reality there was nothing idyllic about rural life or relationships in the South. Nor was there a linear passage anywhere in Italy from the existence of compact communities based on mutual aid to the destruction of communities brought on by modernization.

The next two decades, when Italy underwent a most profound social revolution, with a mass exodus from the rural areas toward the cities and from the South to the North (between 1952 and 1962 more than 15.5 million Italians changed their place of residence) had a profound effect on the family and its relation to the group. The mass urbanization that was the product of individual family strategies (the young who went first used kinship and sometimes village networks in order to survive the first impact and to find work and housing; then they brought other members of the family) certainly reshaped the structure of the traditional family.

As families began to put a new emphasis on home-centered living and consumption, so the family and especially the woman's role within the family changed. In the 1960s, more Italian women than ever before became full-time housewives. Theirs was the responsibility to care for children who were leaving for school later than ever before. Theirs too, especially in the North, was the task of looking after the needs of a husband whose workday often lasted 12 to 14 hours. The women's magazines and the television advertisements of the time exalted this new figure of the modern Italian woman.

The material improvement in living conditions also had an impact on leisure time activities, which were also radically changed. The television set was obviously the most important innovation of these years. At first television was both a socializing phenomenon and an object of political division. People, especially youngsters and adult men, gathered in bars and in their political party's section headquarters to watch favorite programs.

Gradually, however, the collective and habitual way of television viewing disappeared as more and more families bought their own sets and each family watched television in its own apartment. This startling development obviously increased the tendency toward passive and familial use of leisure time, and decreased drastically other more participatory and collective pastimes.

At the same time, a significant number of people from the Italian popular classes became more mobile. The *FIAT Seicento* and *Cinquecento*, because of their relatively low cost, made it possible for popular classes and *ceti medi* to travel as a family unit rather than on the bus or train with others, or remain in the *vicinato*. Sunday outings by car became a possibility for the first time.

The amount of paid holidays increased slowly but significantly, as did the tendency to travel farther. The car and the television further encouraged an essentially private life and familial use of leisure time. All this had an impact on the life in the courtyard and on the extended family. The role of the family unit became even more important than before. The new urban structures served to isolate families, which were decreasing in size, in small but comfortable living quarters, and provided few spaces for collective gatherings or community life. Women became the principal target of the new consumerism, and the increased emphasis on their service role within the home intensified their isolation. The *economic miracle* increased the atomization of Italian civil society; it linked rising living standards with accentuated individualism and introduced into Italy a new model of urban social integration.

The Cultural Ferment of 1968 and Its Aftermath

The Italian student rebellion of 1967-1968, which was seen as a rebellion against all authority and the dominant ideology, was also against the individualist and atomizing values of the *economic miracle*, against the individualism of the new Italy. The extraordinary flourishing of collective action of these years in the major cities, especially in the industrial North, must also be viewed in this context. During these years, for significant numbers of people, time at work, but free time even more so, was filled with meetings, leafleting, mobilizations, demonstrations, and discussions. The activities led to new networks of friendship and solidarity, to contacts between intellectuals and workers, and to a minor cultural revolution.

How did this ferment of collective action in the new, urban Italy relate to the family? Families were drawn out of their isolation and found a new common purpose. It was noteworthy that women played a greater role than ever before. Collective action and sociality often took priority over family needs.

Conversely, however, the most significant development of these years was that some sections of the collective movement called into question the very structure and bases of the family. The critique of the family took various forms, some of which found widespread support. The need to introduce divorce, to allow the family to be dissolved, won majority support in Italian society, as the outcome of the referendum of 1974 showed.

The attempt by the women's movement to combat patriarchy and change the traditional roles within the Italian family also made significant inroads in changing Italian society. The most radical critics wished to attack the very existence of the nuclear family. Attempts were made to find alternatives to this family unit, and to substitute communal living for family life. Such experiments, though, rarely extended beyond student groups in the major cities.

In central Italy, where sharecropping families started up small family businesses, the 1970s witnessed the extraordinary growth of family capitalism, of decentralized and small-scale industrialization, and family structure and *familism* remained rather strong.

In the South, in the rural areas, the agro-towns ceased to be the centers of solidarity and collective action. With the great exodus, the class structure was modified irrevocably. No longer was the population divided into the small elite of landowners and the mass of the rural poor and working-class. Although the class structure had become more varied, human relations deteriorated. In whichever direction they went, the potential for collective action in the rural South had been destroyed. Some evidence of collective action could be found in the industrial working class only. However, the dominant trend in the South was an economic growth and development that was chaotic, unstable, precarious, and mainly without respect for any order or civic discipline.[14] In the interstices of this vital but chaotic growth, criminal organizations like the Mafia in Sicily and the Camorra in Naples increased their networks of influence and protection. Society was divided against itself, and each family fended for itself as best it could. Narrow municipal or corporate or criminal rivalries flourished, leaving little possibility for the sort of solidarities that had existed before the "democratic" chaos controlled by the christian democrats. The political class of the South, corrupt and clientelistic, presided contentedly over this spectacular free-for-all.

Notwithstanding all this, today students and parents are very active in school councils, some neighborhood and block associations have sprung up, and new environmental and consumer groups are active. In Sicily, churchmen and schoolteachers are taking an active part in the fight against the Mafia. The continuing and rising importance of associational life suggests that Italians are drawn together for other reasons than work and consumption. Associationalism (since Tocqueville's time, long considered an index of any civilized democracy) actually increased by 2% in the early 1990s as compared to the mid-1980s. No fewer than 21% of adult Italians belong to an association of one kind or another and more than half of these participate in voluntary groups. Another important observation is that, while in the past such voluntary activity had been almost exclusively organized by Catholic organizations, in recent years the ideological motive has been replaced by a desire to contribute to the life of the community outside the confines of formal politics and work life. Contrary to what one might imagine, the volunteers tend to be reasonably high-earning males in early middle age. This suggests that Italy is witnessing the steady abandonment of strong or party-based political activity in favor of a much weaker, more varied, and dynamic form of social self-realization.

The continuing impression of a national political class operating under conditions of imminent and often actual crisis does nothing to encourage the renewal of political life in Italian civil society itself. But despite the decline in traditional forms of political activity, there has been no appreciable drop in public participation in citizens' initiatives—ranging from support campaigns for the victims of the civil war in Bosnia to the rather less edifying neighborhood protests at the presence of *clandestine immigrants* in larger Italian cities.

Italy is undoubtedly on the road toward democratic maturity, and its people are becoming increasingly involved in public affairs.

Divorce and New Family Structures

The long debate that accompanied the introduction of divorce into Italian legislation is closely related to the issue of the solidarity of family ties. The fear of jeopardizing the strength of this network of relationships was one of the main reasons for the opposition campaign led by the anti-divorce front.

Although the Christian Democratic Party and the Catholic Church opposed it, divorce was introduced in 1970 when the left-wing parties and the small anti-clerical center groups in Parliament surprisingly mustered enough votes to overcome the opposition. True, the new rules called for a five-year waiting period from the moment a married couple had formally separated. Nevertheless, the old principle that an Italian marriage was indissoluble—save through annulment by state or Church court—had been scrapped. The christian democrats remained nearly isolated in the Senate and Chamber of Deputies in their defense of the old, rigid legislation, joined only by the neo-fascists.

Although militant, outraged Roman Catholics collected enough signatures to request a referendum aimed at repealing the divorce statute, and the Church hierarchy and the christian democrats staged a nationwide anti-divorce crusade, the law was not repealed. The referendum that took place in 1974 (59.1% of the electorate upheld divorce) dealt a humiliating blow to the Church and the D.C. Even many Italians who attended Mass every Sunday voted for divorce, proving that they, like Roman Catholics in other countries, were selective in obeying the teachings of their church.

Many couples who had been living apart were at last able to have their collapsed marriage lawfully ended and to remarry. But the large, general rush into divorce that adversaries of the reform had predicted did not occur. In 1987 the legal waiting period between separation and divorce was reduced to three years. By then it was estimated that one out of every fifteen new marriages would end in divorce—a far lower divorce rate than in France, Britain, or certainly the United States, where it is predicted that one out of every two marriages will not last.

Despite almost 60% support for divorce at the referendum in 1974, and the fact that it has been legal since 1970, the Italian divorce rate is the lowest in Europe. Even after they were given legal right to divorce, Italians still were hesitant to dissolve their family unit. In 1981, only 13,000 couples were divorced in Italy. One reason, obviously, is that Italian bureaucracy makes it more complicated. It is also slower: five years—three since 1987—of separation are necessary first, if both partners agree to divorce, and seven if one does not. The influence of Catholic morality on the customs and choices of married life for Italians seems to be considerable. Most importantly, there are economic reasons. The old-fashioned housewife status of a considerable part of the female population, for example, has certainly acted as a check on the divorce rate until recently. The lack of economic independence of the unemployed female, along with the poor protection the law offers to the weaker partner, undoubtedly represents an efficient impediment to the decision to proceed with a request for separation. There are also cultural reasons, as well as the domestic topography that make Italians feel too attached. They cannot separate from a host of friends, from a part of their own lives. But, most of all, the welfare and advancement of children comes first, as always.

Some Italians seem to need the thrills and stress of adultery. Playwright Luigi Pirandello, Benito Mussolini, the leader of the Italian Communist Party, Palmiro Togliatti, film directors Vittorio De Sica and Roberto Rossellini, and thousand of nameless citizens had well-publicized extramarital affairs.

Indeed, *adultery* and unfaithfulness have always been major themes in Italian life and art. From Dante, Boccaccio, and Machiavelli to many modern writers, these themes have provided fertile ground for the imagination of artists. However, despite the fact that the most celebrated works are family tragedies, erotic and adulterous entanglements have mostly been farcical in the eyes of Italians.

Today, even though divorce is legal and fewer marriages are "arranged," infidelity has not diminished. In fact, with more free time and the growth of travel and other form of leisure, infidelity, especially among the bourgeoisie, has increased.

Despite this behind-the-scenes activity, the majority of Italians have always tended to be exceptionally discreet about their love affairs. Many government ministers or other public figures have mistresses, but a public man's private life is his own business so long as he is discreet and does not step outside the law.

Notwithstanding all these changes, there exists one of the most absurd paradoxes of the Italian mentality: the obsessive preoccupation that Italian males, especially those in the South, have with a woman's faithfulness, while they themselves are engaging in extramarital affairs. There is no worse insult to a man than calling him *cornuto* (cuckold). The Italian male seems to want his right to stray from the strict marital path, and knows in his heart and from frequent sociological studies that adultery is not uncommon, but he is obsessed by the fear of being cuckolded, of having his own wife be unfaithful.

Fragmentation and Continuity

Contraception and abortion were legalized in the 1960s and 1970s after lengthy campaigns in both cases. The concern with population growth did not abate after the Second World War. The belief in the intimate relationship between demography and power was extremely strong during fascism, which colored the terms in which social policies on sexuality and the family were discussed and enacted. During this period the encouragement of a high birth rate was interpreted as support for national unity and the future of Italy.

The campaign to legalize contraception and abortion, therefore, had a hard time in the 1960s when the development and popularization of the contraceptive pill gave added weight to demands for repeal. During the 1960s, close analysis of demographic data revealed that a large number of brides were pregnant at the time of marriage, while surveys showed that third and subsequent children were often unplanned or unwanted. Thus, the case for legalizing contraception was made on the basis of family planning, which would allow couples to choose when to have their children and how many to have. The decision to legalize contraception was not made on the basis of any principle of sexual freedom, and it was not until the mid-1970s that contraception became widely used among young people.

The change in sexual attitudes in the last few years, as has occurred in most industrial countries, has certainly had an impact on family structure. It is important to remember, however, that the Italy of the economic boom was still a society full of taboos about sexual behavior. The restrictive codes of official morality were deeply intertwined, especially in the South, with codes of honor, and sexual mores were to change more slowly than anything else.

The early 1960s did see the first stirrings of a new moral outlook. Timid discussions of premarital sex appeared in some women's magazines; one weekly (*L'Espresso*) even published an investigation of infidelity levels among Italian wives. However, profound changes began to occur in the 1970s. For one, the pill was made available everywhere and the whole ferment of the late 1960s and early 1970s had revolutionized mores. Results can be seen in the population figures and family size today. Population growth is approximately zero, which is lower than Great Britain and much lower than France. The number of families with several children has rapidly diminished. Italy now has the lowest birthrates in Europe, 10.2 per 1,000 population, as opposed to 29.4 per 1,000 half a century ago. By comparison, the 1987 birthrate in the United States was 15.6. Naples today produces proportionately fewer infants than Stockholm. The Italian nation is close to zero population growth and may even begin to shrink after the year 2000. The legalization of abortion and the availability of more reliable contraceptives, including the pill, have certainly had an impact on the population growth. Because many women feared the side effects of the pill, abortions became the most widespread form of birth control—more than 360 abortions per 1,000 live births. Abortion rates in Italy are the second highest within the EU, and illegitimate births are, therefore, low.

Although the South of Italy has changed greatly in the last 20 years, traditional thinking still seems stronger than in the North. Research indicates that established families tend to be less worried about their daughters than those who have only been prosperous since the war. Both might take a daughter's boyfriend along on holiday, but while the first group would accept their being lovers, the second would supervise them closely and make sure they were never alone together. The stereotypical picture of a grandmother or aunt accompanying the young couple on a walk is a thing of the past even in southern Italy.

Certainly, the 30% who remain practicing Catholics must be influenced by the pope's adamant refusal to countenance any variation on the Church's teachings on chastity and contraception. However, here again we are faced by Italian flexibility and spontaneity. The point, probably, is that given the pill and free access to abortion, sexual freedom is no longer a menace to the family structure, which itself is the key to Italian thinking.

Italian families are, thus, getting smaller and more nuclear and continue to be cohesive. Even in urban contexts, Italian grandparents remain closely involved in the care of grandchildren; it is still common to see in a public park a child kicking a soccer ball with his *nonno*. Once the older generation is threatened by fragility and immobility, it receives considerable assistance and company, especially from daughters and their families. Nevertheless, some fundamental shifts have occurred in the roles and needs of individuals within the family. There has been an ever-increasing process of *individualization* within the family, of demarcations of activity and consumer rules by age and by sex; women have redefined their roles and responsibilities; youth have increasingly sought their own activities and space at an ever younger age; and individual members of the family relate more and more to their peer groups and the outside world.

Old Bonds and New "Familism"

Notwithstanding the changes, a few characteristics of the traditional family ethos do remain. Curiously, after a tense period of transition, the past few years have even seen a new strengthening of the links that bind the nuclear family. In the late 1960s and early 1970s, Italian teenagers shook off the reins of traditional parental authority. This was a blow to the nuclear family. But today, having asserted their right to independence, young people are moving back to closer emotional ties with their parents, on a basis of greater equality than before. So the family today is united less by constraint and convention than in the old days, and more by genuine need and affection. The autonomy of much of northern youth and its partial challenge to the family in the late 1960s and early 1970s have given way to a new attachment to the family unit. The generational conflict has subsided now that youth has won its rebellion. Whereas the youth of the 1960s rejected the values dictated by its parents, today's adolescents are turning again to the family as a defense and a source of comfort since they no longer find solid values in the public world. The fears created by rising youth unemployment have increased this homing trend. Grown-up children tend to stay at home well into adult life.

Some of the traditional intra-family links remain untouched by modern changes. Above all, there are the strong mother-son bonds, a characteristic shared with other Mediterranean cultures. The classic *mamma* pampers her boy, keeps telling him he is *bello* and *bravo*. After he is married, she is glad to press her mature boy's shirts, cook his favorite dishes, and discreetly and sympathetically listen to the tales of his erotic conquests and troubles. The self-admiring Latin lover is to some extent a product of such "momism." In the dynamics of Italian family life, father-daughter relations also are close. The new family is geared to the production of income and the meeting of needs through the activity of each of its members.

With women's work increasing notably in the eighties, the family is usually living on two salaries. It also has access, thanks to the reforms of the 1970s, to a far wider range of state services than ever before. Consequently, family savings have risen markedly since 1970, as has the overall standard of living. In their lifestyles and in their culture, average Italian families have come a long way.

In the Center and Northeast, where small, family-owned businesses are widespread, extended families appear more frequently than in other regions, though obviously not as abundantly or as numerous as the earlier sharecropping families. In these regions a very strong work ethic, geared to the making of family fortunes, allows self-exploitation and the exploitation of one's relatives at levels that are no longer accepted elsewhere in Italy. There is thus less leisure time and less mobility here than in the working-class families of the North. It is hardly surprising to find that the strong, collectivist subculture of these regions has been severely affected by such developments. Political and Catholic associationism have suffered. The ex-communists, now *P.D.S.*, attract people to their cultural events in decreasing numbers. The secularization that necessarily accompanied urbanization realized the fear of the Church that with the decline of rural communities there would naturally occur a weakening of the links between the family and the Catholic religion.

In the urban South, the majority of lower-class families are nuclear in structure and have significantly more children than the North or Center. In 1971, the average Neapolitan family included 4.7 persons, compared to 3.3 in Bologna. These larger families have to survive in a period of deepening gloom in the labor market. Southern urban families also have to survive in a situation where the services offered by the state are less efficient than the services offered in the Center or the North. In the southern cities the state pays out a high number of disability and social pensions (i.e., poverty pensions) for old people who have never been in regular work.

Family or Money?

Despite the recent changes in Italian kinship structures, millions of families throughout the country keep functioning in the traditional way of providing warmth, security, moral and economic support, and assistance in crisis. Hundreds of thousands of such self-supportive families have also become successful businesses. Countless small or medium-size businesses that have boosted the Italian economy are family enterprises, or started as such: the outstanding case history is the Benetton family.

There are hundreds of families in Italy who dream that their entrepreneurial ventures may one day take-off the way the Benettons' did. Yet, as Italian capitalism is maturing and with fewer brothers, sisters, and children of business clans available or willing to pitch in, outside managers, financiers, and corporate raiders are more likely to get into the act. The decline of the large, close-knit business family is also likely to transform the country's economic landscape.

At the same time, it remains true that most of Italy's privately owned, large industrial companies have retained some features of a family enterprise. Outside the hefty state sector, which now is shrinking, Italy has many fewer corporate giants than do the other leading industrial nations; the largest is FIAT, and it is still, in effect, the family holding of the Agnellis of Turin. To the Agnellis, Benettons, De Benedettis, Ferruzzis, and Gardinis, thousands of other names may be added. On Italy's business-financial scene, it's still largely all in the family.

There is, however, plenty of evidence that family bonds are loosening or even breaking apart. Good times seem less favorable to kinship solidarity than bad ones. Conflicts over inheritance have been very divisive for many families. Scores of ordinary Italian families with sons and daughters estranged from their parents, siblings locked in bitter lawsuits and no longer on speaking terms, and aged widows and widowers abandoned by their children or relegated to old-people's homes with perfunctory visits or telephone calls now and then, do exist.[15] Marital and monetary conflicts bedeviled the descendants of Angelo Rizzoli, who had built a publishing and film empire; of Arnoldo Mondadori, founder of the nation's largest publishing house; and of Gaetano Marzotto, under whom the old family spinning mill at Valdagno, northwest of Venice, developed into one of Europe's largest textile combines. The Gucci family fought for years over control of the Gucci company, which annually sells hundreds of millions of dollars' worth of fine leathergoods throughout the world.

The Problems of an Aging Society

The Italian population not only is decreasing, it is also aging rapidly; life expectancy in Italy has climbed to 79 years for women and 72 for men. By many accounts, however, Italy is not facing up to the aging of its population. At the University of Rome, notwithstanding the rapid decline in the birthrate, there are 42 full professors of pediatrics and just one in geriatrics. In all social classes, couples no longer accept so readily that an elderly widowed parent should come to live with them: *nonno* and *nonna*—grandpa and grandma—are now expected to stay in an apartment of their own. It is estimated that about one-quarter of old people in Italy live by themselves. This has caused a good deal of heartache.

In the absence of family-centered care, the state has begun to realize the necessity to help the elderly, and society is finally accepting that its elderly are no longer solely a family responsibility. In recent years shelters and recreational facilities for the elderly have been opened—a new departure for Italy. However, although public *case di riposo* (retirement homes) do exist, they vary greatly in number and quality, depending on the town. In many northern towns there is a well-developed service for old people, including libraries, places for film viewing, and general recreation. Unfortunately, private rest homes are out of reach for many people, for their cost monthly is equivalent to a worker's monthly pay. The state of desperation of many elderly has caused a big increase in the suicide rate of people over age 65. To see how serious the problem is, you only have to watch what happens to the elderly during the summer months when many of them are abandoned by their children who leave for vacation. The chronic-disease wards of Italian hospitals fill up every summer with elderly patients, whom their relatives park there for several weeks so they can enjoy their vacations.

Municipalities do offer many other kinds of aid and assistance. There are discounts for old people on buses and at cinemas, and inexpensive lunches are provided. Some municipalities organize mini-vacations to the sea or mountains. These services are more common in the North; the farther South one goes, the weaker the central organization and the more the family takes its place. Which solution is preferable is not for us to decide.

An interesting development for old people, mainly in large cities, is the establishment of the *Università della terza età* (The University of the Third Age). Anyone over 40 can sign up for courses whether they have educational qualifications or not. Courses are usually on subjects of local interest and are taught mostly by professors from local universities, who sometimes donate their time.

Whatever the actual effectiveness of the various services, the country is confronted with a new phenomenon that has social dimensions that cannot be easily solved by institutional services. Centuries of family tradition make people reluctant to depend on anything less personal. The average Italian still believes that the best social worker is a relative. In general, there remains a deep-seated moral obligation of children to parents, and in this, as in many other situations, the Italian family and its traditions continue at the center of all social intercourse.

Notes

1. Luigi Barzini, *The Italians* (New York: Hamish Hamilton, 1964).

2. These figures provide some evidence: family with one parent in 1989: 8.2% in Italy, 12% in Germany, 13% in France, and 14% in England and Denmark; and 25% in U.S. Children born out of wedlock based on percentage of total birth in 1990: 6.3% in Italy, 27.9% in England, 30.1% in France, and a staggering 46.4% in Denmark. Divorces per 1,000 inhabitants (1989-90): 0.5 in Italy, 1.9 in France, 2.2 in Germany, and 2.9 in England.

3. After the war, the U.S. also sponsored research projects, mainly in the South, as part of the U.S. plan of capitalist reconstruction of Italy.

4. S. Silverman, "Agricultural Organization and Social Structure, and Values in Italy: Amoral Familism Reconsidered," *American Anthropologist,* 70 (1968): 1-20.

5. A. Gramsci, *Selections from the Prison Notebooks,* eds. Q. Hoare and G. Nowell-Smith (London: Lawrence and Wishart, 1971), 52-120.

6. Paul Ginsborg, *Daniele Manin and the Venetian Revolution of 1848-49* (Cambridge: Cambridge U. P.), 371.

7. A. Pagden, "The Destruction of Trust and Its Economic Consequences: The Case of 18th Century Naples," in D. Gambetta, ed., *Trust* (Oxford: Basil Blackwell, 1988).

8. P. Villari, *Le lettere meridionali e altri scritti sulla questione sociale in Italia* (1885: reprint, Naples: Guida, 1979).

9. See the entry "Famiglia," *Enciclopedia Cattolica*, vol. 5 (Rome, 1950), 994.

10. T. Goffi, *Morale familiare* (Brescia, 1962), 264.

11. The term *amoral familism,* created by Banfield, designates a form of behavior directed solely toward the pursuit of the good of the family, understood here in the more restricted sense of parents and children. It implies, therefore, an endemic inability to act for the common good—what is called a lack of civic consciousness. It is related to societies where the fundamental unit is the nuclear family and more complex forms of social organization are absent. Edward Banfield, *The Moral Basis of a Backward Society* (Glencoe, IL: The Free Press, 1958).

12. "La DC per la nuova Costituzione," in *I congressi nazionali della Democrazia Cristiana* (Rome: Arti Grafiche Italiane, 1959).

13. A. Gribaudi, *Mondo operaio, mito operaio* (Turin: Einaudi, 1987).

14. Manlio Rossi-Doria, "Dopo i fatti di Battipaglia," in *Scritti sul Mezzogiorno* (Turin: Einaudi, 1984).

15. Paul Hofmann, *That Fine Italian Hand* (New York: Henry Holt and Co., 1990), 116.

XII

Women and Gender Relations

The Struggle for Identity

In a 1954 article, Gini and Caranti observed that "the existence of a genuine difference of position of the man and woman in marriage and in social life" constituted a fundamental presupposition of the stability of the Italian family.[1] Since then this difference between the roles of men and women has been steadily disappearing. In its transition from a traditional agricultural to a modern industrial society, Italy has also witnessed a significant redefinition of the role of women. Women have made major strides toward fuller emancipation and legal, professional, and sexual equality. The political action of the women's movement, the changes in lifestyles caused by economic changes, as well as extensive legislative decrees, have all favored the acknowledgment and affirmation of the social condition of women and the formal equalization of the sexes. Along with the quantitative growth of the number of women attending school, there came a "historically" significant change in the labor supply, especially from the start of the 1970s. It was only at this time that significant changes began to appear, and there are reasons.

The latent *machismo* of a Latin society with Catholic traditions may help to explain these delays. But what is more curious is that Italian women themselves, whose social role in some other ways has always been so strong, did not show much interest in this kind of legal equality or in sharing a man's privileges, at least until recently. Women were little concerned with legal equality, but would rather use their "feminine charms" to win their way. Since then, times have changed; but even today the Italian woman prizes femininity above feminism.

It is also relevant to point out that socially, women in Italy have rarely been segregated or treated as inferiors. The Italian woman regards herself, and was regarded, as the equal of man—equal, but different. Given an opportunity to play the same role as a man, she often shied away in fear of losing her femininity, and men cheered her for it. Cliché or not, a woman has viewed herself in relation to the family—where her role has been powerful, in every age and in every social class—and to individual men, rather than to other women or the community as a whole. So it is not surprising that the modern "Women's Lib" movement in its more militant form has never been more than marginal in Italy, and is usually unpopular. However, in the past dozen years a milder and different kind of feminism has taken root among the new generation. Italian girls today expect equality of rights and career prospects, equal personal freedom (sexual and other), and equality in marriage: they no longer expect their husband to make all of the decisions and do none of the chores. They resent, and fight against, *machismo*. But they do not want to become the same as men, and they certainly do not hate or shun men, like some militants. In Italy, men and women alike have a fear and contempt for the bossy, masculine type of woman, and Italian women who emerge as leaders are usually exquisitely feminine people, such as Nilde Jotti and Irene Pivetti, presidents of the Chamber of Deputies.

Italian women today are emerging from a transitional phase. From the old dependence on a man's world they are moving toward real emancipation. However, the road to full emancipation has been tortuous for the average woman, and differences do remain. Because one can speak more of urbanization than of actual industrialization—given a real exodus from the land to the urban areas, and, a peculiar mix of development and underdevelopment, of tradition and modernity, of economic and geographic dualism—the redefinition brought about by the transition has peculiarities that are typically Italian. The process of cultural unification that has taken place, largely because of the spread of the national education system, the diffusion of mass media, and the intense internal and international migrations, has reduced differences in behavioral patterns but not eliminated them.

Until the end of the 1950s, the role of women in Italian society was generally defined in terms of the institution of the family. Urban women were primarily caretakers of the house and of the home and held a subordinate position to men. The situation was different in the agrarian society, which had a more complex family structure. In the South and in the rural and semi-rural areas of the North and the Center, where the extended family was the prevailing feature of the social structure, there wasn't a sharp division between the sphere of production and that of domestic life; women held a very active role in productive activity. As in other countries with a pre-industrialized society, the wife had considerable power owing to her productive role in the family economy. In pre-industrial society, familial and work activities overlapped and the family formed the basic economic unit, making it difficult to characterize family structure and domains; families were patriarchal as much as matriarchal. This was the dominant structure in Italy until the end of the 1950s when Italy ceased to be an agricultural society. "The separation of home and work brought an end to the family economy, and an end to the prevailing family bonds."[2] No longer did the entire family work together, but instead the husband left home early in the morning to go to the factory or office and returned late in the evening. The family ceased to be the basic unit of economic production and social participation. The wife's former productive role in the family economy changed to a subordinate one. Even though she had control over all household duties, she became economically dependent on her husband's earnings; she no longer worked to produce.

The transition to a modern industrial society brought about a more sharply defined division of labor between the sexes. In Italy, because of contradictions that are particularly acute—in which the process of industrialization was rapid, uneven, and riddled with social conflicts—male roles were more strongly defined in terms of the occupational system and female roles in terms of the family system.

The subordinate role of woman as homemaker, mother, and wife was regulated by laws and encouraged by the Church, against the democratic and liberal views of some prominent intellectuals, and civic and political leaders.[3] Mussolini had certainly circumscribed the position of women. Fascism had actively discriminated against women in the matter of right to work by limiting the access to jobs and careers and by mandating separate pay ranges according to sex.[4] Fascism succeeded in promoting sex-role stereotypes that permeated popular mores and behavior, education, and culture in general. In everyday life, for the majority of Italian women—particularly for lower-middle-class women—this meant confinement to menial household chores, made still more difficult by general economic hardship. Under fascism, the state sought to organize the subordination of women around their central role of devoted spouse and exemplary mother. Women were to be guardians of the hearth and subject to the legitimate authority of the husband; they were regarded as mothers whose duty it was to produce soldiers and workers for the state. The Duce went as far as to state that "War is to man what motherhood is to woman."[5] In those years, the Church was also very direct in forging the social functions of people, especially women. In a 1931 encyclical, "Casti connubi," in unison with the fascist policy, Pope Pius XI continued to reinforce the traditional role of women as primarily loving wives and caring mothers. The position of the Church did not change with the fall of fascism and the end of monarchy. In 1946, Pope Pius XII confirmed the previous position of the Church:

> Every woman is destined to be a mother. . . For true women, all life's problems are understood in terms of the family. . . Equality with men, outside the home where she is queen, subjects the woman to the same burdens the man has. The woman who goes to work outside the home. . . dazzled by the tinsel of a counterfeit luxury, becomes greedy for unworthy pleasure.[6]

The Church's position began to change with the election to pope of Giovanni Roncalli. In 1960, John XXIII declared that women's lives pivoted on "two centers, two nuclei; those of the family and of work." He implied that in a post-masculine society women had to be given the opportunity to harmonize family and work lives.

Notwithstanding the social changes and the "economic boom" of the early 1960s, women did not enter the workforce en masse; indeed, the number actually went down. The 6,500,000 women at work in 1959 declined to 5,110,000 by 1972—a unique development in Western nations, where the numbers of women in the workforce had been mounting. There are several reasons why industrial employment for women remained relatively low compared to other well-advanced European countries:

1. In Italy there has never been a condition of full employment for men searching for a job and, in Italian society, male unemployment is considered a greater evil than female unemployment;
2. Wage differentials between men and women are less marked in Italy than in other Western countries, and employers have, therefore, little incentive to hire women because their work is not significantly cheaper;
3. Labor legislation for the protection of women workers during pregnancy and in the period following each childbirth is very

progressive in Italy, but this very fact produces serious obstacles to the employment of married women. Employers tend to avoid hiring workers who are likely to be absent from work for prolonged periods of time and who show a high rate of absenteeism, yet cannot be fired due to the legal protection accorded to motherhood.[7]

Another factor no less important is the fact that the relocation of a considerable part of the population from the backward regions of the South to the industrialized regions of the north radically changed the family's needs and often profoundly weakened kinship alliances. Consequently, the loss of the traditional functions of care and support supplied by kinship relations was not accompanied by the development of new measures of social policy on behalf of the family and its dependent members (the elderly and children). Social ethics had great difficulty in keeping pace with the evolution of customs and ways of living, and the inertia of public policy was justified through the assumption that urbanized families were able to rely on traditional solidarity to carry out a plurality of tasks they had to perform in the new residential context.

The lack of enough public facilities for child care such as kindergartens and nursery schools, the fact that full-time schooling is practically nonexistent, and the demise of the extended family make it extremely difficult for many mothers to have full-time employment.

However, the official data do not tell the whole story about female employment. Because of the peculiar industrial development and the widespread system of *black labor*—of work not officially registered as such and for which employers evade paying for social security and medical care and other kinds of benefits—there is a much higher percentage of working women than is indicated by the statistics.

In the early years of the new industrial Italy, not only were families restructured—e.g., the average number of extended family members declined drastically—but the roles of their members were redefined. The role of the husband and father was to be the wage earner, while the wife's responsibility involved the "preservation of familial unity in terms of love, personal happiness, and domestic felicity."[8] The wife became the proud *casalinga*, housewife.

For many women, especially those who moved North from the South or to the urban centers from the countryside, the image of the woman in a comfortable and secure setting meant progress in a real positive sense. For the husband, too, to be able to keep a wife at home who was the real "queen" of the house meant real success. To be able to return for vacation to the South or to the rural areas of origin and be able to boast about a "well-kept" wife meant a profound social improvement for the new urban man. The transfer to the cities gave women greater freedom from traditional family hierarchies and a greater autonomy in a whole number of ways, too. This was especially true for younger women in the North who came from an agrarian society where the extended family was a common structure. However, the new idealized confinement not only intensified their isolation but also acted to enclose them in a purely private dimension and to remove them even more than previously from the political and public life of the nation. The nuclear family, which was seen as the normative family form in modern industrial society, was not the means toward self-realization that women had hoped for. Instead, the family fettered women, trapping them in the private sphere of the household and in the role of housewife.

In the urban society, the *casalinga* was subordinated to man economically and legally. Until the mid-1970s, the husband was defined as the "head of the household" in Italian civil law. That implied that women had a secondary role in every aspect of Italian society. For instance, before 1969, adultery by women was a crime, with stiffer penalties than rape. The psychology behind this was based on the idea that a man "owned" his wife. Rape was a temporary possession of the female body, while adultery was theft not only of the body but also of allegiance, of the whole woman, love, "soul," body, honor, and pride. As recently as November 1961, the Constitutional Court defended Article 559 of the penal code, which stated that adultery of the woman could be punished with a prison sentence, whereas that of a man was not a criminal offense. The Court maintained that this did not contravene the sex equality article of the constitution because a woman's adultery is an act of "different and greater entity" than that of man. The Court changed its mind only in December 1968.

Women's Movement

The Italian political tradition did not offer much to women. In the marketplace of ideologies there was a version of Catholicism that did offer a role to women, but a subordinate one, that of homemaker and of mother. There was a version of Marxism, which, in spite of the enrichments brought about by thinkers such as Antonio Labriola and Antonio Gramsci, was still concerned essentially with the forging of alliances between social classes that were organized as specific political parties, and not with improving the lot of women.

In the ambience of democratic politics of immediate postwar Italy, women were not offered simple freedom but a hard choice. Each of the two dominant postwar parties bore a powerful ideology with regard to women, the ideology of Catholicism on the one hand and the ideology of Marxism on the other, both deeply affected by attachment to the traditional Italian gender relations of the countryside. On the one hand, there was an implicit message that the business of communist women was to work with women, that is, to do "women's work," and on the other that Catholic women were to remain in the traditional family structure. Therefore, even for the millions of party members, communism was an alternative Italy within Italy. The Party offered nothing but the abstract utopian hope that, one day, all Italy would be communist and, thus, all women would be equal to each other.

As with so many other things, the place and role of women in society started to change with the student movement that began in fall 1967. This movement was, among other things, the expression of a social conflict that could not be defined in terms of class, but it was also a movement that at the same time expressed a critique of authority and of accepted forms of organization and behavior while reproducing—within itself—the subordination of women.[9] Thus, those radical women who were attracted to the politics of the students' movement perceived fairly early on that there was a marked contradiction between the goals of the movement in general and of its patriarchal form of organization. Even though in the first several months women did not play a strong role (indeed, they experienced considerable ambivalence in their attitude toward the movement), more young women took part in politics than at any time since 1945. Although most of them remained subordinate within the movement, unable to express their own needs and desires, there were strong positive elements of new political commitment and an extraordinarily intense sociality. These were important years of fermentation, which culminated in the formation of several women's groups, which by 1975 constituted a strong national women's movement, a movement that was mostly political rather than intellectual.

While some of the impetus for the women's movement in Italy came from the student protests of the late 1960s, it was mainly because of the outgrowth of small feminist groups that were formed by mostly middle-class women at the beginning of the 1970s in major urban centers. Though certainly a consequence of the many economic, social, and cultural changes that had been transforming Italy, during the 1970s the movement took on a life of its own. It became an important interlocutor of political parties, trade unions, and social movements. In the first stage, the movement found its propulsion mainly in the American women's movement, with its emphasis on separatism and gender consciousness-raising. However, the impact of inflation and the stagnation of the economy, caused especially by the oil crisis, cannot be underestimated either. Working-class women especially found it increasingly difficult to balance family budgets. Their own potential for contributing to their families' resources through paid work was constantly menaced by the economic crisis. Political action to meet specific social needs became their initial primary demand.

Contrary to the American counterpart movement, which was for the most part elitist and engaged in having token women appointed in top visible positions, the Italian movement attracted most of its adherents from the middle and lower classes and worked to develop a collective consciousness. Italian women became involved in social struggles on an unprecedented scale. The battles for housing and for improved services in the neighborhoods, among others, saw women emerge from the private sphere and take a leading role in collective action. By this we do not mean in any way that they were not interested in gender issues. They were certainly interested in dealing with their experience in a man's world (patriarchal, fraternal, etc.) that was hostile to them. They did pool together their experiences to analyze their own sexuality and women's oppression by men and to formulate demands that were less for parity than for women's rights. They wanted a loose and non-authoritarian organization of all forms of institutions. In a sense the movement was understood as a movement that sought to discover and affirm female subjectivity. Whether or not it proved possible to do away with the mediation of men, women within the movement saw themselves as women, laying claim to a gendered identity and seeking to understand and live out that identity. However, for the most part, women worked with men in passing legislation that affected the lives of women in the private sphere and in the social and global environment.

Different groups in the Italian women's movement raised different demands and issues. *Lotta Femminista* (Women's Struggle) raised the slogan of "wages for housework"; the issue, which touched all classes, was meant to equalize the household environment and provide a healthier context for decisions on procreation and sexuality and to improve the poor relationships between men and women, which the group attributed to women's economic dependence on men. The *UDI*, *Unione delle Donne Italiane*, the traditional movement of communist women, put more emphasis on the intervention of the state to relieve women's oppression, while *Rivolta Femminile* denounced marriage and the family as the site of male domination. One of the most influential groups was the *MLD*, the *Movimento della Liberazione delle Donne Italiane* (Movement for the Liberalization of Italian Women). *MLD* combined demands for equality—the elimination of gender discrimination in the schools, of sexual discrimination at work, etc.—with those that would increase women's autonomy—the right to control their own bodies through free contraception and the liberalization of abortion. In 1975 the *MLD*, with the support of the small Radical Party, organized the collection of signatures for a referendum on the abortion question. Five hundred thousand signatures were needed; 800,000 were collected. Women's mobilization on this issue was able to transform it from an important civil-rights question into a wide-ranging discussion on woman's position in Italian society. The concept of adultery as a criminal offense was abolished and legal separation could be obtained when the marriage had broken down, and no longer, as used to be the case, only when one of the two parties was "guilty." Children born out of wedlock were given the same rights as "legitimate" children. Moreover, it also dealt in a more egalitarian manner with economic and patrimonial relationships inside the marriage bond. In 1978, against strong *D.C.* opposition, a law legalizing abortion was passed by the Italian Parliament and the attempt to reverse it with another referendum (May 1981) was clearly defeated with a majority of 67.9%. Law 194, on the termination of pregnancy, regards women as the principal authors of that decision, but it also set limits on women's rights to choose: it allows voluntary termination of pregnancy during the first 90 days when the woman can show cause why continuation of pregnancy or the birth of the child would entail a serious risk to her physical or mental health. The law also allows medical and ancillary workers to refuse on grounds of conscience to take part in abortions.

Pressures from the women's movement were also a determinant in bringing women legally on a par with men. In 1971, women obtained equal rights in the matter of acting as guardian in the case of separation or divorce. In spring 1975, a long-awaited reform of the family law was approved. The most important principle of the new law was the one that established parity between the two partners in marriage. Previous insistence on the supremacy of the male head of household and of the right of the husband to control his wife's behavior and activity was abandoned definitively. The new laws also stipulated that the housewife share equally in family property, thus acknowledging the contribution represented by the domestic work. In 1977, a law was passed giving men and women equal status at work, including equality of pay for the same kind of work, regardless of the value of the product, and retirement rights at 60. Also, a wife now has personal ownership of any property she has brought to the marriage, while those working in the civil service can get a pension after fifteen years if they have one child. Of particular interest is the recognition of the right of fathers as well as mothers to be absent from work in order to look after children—and not just children by blood: adoptive children and other children for whose care the worker is responsible are included.

Working life has been regulated by sweeping pieces of legislation. Legislation hinged on the idea that women's basic rights—the right to work and have economic independence—should not be infringed because of childbearing. Starting in the 1960s the Italian Parliament responded to the protection of motherhood with very progressive laws. Maternity leave lasts five months (two before giving birth and three after) at 100% salary for employees and 80% for self-employed and professionals; an additional six months of unpaid leave are available, with the right to return to the same job afterwards. The Constitutional Court has issued a ruling that in the absence of the mother, due to death, disease, or other serious cause, the father may make use of the leave after childbirth, thereby guaranteeing child care. The laws also provide for optional leaves in the event that the child is sick or handicapped.

The concept of the "social value of motherhood" also fueled a drive for kindergartens and day-care centers. In 1968, kindergartens (for children from age three to six) came to be part of the educational system in many towns and cities; the system has expanded remarkably over the past years, in spite of much criticism of the schedules, which often do not meet working women's needs.

To accommodate the new role of men and women in the family, the pension system has also been changed so that a pension plan can be transferred not just from a husband to his widow but from a wife to her widower. The most important instrument of change was Bill 903 of 1977 because it eliminated all discrimination in hiring practices, promotions, salaries, and social security.

The first major demonstration of the women's movement, some 20,000 strong, took place in Rome on December 6, 1975. Throughout the following years the women's movement developed rapidly. Women had become the center of political controversy. Another good indication of changes is provided by the 1976 general elections, for here, for the first time, every political party felt the need, in its campaign, to address itself specifically to the female electorate, to include many women in its lists of candidates to Parliament; and, finally, to manage to have them elected with an unprecedented number of votes. Women had become social actors and, probably, a social force in their own right.

There were also some structural preconditions behind the women's movement, such as an increase in female education; it would make women more competitive with men in a number of occupations. Another consequence was a decrease in the birth rate. As a result women were anchored to domestic chores for a shorter period of time.[10]

As the women's movement gained momentum, the two leading parties increasingly cultivated women's support. Although the P.C.I. had always had a smaller proportion of women members than the D.C., it certainly did more to promote the advancement of the women in their party than did the D.C. In the Chamber of Deputies that was elected in 1983 19.9% of P.C.I. deputies were women (38 out of 198) against 2.6% for the D.C. (6 out of 255) and 1.4% (1 out of 73) for the P.S.I. The total of women corresponded to 7.9% of all deputies' more than twice those in the British House of Commons or the American Congress. The highest office in Italian politics ever held by a woman was held by Nilde Jotti, a communist leader, when she became president of the Chamber of Deputies in 1979 and held the position until 1992. Another woman, Irene Pivetti, filled that high position in government for a shorter period.

About 25 years or so have elapsed since the birth of the new feminism in Italy. There is no doubt that it has scored some remarkable successes both in the domain of ideas and in the institutional field. Nevertheless, it too, is in crisis. On the one hand, modern feminism criticizes institutions (parties, government, religious institutions, etc.), yet at the same time it accepts the fact that the necessary legal changes require the intervention of these institutions.

The women's movement of today has come to the understanding that it needs the cooperation of men on the political level to create enough mass support for change, to bring women's issues from the fringe to the forefront. This generation of young women generally welcomes men into the movement. Feminists do not speak anymore in terms of "us" vs. "them" but of cooperation and of natural and social relationships. They recognize that men are basic to women's life as women are basic to men's, and young women have been able to create a discussion about men's stake in the women's movement and reasons for which they should contribute to social and political change. Italian men have understood that the solution of women's issues directly benefits men too.

Moreover, the number of grassroots groups has grown larger, especially women's networks in various sectors of professional life. The same is true of women's cultural centers, resources, and support centers, which have opened in various larger and middle-size towns, with the purpose of providing counseling on matters of sexual violence, battering, harassment, etc., or advising women on issues of professional and work discrimination.

Women's participation in political life has had a determining effect on the Italian democracy. Since they were given the right to vote in 1946, women have always participated in elections in numbers that exceed 80%. Nevertheless, there are still not enough women holding public office. In the administrative elections in 1990, 8.5% of the candidates elected were women; in the political elections in 1992, the figure rose to 10.2%. Although these figures appear very low, they are not when viewed in comparison to other countries.

It is in the participation in social life through volunteer associations that the number of women becomes predominant. Women volunteers are not rejecting traditional values but trying to use them to change society and the condition of women from outside the political system.

Women's biggest social advancement has been registered in education. In 1945 Italy was third from the bottom in the ranking of European countries in the number of illiterates, and women represented the highest percentage of those illiterates. Today more women receive high school diplomas than men, and there are as many women as men in the universities, even if the percentages vary from department to department, with the highest concentration of women in the humanities. Women's increased level of education has had a positive impact on the work market.

Another important development in the sphere of culture was the growth of women's writing, in a range of forms, from narratives to diaries to journalism. This new output drew on a long tradition of women's participation in literary work. When the movement was at its height, there was a great flowering of women's writing and feminist writing, born of the sense that women now had the chance to produce and express new forms of thought. On the one hand, female voices came from the experience of consciousness-raising groups, from the pages of the new women's periodicals (*Effe, Sottosopra, Differenze*), and from feminists' encouragement to one another to take their old writings out of the closet or to embark on fresh ones; on the other hand, women's literature showed itself more and more aware of its cultural context and its new character. There was a complex interplay between these dimensions, a matter not of casual relationship but of common participation in the process creating language, values, and consciousness. In the subsequent decade, women's literary and auto-biographical writing continued to grow impressively in energy and in quantity, engendering whole series of works, publishing houses, and bookshops, and giving rise, too, to a body of critical and reflective commentaries. Feminist publications celebrate the discovery of the other woman, of other women, of their speech and their bodies. As women made their presence felt in the world of publishing, the boundaries of gender shifted in the cultural sphere and a huge new market was created. All these developments combined, by highlighting the growing creativity of women, highlighted also the contradictory fact that they received little institutional recognition; it fostered closer ties between members of the same sex, but it sometimes sharpened conflicts between women and men in the public sphere.

Gender Difference

A radical change in achieving equality with men is the way women are treated in cases dealing with sexual issues. Today police investigators and magistrates are showing greater respect for victims of sexual violence than they did only a few years ago, even though rapists often still receive lenient sentences, which may be even further reduced on appeal. In the past a man facing assault charges got away scot-free if his victim was unwed and he then married her in what was known as a "reparative marriage." A legal reform in 1981 abolished that semi-barbarous institution. Another archaic usage—elopement to force reluctant parents to give their consent to an undesired marriage—still survives in the South.

What survives, too, mainly in the South, is violence caused by outrage over real or presumed sexual looseness: fathers or brothers chastising the seducers of girls, husbands killing their wayward wives and their lovers, betrayed wives taking revenge on their rivals. Italian courts have long conceded extenuating circumstances to perpetrators of violence assumed to have acted to defend their own or their family's reputation. (The judicial recognition of the "crime of Honor" lingers on.)

Between 1979 and 1980, the criminal code dealing with rape, sexual violence, and extenuating circumstances by reasons of "honor," came under scrutiny. An all-encompassing and radical reform bill was introduced in Parliament owing to the action promoted by women groups. The cases of the extenuating circumstances on account of "honor" were repealed in 1981 and so, too, "crime of passion" vanished from the criminal code.

As late as the 1960s, the old codes of this Catholic society remained in force; all evidence still suggested that Italian unmarried girls as a whole, especially in the South and in the provinces, were still among the most virginal in Europe. Virginity in unmarried women is still highly prized by many Italians despite the changes in sexual mores. When a nationwide sample of 1,000 people of both sexes was polled in 1987, 57.1% were found to attribute prime importance to female virginity before marriage. Predictably, the strongest response against premarital sex for women came from the South.

However, following the lead of the Nordic countries, in the 1970s sexual freedom had finally began to spread. Parents had become readier to allow their daughters to go out with boys; young people had more leisure and money for going off together. At the beginning, the new freedom was welcomed with mixed feelings: on the one hand, they welcomed the growing climate of frankness between the sexes, on the other, they felt uncomfortable without any form of convention.

The major shift in values in the 1970s was due to several factors: foreign influence, the freeing of legal controls of contraception, the steady decline in the role of the Church. The majority of teenagers are now promiscuous for a while. Sex in this phase is rarely linked with love; it is simply a means of communication and self-discovery. For most teenagers, virginity is no longer considered a virtue. It should be pointed out that, once again, the liberalization is far less evident in small towns or rural areas than in large urban centers. Some social classes, too, remain more strict than others. Working-class families tend to retain a more stringent sense of morality, a tighter watch over their daughters, than the middle class. But overall, the fathers cannot expect to bring to the altar a virgin daughter, and the groom, after having slept with so many girls, cannot expect to marry a virgin.

Until the early 1960s birth-control was almost as taboo in public discussion as it was during the Fascist period. Hypocritically, on the pretext that they limited syphilis, male condoms had always been freely on sale in drugstores. Abortion was legal only when the mother's life was in danger, and most doctors interpreted this with a religious literalness. Consequently, death from clumsy self-abortion ran into several thousand per year. Certainly, rich and informed women would avoid these problems by visits to private doctors in Switzerland or England. But millions of working wives, faced with the horrors of raising a large family under Italian housing conditions, came to regard sex and their husbands' desires with panic. Reform had been blocked mainly by Catholic opinion, but the 1960s saw a steady change of heart among fervent Catholics, including the clergy. The campaign of a few pioneers forced a breach in the curtain of social prejudice and brought the whole issue into the open. The prejudices waned first in the middle class, while working-class wives remained reticent far longer. It seems there was a political element here, since official communist policy for many years was to oppose birth control as a capitalist trick to reduce the numbers of the proletariat. But since the early 1970s the P.C.I. swung in favor of contraception, as of abortion, and this change in attitude paved the way for a steady change in working-class attitudes.

As with birth control, the government for years was afraid of legalizing abortion for various political reasons. Not only was the opposition from the Church and traditional Catholics far stronger in this case, but there was a clear hostile majority among the pro-government parties in Parliament. The law gives women, married or single, the right to claim an abortion within the first 12 weeks of pregnancy; after this, termination can take place only if there is medical evidence that there is grave risk to the health of the mother or the child, verified by two specialists. There are some other restrictions: minors (under 18) must obtain parental consent; a woman must first be interviewed by a psychiatrist to establish that the abortion is desirable. Abortion is not free; it is covered within the social security which reimburses a percentage of the cost. So today, very few women are going abroad or resorting to the back-street hacks; the situation is certainly helped by the continuing spread of contraception. However, problems do exist, caused partly by a shortage of hospital facilities and especially to the fact that many doctors, nurses, and hospital directors are refusing to cooperate. Practicing Catholics have the right to invoke a conscience clause.

The belated legalization of contraception, and then of abortion, has been a major factor behind women's great leap forward in the past decades. Psychologically and practically, it has liberated them in many ways. It lies at the basis of their new pre-marital sexual freedom, and inside marriage it has helped them to order their lives as they would wish. But these advances are still contested by traditional Catholics.

Despite the new sexual freedom and equality, traces of the old Latin mentality persist, at least among the over-30 crowd. Even today, a woman must not be too brash or assertive, she must use guile to achieve her sexual ends, or she will not be found attractive, and what she treasures above all is male appreciation of her femininity. This she is given abundantly. The Italian male's demonstrative pleasure in female company gives to relations between the sexes a certain romantic tenderness and intimacy not always equaled in countries with an older tradition of emancipation. In spite of his egotism, and partly to flatter his own vanity and sexual power, the Italian man is more sensitively concerned than most males to see that his woman, too, is fulfilled.

All these changes have also had an impact on the political behavior of women. Education and work opportunities have freed many women from the pervasive electoral influence of the pulpit. This is especially notable in the South and in the Northeast, traditionally Catholic regions where the D.C. enjoyed until very recent years its most impressive bedrock strength. In fact, in these regions, electoral shifts away from the Christian Democrats could not have occurred, or would not have been as strong, were it not for some radical changes in the voting patterns of women.

Women in the Work Force

As a result of the progress women made, there has been an increased complexity of women's roles in society and their relation to it. Because a woman's role is no longer defined exclusively or mostly by family but instead by work, it is important to see women in the job market.

Italian women's entry into the world of work occurred at a rate which was much lower than that of other Western countries. Although women were given the chance to obtain the same education as men, as we have seen, there are many reasons why in Italy women have not been competitive with men in the labor market.

The fact that Italian legislation does protect the institution of motherhood to a very high degree makes young married women less attractive in the job market. The Italians have made it a criminal offense for a woman to work during the two months before the birth of a child or in the three months after, and there is no reason for women to work during this time because by law they are entitled to full pay. Afterwards, they are entitled to flexible working hours to facilitate their nursing responsibilities and needs. Although maternity leave plans do vary from company to company and from the public to the private sector, Italy is the most progressive country in the world when it comes to statutory rights to work-leave for birth and marriage.

However, the issue is much more complex. Female employment decreased by 1.1 million units between 1959 and 1967 as women were replaced by young male migrant workers from the South. This did not take place through the deliberate firing of women workers, but by taking advantage of their high turnover in the labor market (due mainly to pregnancy and child-rearing). Female labor was eliminated from agriculture because of the general shrinkage of employment in that field because of the wide use of machinery. It was edged out from industry because of the competition from migrant male labor. The proletarianization of the rural labor force thus followed the pattern of employment in industry: a preponderance of male labor. Furthermore, the crisis in the textile industry, a traditionally large employer of female labor, accelerated this tendency. The rise in the standard of living facilitated their being kept out of the labor market. The wages earned by male workers increased. This dichotomy maintained and reinforced the division of labor between male breadwinner and female homemaker. It should be added that Italy was the only industrialized country in Europe to exhibit the dual feature of growing industrialization and a decrease in female employment. One could speculate as to the political reasons behind the inadequate support for women in the workforce. Could it be that the government feared that rapid entry of female labor into production would further disrupt the foundation of the family (already profoundly modified by industrialization and emigration) thus generating social pressure difficult to control? In other European countries female employment was on the increase throughout this period owing to the growing introduction of part-time labor; but part-time labor was resisted by the Italian trade-union movement.

When the "miracle" was over, women began to return to the labor force, but they tended, on the whole, to take jobs in the so-called hidden economy of casual labor and small family firms. Women workers can stay at home and look after their children, and at the same time contribute to the family income. But there are many factors that have influenced the entrance of women in the job market. It seems that women born between 1936 and 1946 who had their adolescence during the emergence of the culture of consumption and the availability of washing machines, refrigerators, cars, and televisions, moved into the labor force in large numbers in the mid-seventies, after they had raised their children.[11] Women born between 1947 and 1957, who experienced the political turmoil and changes of the late sixties and early seventies and faced gender debate and changes (including the legalization of abortion and contraception) at the onset of adulthood, while dealing with the consequences of their first adult choices—marriage, childbearing, and holding or giving up a job—were the first to enter the labor force in great numbers and to remain in it after marrying and having children. Women who entered adulthood in the middle eighties born between 1962 and 1968 seem to have a different social identification from older women because they have greater equality with men and have benefitted from the gains that the preceding generations obtained. However, these women no longer have a sense of collective identification and goals as previous generations had. Thus, older feminists complain that communication with those under 30 is difficult or nonexistent.

A survey taken in the mid 1980s showed that 22.5% of Italian women had full-time jobs, 5.8% had casual employment and 71.8% did not work. However, it is difficult to have exact figures in this area because many Italian women carry on industrial production in their living rooms ranging from knitting and sewing clothes to being mechanics and making electronic components. It is estimated that women make up 70% of the unofficial labor market.

If we examine women's employment in various categories of the service sector we find that, without exception, they tend to be concentrated in the lower-paid jobs, although there has been a marked improvement since the 1980s. The increase of women's entrance in the civil service occupations occurred concurrently with a lowering in the prestige in such occupations. It has been found that women, unlike men, are attracted to civil service jobs not because of status but because of the security of tenure of work and welfare benefits as well as the formal criterion of "equality of opportunity." Women's presence in the labor force increased steadily from the mid-seventies onward, from 27.3% in 1972 to 35.7% in 1986. Their activity rate (the proportion of women in the labor force measured against all women) went from 21.3% in 1972 to 28.9% in 1986. And their specific occupation rate (the proportion of those holding a job measured against all women of working age) went from 31% in 1972 to 38% in 1986. More than 80% of the increase in the number of workers, both male and female, in the period is thought to be due to the increase in women's labor force participation. Women make up 66% of the education work force: 79.4% of elementary school teachers, 63.7% of middle-school teachers, 49% of high-school teachers and 21% of university professors are women. The health profession also has a strong presence of women; 22% of physicians and over 65% of nurses are women.

Unquestionably, women now in their mid-twenties entering the job market experience a greater equality than their mothers, legally and in daily practices and behavior, although these experiences vary according to social contexts. They enter the job market with the same expectations as males; they sometimes want to work throughout their adult lives without leaving their jobs to get married or have children. In addition, the mothers of these young women support their daughters' plans to find a job and keep it throughout the years of raising a family. Work for women is increasingly viewed as valuable for reasons of personal autonomy, as family insurance in a time of insecure employment, and as personal insurance, perhaps against the hazard of divorce.

The less a job offers them rewards, the more likely it is that young women will perceive marriage and motherhood as the only place to find a sense of self-worth. Certainly, women's lifestyles and desires depend also on the level of education achieved and the urge to prove themselves. Indeed, education was a key factor in changing the role of women in society. Studies have shown that a woman's education is consistently and strongly related to gender-role attitudes.[12] Formal education is a means of social mobility, and the right to an equal education has made women more competitive with men. Education has empowered the process of change in women's roles in Italy, but this process has met with definite constraints. Women must confront the problem of the outside labor market while trying to assure that the family organization functions adequately.

The New Complex Role of Women

Younger women have more education, enjoy equal social status to men and full emancipation. At the same time, women's lifestyles and life strategies have become explicitly more diversified, as resources and options have opened up. Childlessness, celibacy, divorce, and remarriage increasingly are acceptable options. At the same time, the social competence women show (and are expected to have) in dealing with social institutions on behalf of themselves and their families is significantly changing the public/private boundaries, creating new resources for social relations and self-definitions and perceptions. It should be clear that class differences matter a great deal in the analysis of women's changing roles in Italy.[13]

Many young women still think that marrying someone they love and are loved by, and having one or two children is the most valuable option they can choose. More often this type is found where there is no rooted tradition of women's work. An increasing number of young women, however, do not focus on marriage and motherhood as an important goal in their near future. Rather, they see having a family as a potential burden for their career and as a hindrance to having a "full life," in terms of interests and social relations. Although they do not reject the possibility of a family, they put it off into a still indefinite future.

Moreover, the decline of the extended family and the lack of support from grandparents to rear children has put an additional burden on women. The growth of the welfare state did not compensate for the service that the extended family was providing. "The services of the welfare state are available only if there is an individual who is prepared to engage in the necessary bureaucratic practices needed to obtain these services" (Sassoon, p. 103). This job falls in the laps of the women—who must also compensate where public services fail. Moreover, the extension of the consumer society and the constant and dramatic decrease in the self-sufficiency of the household (compare a peasant family with an urban family who must purchase virtually everything it needs) adds on another task for women: the purchase of private services. Regardless of their occupation, employed women spent on average 2.5 to 3 hours more per day on housework than employed men.

By entering the male working world, women gained freedom of movement in society; but they also brought to their lives a burden: the splitting of their roles and identity. Many young wives have found it a great strain, both physically and psychologically, to combine a career with running a home, especially in the North where the tempo is so fast and standards so exacting: office hours are long, bosses are demanding, and a husband will expect everything just perfect when he wants to entertain. By entering professions or jobs—teaching, caring services, and so forth—that somehow required the same behavior and values of the activities performed at home, the internal conflict is lessened, but they still need to readjust and redefine their role and the roles of other family members. Nevertheless, what is appropriate for a woman is less and less dictated by tradition and more and more by the highly educated career woman.

To sum up, women work before they have children, then they abandon their work in order to look after their children. However, they often return to work when they must function as the agents of the welfare state within the family, as the agents of the consumption sector of the economy within the family (purchaser of private services). Furthermore, they must also compensate for the deficiencies of the welfare state. Finally, they must also fulfill their natural role of procreators and traditional role of homemakers. They are citizens of two worlds: they have full-time responsibilities in both, family and work. Not only do they assume two roles, they also belong to two complex social systems that are interrelated, yet separate; and they have full-time responsibilities in each. Working women generally have a different experience from working men, because the latter do not have full responsibility for the everyday maintenance of the family and, therefore, are not penalized by society for their reduced participation in it. As Sassoon indicated, compared to women's life, the life of the man is a rather simple one: "work, leisure, and sleep" (p. 104).

In the process of female emancipation, married women have found it especially difficult also because the man had found the adjustment hardest because of his *machismo*. Traditionally, in this Latin society, women have exerted their greatest power within the family or in relation to one man, or to individual men, rather than to the community. Pleasing a man had the reward of remaining queen of the house. For Italian men, notoriously egotists, have exploited their advantage both emotionally and in practical ways, down to refusing to help with the chores because it is thought unmanly.

This has been the general pattern, but in the past 20 years Italian women, mainly younger ones with a college education, have rebelled against it. These are the generations influenced by British and American societies via the media. Today, if her man behaves with thoughtlessly arrogant *machismo*, a woman will simply walk out on him. She expects the same degree of sexual freedom as a man; and, conversely, the same degree of fidelity from a man. Inside marriage, she demands equality of decision-making and equal control over shared finances; and she insists that her own leisure interests and her own cultural or other needs be taken as seriously as her husband's. Younger men generally adapt easily because the egalitarian experience of their student days is carried on into marriage.

Homosexuality and Individual Difference

The 1970s were crucial years for the history of gender relations in Italy. Long-standing tensions and dynamics came to the surface, expressing themselves both in legislation and in the sphere of symbolic representation, and this led to far-reaching changes in the ways people spoke and behaved.

There is greater freedom for lesbian and gay male relationships, though more for the latter than for the former. Women have become more visible in a range of places and situations and more visible to one another.

Legislation on sexual matters, as on matters concerning the family, has been brought into line with advances in medicine and with common practice. The pro-abortion campaign, in particular, brought together demographic pragmatists, those campaigning for greater social justice, and those who believed in the freedom of the individual and refused the right of the state to regulate in this private domain. At the same time as such campaigns were being organized by women to defend and promote what were essentially seen as women's rights, campaigns were launched to secure equal legislative treatment for homosexuals. The homosexual movement echoed many of the practices of feminism—the collective-based structure, the emphasis on beginning with the personal, the critique of psychoanalysis, the celebration of the body and sexuality, the critique of the bourgeois family and of formal politics. The campaigns focused on matters such as attempting to secure harmonization of the age of consent for homosexual and heterosexual acts.

From June 1972, *FUORI* (*Fronte Unitario Omosessuale Rivoluzionario Italiano*—The United Italian Homosexual Revolutionary Front) published their monthly magazine of sexual liberation, also called *Fuori!,* which means "out." In its pages we find all these themes, addressed in direct, impassioned, and unsparing words and images. The movement embarked on a "critique of normality" based on a critical consciousness that went "well beyond the problem of homosexuality." This drew upon the tradition of Left intellectual culture, and referred, in a more or less critical spirit, to the works of Marx, and Freud, Adorno, and Sartre. The movement proclaimed the New Revolutionary Homosexual, who, while he criticized the limited nature of class politics, preferring a trans-class approach, nonetheless emphasized economic and social oppression and paid attention to such questions as homosexuality in the factory. The publication of the movement offered a generalized critique of the violence of the capitalist world. The year 1975 saw the murder of Pier Paolo Pasolini, who was recognized by homosexual culture as one of its own, which served as a grim reminder of the daily violence surrounding gay men's lives.

The question of homosexuality was brought into sharp focus by the AIDS epidemic. The country has one of the largest number of AIDS cases in Western Europe. Hitherto these have been mainly confined to the male homosexual population, particularly those between the ages of 25 and 45 who are middle-class and who live in large urban centers. A significant number of hemophiliacs have also been infected with HIV as a result of receiving contaminated blood, and, as elsewhere, HIV is also spreading to the heterosexual population. The relatively large number of cases may reflect more efficient notification, especially in the early years of the epidemic, and better facilities for treatment. Certainly, in the absence of a vaccination against HIV or a cure for AIDS, there has been considerable resistance to proposals for mass testing, together with a reinforcement of measures to ensure that those infected with HIV do not encounter discrimination.

Notes

1. C. Gini and E. Caranti, "The Family in Italy," *Marriage and Family Living*, 18 (1954): 354.

2. E. Lupri, ed., *The Changing Position of Women and Society: A Cross-National Comparison* (Leiden, The Netherlands: E. J. Brill, 1983), 5.

3. Already during the Risorgimento, in the pursuit of a just unification of the country, Giuseppe Mazzini was proclaiming the parity of women: "Cancel in your minds every idea of superiority over women. You have none whatsoever." D. Meyer, *Sex and Power. The Rise of Women in America, Russia, Sweden and Italy* (Wesleyan, Connecticut: Wesleyan U. P., 1987), 141.

4. The fascist legacy in matters of pay differential between men and women ranged in 1945 between 30 and 50% in manufacturing as well as in services. In the textile industry, where women made up 75% of the workforce, they were paid from 20 to 40% less than men for the same work.

5. As reported in M. Clark, *Modern Italy 1871-1982* (New York: Longman, 1984), 276.

6. G. Ascoli, "L'UDI tra emancipazione e liberazione (1943-1964)," in *Problemi del Socialismo,* Oct.-Dec. 1976, 119.

7. A. Cavalli, "The Changing Role of the Women : The Case of Italy," in E. Lupri, ed., *The Changing Position of Women in Family and Society* (Leiden, The Netherlands: Brill, 1983), 183.

8. E. Lupri, ed., *The Changing Position of Women and Society,* 4.

9. G. Filippini, "Movimenti femminili, femminismo," in *Istituto Gramsci, La crisi della società italiana e gli orientamenti delle nuove generazioni* (Rome: Edizioni Riuniti, 1978), 110.

10. F. Alberoni, "Movimenti e istituzioni nell'Italia tra il 1960 e il 1971," in Luigi Graziano and Sidney Tarrow, *La crisi Italiana* (Turin: Einaudi, 1979), I: 263.

11. In a very informative study, Chiara Saraceno gives persuasive evidence on women's shift in working patterns in the last twenty years: "Changes in Life-Course Patterns and Behavior of Three Cohorts of Italian Women," *Signs: Journal of Women in Culture and Society*, 16 (1991): 502-21.

12. K. J. Diecplt and A. C. Acock, "The Long-Term Effects of Family Structure on Gender-Role Attitudes," *Journal of Marriage and the Family*, 50 (August 1988): 711.

13. See Alessandro Cavalli, 186-189.

Regardless of where one goes in Italy, over two thousand years of past history are visible and may be appreciated in many human manifestations. Large cities, small villages, and countrysides constantly offer a reminder that the present is the evolution of a most fascinating past. Printed by courtesy of *America Oggi*.

XIII

A More Open Society

A New Affluence

Overall, during the last 50 years Italy has become more industrial, more educated, more urban, and more secular. All of these changes have struck at the very heart and soul of the country. There have been profound alterations in well-established ideas about compulsory public education, marriage, procreation, abortion, divorce, exposure to the views and lifestyles of others, separation of Church and state, the relative responsibilities of spouses and their children, and the nature of work and leisure; in short, in almost every aspect of Italian life. But perhaps the most influential change has been the new affluence that has come to Italy.

The postwar rise in prosperity has touched practically everyone, even though in some social areas the increases have been somewhat fictitious because they are due only to a generous policy of awarding old age and disability pensions. Albeit unevenly, living standards have risen faster in Italy than in most other Western European countries. The upper-middle class in particular today lives better than in Britain and the United States mainly because it rarely inflicts on itself the same burden of high private school tuition bills. Many families can thus afford expensive clothing, frequent dining out, and two long vacations each year. Surveys indicate that Italians have improved their traveling habits; indeed, in the last 20 years the number of Italians going on vacation has doubled from 28% in 1969 to 56% in 1991. Taking two vacations a year and going abroad is the popular trend: 17.3% have chosen to go abroad in 1991 versus 15.3% in 1988. Among those who travel 43% have taken two vacations, while 21%

have taken three or more vacations. In this as in so much else about Italy, the percentage of those going on vacation is still much higher in the North than in the South—64% versus only 41%.

The Italians are less insular than they used to be; they have become more aware of other peoples and are curious about how they live. Many of them have become less ready to spend long weeks at the Italian seashore or in a country villa; instead they go to Spain, Greece, the Balkans, France, and Eastern Europe. America especially is now popular, at least when the currency exchange is favorable. Among the middle and upper classes, the trend for some years has been toward more unusual, varied, and active kinds of vacation: a growing minority of people may opt for an archaeological dig in Mexico or even a safari in Kenya.

In the urbanized Italian society, the middle classes have become the dominant social sector of the Italian population. It is a population, however, that cannot be viewed as a very composite stratum because it includes people coming from many sectors of employment and of the economy.

There has, of course, always been a strong middle class, never a real aristocracy. Since the days of the mercantile city-states of the twelfth century—the Florence of the Medici excluded nobles from the government of the city—until 1922 when a definitive *Debrett's* of the Italian nobility was drawn up, the middle class was *the* social class. And even after 1922, aristocracy was a vague term that included people so diverse that they had little in common.

Today's affluence has been particularly strong in the new middle class that has arisen and whose influence has been growing fast. Economic expansion, especially of the new tertiary services, has elevated from the ranks of the lower bourgeoisie a new group that lacks inherited property but has achieved significant affluence: sales and advertising executives and skilled technicians, together with shopkeepers, artisans, and small industrialists who have modernized and moved with the times. This is an assertive status-seeking world of new social mobility that is immensely in love with American material values. Elsewhere in the middle classes, achieving prosperity has been more uneven. The less-enterprising artisans and small traders, outclassed by the new consumer economy, are sliding into decline. The public servants—postal workers, clerks, and primary school teachers—have seen their wages rise less rapidly than in the private sector. Their ranks have now been infiltrated by the sons and daughters of the peasantry and the working class—young people who prefer soft jobs as clerks or typists to the drudgery of farm or factory.

In all these changes, class divisions have been fading, even though *class-consciousness* is still very much alive, especially in the South. In fact, it is another paradox of Italian life that the Italians are far more class-conscious than the Americans and French, but are less class-divided. It is a psychological more than an economic division. In fact, except between families and groupings, there are few social barriers in Italy. Snobbishness exists, but playing a role is more important than any innate sense of superiority. The boss of a firm will probably treat the employees in an authoritative way because he is in charge; however, when he is outside his firm that power is no longer present. There is no equivalent at the high school level of the British fee-paying public schools or American private prep schools, or of Oxford, Cambridge, Harvard, Yale, or the many other prestigious colleges to separate people socially. There is no upper-class in a permanent, innate sense.

The gap between the extremes of wealth and poverty has been reduced, unlike in the United States; however, there is not the same social mobility and, therefore, not the same freedom of opportunity. Certainly there is more mobility than before the war, and children of all classes now mix in the same state schools until age 14; but there is little sense of a classless meritocracy where a worker's gifted son can rub shoulders with a doctor's or a university professor's. The causes of this division lie deep in Italian history and character. Class patterns are certainly changing, more through the economic merging of different classes than a blurring of the outward distinctions between them. Under modern conditions, their interests and habits have drawn closer. A skilled worker may own the same kind of car as a member of the bourgeoisie, and off duty he may dress much the same way; the new working generation has given up its old class "uniform" and is dressing like the middle class, so it becomes harder to tell them apart. A lot certainly has to do with the *bella figura* (the facade) that everyone wants to present to the outside world.

Bureaucracy: Twenty-first Century Baroque

If there is one "class" that all Italians could agree to despise, it is the bureaucratic class, *la burocrazia*. There persists a general consensus that public officials do not work and are not to be trusted. In Italy, the idea that any official organization is there to serve the citizen is not only unfamiliar, it is laughable. Most civil servants are neither "civil" nor "servants." It is a known fact that people join the bureaucracy not out of love for a certain kind of work or out of a calling for public service, but mainly because they want stable employment, a secure job, and very little hard work. After all, most government and municipal offices are only open from 8:00 a.m. until 2:00 p.m.; there isn't another organization in the universe with such a schedule! Anyone who goes to an Italian consulate abroad can easily get a good taste of what happens in Italy! Government employees think in terms of rights, not obligations.

This sprawling bureaucratic maze conceals all sorts of illegal or quasi-legal activities on both small and large scales. It is impossible to get anything accomplished rapidly. In a request for a driver's license or a permit to use public space, a citizen may easily be tempted to pay for speed or to create a network of mutual favors. On a larger scale we need only look at the scandals uncovered in 1992-1993 that revealed wholesale kickback abuses, *tangenti*, in every sort of government control. The increase of scandals to the level of shameful obscenity has finally turned public opinion against dishonesty in the public services, and magistrates are conducting a campaign clean-up by jailing hundreds of public officials, including major political personalities in the "clean hands" (*mani pulite*) campaign.

There is a complete mistrust of the bureaucrats by the public. The mask of anonymous authority stands between them. No attempt has ever been made in Italy to personalize the employees' relations with the public, for example, by putting name-cards on desks and guichets as in the United States. Some change is taking place slowly in certain areas. The telephone service in particular has made a real effort to improve its relations with the public, and operators are now far more polite and helpful. Overall, however, the situation is still deplorable and Italians dread those occasions when they must deal with governmental offices.

Unfortunately for those who need to be served and must pay for the "service," the total number of bureaucrats is very high. Almost four-fifths are from the South, and it is ironic that the heirs of the conquered Bourbon state now administer a united Italy.

Italians spend their lives devising ingenious rules and then finding equally cunning ways of evading them. Thus they are able to cut corners and circumvent some of the bureaucratic absurdities. That is, everyone, including officials, accepts the fact that red tape can be tacitly ignored from time to time, especially when it is done between pals.

One basic problem in the bureaucratic system is the Italian concept of authority as an *absolute* entity. Consequently, there is much less delegation of power than in Britain or America. There is less sense of a team responsibility: the head of an office or department will tend to concentrate the key work in his own hands rather than sharing the load. This extends even to relations between a boss and his secretary, for Italian managers tend to make inadequate use of their secretaries. The reluctance to delegate is one more aspect of the Italian centralist tradition, which operates just as much within a firm or other small unit as on the wider level of the government. And it has some unfortunate effects. It tends to create a gulf, more noticeable than in most countries, between the dynamic few at the top and the frustrated or time-serving many at more junior levels.

In the private sector, however, the efficiency of individuals and groups is remarkable. For example, the attitude and performance of the working "class" is relatively high now; there has been a considerable improvement since the 1970s. The industrial transformation may have had an effect on work ethics and workers' behavior. Today, the number of employees in industry has declined. The balance between those working in large factories and those in small ones has tipped significantly in favor of the latter. Because of the upsurge of small firms, family-owned businesses, and the underground economy, it is difficult to assess change. Nevertheless there has been a significant change in the number and the make-up of the working class.

One of Italy's most significant achievements since World War II has been its expansion of social insurance coverage to include the entire population; but that has also been the major cause of the financial disequilibrium. In 1982, 13% of the GDP was spent for pensions; that is equivalent to one-quarter of the total public expenditure. The major problem is certainly the high numbers of those who receive aid; in the South, especially, pensions are a form of welfare assistance. Another serious problem is certainly the low contribution to the pension plan by employer and employee and the concomitant heavy subsidy by the state. Moreover, the Italian pension system is the most generous in the EU in terms of age. While in most countries men retire at age 65 and women at 60 if they do not follow the same age limit as men, in Italy, as in Japan, men are eligible for retirement at 60 and women at 55.

However, Japanese pensions are calculated on the earnings average of one's entire career, whereas in Italy the average is based on the last five years of employment. Because of low birth rates and an increase of the elderly population, Italy, like France and Great Britain, is reviewing its pension system. The OCSE (the Organization for Cooperation and Economical Development) has anticipated that Italy may, in the near future, end up spending more than one-third of its national product for social security expenses, if no changes are made. This growth in increased social benefit will, of course, cause a further increase in the bureaucratic machinery.

On the positive side, one result of the vastly improved health care system has been an improvement in longevity and average height. In addition to eating better and being better housed, the Italians live longer and have become taller. A 1991 survey conducted by ISTAT, the Central Institute of Statistics, revealed that the Italian lifespan has increased: men's average life expectancy is 73.2 years while women's is 79.7. Italy is preceded in this category only by Japan, Sweden, and Switzerland. Better diet, living conditions, and health care not only have improved longevity, they have also disproved the common stereotype that Mediterraneans are genetically short. The average Italian height is now 173.67 centimeters; an increase of five centimeters since the 1930s.

La Bella Figura

All of those improvements in personal health and individual well-being are important, for Italians have always been concerned about appearances. From the way they prepare their food to the way they dress, there is always an attempt at style and beauty.

To most foreigners, Italian "style" often means extraordinary elegance and dignity. Italians lavish much attention on presenting a good appearance, and compliments in that regard are an ordinary practice. In fact, compliments are an essential part of a mutual admiration society. This tendency to comment on positive physical attributes partly explains the success of Italian men with northern women as well as the disappointment which Italian women feel when they go to northern Europe where compliments tend to be regarded either as insincere or as a way of playing on vanity.

This *bella figura*—putting on a beautiful facade—and the slavery to fashion, can be irritating. But of course it is the surface of personal living. Much of the attitude to fashion and *bella figura* comes originally from village life where everything is personal, one knows everyone, and one's appearance and behavior are important. That attitude was brought to the cities; today, only a small percentage of the people living in the city were born there, but, notwithstanding the profound changes, it is impossible to suddenly eradicate attitudes that are two thousand years old.

An interesting indication of their sense of proportion and their concern for *la bella figura* is that Italians rarely get drunk. They seem to know that alcohol, after all, does not generate exuberance, but rather it deadens the senses and makes people sloppy. Even at soccer celebrations most fans do not fall prey to the excesses of alcohol—contrary to what occurs in many other parts of Europe. Italians drink alcoholic beverages mainly at dinner time to complement a meal or at a *caffè* to enjoy a conversation with a friend.

Italy's new postwar affluence, as in other countries, brought great changes in spending and leisure habits. Italians are eating far more meat than before the war; it was served only once a week on Sunday, whereas today it is daily common food. They have also been adopting American spending habits. Cars, televisions, summer vacations by the sea, and other new privileges have been altering their lives. Relatively speaking, Italians still place more emphasis on enjoyment, but their former reluctance to spend their money on useful possessions has waned sharply. During the boom years, the Italians steadily increased the share of their budget that went on their homes, not only on rent and mortgages but on comfort and equipment too.

With the growth of individual housing and the middle-class vogue for buying and restoring crumbling villas, castles or old farmhouses for weekend retreats, skilled hand work has also become a major pastime. For example, in the outskirts of many towns, one sees big new garden center supermarkets attracting a new generation of gardening enthusiasts. Even a respectable doctor no longer considers it undignified to be seen by his neighbors doing work around the house.

Urbanization

The Italian concept of *la bella figura* was put to a stern test when the country attempted to respond to the need for more and better housing for everyone. In the postwar decades of growth and modernization, the main urban emphasis went rightly to solving Italy's terrible housing shortage, a legacy of many years of neglect. New high-rise buildings were erected often with little regard for aesthetics or amenities. But after the high-rise boom in suburbia of the 1970s, which, unfortunately, spoiled the old charm of many Italian cities, the accent today is on much needed improvements to quality of life—more parks, fountains, traffic-free streets, rehabilitation of poorer districts, and so on. There was also a shift in priorities, as an affluent society began to react against the negative aspects of too rapid urbanization. Italians demanded that their new individual prosperity be matched by better public amenities and by steps to make city life more tolerable. Since the late 1970s many town councils have shifted their emphasis from building monolithic housing projects to developments that paid more attention to ecological or aesthetic considerations. However, because of their *socialità* and love for nature, Italians always built housing that made for easy human relations—houses giving onto squares, balconies, and so forth. The new environmental trend took many forms and often arose from local or private, rather than state, initiative. Throughout the country there are new open-air or heated public swimming pools, well-equipped leisure and sports centers, advisory clinics, new homes for old people, renovated *palazzi* and castles, new museums—and campaigns against noise and litter abound. The urban revolution has steadily molded new lifestyles and new social attitudes. The many millions who moved from the farms or from slum districts to the new dwellings had to adapt, sometimes painfully, to very different needs and patterns of modern suburbia. Many people reacted by a scared retreat into privacy, others by trying to form new clubs and associations—for sport or culture, for example.

Slowly a new style of local community life is emerging in Italy, more informal and less institutional than that of the old urban bourgeoisie society but less warm and less relaxed than that of the old village or agrarian world. Among the cities' zestful, nervous crowded terrace-*caffé*, smart shop-windows and frenzied *piazze*, these new citizens had to get used to a new tempo. The congested narrow streets with their more aggressive and angry drivers are not easily acceptable to the newcomers. Even italophiles who spend a month or two in an Italian city, finding it fascinating and exciting, find it difficult to adapt to the strains that cities such as Rome, Naples, or Milan present.

Italy has solved the housing shortage, but at a price. In the mid-1950s only about 10% of all Italian homes had a bath or shower and only about 30% had flushing lavatories. The Italians used to live in overcrowded and often squalid conditions, but cheaply. Since then homes have been built for over half the population, and every town is ringed with modern blocks of flats—a common enough sight in the Western world. In many parts of the country, the new housing complexes built around cities, called *borgate* around Rome, were usually poorly planned. There are no meeting places, apart from the occasional *caffé*. Cafés, however, are reserved for men in the evenings, and the very few cinemas show only films of the lowest quality. There is a striking shortage of parks, hospitals and cultural services, schools, libraries, theaters, concerts halls, cinemas, and sport centers, relative to what is available just a few miles away.

Another feature is a distorted pattern of consumption. As in the fast-urbanizing capitalist countries, a burgeoning consumer-goods sector goes hand in hand with inadequate social spending (for houses, roads, sanitation, hospitals, social services, etc.). It is characteristic of all capitalist societies in the course of their development that economic activity and the population it supports become polarized spatially. Wealth and people become concentrated in core regions occupying a relatively small part of the territory, and the rest remains underdeveloped. According to recent statistics, over 60% of the Italians own their own homes, and many have also purchased vacation homes as well.

Today, housing is far more plentiful and very comfortable, but prices have skyrocketed. The average share of family income devoted to rents or mortgage, plus basic charges, has risen since the war from the incredibly low figure of 3.4% to over 25%. But the burden is unevenly shared. State housing policy has made repeated U-turns since the war, and its complex bureaucratic system of controls and subsidies has relieved some injustices but created others.

Nevertheless, now that the Italians are well-housed, they are freer to pick and choose the kind of homes they really want, and this freedom has triggered some striking changes. In the first thirty years of the postwar period, new high-rise blockstyle housing was constructed as this was the quickest and cheapest way of solving the shortage. Later, there was a shift toward buying rather than renting and an emphasis on single dwellings. In fact, in all classes there is a steady trend toward buying rather than renting of new property. This tendency satisfies the Italian's property-owning instincts, and it provides developers with quicker returns. The Italians have become quite "house-proud," and no longer do they readily reject home comfort in favor of food, vacations, or other pleasures. Their expectations have risen; they no longer tolerate the old overcrowding, and they want larger and better-built apartments or houses.

The housing urge has also expressed itself in the increased construction of second homes, and Italy is supposed to have more of these than any country in Europe. Some are ancient family houses deserted by emigrants to the city who, once they were earning well, returned to modernize them and turn them into summer resorts.

Foreigners are amazed by the type of first and/or second housing that even the Italian with modest income is able to afford. One possible explanation is that in many cases the houses are inherited. As for the new housing, money comes through parents' sacrifice and personal *arrangiarsi*; with a peasant background, Italians have maintained the habit of saving frugally for something they really want. However, the enthusiasm for second homes has tended to deaden some small towns. Moreover, many of the old houses are being bought by foreigners; parts of Tuscany have been referred to as Chiantishire because so many British own property there. But these foreigners or the rich Italians occupy them only for a few weeks a year, with the result that villages are losing their identity.

Speculation over land and property has for many years been a major cause of the soaring rents and house prices. However, the tempo of new building has now slackened considerably since the main needs have been met and the birthrate has been declining. Conversely, the new trend in modernizing old buildings instead of demolishing them has been strong. Especially for historic city centers, Italy has turned toward a policy of rehabilitation; regulations for rehabilitation of old housing in *centri storici* are very strict and detailed. The restoration of old housing is seen as the best socially human way to preserve Italy's architectural heritage and reanimate city centers. Any visitor is bound to be impressed by the way Italy cares for its "historical centers." And so today there are two trends, going in opposite directions. On the one hand, more people want to move back to city-center living when good housing is available; on the other hand, more people are wanting their own individual houses, amid greenery in the outskirts or at least within commuter range. Both groups reject the sad high-rise apartments of the expansion years.

Italians tend to buy instead of lease because living in dwellings for a short time is incompatible with the Italian idea of *domus* which evokes solidity and permanence. And if you have a house, you do not normally sell it to buy a better one as you get more prosperous with age. You keep it for your children, who were brought up in it, and add to it if you can when you need more room.

Decadence or Renewal of *Gastronomia*

Italians also like to spend their new wealth on eating. They spend as much as 38.8% of income on food, of which only about 6% goes for restaurant meals. Traditional Italian good eating has undergone many changes in the past decades and has come under various conflicting and complex pressures, pushing it simultaneously toward decline and recovery, and a foreign visitor may at first be baffled by what he sees, hears, and tastes. Fast-food places serving hot-dogs and hamburgers or pizza abound all over Italy. These are crowded, cheerful places, popular with youngsters in the evening and office workers at lunchtime, and they compare favorably with their American equivalents. The *McDonald's* in Rome is the most successful of the chain worldwide! Certainly, the social change has affected eating habits. A modern nation in a hurry no longer has time or concern for serious daily cooking and eating: both at home and away from it, routine meals have become more simple, slapdash, and utilitarian.

Yet, the Italians' gastronomic zeal is not dying; Italians are increasingly channeling it toward the once- or twice-a-week occasion or ritual with friends, at home. There is a national style of cooking and an assortment of different regional styles that overflows into neighboring provinces. Pasta is certainly the common denominator of most cooking from one end of the peninsula to the other. And pasta comes with hundreds of names for hundreds of types: *spaghetti, tagliatelle, rigatoni, lasagne, orecchiette, ravioli, cannelloni, tortellini, linguine* are only the more obvious. Depending on the locale you may be offered *strangozzo, trenette, strozzaprete* or dozens of other varieties. And then you may choose among the hundreds of rich flavoring and sauces that may be used: *all'arrabbiata, puttanesca, bolognese, carbonara, pesto, napoletana,* to name just a few.

Home-cooking habits are not as consistent as just a couple of decades ago. Television, cars, foreign vacations, better housing, and other possessions all developed new rival claims on the average family's budget and interests—and especially on the wife's time. In the middle class, far fewer wives now have servants than before the war, more have jobs, and life is more hectic. Some younger wives do not want to be a "slave" in the kitchen.

The Italian housewife still has a far wider variety of fresh foods to choose from than homemakers in most parts of Britain, Germany, and even France. But after a long period of resistance her opposition to the idea of frozen foods is now thawing out. Even today, the Italians eat less than half as much frozen produce as the British and the Americans, but the consumption figures are increasing each year, and frozen-food freezers in supermarkets have been lengthening. The main difference is that while in the U.S. the best-selling frozen foods are ordinary items, the Italians prefer much more complex and expensive deep-frozen pre-cooked dishes.

Other changes may be inevitable. It seems that Italians are starting to move over to the light-meal habit for at least one of their main meals of the day. It should be possible for the light snack and true gastronomy to coexist, each for its own occasion. Italy has long been a nation of overeaters where too much stress has been set on the convention that a meal must contain three or four full courses—a tavola non s'invecchia (at the table one doesn't grow old) the saying goes. Fortunately, being the masters of the now-fashionable Mediterranean diet, Italians are on the average less obese than Americans. Nevertheless, with the nervous speeding-up of life, today far more care is being given to dieting.

Consequently, as in America and Britain, sales of cookbooks have soared; in Italy another reason is that after the war many middle-class urban mothers ceased handing on their culinary lore to their children, who are now having to learn it for themselves.

We have mentioned that Italians find it disgraceful to get drunk, but this self-restraint does not mean that good food goes unaccompanied by good wine. Italians have not made a religion of their wine-drinking as perhaps the French have done, but an appropriate *vino* is an integral part of a good meal. There is an expression: "*un pranzo senza vino è come un giorno senza sole,*" which translates as: a meal without wine is like a day without sunshine. Today Italy produces and exports more wine than any other country, yet there is a suspicion that they keep the best for themselves. From cold, dry whites like frascati, soave, pinot grigio, and verdicchio, to smooth, hearty reds like chianti, brunello, amarone, bardolino, and barolo, there is a vino to accompany any dish. To whet the appetite, there are dozens of *aperitivi*, and after the meal one might try a *digestivo,* often an herbal alcoholic drink "to aid digestion." Italian cordials are world famous—anisette, sambuca, amaretto, galliano, strega, just to name a few—although two fingers of *grappa* might be a more usual way for an Italian to end a good meal.

Sexual Behavior

Whether it is enjoying a good meal with friends or just greeting someone on the street, Italians are personal. Often, however, it is difficult

for the American or Northern European visitor to accept the natural-
ness with which Italians touch each other. Usually it is simply an extension of the physical warmth and affection of the family. The way
men embrace each other without self-consciousness can also be surprising to an Anglo-Saxon. The fact that the "northerners" recoil from
touching or embracing each other is possibly due to excessive consciousness of sex. Certainly the fact that they are less demonstrative
within their families could mean that for them touching is associated
more with sex and less with warmth and spontaneous friendliness.

Despite strictures by the Vatican and the clergy, Italians have always had a reputation for sexual permissiveness, and foreign artists
and writers, such as Goethe, Stendhal, Byron, Schopenhauer, and
Tolstoy learned much about the country from their Italian loves and
praised the passionate nature of its women. The Italian lover, a movie
cliché since Rudolph Valentino, is still an unadvertised asset of the
Italian tourist business. *Summertime,* in which Katharine Hepburn
falls in love with the dashing Rossano Brazzi on her first visit to Venice
perhaps epitomizes this romantic vision of Italy.

In fact so much about Italy is part of this image: the gondolas, the
songs, the wine, the sunlight, the Ferraris, *la dolce vita.* And the
magic and romantic associations of names: Capri, Sorrento, Positano,
Venice, Verona, the Trevi Fountain, the lakes. A number of women
visitors to Italy seem to look forward to instant masculine attention
and feed the notion that a lot of foreign women are coming to Italy in
search of erotic adventures. Unquestionably, what is known as *caccia
alle straniere* (hunting for foreign women) is also a pasttime of young
Italians to prove their virility and seductiveness.

The most striking change in sexual behavior certainly happened
with women. Today, the Italian woman expects the same degree of
sexual freedom as a man and, conversely, the same degree of fidelity
from a man. She no longer accepts that his peccadillos are more for-
givable than her own. The sexual attitudes and behavior of Italian girls
have also been changing dramatically, though the new permissiveness
is still very recent, more so than in most countries. As late as the
1960s, all the evidence was still suggesting that Italian unmarried
girls as a whole, especially in the provinces, were still among the most
virginal in Europe. Well into the 1960s the old code of this Catholic
society remained in force, at least on the surface. According to a survey in 1960 more than half of Italian mothers still thought a girl should
not be allowed out with a boy till she was 19, and many still acted on
that belief. And less than one-third of girls said they approved of pre-

marital sex even between fiancés, while about 70% of married women under 30 claimed to have been a virgin on their wedding night.

However, following the lead of the Nordic countries, sexual freedom began to spread. Parents became readier to allow their daughters to go out with their boyfriends; young people got more leisure and money for going off together. In some student circles, relations had become very free by the mid 1960s. The 1970s saw a further change, essentially among the very young and in parental attitudes toward them. This attitude change came from foreign influences, from the freeing of legal controls on contraception, from the steady decline in the role of the Church. Today at school teenage girls treat boys as sex objects in a free market, just as boys treat girls. However, lately there has been a swing away from promiscuity, mainly because of the spread of AIDS. In general, sexual freedom in Italy has now reached the same level as in France, Britain, Germany, or Sweden—and that, for this so-called Catholic country, is quite a transformation. It would be wrong, however, to infer from the teenage revolution that every adult woman has become *leggera* (easy) overnight. Most of those in their mid-twenties or older are still *serie* (serious) and will not give themselves except for love.

La Gioventù: Footloose but More Sincere

Naturally these changes in social behavior have had their effect on Italy's youth, *gioventù*. Young people have their own consumer markets for music, clothes, and cars; they have their own world of rock groups and other singing idols. All enjoy far more freedom from parents than cloistered Italian youths had 20 years ago, and far more sexual license, too.

Today's *gioventù* is not rebellious and is not fired with revolutionary ideals for trying to change society, very much in contrast to the seething youth of the late 1960s. Tolerant and reflective, today's young people seem curiously passive. Only rarely do they show much sense of public initiative.

It used not to be so. Many of the most important changes in postwar Italy occurred because of a new generation rising against the standards of its elders. The postwar climate was very different from today's: more austere, but also more open and adventurous. The upheavals of wartime had broken down some of the barriers that previously kept youth in its place, and an idealistic new wave was gradually able to make inroads into the fossilized hierarchy. It is remarkable how youthful many of the postwar pioneers were at the outset: former Prime Minister Andreotti was in his early twenties, President of the Republic Scalfaro was in his early thirties. Today these and other pace-setters are established old figures, some of them still in key positions, corrupted, and without vision; but the new generation, born into an age of greater affluence but also of greater skepticism, has seldom shown the same innovating spirit. The spirit that animated neorealist artists, who so accurately captured those years of ferment, was replaced by a spirit of desolation that was seen in the prophetic *La Dolce Vita*. Italy's young people, it seems, became too much attached to the world of *Dallas* and *Falcon Crest,* which were just as popular in Italy as in the U.S.

In the 1960s, a new generation, sipping its Coca-Cola and listening to pop music and singing American rock'n'roll was born. Quickly, the Italian pop was born. At first the movement was highly derivative. Not only did the stars borrow American tunes, several of them found it smart to adopt Anglo-Saxon names as well. Open-air concerts attracted tens of thousands of teenagers. These gatherings reflected the high sense of solidarity of the new generation. There was a tone of revolt in all this, but the revolution was purely one of music and rhythm, not morals and standards.

The situation changed from the end of the 1960s on. Italy's youth today is something of an enigma, and one that many adults find disquieting. Through the 1950s and 1960s it remained very much under parental influence, leaving a dominant impression of docile reticence. Then from the end of the 1960s, giving vent to the frustrations that had lain beneath the surface, youth became almost an independent political and cultural force. This period was the golden age of faith in ideologies and the belief that the new generation could after all change society. Youth burst into action. But when the dust had settled, and society had not been changed very much, it soon became clear that the crisis between 1967 and 1969 had not turned the entire Italian youth into revolutionaries.

However, those years were not without their permanent legacy, notably in the way they modified the relations between Italian youth and its elders. The old barriers of authority were broken, and this was true as much within families as in schools and universities. But, almost 25 years later, what use has been made of this freedom by the ensuing generation? Well, most of today's youngsters were born after those years of *contestazione.* For most of them those years of high ideals are history and are seen with skepticism and passivity. Recently, whenever the youngsters have engaged in demonstrations, they have done so more in opposition to change, than as a constructive demand for change. They are much closer to their parents' interests and attitudes: rejection of ideologies and formal organizations, concern with private pleasures, and "feathering the nest." The new Italian concern with an ethos of personal fulfillment and hedonism is even stronger among the young than among older people. It is easy to lament this apparent shift toward egotism and rejection of ideals of wider community service. They cling to their own trusted circle of family and friends and reject any wider allegiance.

One feature common to most young people in the past decade, even the more conformist ones, is that leisure and privacy have been replacing work as the essential paths to self-fulfillment. The young attitude to a job or career is frequently utilitarian; work is seen as a means of ensuring the quality of their leisure lives; and few of them share the passionate work ethic that drove their elders to build the modern prosperous Italy. The country should, certainly, be concerned about the decline of the old dedicated work ethic. It seems, however, that there have been signs of a new swing of the pendulum among some very young people. Although very often individualistic and self-centered, they are more ambitious and are prepared to work harder. They have drive and initiative, but they do not challenge the system or seek to change it for the good of society as a whole; in fact, usually they would rather run their own business than work for a large organization or institution.

Idealism over a united Europe has also waned recently, for young people as much as their elders have grown cynical about the EU as an institution. Yet in a more general sense they still feel "European," more so than the French, and much more so than the insular British. They have less sense of frontiers than the older generation. These young people not only are not racist, they take pride in showing solidarity with new immigrants, mostly of color, and also feel a strong concern toward the Third World.

Overall, however, *la gioventù* has won a new freedom from parents and teachers, but it has also lost its sure moral leadership. It cannot trust the values of an adult world that is corrupt and no longer offers certainties; hence, in the search for its own values it retreats into a shell.

Part IV
Cultural Changes

Introduction

The old concept of *culture*, at one point exclusively identified with education, literacy, and "print culture," as well as the high arts, has changed also in Italy, even though it took much longer than in other Western nations. A number of reasons may explain the resiliency: the combination until the 1960s of restricted-access institutions of higher learning with low national rates of literacy of post-primary school attendance, particularly in rural areas; the prestige and durability of a humanist intellectual tradition—the neo-idealism associated particularly with the philosophers Benedetto Croce (1866-1952) and Giovanni Gentile (1875-1944)—which identified culture with intellectuals, cultural history with intellectual history. This tradition continued to hold sway over higher education and publishing in Italy until at least the mid 1960s.

Today the prevalent concept of *cultura* among Italian intellectuals is very broad and encompasses many social manifestations. It seems that they have also come to accept the view that identity is molded by consumption; that there is something one could call consumer identity. The Anglo-Saxon term *commodity aesthetics*, referring on the one hand to beauty as an appearance appealing to the senses, and on the other hand to a beauty developed in the service of the realization of exchange of value, has had an impact on Italians' view of culture and how it is produced. The creation/production of culture as a product is part of the system of selling and buying, of aesthetic illusions, of commodities bearing value and, therefore, the use of values. The more affluent a society is, the broader and stronger is this culture and cultural phenomenon.

The economic development and rapid urbanization has been accompanied by a remarkable rise in living standards as reflected in the consumer modes, lifestyles, and leisure activities. From the new fad for clothes to the kind of vacations they take, Italians have become more able and willing to spend more *lire*, more mobile, more open, and socially more homogeneous.

The passion of the Italians for good clothes and anything that displays good taste is well known, as is their leading role in the fashion world. Although Milan has become the unquestioned world fashion center, trend-setter, and a Mecca for foreign talent, the whole country is rich in high-level designers. The new fashions have for many years been quickly copied and mass-produced for the major stores at prices within the reach of all strata of society. Today, the ordinary woman dresses more elegantly than 30 years ago and does not dress much differently from those coming from wealthier families. Fashion magazines and television have certainly been drumming the notions of elegance into the heads of ordinary Italian women who, as a general breed, always had a special claim to being very well dressed.

Popular magazines and television can also take some of the credit for improvements in housekeeping, general personal appearance, and especially hygiene. New campaigns brought about a rise in the sales of soap, deodorants, and toothpaste. Modern techniques of advertising and public relations arrived late in Italy, but then swept through the land with torrential force; in the process, the experts decided that Italians could be conditioned to accept a commodity as new and smart if it were given an Anglo-Saxon name; therefore, the clothing and cosmetics worlds virtually adopted English as a lingua franca.

Such social transformation was not separate from the cultural modernization of the country. In many of their new leisure habits (discotheques, weekend pleasure, and various sports), as in so much else (the spread of television, personal computers, hi-fi), Italians have surpassed most industrialized nations.

The social, economic, and political changes discussed in the previous chapters were accompanied by a dramatic decline in illiteracy; the surge of mass media brought about for the first time in Italy a uniform, nationwide mass culture. New interest in books and cultural products has also had profound effects on every aspect of literary culture in Italy. Everything surrounding the actual literary texts has been affected too—production, distribution, sales, and, above all, the reading public. Changes in all these areas in turn have had their effects on writing itself, on its general role and status in society, and on the role of those who write. At the same time, traditional practices and long-standing social factors have continued to play an important part, exerting a conservative, braking pressure on the drive toward innovation and expansion.

The Dialects and Languages of Italy (adapted from C. Duggan, *A Concise History of Italy*, Cambridge, 1994, p. 29)

When the Second World War ended in 1945, Italian filmmakers were freed from the restrictions imposed by the fascist government and began to produce movies about real Italy (the devastation of the war, the difficulties of reconstruction, the poverty of their country, and the peasants' world. The economic boom of postwar Italy pushed the cinema in new directions. In the late 1950s, Federico Fellini began to make films that clearly broke with the tradition. Fellini injected fantasy, dreams, and his own memories into his films, and broke many taboos. The cinematic world of sex became an area of great interest. Printed by courtesy of Editions Soleil.

XIV

Cultural Modernization: Changes and Conflicts

Language Changes

A greatly increased demand for books was first registered in the euphoric period immediately following the liberation from the Nazis. This demand seems to have come from the working class as much as from any other section of the population. But before the initial demand was satisfied, several problems had to be overcome. There was a shortage of paper, and the little that was available was very expensive; publishing houses were not geared to large-scale production; much that was actually written and published was still uncompromisingly literary; and, most importantly, the great majority of Italians spoke only dialect. This last issue needs clarification.

Italian is assumed to be Italy's national language. It originates as a written language based on the literary Florentine of the fourteenth century. Although literary Italian had been adopted as a written language, the vast majority of Italians until recently were in fact illiterate because their mother tongues were Italy's local dialects. These dialects are in effect separate Romance languages, and they can differ from each other as much as French differs from Spanish. These Italian dialects are not derived from Italian, nor are they varieties or adaptations of the national language. On the contrary, it is Italian that is based on one of the dialects (i.e., Florentine), or rather, on the standardization of its literary variety of the fourteenth century. But Milanese, Venetian, Genovese, Bolognese, Florentine, Roman, Neapolitan, Sicilian, and so forth are all 'sister' languages derived from Latin. They differ from each other in phonology, grammar, and lexis.

We said that these dialects are separate Romance languages. But it should be understood that, from a strictly linguistic viewpoint, there is no difference between a language and a dialect. The distinction is not linguistic but cultural, social, and political. It should also be said that many dialects have a long-standing and rich literary tradition, in many cases going back to the Middle Ages. In fact, they are part of the Italian literary tradition. We should also underline that what we call Italian literature finds expression, up to the sixteenth century, mainly in two languages, Latin and its vernacular, and from the beginning of the sixteenth century a third medium is added—dialect. Dialect literature is of course not the same as popular literature, and normally belongs to a sophisticate level of elaborate, self-conscious high culture, rather than to spontaneous popular culture.

How many different dialects are spoken in Italy? The question is problematic; as it is difficult to assess the number of languages in the world, so it is difficult to assess the number of Italian dialects. Linguists agree on about fifteen main dialect groups, clearly different from each other, and roughly corresponding to the traditional subdivisions into regions. But it is clear that often there are noticeable differences between neighboring towns, and even within the same town. The issue of the dialects is separate from that of *linguistic minorities*. These are enclaves of speakers of foreign languages, often established in Italy for many centuries.[1]

The attempt to establish how the use of dialects has changed and/or how many people use Italian and how many use dialect poses considerable difficulties. Only since 1951 do statistical data distinguish between "literates" and "semiliterates." The census of 1951 revealed that 12.9% of Italians over the age of six were illiterate; in the South the illiteracy rate reached 24%. We must remember that, at this time, Italy had been unified for less than 100 years and having been dominated by so many diverse countries and cultures, there were dozens of dialects that were still in common use immediately after the war. In addition, until recently the agrarian and peasant population was largely illiterate. This situation has changed greatly in the last forty years.

It is well known that very many people in Italy still normally speak dialect and that dialects are very different from each other; indeed, they are mostly unintelligible to speakers of other dialects. In 1862 the number of people in the country who could speak Italian (i.e., either the old Florentine-based literacy language or the dialects of Tuscany and Rome that were close to it) has been estimated at between 2.5% and 10%. In other words, the "national" language was not used by at least 90% of the Italian population. Italian was essentially a written language that had yet to enter into common spoken use. Even when it did, it would take several generations to start supplanting the dialects.

In more recent years the figures, as we may expect, are very different. The following data based on Doxa polls give a clear view:

Usage in the family	1974	1982	1988	1991
dialects with everyone	51%	47%	40%	36%
Italian with everyone	25%	29%	34%	34%
Usage with friends and colleagues				
Only or mainly dialect	42%	36%	33%	23%
Only or mainly Italian	36%	42%	47%	48%

The data are not based on direct observation of linguistic behavior, which would be extremely difficult to assess, but on answers given by 2,000 adults to a questionnaire concerning linguistic behavior. The questionnaire asked whether the informant spoke Italian, or dialect, or both (a) in the home, (b) with friends and colleagues. Since, in general, more prestige is attached to the use of Italian, it is possible that the answers were biased in that direction. The figures are also interesting when they are interpreted analytically. There are proportionally more dialect speakers (1) among women than men; (2) among older than younger people; (3) in the South and the Islands than in the Center and North; (4) in the country than in the urban centers; (5) in the lower than in the middle and upper classes. These data obviously show a fall in the use of dialect and a rise in the use of Italian. Italy today is a largely bilingual country, whereas before it was effectively a monolingual one, consisting of dialect speakers.

The main processes leading to the diffusion of a national standard language (in reality, a set of regional and social varieties of Italian) were mass urbanization, geographical mobility, schooling, conscription, and the mass diffusion of radio and television. Radio and television certainly had the major impact because they touched in the same and more direct and profound way every citizen.

Although schools could be an important site of dissemination of the national language and acquisition of literacy, one must not assume rigid and automatic correlations between state education, the learning of the national language and literacy. While it is true that most illiterate people spoke only their local dialect and were not speakers of Italian, the converse did not necessarily hold. That is to say, a person who learned to understand and speak a form of Italian did not necessarily acquire literacy skills. Illiterate or semiliterate people could learn Italian through social contact, for instance in the labor migrations to the cities or the mass conscription of peasants into the army, and later through radio, sound films, and television. The printed media (books, newspapers, and periodicals) have a lower impact because of social barriers. For the rural and blue-collar working population, because of lower levels of literacy, lower incomes, and lack of free time, the print media have always had only minimum impact.

Although it is an indisputable fact that the number of people who use Italian rather than dialect has been consistently growing, some linguists question the "sort" of Italian that the "mass" population speaks. Many linguists, especially on the right side of the political spectrum, feel that Italian is "going to the dogs," that the language is in decay. The complaints are, of course, not maliciously concocted; they are based on the fact that many more people than before go to high school and also to university and come from more varied social backgrounds. As a consequence, there are many more students than in the past who, at the level of secondary education, and even at the university level, make elementary grammatical mistakes; a sizable proportion (particularly among those who come from the more disadvantaged socioeconomic groups) do not have a full command of the traditional literary idiom. What we are witnessing is the emergence or the establishment of varieties of the standard language that have been called "popular Italian," "regional Italian," and "media Italian." In this process one can observe a slight narrowing of the gap between spoken and written usage, with the penetration of certain features of the former into the latter. One has the feeling that written Italian is becoming less formal and elaborate than it used to be. The notion is a positive one because it carries progressive and democratic connotations because "popular Italian" is a symbol of the social, economic, and cultural achievements of the working class.

Some linguists establish a connection between the emergence of this brand of Italian and media Italian.[2] On the one hand, it seems clear that television has played a crucial role in spreading the knowledge of Italian; on the other, one would need detailed studies providing serious evidence for the specific influence of television in modifying the grammar of modern Italian. Most people complain about the negative effects of television, of the impoverishment it has brought to the language; rather, this attitude indicates a confusion between the low intellectual level of much that appears on television and linguistic impoverishment.

If we would compare grammar books and some language texts, from the end of the last century to the present, we would find some unexpected results. Some of the modern grammars are obviously more open to linguistic reality than earlier ones; on the other hand, some of the grammars from the end of the last century take the line, suggested by Manzoni, that the language of the new Italian state ought to be based on the living speech of Florence; accordingly they include many examples belonging to the spoken language rather than to the literary tradition. However, if one analyzes some prose and considers spelling, vocabulary, morphology, and syntax, the impression one gets is one of great stability today and not at all one of linguistic upheaval.

Italian has been changing, and the gap between the high and low level is closing. The question is desirability: whether the gap should be bridged by lowering the high level or by raising the low level, or by making them move toward each other.

Political Cultural Strategies

The process of language change and the increase of the literacy rate affected literary art and the related industry. If the overall expansion of book production and sales took time, from the late 1950s the phenomenon of the large-scale best-seller had appeared in Italy, and what is more, best-sellers included works of contemporary Italian fiction. The first of these was *Il gattopardo* (*The Leopard*) of Tomasi di Lampedusa; it sold an unheard-of 100,000 copies in the 12 months following its publication toward the end of 1958. Similar sales were achieved in the early 1960s by various novels of Carlo Cassola and Giorgio Bassani. By the early 1970s it was possible in a few cases for a best-selling paperback to reach sales of half a million or more. The best example was *La storia* (*History/Story*) by Elsa Morante, which within a few months of its appearance in 1974 sold over 600,000 copies.

In this process of accessability to literary work and change in literary tastes, once more the 1960s were a turning point in Italian affairs.

This was the decade during which the economy took off, consumerism was born, education spread, culture found new markets, and social tensions exploded. Inevitably literature, too, was deeply affected.

Probably, the new appetite for the "book" would not have reached such levels so quickly if it were not for well-orchestrated publicity on the part of the publishers. By the end of the 1960s, book publishing had become a business like any other. In the process of expansion and reorganization by the major publishing firms, one important step was the introduction of the modern paperback. Cheap series had already been introduced in the 1950s, most notably the *B.U.R.* (Biblioteca Universale Rizzoli); it included a wide range of Italian and foreign classics. But the more attractive paperbacks did not appear in Italy until 1965, partly because publishers were not aware of potential markets, as they would later become. When Mondadori launched its *Oscar* series in that year, there followed a paperback boom, which gradually drew in the other principal firms, including those which initially felt that, with the paperback, literature was being all too blatantly made into a commodity. In fact, that was what Mondadori was doing with some force; this aggressive publishing enterprise was looking for new markets among the mass of habitual non-readers.

By the mid 1970s sales of books had increased tremendously; however, the expansion had limits. Although there had been a significant change in the volume of publications, the reading public was still concentrated in particular areas of society. The sale of about 140 million books in the mid 1970s, an average of three books per inhabitant per year, did not mean that every Italian read a few books, rather that large sections of the population read a great deal, while others read hardly anything. The reason has to be found mainly in the *literaryness* of Italian prose. In fact, even commercially successful narrative prose is commonly a good deal more refined than is the case with its American or British equivalents. In creative writing there has been a remarkable survival of a highly literary style. Italian discursive prose, as it is used for historical, sociological, philosophical, and critical writing had remained remarkably complex and abstract in vocabulary, Ciceronian in syntax, and conceptually sophisticated. The positive aspect of all this is that the intellectual and stylistic level of Italian writing has been high; the negative aspect is that it maintained a barrier between insiders and outsiders.

Partly because of a new concept in mass culture and partly because of the arrival of a new intellectual sophistication—semiotics, structuralism, modern Marxist thought, new theories of psychoanalysis quickly penetrated Italian literary culture—there developed a shift away from conventional fiction. In the nonhomogeneous literary culture, there emerged two main bodies of fictional writing, "elitist" and "nonelitist." The elitist, restricted to a small reading public, has consistently set its face against the established order and against the consumerization of literature. Its overwhelming tendency has been to denounce, from a variety of points of view, the new industrialized and consumerized Italy as a physical and moral wasteland to which alternatives must be found. The nonelitist writing has been more accepting of the social, political, and economic order of the country. Whatever its critical position, it has inevitably been deeply involved in the commercialization and consumerization of literature, and it has been commonly perceived as providing consolation or escape.

By the beginning of the 1980s, in Italy more people were engaged in services than in the production of industrial goods. In the 1981 census, the service sector emerged for the first time as the largest broad occupational category, employing 50.2% of the active population, followed by industry with 36.8% and agriculture with 13%. The respective figures for 1987 were 57.4%, 32.2%, and 10.4%.[3] Like other advanced economies, Italy had evolved from an industrial society to a "post-industrial" society, with the difference that the change in Italy was rapid—the changes from pre-industrial to industrial to post-industrial are concentrated in the space of less than two generations.

As we had occasion to note, the entry into a post-industrial era has not meant that the manufacturing economy has become unimportant, or that there are no longer depressed regions. The term "post-industrial" society is mainly equated to "information society" in the sense that the majority of its working population is engaged primarily in the handling of information—communications, computer data, cultural services. All of them have characterized important changes in production and distribution and the organization of the labor process. Certainly one can say that the development and marketing of telecommunications and information technology, together with other changes in the economy, education, and social habits have profoundly restructured Italian society and culture over the last generation.

In fact, Italy's formation as a post-modern nation encompasses profound cultural changes especially in the area of mass culture. The development of industries engaged in the production, reproduction, and distribution of cultural products brought in its wake an "anthropological revolution," a break-up of old ideologies and class identities, and a new cultural homogenization around a petty-bourgeois consumerist ethos.[4] The industries that produce or reproduce and distribute books, newspapers and magazines, films and radio and television programs were central to these changes.

To fully assess the change of the country, therefore, one cannot neglect to consider the impact of modern cultural industries on Italian society as it unevenly developed and the development of mass audiences and markets.[5] In so doing, a clear synchronization should be established between cultural and political changes, and an attempt should be made in measuring the degree of political influence upon culture. However, we have to keep in mind that although cultural industries operate within political constraints, they are not driven by political interests alone. There tends always to be a reciprocal play of interests between cultural entrepreneurs and political forces. And we cannot ignore the peculiar nature of the relation of cost/consumer of the cultural products. The fact that modern cultural artifacts (newspapers, magazines, films, records, television programs, etc.) possess the unusual character of commodities, for trying to combine high original costs with mass distribution and low unit costs cannot be neglected, nor can the relevance such production acquires in the realm of mass culture.[6]

In judging modernization and the consequent advent of mass culture one should consider how positively or negatively it affected Italian society. Did modernization "denature" Italian culture by breaking up its traditions of regional differentiation? Or did it bring a beneficial transformation? Has it standardized and "leveled" cultural consumption? Or has it brought new forms of cultural "distinction"? How has the complexity of these changes in the supply and consumption of culture, i.e., the prevalence of popular genre cinema, continued predominance of film imports, development of popular magazines and strips, development of television, been seen by contemporaries?

The most typical approach in the fifties and sixties was to interpret these changes largely in negative terms as the advent in Italy of a low-quality "Americanized" mass culture. The conservative minority lamented this cultural leveling. Most Left-wing critics tended to interpret the cultural changes, which began in the postwar reconstruction period, as being one-dimensional: as functional only to a politics of conservative legitimation. Mass culture, in their view, was simply a "fabrication," part of an "ideological operation." These critics lamented above all the alleged dismissive attitude toward annihilation of popular culture by the political class in power. Thus, the Left interpreted mass culture in an overtly political manner and as a more or less direct agency of class domination presided over by the christian democrats with the support of the Americans. The political forces of the Center and of the Right correctly argued, on the other hand, that cultural "products" do not have the same meaning for everyone and that mass cultural forms may assume complex and diverse meanings for different individuals and social groups.

In general, it is hard to make such a view of the connections between cultural modernization and political domination fit the facts. The advent of mass culture seems to have contributed to socially liberal forms of "consumerism" and to a "revolution of rising expectations." For example, it has brought about the formation of a cultural youth market (records, scooters, fashion, e.g.) which probably helped to catalyze, by the later sixties, the first substantial rejection of the styles of an older generation. Only by shedding some prejudices of a narrowly "ideological" reading of the development of mass culture and adopting a less one-dimensional view of the politics of the period will it be possible to "tease out" some of these cultural contradictions of the postwar era.

Nevertheless, political presence was very strong in Italian culture and had a profound effect on the changes of mass culture and culture in general. In this regard, the primary role played by the Communist Party cannot be underplayed. The *P.C.I.*'s influence was particularly strong and important in the first twenty years of the postwar period.

In the first few years after World War II the *P.C.I.* tended to identify culture largely with print culture, to associate it with books and education. In this respect, of particular importance were the "Communist Book Clubs" and reading groups that sprang up at the end of the war. They provided a form of public, civic participation in an associative, collective cultural activity outside the home, and linked to education and the development of public forms of political consciousness. One went to the *Centro del Libro Popolare*, just as one went to the *casa del popolo* (civic center) or to an education class at the party club; the culturalization charged with political consciousness was implicitly confrontational in nature.

The confrontational attitude of the party, as one may expect, was strong also toward the film industry because the party claimed that "the vulgar commercial film production" pandered to the most facile tastes of the public, avoided films of ideas, and therefore denied cinema its natural cognitive and formative function.

The Communist Party tended to conceive of the people as dispossessed of real culture and therefore in need of access to culture and knowledge: the "guard-dogs" of the bourgeoisie defended as a privileged class inheritance. The people were seen as possessing cultural "aspirations" that needed to be satisfied by recommended reading of "progressive books" or films that presented an "authentic" reality. They allegedly needed to be protected from the aspirations created by American films and the *Reader's Digest*, which pushed them into a "world of dreams" and tried "to make them forget the problems that assail the working class."

In the communist worldview, there was a contradictory attitude toward the people's culture. On the one hand, progressive or authentic forms of popular culture were invoked as positive alternatives to the debased forms of an incipient mass culture; on the other, it was claimed that the masses were delegitimized by a cultural policy fighting to give the people access to "real" culture. It is significant that well into the 1960s, and even beyond, the party continued to pose questions in terms of *exclusion from* and *access to* culture. Therefore, despite all the positive things the party may have done in its own terms, it brought about two negative consequences. First, it reinforced a sense of real popular culture as lying outside the market, the home, and the sphere of private consumption, even though people's culture was becoming increasingly bound up in this period precisely with market relations and transactions and home-based leisure, notably television. Second, it rendered invisible or only very vaguely visible those popular cultural forms and activities based on domestic life and labor or on individual consumption, such as magazine reading, popular particularly among women.

In all this, the concept of the intellectual having to have "common utility" was very strong. Such a concept was Gramscian but by no means exclusively so. The notion that culture resides within intellectuals was part of the legacy of idealist thought—Benedetto Croce had viewed culture as a patrimony of educated elites acting as the motor forces of history—and this notion was to a large extent reproduced by Gramsci, despite his much broader and more democratic conception of the intellectual's role. This explains the cross-fertilization between idealist and Marxist thought in postwar Italian cultural, theoretical ambience. In this period, the idea that the intellectual had to go through a process of proletarization and complete assimilation into the vanguard class to be useful to the service of truth acquired a stronger significance. Because general and ideal service of truth and humanity is always produced in reality as a binding together with those forces that are really operative in the concrete situation, the intellectual can operate properly and effectively only in full contact with the people's life.

Literary Representation

It is this kind of thinking that was at the base of the promotion of a cultural system centered upon *realism* and collective solidarity and a corresponding critique of *decadence*. Realism—or neorealism as it reemerged after the war—at the level of artistic practice and aesthetic evaluation, was associated with engagement or commitment rather than detachment, with the involvement of intellectuals in the working-class movement as opposed to ivory-towered intellectualism, with the concrete versus the abstract, with clarity of expression and the need for divulgation against stylistic preciosity and difficulty. Art, literature, or cinema was valued positively only when it could be interpreted in a realist or a socially committed key. Otherwise modernist works tended to be consigned as cultural waste and labeled as "formalist," "decadent," "abstract," "irrational," "sterile," "snobbish," or "bourgeois." The truth and sincerity of realism was opposed to the supposedly phony commercial tinsel of the Hollywood entertainment film. The social dimension of realist art, its essential mass, popular nature, and its human warmth were opposed to the minority appeal and arid intellectualism of the avant-garde.[7] Realism became, in its appropriation by the forces of the Left, a slogan heavy with connotations, one in which many new meanings and oppositions were condensed.

Neorealist writers focused on the years of the Resistance and the German occupation of Italy. Cesare Pavese, *La casa in collina* (1947-1948), Elio Vittorini, *Uomini e no* (1945), Beppe Fenoglio, *Una questione privata* (posthumously published in 1963 with the title *Un giorno di fuoco*; the new definitive edition appeared in 1965), and Italo Calvino, *Il sentiero dei nidi di ragno* (1947) are the novels that have come for many to represent the writing of this period.

The realist aesthetic strongly favored an art that was social, public, and political as opposed to one that dealt with the personal, private, or inner life. In this aesthetic, there was a noticeable anti-Americanism. Although there was a positive critical evaluation of some aspects of American culture—for instance the films of Chaplin or the social fiction of Steinbeck, Dos Passos, and others, there was a strong deprecation in the postwar period of what America represented in terms of mass culture and cultural imperialism. In the Cold War climate new vigor was also given to the idea of the dominance of an essentially decadent and bourgeois culture. In a sense, during the Cold War, the Left made and associated the concept of a progressive national tradition with the Left and the working class as its legitimate standard bearers; at the same time, it reinforced the idea of a decadent culture belonging to American and capitalist society.

During the same period, the christian democrats tried to popularize their democratic views by linking them with corporate collectivity, the family unit, the rural hinterlands, the Catholic tradition, the economic reconstruction, and the new industrial civilization. They identified democracy with property rights, a *laissez-faire* economy, freedom from totalitarism, in short, with the "American way of life." Consequently, they, too, pushed neorealism as a democratic form of artistic expression and carried out their own strategy with regard to the spread of popular culture. However, in the first decade of economic recovery, the acculturation of the masses was not taking place through the printed medium. In 1956, merely 5,623 books were published, including original works, translations, new editions, and reprints. And in 1957, 40.8% of Italian families, according to official figures, did not habitually read printed matter of any kind.

The cultural strategy of both the Communist and Christian Democratic Parties came to a crisis with the rapid rise of living standards, the spread of consumer culture, and increasingly centralized ownership and control of the cultural industries. The strategy of capillary penetration in a democratic society through the level of popular culture had made a good deal of sense in the conditions of the early postwar period, but it could not deal with the natural change that was taking place beginning in the early sixties, a process that involved the elimination of traditional popular cultural practices in many parts of the country and the introduction of new forms of popular culture mediated by mass communication technologies. The communists were slow in realizing the crisis of their strategy, and the gap between the still *artisanal* cultural attitudes of the party's intellectuals and the industrial forms of culture developing around them widened.[8] Italy was also going through a profound change that involved interrelated trends: a shift in occupational patterns resulting in a gradual decrease of blue-collar workers; a relatively fast growth of tertiary (service) sector jobs within the labor market as a whole; an increase in the number of people trained to enter the professions (teachers, doctors, lawyers, journalists, civil servants, etc.). These changes were connected with the downward social mobility of intellectuals that reduced them to the status of salaried employees (in the professions and the fast-expanding cultural and communications industries), to intellectual workers on a par with other workers. All these changes were bringing to a crisis the notion of the national-popular culture and the outlook that had sustained the neorealism concept in the critical discourse of the Left.

Therefore, although the cultural and ideological significance of neorealism within postwar culture should not be undervalued, it was a relatively short-lived movement, undermined by three important developments in Italy's economic and cultural life as a whole. These were the shift in attitude toward historical events, World War II in particular; postwar economic growth, which created a climate favorable to new writing practices; and, very significantly, a change in the critical understanding of neorealism as exemplified by one of its most famous practitioners, Italo Calvino.

First of all, there was the question of attitudes to the country's recent history. In addition to the neorealist narrative of the 1940s and 1950s that featured the partisans ultimately as history's victors, who entered the national consciousness as patriots and heroes, gradually there was greater readiness to listen to the quiet inflections of the victims of war and the defeated—the Jewish communities, women, children, civilians in general. In 1962 Giorgio Bassani's *Il giardino dei Finzi-Contini* was published. Primo Levi wrote remarkable documentary narratives, *Se questo è un uomo* (1947) and *La tregua* (1963).

The second factor that contributed to the undermining of neorealism was the accelerated growth in the postwar economy that was to bring about a shift from a predominantly peasant to a neocapitalist society. At the same time a new generation of writers, most of whom had been educated after the fascist period, launched a confrontational attack on neo-realism and its aesthetics, became known as the *Gruppo 63* or neo-avant-garde.[9]

The writers and critics of the *Gruppo 63*, for instance, were concerned not with mimesis but with exploring the formal resources of language. The 1960s saw writers exploring new paths largely in response to changes in the society in which and for which they were writing. Put in general terms, this meant that a great deal was written that attempted to interpret the reality of the new Italy and, in some cases, to act upon it. But it also meant that new areas of language and new techniques were investigated, often on the basis of advanced theories of literature. Indeed, experimental modernism became one of the strongest trends in both verse and prose of the 1960s, but even poets and novelists, who were more cautious in their approach, found themselves modifying and modernizing the way in which they wrote.

By the early 1970s the *Gruppo 63* and all the *neoavanguardia* were expiring. Today they no longer have imitators among young writers, and their leaders have mostly ceased producing novels. In the academic world, from the *licei* to the universities, their names rarely appear among the authors who are recommended. So what has the *neoavanguardia* achieved? Some critics feel that it has been useful as a language laboratory for the search of new forms of literary representation. For others, their influence seems to have been mainly negative for its passion for nonsense. For some years they used their influence over the younger novelists, making them feel unable to write in a traditional manner.

Today their particular brand of nonsense is no longer much in vogue, and the Italian novel is returning to humanist values. In fiction today there is no dominant school or trend at all. A few modestly successful writers have emerged. With the waning of the experimental novel, the literary trend now is back to books that tell stories and develop characters. But there has been a burgeoning of critical forms to the detriment of creative ones; a takeover of the literary heritage by pedagogues, linguists, and psychoanalysts has stifled the literary spirit of adventure, the ambition and taste for imaginative writing. Yet, it is remarkable how few of these deal squarely with themes of contemporary Italy. Serious writers seem to prefer to set their books in the past, their childhood, or abroad, rather than to analyze Italian society today. They are not concerned with exploring the social tensions or crude consumerism of modern Italy; they rather concentrate on private life and the refinement of style. So the novel survives as a fragile, anemic creature, cut off from the mainstream of life. It is a pity, considering that Italy's society has been going through so fascinating a period of change, that the novel has virtually abdicated its classic role as chronicler of that society.

Who are the new novelists, poets, playwrights, and thinkers who have emerged in the last twenty years to make any lasting impact? There are several names: Franco Fortini, Andrea Zanzotto, Mario Luzi,

Pier Paolo Pasolini, Leonardo Sciascia, Dino Buzzati. The intense interest in Alberto Moravia, the growing reputation of Italo Calvino, the success of Dario Fo (winner of the 1997 Nobel Prize for literature), the impact of the ideas of Antonio Gramsci, and the reception of Umberto Eco's outstanding work in semiotics testify also to the Italian presence in the Anglo-Saxon literary and intellectual circles. Their works also reflect accurately the social and cultural transformation of Italy after the war. In their work, from different and changing perspectives, what has been happening in the country is articulated, interpreted, and in some cases resisted and denounced. To read them is both to see rapid changes in the society, culture, and economy of the country reflected, more or less directly, in writing, and it is also to see how those changes might be given form and significance in words, to gain some idea of what they might mean in other terms than those of statistics, sociological analysis, or political economy. And despite the particularity of the Italian situation, their interest is not purely local. For in their work the general problems of literature and of articulate understanding in advanced capitalist society in general achieve intense, sometimes brilliant formulation.

These are authors who recognize the widespread sense that the boundaries of literature are shifting, that new demarcations are in the process of being drawn between literature and history, between literature and ideas, between one form of writing and another.

Again, this panorama confirms the fact that in literature, more than the other arts, this is an age of criticism and documentary rather than of creativity; consequently the novel suffers, in Italy more than in Britain and the United States. One could say that the Italian novel has either grown stale through remaining too conventional, or has suffered from the terrorism of the avant-garde and its technical experimentation with language and form.

The 1970s is also the decade when women emerged in large numbers on the literary scene. Although women participated in large number during the Resistance movement, they showed a muted response to the war. One explanation as to why women did not contribute to stories of the Resistance is provided by the nature of the genre itself. The Resistance, as it was relived in the collective imaginary, shared many of the attributes found in the world of boys' adventure stories where life is lived, often literally, in the wild, beyond the reach of home and family. Missions have to be carried out, dangerous open spaces crossed, enemies killed. Conventions of the genre were established very rapidly, and they excluded women.

In fact, a substantial body of women's fiction was produced during the years of neorealism: in the decade from 1943 to 1953 there were publications by, among others, Elsa Morante, Gianna Manzini, Anna Maria Ortese, and Anna Banti alongside Maria Bellonci, Natalia Ginzburg, Lalla Romano, Livia De Stefani, Alba De Cespedes, and Milena Milani. Many of their narratives did not address either fascism or the war.

When in the 1970s a generation of women writers emerged whose writing took three forms—testimony, autobiographical narratives, and fiction—one of the most noticeable features of what otherwise manifested itself in a diversity of narrative practices was their constant recourse to first-person narration. To understand the nature of this public position, one has to contextualize what became for a while a culture industry for and by women, often conducted in separatist bookshops and publishing houses. In the early 1970s a number of women, many of them associated with radical groups, realized that neither these groups nor the *P.C.I.* appeared to have much interest in women's issues. It was a decade when, as part of the general process of modernization that the country was undergoing, social legislation began to catch up with the demands of a modern industrial state.

Born of the need to document, in one sense these books continue with the project, presented in the first instance by realism and later neorealism, of unveiling Italy's hidden face, this time by creating a space for the marginalized to speak for themselves. They speak only for themselves, of experiences that are uniquely theirs. The public's continuing desire for documentation about the realities of Italy is reflected in the fact that these testimonies were published, in paperback, by mainstream houses. Important narratives were given by Gabriella Para (*Voci dal carcere femminile*, 1973), Armanda Guiducci (*La donna non è gente*, 1977), Dacia Maraini (*Memorie di una ladra*, 1972; *Donna in Guerra*, 1975), Francesca Sanvitale (*Madre e figlia*, 1980; *Il figlio dell'impero*, 1993), Natalia Ginzburg (*Caro Michele*). To reject memory is to reject one's own experiences and the ability to connect self to other, life to history, present to past. The project of so much postwar writing by women writers in Italy is to salvage and make sense of experiences that otherwise will be lost, forgotten.

One big novelty in the Italian literary landscape of the decade is the appearance of literary works by immigrants.[10] Small publishing houses tend to publish the texts in this growing genre, and many are not widely available. These works have been published in the last few years, and thematically they all concern, however loosely, the immigrants' experience in Italy. The structure and format of these texts, though, varies: from diary format, to collections of transcribed oral narratives, to a novel-like text that includes a glossary and exercises about immigration and racism.

The Arts and Intellectuals: Low Creativity

In Italy's postwar cultural modernization and democratization process, more than in most Western countries, the performing arts have displayed a lively activity in collective cultural manifestations rather than high creativity by the individual. In fact, much of the best creativity has not been given by the solitary playwright or sculptor, but by little groups of actors, dancers, and musicians, or workshops of sculptors, decorators, weavers, video directors, all in close touch with their public and very much part of society. It is a kind of culture that is less philosophical and spiritual, in many ways more ephemeral, and certainly much more social.

The revival of the performing arts, and popular enthusiasm for them, began soon after the entrance of the Socialists into government in 1963. The renaissance of theater, especially in the provinces, was followed by the reemergence of musical activities. Museums and art exhibitions, too, have attracted big new audiences. This widespread thirst for culture was not balanced by a high creativity of the first rank by writers, painters, and playwrights. Even the cinema, except for the heyday of neo-realism and a few single works, has not maintained a high level of creativity; and the music revival, fecund in performance, has yielded little as yet in the way of gifted new composers.

In philosophy and literature, Italy no longer appears as the great champion of Western thought and creativity. Italian thought and humanism have lost their old radiant universality and have yielded to the arid form of today's critical inquiries and the loquacious void of the *pensiero debole*, weak thinking.

The decline of creative writing has been even more apparent in the theater. No new playwrights of any great substance have arisen in the past 20 years to take the place of the Betti, Fabbri, De Filippo generation; and in most Italian theaters, nearly all the good plays are foreign imports, revivals of classics, or free-wheeling adaptations. So, today it is commonly said that the Italian theater is moribund. However, this is not a fair assessment; it is still lively, innovative, and international.

This is due above all to the exceptional creativity of some outstanding directors—Giorgio Strehler, Luigi Squarzina, Memé Perlini are among the big names—who become the real stars of the plays, more than the actors or the playwrights. For better or for worse, they impose their own personality on the texts, often reworking them totally. This is a new theater of gesture, lighting, movement, more than, in many cases, of the spoken word.

The bourgeois commercial theater has been kept alive, together with the state repertory companies that attract younger audiences and can afford to experiment with the help of government subsidies. The major subsidized theaters are *teatri stabili* because of heavy state patronage and hence present a picture of greater success. With the help of generous subsidies, these theaters have been able to pursue a policy of low prices and build an audience very different from that of the prewar period—students, young intellectuals, even some workers who would never dream of rubbing shoulders with the elite—for a repertory that today continues to mix the Italian classics with a few modern or foreign plays but with the accent on stage craft.

There is a clear difference between New York's and Italy's stage. Classical revival apart, New York's and Britain's forte is the craftsmanlike production of well-written new plays; Italy's accent is on the fireworks of experimental *mise-en-scène*. What good new playwrights, if any, have emerged in the past thirty years? Not many. Young playwrights find it hard to get a break; private theaters are wary of taking the financial risk of presenting a serious play by an unknown writer, while the big national theaters make far less effort than their British and American counterparts to seek out new talent. So Italy fills up its stages with revivals and imports. English and American plays are in vogue with the public. Many producers and actors feel that foreign playwrights, far more than Italian ones, provide them with meaty subjects and strong acting roles that relate to the real modern world. As in the case of the novel, too many new Italian plays are about hang-ups of writing a play, or some equally hermetic theme.

Yet there may also be quite another explanation for the dearth of new talent. This lies in the dominance, during the 1970s especially, of a school of clever and fashionable directors who have an entirely different concept of doing theater. They are simply not interested in receiving a text from an author and then faithfully staging it, like a kind of publisher. To them a live author is a potential nuisance, an impediment to their creative fancy. They prefer either to reinterpret the plays of dead authors or else to devise their own texts.

Some directors have been taking literary texts, or political ones, and working them into a kind of play. Even more controversially, some of these new star directors apply their creative gifts to reworking the classics. The intent is to give a modern force, a twentieth-century resonance to the old texts. However, one could easily say that the classics have been put under torture as they have been chopped up, rearranged, reworded, and replotted. Either in mockery, or through dogmatism, the directors try to make the author say the opposite of what he or she thinks. In a director of this kind, one could sense the jubilant sadistic streak of a failed would-be writer who is trying to take it out on a colleague, who has been dead for a few centuries!

What are the reasons? It could be argued that the arts and ideas, in Italy or elsewhere, flourish best either in times of settled prosperity, or under oppression and austerity, but not in an in-between period of industrial transition and social changes when the nation's energies are elsewhere. Unquestionably, the politicization of the arts was damaging to cultural creativity, and so was the attitude of the artists and intellectuals toward society. Many intellectuals, being mostly from the Left, not only disliked a capitalist regime, but also felt embittered frustration at the rise of a new way of progress that brushed aside their own theories and precepts. How could they reconcile the fact that a cookbook would sell more than a supposedly good novel?

There is another major explanation for the status of Italian performing arts. The Italians have a tradition of promoting the arts; and in the welfare state Italian-style that means that funding comes from the state. In the original government plan of supporting the arts there was undoubtedly the element of national prestige, but also the strand of socialist idealism, the desire to popularize the arts, and to bring them closer to people's daily lives. There was the intention that a better cultural climate might stimulate new creative work and revive the flagging Italian genius. Moreover, at the basis of the government thinking was that *all* the arts matter, even minor ones, and that culture must be truly popular. So state patronage was extended to many spheres previously neglected by it. And money came raining down in buckets.

But like every other aspect of Italian life where the state is involved, the arts and cultural manifestations in general were not immune to political muddling. Financial support for the arts, therefore, easily became part of the clientelistic system which, as we know, is very politicized. Unfortunately, for the Italian artist, the dependence on state money is particularly acute because private philanthropy for the arts has been practically unknown in modern Italy.

By heavily subsidizing the arts, the government increasingly made political decisions and allocated funds on the basis of straightforward political criteria. In the 1970s, theatrical companies made it to the stage only if they were supported by one or more political parties. Visual artists, too, were unlikely to go far unless they received the blessing of a political party or an interest group associated with a political party. Parties had their favorite painters, sculptors, filmmakers, writers, poets, dance groups, musicians, art galleries, photographic studios, and so forth.

Parties sought out these symbols of culture in order to demonstrate that leading exponents of the fine and visual arts were located in their ranks or approved their programs. The Communist Party boasted of having among its members some of the most prominent painters, sculptors, architects, filmmakers, musicians, writers, actors and actresses—L. Visconti, F. Fellini, R. Rossellini, P.P. Pasolini, V. De Sica, F. Zeffirelli, C. Cardinale, M. Mastroianni, I. Silone, Manzù, Guttuso, C. Malaparte, all were members of the PCI. Because so many of the obviously outstanding artists were long associated with the Communist Party, it and the Left in general counted on a good portion of available patronage.

In such a situation, the basic understanding was that for any creative person in search of support, the correct political party connection was as important as sheer talent. Awards were almost never made without regard to the applicant's ideological or political coloration. As one may expect, intellectuals were concerned even more with politics and were openly lined up with political parties; indeed, many of them held prominent roles in all levels of government. It was rare to find intellectuals or artists who were relatively autonomous or distant critics of social, political, and economic structures. As a group, they have been engulfed by politics and happily have thrived in it. Because they knew it was risky to be independent, artists got trapped in a vicious cycle: once a person became a slave of the political system, he or she could not survive without it. The reasons of this are easy to understand.

Certainly, the emphasis today, as we have seen, is on success, enjoyment, and quality of life, and culture plays a sizable role in this new leisure world and will continue to do so under any regime. But whether it will lead to any upsurge of real individual creativity, especially in literature, is still far from certain. Of a revival of serious literature, or playwriting, there is not much sign. In fact, a discernible trend in Italian culture as a whole over the past decade or so is that its emphasis has become less solemn and cerebral, more colorful and amusing—or in some cases, the pretentious gives place to the superficial.

Although Italy is bereft of playwrights today, its theater has virtuosity and vitality. Its highly sophisticated directors have been giving a new vision of theater.

Cinema: Ups and Downs

In the mass culturization process of the country, cinema also played an important role and, as one may expect, was even less nationalistic in character than TV, as we shall see, mainly because of the excessive presence of American imports.[11]

Notwithstanding the excellent Italian film tradition, cinema did not become a mass cultural phenomenon until the end of the 1950s. The Catholic Church was instrumental in the creation of over 5,000 parish cinemas, often in rural areas, and the whole Italian industry expanded both in production and exhibition, so that by the late 1950s we can identify films as directed toward the more rural South, and we can find the box-office returns for Italian films coming as much from provincial and rural cinemas as from the urban ones.

The Italian production sector picked up gradually during the late 1940s also for other reasons. Some films of the period dealt in a remarkably realistic way with the social and political conditions of Italian life in the aftermath of the war and established a movement (already discussed) that became known as neorealism. In its short period of popularity, neorealism began to find a warm response in the art cinema circuits abroad by redefining the function of cinema and introducing to popular audiences a different sort of engagement with reality. Some of the commercially successful films of this genre were Rossellini's *Rome Open City* (1945), De Sica's *Bicycle Thief* (1947), Zampa's *Living in Peace* (1947), and De Santis' *Bitter Rice* (1948). All the stress in neorealism was on the hidden underside of Italian life—poverty, backwardness, the legacy of fascist neglect, and the difficulties of postwar reconstruction.[12] It should be pointed out that just as fascist cinema tried to ignore the Depression, so the postwar cinema seemed oblivious of the "economic miracle" that was gathering pace throughout the 1950s.

But ignorance of what was occurring in the economic lives of Italians was not the most obvious defect of Italian cinema. It is particularly in representations of the sexual question that Italy fell out of step not only with America but with much of the rest of Europe. Although Italian films of the 1950s were more sexually explicit than American films of the period, their morality remained conservative. Not only did Italian law not recognize divorce, but the subject was virtually taboo. It was not until 1961 that a film such as Pietro Germi's *Divorce Italian Style* could be produced. Italian marriage law was only one aspect of sexual double-standards that went uncriticized in Italian films until the 1970s.

The christian democrats, who had practical control of the government until the 1960s, exercised a rigid control on cinema as well as on TV. They did not attempt to dictate what the cinema should be but took active steps to ensure that it did not become anything they did not want it to be. The postwar christian democratic governments were in fact more repressive toward the cinema than the fascists had been, but then, they had to be. Whereas the fascists could rely on general quietude and an ignorance of the formative role of cinema in popular ideology, the christian democrats saw that they had a real struggle on their hands, not only to establish a national cinema competitive with Hollywood but to ensure that this cinema expressed a concept of Italian nationality they approved of, rather than the variant of the "national-popular" espoused by the Left and expressed through neorealism.

Another factor influencing the protection of many films in the early postwar period was a strong public interest in comedy, inspired, in large part, by the great vaudeville tradition of comic persona and performance. One of the major stars of this type of films was Totò; he entertained audiences in dozens of films and became one of the great comedic performers of the twentieth century.

In fact, one cannot help being struck by the extent to which comedy has always been a staple of Italian cinema, a comedy that is built around a comic actor of a certain kind, the clown. Erminio Macario was the little man lost in a world too complex for him to understand; Totò was the Neapolitan clown turning the world upside down in the anarchic expression of his vitality.

At the beginning of the 1960s the Italian film industry needed to expand production, and imitation and repetition offered a way of achieving this in the absence of a large pool of untapped creative talent waiting to be exploited. In 20 years some 450 "spaghetti westerns" were produced, most of them shot in Spain and distributed also abroad. Sergio Leone's film, *Per un pugno di dollari* (*A Fistful of Dollars*, 1964), cost 200 million lire to make, and netted over fifteen times that amount worldwide. This genre was very successful and lucrative but did not establish a tradition. At the same time, however, Italian cinema was building for itself an international reputation for art cinema, films whose origins lay in the ideas and artistic creativity of their directors. They were viewed by sophisticated, middle-class audiences in Italy, in art cinemas of the major cities of the world, at film festivals, in universities, and in film clubs and societies. The reputation created by the neorealist films was reinforced by the films of Federico Fellini, Michelangelo Antonioni, Pier Paolo Pasolini, Bernardo Bertolucci, Liliana Cavani, Ermanno Olmi, Lina Wertmuller, Elio Petri, Marco Ferreri, Marco Bellocchio, and the brothers Paolo and Vittorio Taviani. Probably the most innovative was Antonioni.

Characteristically the typical Antonioni character is economically secure and emancipated from Catholic morality, but troubled by neurotic anguish and doubt. Sexual relations provide little fulfillment but a certain limited consolation to individuals oppressed by the techno-bureaucratic machine. For Antonioni the modern world is an already realized "utopia" with its bad consequences, and his images of unpleasant modernity are merely the obverse of the sentimental portrayals of Italian backwardness elsewhere in the cinema.

The vigor of the Italian art cinema in the 1960s, relying on the creativity of great directors, depended on the general vigor of the Italian production sector, particularly at the popular level, supported by ticket sales of 700 million a year and plentiful American investment in production. There was a brief period in the early 1960s when it looked as if the tide had turned. RAI television was resolutely protectionist, while in the cinema the share of Italian box-office receipts obtained by American films plummeted to less than one-third. Italian national production, supplemented by that of other EU countries, seemed to be sufficient to satisfy public demand, prompting the illusion of a European cultural revenge against America. In fact, the idea of a shared European culture turned out to be the most illusory. While European co-production made economic sense in the cinema, the cultural character of the co-produced films could rarely be described as distinctively "European." The cultural contest therefore remained to be between Italian and American products, with a handful of nebulously European films and television programs playing a marginal role.

In the mid 1970s American finance was withdrawn, and the reorganization of distribution led to rapid drops in ticket sales. This change was escalated by the arrival of television in Italy; television replaced the routine of cinema-going, and with this contraction of the "base," higher-quality film production became starved of finance. Between 1950 and 1969, Antonioni directed 12 films; between 1970 and 1990 he directed 4. From an annual output of up to 300 films in the late 1960s and ticket sales of over 700 million, more than half of them Italian films, annual production in the mid 1990s was around 100 films and ticket sales just over 100 million, with 80% of the money going to U.S. films.

As popular culture in general, cinema and TV became Americanized by default. To compete at the box office, Italian films were forced to imitate American models, which they did fairly well. But it was American films that seized the popular imagination, and it was not long before the Italian film industry reestablished itself in a role very similar to the one it had assumed in the fascist period, supplying cut-rate versions of popular American genres, though with a distinct national inflection. The return of American cultural products is one of the significant features of the media explosion of the 1970s and 1980s.

Today, even though American films are maintaining their traditional dominance, in 1992, for the first time in years an Italian movie, *Johnny Stecchino*, starring and directed by Roberto Benigni, outran star-laden American imports to earn the biggest profits ever recorded for a movie in Italy (it grossed $25 million). Moreover, Italian movies brought home coveted foreign prizes, including an Oscar for *Mediterraneo* as the best foreign-language film and the Cannes Grand Jury Prize for Gianni Amelio's *Ladro di bambini* (*Stolen Children*). In 1996, *Il postino* (*The Postman*) was up for several academy awards. These honors are signs of new vigor for what was once Europe's most robust movie industry. Clearly, this success, attributed to the emergence of a new generation of actors, directors, and scriptwriters remains overshadowed by the unanswered question of how public tastes, attuned to television, will affect the reviving movie industry; after all the public at the movies is a public that was formed in the bosom of television.

These events come after three decades in which the Italian movie industry generally followed a downward curve, both in theater attendance and in quality. In the fabled year of 1955, Italian movie theaters sold a record 819 million tickets, more than eight times the present-day figure. Not only that, the number of movie theaters has fallen from 7,500 at the beginning of the 1980s to around 3,500 at the end of the 1990s. Only 1,200 of them qualify as "active theaters," and, in any event, such are the peculiarities of the Italian movie theater season that they are open for an average of only 240 days a year. For many Italians, the lure of television sitcoms and game shows remains irresistible.

The Italian film industry also cannot rely on the American market. For directors who work in foreign languages, America today has scant appreciation of foreign movies. Few foreign-language films are released in the U.S. these days, and those that are attract fewer viewers. Americans, absorbed in their junk culture, are shuttering a window to the rest of the movie world.[13]

On the cultural level, regardless of what will happen to the movie industry, Italy will always enjoy a prominent position in the world. Italy's main cultural export is itself. It has enough heritage not to need a heritage industry. So long as the tourists can be packed into the Uffizi or the Sistine Chapel, or the Pompeii excavations or the Arena at Verona, the other Italies—where American soap opera, the imitation of American game shows and American movies top the ratings—can be ignored.

Notes

1. From current literature the following list emerges, with the estimated (and very hypothetical) number of speakers in brackets. There are small historic relics, often going back to the fifteenth and sixteenth centuries: Greek (30,000) and Albanian (100,000) in several villages in Southern Italy; Catalan (15,000) in Alghero, Sardinia; German (13,000) in small communities in Piedmont and in the Veneto; Croat (3,000) in Molise; Occitanic and Franco-Provençal in small colonies in Southern Italy. Stronger groups, adjacent to bordering foreign countries: German (280,000) in South Tyrol; Occitanic and Franco-Provençal (115,000) in Piedmont; Slovene (53,000) in the Veneto. There is a large group of recent immigrants (estimated to be about 1 million), mostly from North and Central Africa. It is difficult to evaluate to what extent these will become part of the permanent population and whether they will preserve their original languages.

2. Tullio De Mauro, *Storia linguistica dell'Italia unita* (Bari: Laterza, 1976), 430-59.

3. *Le regioni in cifre* (Rome: ISTAT, 1988), 92.

4. See Pier Paolo Pasolini, *Scritti corsari* (Milan: Garzanti, 1978), pp. 50-81 and *Lettere luterane* (Turin: Einaudi, 1976), 77-91.

5. An interesting and informative discussion of this issue can be found in Silvio Lanaro's *L'Italia nuova. Identità e sviluppo 1861-1988* (Turin: Einaudi, 1988).

6. It is very expensive to make the first copy, but once these first-copy costs have been recovered, it is relatively cheap to run a few hundred more copies. This impels cultural firms to go for large runs and to create large markets. It also encourages them to take control of distribution, because it is with mass distribution that big profits and high returns on economies of scale are made.

7. For a useful general discussion of realism in the *P.C.I.*'s cultural policy during this period, see Nicoletta Misler, *La vita italiana al realismo. La politica culturale artistica del PCI dal 1944 al 1956* (Milan: Mazzotta, 1973).

8. Francesco Pinto, *Intellettuali e tv negli anni '50* (Rome: Savelli, 1977).

9. Although *Gruppo 63* and the *Neoavanguardia* faded from sight quickly, in their heyday they caused more journalistic ink to flow than they deserved in terms of achievement. They were never really a "school," for their leading exponents were quite different from each other and frequently quarreled; yet they did have some things in common. The most obvious shared feature of their work was an obsession with the rejection of the moralistic or social-comment conventional narrative and an attraction for minute, physical description whether of objects or sensations, to represent a very dehumanized situation. Their semi-scientific approach to literature had a clear link with structuralism, emerging at about the same time.

10. Some of the titles are: Mohamed Bouchane, *Chiamatemi Alì*, eds. Carla De Girolamo and Daniele Miccione (Milan: Leonardo Editore, 1990); Giuliano Carlini, ed., *La terra in faccia: Gli immigrati raccontano* (Rome: Ediesse, 1991); Nassera Chohra and Alessandra Atti di Sarro, *Volevo diventare bianca* (Rome: Edizioni e/o, 1993); Amelia Cristiano, ed., *Ho trovato l'occidente: Storie di donne immigrate a Palermo* (Palermo: La Luna, 1992).

11. In the period up to 1915, Italy was one of the world's major exporters of films. A few large production companies had grown up, and around them there existed a multitude of smaller companies. Italy became known as a producer of spectacular films on historical themes, and these films exported partly because of their exotic value. With World War I, and the rapid growth and organization of the US film industry, Italian production went bankrupt and collapsed. Whereas in 1915 Italy produced 562 films, by 1930 that number had dropped to 12. The fascist government set about reorganizing the industry along more efficient and less wasteful lines, eventually finding itself owning studios, distribution companies, and a cinema chain. The Cinecittà studios were built with state money and were taken over by the state; the Centro Sperimentale di Cinematografia, a university-level film school, was established; and the Venice Film Festival was launched as an international showcase for Italian films. The result was that by 1942 Italy was producing over 100 films a year.

12. This is a departure from the tradition. One of Italy's most successful exports before World War I was the historical genre, representing great moments in Italian medieval or Renaissance history. It should be said, however, that Italy never abandoned completely this genre of film, which adopted a pose of cultural dignity, and which had the virtues of being spectacular, of reinforcing nationalist notions of Italy's great past, of inviting comparisons between the politically righteous and the dissolutely opportunist.

13. What did go wrong? In the 1950s and 1960s the allure of foreign-language films was twofold—they had class and they had sex. Ritzy Manhattan soirées were spiced with debates about what was real and what fantasy in Fellini's *8½* and *Juliet of the Spirits*, about Antonioni's seductive use of existential ennui. And when foreign films did not tax the brain, they stirred the loins. The three breakout foreign language hits of the 1990s—*Cinema Paradiso* and *Il Postino* from Italy and *Like Water for Chocolate* from Mexico—are nice romantic dramas about love and loss. They were brilliantly promoted by Miramax. But they did not extend film language as Fellini's or Antonioni's films did; instead, they gave audiences that warm-puppy feeling. Any Disney movie can do that. So can many of the American independent films that have filled the old foreign-language slots at art houses. And you do not have to read subtitles. However, the real problem is our boredom with anything outside ourselves; Americans are obsessively and exclusively interested in American culture. Even college students now tend to like the same films everyone else likes, and that is pretty bad.

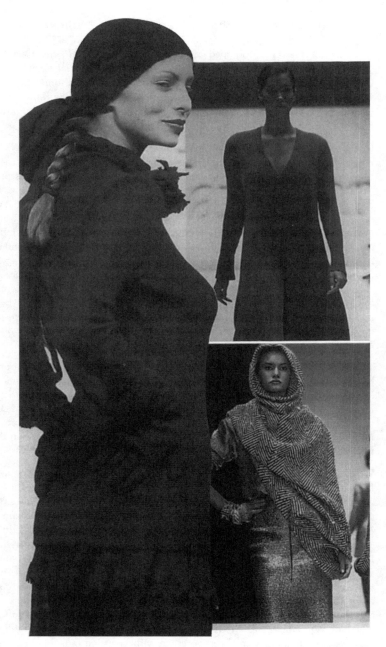

Fashion and clothing is an important industry in Italy. Some of the world's top designers are Italians: Armani, Gucci, Fendi, Valentino, Missoni, Ferragamo, and Krizia. As their counterparts have done in the car, furniture, and office machine industries, Italian fashion designers have been able to continue the long tradition of superb craftmanship and combine it with high technology.

XV

Communications Revolution and Cultural Consumption

Communications

In its process of modernization, Italy needed to profoundly improve its communications structures. That had to be done not just to stimulate economic growth but also to bring about cultural changes.

Since only 20% of the country area is flat, communication had remained difficult until World War II. Of course, communications had improved dramatically with the advent of the railways and the construction of roads to serve them. Even so, many rural areas had remained practically inaccessible right up World War II, and it was not until World War II that many people traveled more than a few kilometers beyond their native village. The postwar period saw huge improvements in the roads and the rise of public and private motor transport as well as the beginning of tourism based on the private motor car. The publication of road maps and the creation of the *Michelin Guide* fostered this trend. World War II and particularly the invasion of the Allied armies and the retreat of the German forces caused considerable damage to the communications infrastructure. Consequently it underwent reconstruction and modernization in the 1950s and 1960s. Italy built an impressive highway system, *autostrade*, only matched by Germany in Europe. Private car ownership also grew significantly, with manufacturers like *FIAT* developing popular models like the *Fiat 600* and *1100*. After a slow start in the second half of the 1950s, television also became a feature of most Italian homes during the 1960s, with nearly 80% of households owning at least a black and white television by the 1970s. By the early 1970s, people were able both to travel more easily and to receive in their homes immediate news of national and international events.

The decades of the 1970s and 1980s, however, witnessed a qualitative transformation of communications in Italy, based in many cases on the application of new technologies to existing systems. Today, as might be expected, 97% of Italian households are equipped with the telephone. In 1970 the figure was a mere 11%. In the 1970s telecommunications underwent a profound program of expansion and modernization. It not only eliminated lengthy waiting lists for telephones and created a network of public telephones, but also introduced fully automated connections for national and international calls. Other Western countries similarly modernized their telecommunications systems in the 1970s and 1980s, but in Italy the process was both exceptionally rapid and extremely thorough. In 1970 Italy was very much like East Germany in 1989, and its backwardness created a similar hindrance to economic expansion. By the end of the decade, however, it had acquired one of the most advanced telecommunications systems in the world.

The rail network did not undergo a similarly fast and qualitative transformation because Italy put its focus on developing its highway system. However, the development of a high-speed train system now in progress is radically reducing traveling time throughout the peninsula.

Thus, in the space of a generation, the individual's relationship to, and perception of, space has been profoundly transformed in Italy through greater possibilities for rapid transit combined with highly developed *in situ* communications, making it possible to access information sources from throughout the world much more easily. The accompanying cultural revolution is much greater than that brought about by the railways in the nineteenth century. It is now extremely easy to travel the length and the breadth of the country, while new road, rail, and airport links facilitate communication between Italy and its geographical neighbors. Other communications systems have been massively modernized and improved. The psychological impact of such changes is hard to overstate.

Television: A New Cultural Medium

Of all the media, probably the advent of television had the most profound impact on every sector of the population, and it was most responsible for the cultural revolution that took place after World War II. The development of a mass television audience predated mass ownership of sets because of the widespread practice of public viewing in bars and other public locales. Collective viewing was more widespread especially in the lower-class and working-class neighborhoods, and it functioned as a "social cement." By 1964, a decade after regular transmissions began, there were 5.22 million licences, of which 95,200 were for sets in public places, and the average audience between 9 and 10 p.m. was estimated at between 12 and 13 million. Surveys in the same year established that between 23 and 24 million adults watched television each year, and that 38% of people between the ages of six and seventeen watched at least four or five times a week.

In its first decade, the one-channel television had a profound impact on the life of the country. In 1951 the government granted *RAI* a monopoly of radio and of future television broadcasting services. The license lasted until December 1972. Television was required to inform, entertain, and educate; at the same time it was expected to reflect the ideas of the political majority. Being state-owned, the D.C.-led governments thus made it essentially an instrument for holding power by controlling public opinion. People were fed programs that were in line with the cultural policy and ideology of the government. For the first decade of its existence, *RAI* was slavishly christian democratic in its politics and piously Catholic in its cultural values.[1]

As one may expect, during the first phase of expansion, television was not supported by many intellectuals; it was criticized and rejected by the Left and suspected by the Church. It was a matter of elite culture rejecting popular culture, either because (in the case of Left intellectuals) it saw television as a diabolic invention of the corrupt capitalist West or because (for Catholic and conservative intellectuals) television threatened to undermine traditional religious and ethical values. They saw television as the bearer of a massified culture, a commodification of art, and as lowering the status of the intellectuals who wrote about it.

In the 1960s state television perfected its educative model and reacted to some of the criticism by adding another channel and increasing broadcasting hours with informational, cultural, and school programs. *RAI 1* would "represent" the government view from the christian democrats' perspective, *RAI 2* would "represent" the government view from the socialist perspective. Even with these changes, no channel had complete freedom to take cameras out into the streets to make its own probing reports on controversial topics by actually asking people what they thought on a particular issue. All the parties considered this kind of freedom far more dangerous than safe studio talks with party "representatives." Certainly, however, the two channels offered more of a variety of views than the previous monolithic network. This change, however, did not neutralize the criticism of the political parties because they did not have any control on the flow of communications to both the general public and specific sector.[2] However, the kinds of cultural and political strategy characteristic of the 1950s that were premised upon a polarization of the political and cultural climate, and on the ability of political parties and the Catholic Church to shape the cultural formation of its followers through their own apparatus, started to come to an end.

In giving an objective evaluation of the first phase of Italian television, that is, the period of *D.C.* control, it must be said that Italian television quickly became noted for its fine programs. The state gave the needed support to create an Italian BBC; and the system did acquire the prestige or self-confidence that is essential for creating the standards and attracting the talent required for good programs. In fact, the state always financed the system very generously while it was a state monopoly and even afterward and, therefore, some very good productions went on the air.

Indeed, the brighter side of the coin was that in the christian democrats' days, Italian television at least tried to keep up a certain cultural tone. State monopoly did offer the advantage that there was no need to compete with commercial television for audiences; hence, the proportion of serious cultural programming could be kept fairly high. *RAI* bought cheap American soap operas and other kinds of programs; and however banal its own quizzes and variety shows, at least they were balanced by long hours devoted to the arts, history, and other educational programs. The approach was often comformist and uninspired, but no one could deny the cultural intent. Television was didactic in the Italian pedagogic manner and took relatively little account of audience tastes. Unfortunately, for a nation with such a talent for film-making, there was also a relatively high percentage of programs of low quality. The trouble here was that most of the top *RAI* executives, unlike their BBC counterparts, were not broadcasters but men brought in from the civil service or even industry who were given the jobs for political reasons—few of them had much experience or understanding of creative work, and so they failed to set high standards.

Profound changes occurred in the 1970s. As a result of the tremors caused by the social unrest during 1968 and 1969, christian democrat hegemony started visibly to crumble. The Left began to elaborate a program of a decentralized broadcasting service, on a regional basis, and for internal reforms in *RAI*'s structure. This movement for decentralization was in line with the policy of devolution to the regions, envisaged in the constitution of 1948 but not put into effect until 1970. Decentralization would mean, in broadcasting terms, reversing the trend that had dominated in *RAI* since 1946, for it entailed devolving decision-making about scheduling to the regional studios, greatly enhancing the latter as centers of production and as local newsdesks, dealing with regional and local realities, giving airtime to local groups (schools, unions, etc.), and enabling them to make programs using the *RAI*'s technical and artistic expertise, equipment, and space.

At the same time as these changes were being proposed by the Left, demands were also coming from the private broadcasting lobbies for a "liberalization of the airwaves." The privatizers wanted *RAI*'s broadcasting monopoly to be declared unconstitutional on the grounds that it violated Article 21 of the constitution which states: "All people have the right to express their thoughts freely in speech, writing, or any other means of communication." What the private broadcasting lobbies were really interested in was not simply freedom of expression but freedom to exploit the lucrative advertising markets and attract revenues from local and national business clients. Their argument was convincing enough to sway the Constitutional Court and some sectors of public opinion.

In July 1976, a Constitutional Court decision not only abolished censorship, but also approved private broadcasting as long as it was not on a national scale. From that moment on, things developed rapidly, but along different lines from those originally envisaged by Parliament and the Constitutional Court. The court's decision opened a large loophole because precisely what "local" meant was not defined, while it was left to Parliament to regulate the newly emergent private sector. The legal vacuum that developed also meant an absence of rules concerning the use of frequencies, the ratio of advertising to programs, the proportion of domestically produced to imported products, the construction and siting of transmitters, and the concentration of ownership and control. On the one hand, *RAI* remained tightly regulated, because a legal ceiling was placed on advertising finance and the license fee was subject to the periodic decisions of Parliament; on the other hand, the lack of regulation for intending competitors in the field of radio and television left open a rich field for commercial exploitation.

The ambiguities of the law turned out to favor not the decentralized building up of community based alternatives to *RAI*'s national channels, but rather an accelerating tendency toward oligopolistic concentration. After the court's decision in 1976, a few thousand commercial radio stations and about one hundred television stations rapidly sprang to life; there are so many radio stations that if you are driving with the radio on, you are switched automatically to a new station practically upon every turn of a corner. Since the 1980s Italy has had the highest number of television transmitters per capita of anywhere in the world. The passage from hyper-regulation to capitalist free-for-all was so abrupt that it did not allow for the crucial stage—experienced by other Western countries—of negotiation between television and state on how best to regulate the medium, and between television and its audiences over what service should entail.[3] Technological developments have made more complex the preservation of constitutional rights and the regulation of the communication system. The advent of satellite broadcasting will enable the owners of a special aerial to watch hundreds of programs and will further weaken public broadcasting and the control of the nation-state over television.

The judgment of the Constitutional Court of 1976 profoundly changed the general framework within which *RAI* had been accustomed to operate. Even if this did not immediately produce notable effects on the *RAI* agency, it did mean the beginning of competition between it and private operators; competition, furthermore, affected every area of its activity, from programming to the acquisition of copyrights, and from its relationship with its personnel and its audience to advertising. To better understand this picture, we need to remember the new type of television audience produced by the transformation of Italian society during the 1970s. It consisted of new viewers, most of whom had been freed from financial hardship, were better educated, more independent in their views, had more free time, and wanted a wider range of information, culture, and entertainment. Over a short period of time, therefore, *RAI* found itself operating in new and unforeseen political, social, and market conditions. The problem facing *RAI* was that of rethinking its relationship to political power, to its audience and to its privately run competitors.

The new environment created a landscape that presented unexpected beauty and traps. For example, the political forces that imposed radical changes on the TV system and on the structure of *RAI* were not completely correct in their assessment of the impact of television on shaping political views of spectators. With the liberalization of the medium, the ability to control the output of television news is necessarily very limited, primarily because political messages must be transformed by the media; in other words, the political parties are less and less an independent source of information; they tend to become mere items in an information system dominated by television. Moreover, overall mass behavior is affected by the entire information system and not just by television. Therefore, political control cannot be established over the totality of television output because it depends on the entire cultural industry. In fact, when in 1978 the Communist Party also acquired a voice by the establishment of *RAI 3*, the party did not register a significant change in the results at the polls. Thus, it should be stressed that there is no evidence that the media are able to influence the results of elections to any significant degree. There may be some influence over a small percentage of the population, which inevitably contributes to the small electoral swings. With a proportional representation system in place in Italy until 1994, these small swings could have affected the overall result and did affect the composition of the ruling majorities and the strength of the opposition.[4]

The major problem for *RAI* was its inability to organize a united response to the private sector, which from the very outset displaced *RAI* or created a new audience by filling the most important slots with entertainment programs—quiz shows, talk shows, and, above all, television movies, serials, and cartoons purchased on the international market.

Instead of opting for a course that differentiated public television from the private networks, by stressing its institutional role as a public service, *RAI* decided to challenge private television on the very ground that was most favorable to the latter, namely, in the area of entertainment, quiz shows, escapist amusements, and in the number of hours broadcast each day. It found itself in the contradictory situation of concentrating its financial resources on the purchase of foreign films, television movies, and serials (private television's most competitive genres), and thus diminishing the available resources for in-house production. One of the most absurd effects of this situation occurred in the early 1980s, when Italy became the world's principal importer of television programs from the U.S., Japan, and Brazil, and competition between *RAI* and the private networks for the rights to foreign programs caused a sharp rise in their prices.

A serious attempt to change this process was made in the early eighties when *RAI* began a comeback strategy. That meant moving into an industrial phase of fiction production and training producers, directors, screenwriters, and actors for their new jobs. The aims of this strategy were, first, to put a check on the growing number of imported television movies, serials, and cartoons; second, to produce drama and serials whose contents were more in keeping with national and European culture; and, third, to begin exporting these products, first of all to Europe, but then also to North America. These primary objectives were linked to the attempt at establishing greater cooperation throughout Europe based on the development of co-productions and on the creation of an efficient continental commercial network. *RAI* thus managed to become one of the principal Italian film producers.

In 1978 an important milestone took place: television, with just the *RAI* license fee, started to earn more revenue than the cinema. Thus, the crisis and restructuring in the entertainment industry generated a new framework in which the main player was clearly television. It is not that the consumption of entertainment fell overall; rather that it was distributed in a different manner. This period witnessed the defeat of the public place of entertainment by home-based entertainment, which had the not inconsiderable advantage of being spread around the entire country with fewer inequalities. Television became the most fertile ground for advertising investments; consequently, private broadcasters sprang up everywhere. The penetration of television as a mass consumer medium into the home, together with the rise of other forms of home-based leisure and cultural consumption, profoundly restructured the notion of community upon which traditional forms of collective political and religious participation depended. Also, the increase in television watching, together with other changes like mass literacy and mass post-primary education, helped make working-class people better educated and more aware of the political, social, and cultural issues, and thus less dependent on the party apparatus or the Church as sources of information and values. The media, through their focus on individuals and on dramatic rather than routine aspects of the political process, shifted the popular perception of politics away from party programs toward controversy, personalities, and spectacle. Moreover, the rise of the private networks unhitched the media from state tutelage and created in the people the idea that mass media would respond to the needs of all, free from political goals. By the end of the seventies, public cultural manifestations and events intended for the masses no longer had a content that was packaged to contain a specific message, but they were organized to meet public satisfaction and appreciation.

Private Television and Low-Level Mass Entertainment

Today the Italian system is more open to the logic of industry and competition than to that of politics and cultural institutions. In the liberalization of broadcasting, what was revolutionary was an interactive use of the medium. Instead of being given information by studio experts about issues that often had little relevance to their lives, local people could themselves speak on radio and television and discuss questions of immediate importance to them, either by coming into the studio or by phoning in. With two or more telephone lines on the air simultaneously, people could talk not just to the presenter and to the audience, but with one another. Radio and television were not only a means of distribution, but also of communication. Instead of being the mouthpiece of a political group, they became the "platform" on which different voices could come together.

However, it is television, naturally, that has had the most profound impact on the wider population. Television became fashionable, along with light entertainment and everything else that had once been so despised. This was a real cultural transformation. Television was perceived no longer as an educative instrument but as an integral part of the cultural industry, which could be run as a competitive business, thus leading, among other things, to market segmentation.

In all this, private television seems to better reflect an aspect of the thinking of the general public. The distaste for long narratives, which according to Lyotard, the French philosopher, is the mark of our times, goes along with a greater capacity to grasp fragments, contradictions, differences, and redundancies:

> We can consider "postmodern" the scepticism towards certain types of narrative. The narrative function loses its actors, the great heroes, the great dangers, the great journeys and the great ends. . . Postmodern knowledge is not exclusively an instrument of power. It refines our sensibility for differences and strengthens our capacity to face the immeasurable.[5]

In the era of new media systems and new information and communication technologies that interact with new production regimes and advertising markets, there is a decline in the notions of *mass culture* and *mass communication*. Technology and advertising have made broadcasting a segmented and targeted communication. Indeed, especially because of advertising, there has been a shift from mass audience to segmented audience, in Italy as elsewhere. There is a switch from broadcasting to "narrowcasting," or from mass communication to segmented communication. Firms can insert an advertisement where it will reach its target public, which need not be a "mass" public. A firm that manufactures personal computers or expensive cars is likely to be more interested in reaching 200,000 people in the right income and occupational bracket than 2 million whom it knows nothing about. "Italian commercial television, in the absence of any plan or legislation, did not develop on the classic model of the European broadcasting industries. It followed in the wake of advertising, it developed as an outgrowth of advertising messages and of the means of distribution and consumption specific to those messages."[6] It was the concessionary that determined the program content on the basis of attractiveness to advertisers, not the stations on the basis of any cultural policy or perceived public need or demand. The television system became geared almost entirely to the distribution end, with advertising "piggy-backed" onto prepackaged programs, rather than to the production end. The "product" that one sees on private television is determined by the power of money.

Competition for advertising dollars has also lowered standards. There are no programs for schools, except on videotapes, and no exclusively cultural channel. The struggle for advertising produces gimmicks like sudden stopping of a film at the most exciting part in a bid to hold viewers. Pornography, too, is used as a bid for advertising, as it is used on the covers of magazines.

Private television stations are vertically integrated with advertising agencies and main publishing groups. In the absence of regulation, three or four television groups emerged in the 1970s that eventually took control of the entire sector. Among these, Silvio Berlusconi has built up a television conglomerate that not only dominates private television but also has overtaken the state network in advertising revenues and in viewers. Since 1984, after flattening the last of his major rivals, Berlusconi, through his highly diversified holding company, Fininvest, has dominated Italian private television. He controls the three principal private networks, *Canale 5, Italia 1* (1983), and *Rete 4* (1984).

The success of Berlusconi is a clear indication of how influential were advertising and a purely business approach to television. In 1981 Berlusconi first imported the Lorimar television series *Dallas* for around $20,000 an episode, to compete against *RAI*'s costly prime time in-house productions. Berlusconi's success had little to do with any media skills he may have possessed, even though he was shrewd enough to open up previously untapped viewing slots. His background was in the construction business, unlike Rusconi (*Italia 1*) and Mondadori (*Rete 4*) who were publishers and would have seemed more natural media entrepreneurs based on the model of the multimedia tycoons elsewhere in Europe (Hachette, Murdoch, Maxwell, Bertelsmann). Instead, his success had everything to do with his ability to sense potential advertising markets and to sell advertising space, confirming the point that it was advertising that drove the expansion of the networks.

Berlusconi was also able to target his products to specific kinds of viewers. In 1982 he began to use *Italia 1* in tandem with *Canale 5*, differentiating them for different markets. *Italia 1* was given a schedule that was oriented to a popular-youth market, whereas *Canale 5* had a family-feminine profile. The two networks began to trail one another's programs in 1983 and Berlusconi shifted personnel and programs between them to try to secure maximum competitive advantage.

The emergence of private broadcasting has had negative cultural consequences. In the absence of any form of effective state regulation (such as protective quotas or rules stipulating a certain proportion of in-house productions) and because it is much cheaper to import someone else's programs than to make your own, Italian television companies have increasingly become creatures of advertisers and importers of other countries' television. This domination of imports on Italian screens leads one to question the validity of traditional notions of a national cultural space, both popular and high culture, and ask the reasons for this and what are its implications.

Besides the economic reasons, there is the problem of Italy's history and the specific economic forces and policy choices that have affected the flow of cultural goods into the country. Italy's history of regional fragmentation, late unification, late diffusion of the national language, and, very importantly, the low level of "national-popular" integration, that is to say of voluntary participation by the mass of the people in the formation of the nation-state and in post-unification national culture—all have left an imprint. The masses were alien to the nation-state; the unification was done without a revolution and without their full participation. Italy may have been unified in a political and administrative sense in 1861 but outside the sphere of its ruling elite there was little or no shared cultural identity at the national level. This was partly because local and regional cultural traditions remained strong for a long time after unification, and partly because the various attempts to construct and define a national culture from above were either restricted to an educated minority or were of a coercive, rhetorical kind.

In this respect, the "openness" of Italy to non-Italian cultural material can be seen in part as a result of its relatively weak national-popular integration, its regional fragmentation as a community, and possibly the "cosmopolitanism" or "non-national-popular" character of its intellectual elite.[7] However, it should also be said that the imports were often cheaper to buy than Italian-made equivalents and, in so far as they had already been tried out on foreign markets, represented less of a risk for the cultural entrepreneur. Therefore, on one hand, the cultural dependency is a danger to the national character of the country, and on the other, Italy's openness to non-national culture could be seen as an index of cultural pluralism and vitality and a means by which diverse lifestyles have been absorbed and creatively reworked. It may be that while we wait for the "utopian" television of the future, in which the intermingling of national cultures will be generalized and intercultural viewing will be possible, Italy can currently offer us today the interesting spectacle of a system in transition.

Because of the nature of the medium, television has naturally become one of the cheaper forms of entertainment. After expenditure on a set, installation, and servicing, it provides virtually unlimited material in the home at very low cost. In non-metropolitanized areas with little or no book production and limited book consumption (Marches, Abruzzi, Calabria, Basilicata, and Sardinia) there are high levels of television consumption. By contrast, the cities of the North, with more money and a greater diversity of available entertainments, are areas where viewing rates are slightly lower. Television programs have the competition of more sophisticated forms of entertainment.[8]

The popular view that the new media offers a proliferation of low-level mass entertainment is, in many respects, true. However, it should also be said that segments of the public who were either not previously catered to adequately by RAI (for instance women, who constitute the majority of the audience, or youth) now are receiving proper attention. One could also say that a positive effect of the competition from the private networks has been not only to put better films on RAI at prime time but also to propel it to experiment with some imaginative entertainment shows. Moreover, the private broadcasting has put an end to the monopoly of state-regulated broadcasting, which was frequently dull, patronizing, party-obsessed, and party-manipulated, while opening new ways of reaching the public. The importance given to the broadcasting of rock videos, low-intensity talk-shows ("Oprah" and "Donahue" style), and variety programs, panel games, game-shows, quizzes, cartoons, etc., while lowering the cultural level of broadcasting, shows the strong intent to make television profoundly democratic. It also shows that Italian television, like other television in the West, has become more and more an environmental medium than a representational or expressive one. The television set is becoming more and more like the radio, switched on and running permanently in the background. In the Italian household it is not rare that the television set is not in the same room as the people, and, as a consequence, the sound volume is turned up very high. Television has become a domestic companion.

So today it is the low quality of the programs in the entertainment, arts, and documentary genres that is a much worse problem than the old issue of political bias. Italian television may be more free and outspoken than in the old days, but it is even more culturally mediocre. Today the cultural output has dropped drastically and is much lower than in Britain. The new commercial rivalry between the networks has led to a non-stop tussle for high ratings and has pushed the companies into putting more stress on easy entertainment programs with a wide appeal. This would matter less if they were at least well done. But the competition has led the networks to rely heavily on cheap foreign products and reruns. As compared with 20% in Britain, over 50% of Italian TV material is imported, much of it American soap opera.

It is true that some good new work by talented people does reach the screen, but such programming is far too rare. For example, serial adaptations of classic novels rarely come near the quality of the best BBC work. When it comes to new television plays on modern subjects, the results are very disappointing.

In the matter of morality there has been a major relaxing of standards. Until the early 1980s TV drama was still influenced by the Catholic ethos. Italians have always been highly tolerant toward all kinds of private behavior, so long as it remains private and is not aired in public, and television was a surviving bastion of this attitude toward public morality. However, new, freer values have reached the screen: nudity and sexually explicit scenes are now permitted almost as much as in cinema, and the Italian TV has even moved ahead (or behind!) of America with respect to the presence of sexually open programs.

On the other hand, Italian television remains more reticent than British or U.S. when it comes to satire or very frank analysis of delicate moral issues. There are discussions and features on such topics as AIDS, homosexuality, and abortion, but television might still shy away from screening the kind of programs seen recently in America, where gays face the camera and openly talk about their lives; a respected public figure would not admit on the screen to being gay or being promiscuous even though he is not very discreet in his private life.

The presence of private television networks has proven valid the fears of those who opposed the liberalization of television: fears of a further lowering of cultural standards, fears of the growth of powerful monopolies, and fears of political pressures of a new kind.

Technologically, Italian television is very advanced, in its way. It makes full use of the latest electronic news-gathering techniques, and it uses split-screen and montage effects with a virtuosity verging on gimmickry. But while the Italian government pours money into the subsidizing of theater companies and feature filmmaking, concerts, operas, and art exhibitions, and these activities draw good audiences, even so, in terms of sheer time devoted to it, most adults nowadays get most of their cultural exposure from television. It is a far more potent vehicle for the spreading of culture than any other, and, more than in most major European countries, the Italians are meagerly fed by that small screen.

Dailies in Search of Readers

The printed press also presents features that are rather uniquely Italian: (a) it is not truly national; (b) only a small percentage of the population read newspapers in Italy, therefore, the overall circulation has remained quite low; (c) the press is not independent; (d) most dailies, including almost all of the large ones, have piled up sizable deficits year after year; and (e) the government controls newsstand prices, and the advertising base still covers a very small percentage of the expenses.

Italy lacks a national press as it is known in Britain or France. There is no equivalent of *Le Monde,* the *Times,* or the *Sun.* It is sufficient to compare this with the daily sales of 4.2 million of just one newspaper, the *Sun* (estimated readership 12 million), in Britain, which has a similar population size. It is significant that the newspaper market was, and has remained with a few exceptions, characteristically a local or regional market, not a national one, and the economic success of a daily paper was measured by how far it managed to dominate its particular regional market. Thus, in the 1990s such major newspapers as *La Stampa* (400,000 copies, Piedmont), *La Nazione* (Tuscany), *Il Resto del Carlino* (Emilia), *Il Mattino* (Campania), and *La Gazzetta del Mezzogiorno* (Apulia) all still sold between 75 and 95% of their copies in their region of production and even *Il Corriere della Sera*, then the only paper which could be said to have had a national presence, sold 66% of its copies in its native Lombardy. The paper with the most convincing national profile is *La Repubblica*. Launched in 1976 and based in Rome, it is not associated with a particular region or city and it has carved a niche of readership among the younger generation. Although change of ownership and a more national orientation helped *Il Corriere della Sera* to reestablish itself as the leading paper in terms of sales (with a circulation of 778,000 in 1994) and reputation, the regional bias remains. Apart from these pluri-regional or regional papers, each city or major town often has its own daily paper that is distributed in the surrounding province. Finally, there is a smaller provincial press that comes out once or twice a week and which is exclusively local. The papers which, at least until recently, had the best national distribution over the peninsula, were *L'Unità*, the daily of the former Communist Party (now the Democratic Party of the Left) and *L'Osservatore Romano*, the official paper of the Vatican. Probably the paper that has the most even distribution and sale across the country is *La Gazzetta dello Sport*, which is also the most-read daily! What is evident is that the Italian press has a strong regional character and that this continues to be the case.

Why does Italy not have a paper with a genuinely national readership, whose authority within the country is the basis for an international reputation? Provincial papers account for over two-thirds of the dailies' total sales. This localism can be explained in turn both by the strength of regional traditions and by the difficulties of nationwide distribution, given the physical features of the country (length, mountains), the poor communications in many areas, and the lack of a developed network of distribution and a sufficiently high number of retail sales points. The strength of local identities has been an important factor and something that the Catholic Church has long cultivated, celebrating the values of family and community. The regionalism derives in part from Italy's lack of a historical metropolitan capital comparable to London, Paris, or Berlin, from whose central position the rest of the country could be dominated. Whereas Rome is the political capital, Milan is the economic and cultural capital. Italy is a country of multiple urban centers that have not only maintained their identities but that are currently reclaiming their distinctive traditions in the name of a greater degree of self-government. With the prospect of regions becoming more powerful as centers of government and economic activity, the justification for this kind of press is enhanced. The strength of the regional and provincial press is not uniform throughout the peninsula. Because of the need for an advertising outlet for local business, the Center and the North had a more vigorous press than the South and, as a result, Italian newspapers have endemic weaknesses of their own, both economic and editorial. One major problem is that the Italians by inclination have never been great newspaper readers and are becoming even less so.

Italian newspapers continue to have a relatively small readership (the number of readers has been around 5 million for nearly fifty years). A survey of 1956 found that 64.5% of the population never read anything at all. Although by 1990 some 6.5 million Italians were buying a daily paper, the readership pattern was still regionally skewed.[9]

Today's relatively low readership in Italy is due to several factors. Because of historical, economical, and cultural reasons in Italy, only an elite readership was formed. In the second half of the twentieth century, when the majority of Italians became literate, the newspapers had ceased to have a monopoly of information, owing to radio and, above all, television. Language use is not a small drawback. Newspapers made no attempt to make themselves more accessible. The lack of transparency and high level of abstractness of bureaucratic and political discourse reproduced in journalism have not helped in breaking the barrier for a very high percentage of readers. The Italian journalistic establishment still considers the newspaper market a "quality" market. Newspapers and newspaper advertising are targeted at a high-income, educated reading public, not a mass public; there is an absence of popular "downmarket" newspapers of the British or German or U.S. type. Sport not only is massively covered in the press with regional and local publications, but enjoys coverage by three daily sports papers—*Corriere dello Sport, La Gazzetta dello Sport,* and *Tuttosport.* If sports papers and weekly magazines are included, the Italians are a nation of readers. Soccer, the most popular sport in

Italy, attracts with equal enthusiasm fans from every social class. The nonpresence of tabloids may be explained by the following facts: first, regional and local identity and its journalistic representation cut across the division of social class; second, popular issues such as sports and crime are covered by the Italian press in a different way—crime stories are covered by the national television news even when the individuals involved are not famous; third, the well-established large readership of weekly magazines remained faithful to their publications. For a number of reasons, tabloids have never taken off in Italy where similar cultural functions appear to be fulfilled instead by weekly magazines. These magazines have a very high total circulation owing to their strong visual element and in certain cases a typical tabloid content (scandal, sports, sex, television). But even this sector is not comparably popular because most Italians find them difficult to read. The effects of television on the press are described as uniformly deleterious. It is not just that television puts importance on entertainment values, making news into a spectacle for consumption, nor just that television has overtaken the press in speed of reporting, establishing itself as the chief source of news for the majority of Italians. The problem is that the press in Italy has allowed television to set its agendas so that anything in the *telegiornale* (TV evening news) has to be covered in the morning edition.[10] It has also tried to become more entertaining, symptomatically giving extensive coverage to television personalities and events.[11]

The most obvious explanation for this low level of readership is, however, that Italy is a latecomer in the field of mass literacy and mass education. And when this was finally achieved the age of television had already come. It should also be noted that the newspapers are highly politicized and full of special vocabulary and esoteric language. All the newspapers are much more wordy than their equivalents in the Anglo-Saxon press. They are also more serious and probably go into the news in greater depth than their British or American equivalents. Since Italian universities do not offer degrees in journalism, journalists enter the profession without special training, usually coming from an academic background rich in classical studies. Moreover, Italian journalists belong to a "registered" profession with restricted entry and high salaries. As a result, newspapers cannot compete with news reporting on television, both for the cost and the ability to attract a large audience.

Certainly the fact that the Italian press is not independent does not help. Italian newspapers are strongly connected to centers of power, political institutions, and political parties on the one hand, and economic groups and forces on the other. The "party press," which has been in rapid decline since the end of the Cold War (*L'Unità*'s circulation dropped from 500,000 in 1952 to 111,000 in 1997), differs profoundly in its political orientation and therefore differs equally profoundly in the way it reports and interprets news. It is a press that is protected from the market in that it does not depend financially on sales and advertising; however, it is expected to respect the orthodoxy of the party and is subject to its censorship. Even so, the majority of influential newspapers were, and are, controlled by the business enterprises. Through newspapers, generations of Italian entrepreneurs have exercised strong influence on the economic and political affairs of the nation.

Although almost without exception newspapers are unprofitable and depend on government subsidies, this state of affairs has never unduly troubled the newspaper owners. Whether businessmen or other wealthy individuals, corporations or economic groups and associations, they do not look upon their journalistic holdings as money-making ventures. In a country where political influences are omnipresent, the corporate-controlled press is an important weapon, providing entrepreneurs with a means of influencing public opinion and the parties. They regard them as tools to protect and promote other, more important interests of their own through a complex combination and interplay of pressures and counterpressures, favors, and concessions involving the government and the political forces which share, or are expected to share soon, in running national or local affairs. This web further widened and thickened as government aid to the press, badly hurt by skyrocketing labor and newsprint costs, came to include not only indirect subsidies but direct allocations running into the tens of millions of dollars a year.

Indeed, a striking feature of Italian private industry is its role in the media. Virtually all the major daily newspapers are owned entirely or in part by corporate powers: *La Stampa* by Agnelli; *Il Messaggero* by Montedison; *Il Giornale Nuovo* by Silvio Berlusconi, former prime minister; *Il Sole 24 Ore* by Confindustria (the industrialists' organization); *Il Tempo* by Italmobiliare; *La Nazione, Il Resto del Carlino,* and *Il Piccolo,* by Monti; and the *Corriere della Sera* by a consortium controlled by Agnelli, Pirelli, Bonomi, and Montedison. *La Repubblica* is owned in part by *L'Espresso,* a weekly in which Mediobanca and De Benedetti have interests. Carlo Caracciolo is the principal owner of *L'Espresso, La Repubblica,* and seven local dailies. Agnelli, Monti, and Confindustria have absolute editorial control over their papers; the others have varying degrees of influence.

In spite of the connections between the press and the governing parties, much of the Italian press, particularly since the mid 1960s tends to favor the parties of the center-left. Ideologically the press tends to espouse various aspects of liberal tradition no matter who owns them.

La Repubblica is the best daily; during the first republic, it criticized the socialists or communists as much as the christian democrats. It is perhaps the most bulky newspaper in Italy with many long pieces and extensive cultural and financial sections; politicians also have an opportunity of expressing their views or answering points made against them, and there are sometimes long forums on the ills afflicting *Italia*.

Some of the changes, such as the greater proportion of women in journalism and the greater attention to social rather than narrow political issues, are positive. Newspapers are freer to focus on commentary and analysis of news that has already been delivered by the other media.

The Italian Press and the United States

It was hardly surprising that the media thus controlled or influenced by the political and economic establishment should project an image of America that reflected the basically conservative bent of that establishment and a pro-American stand. However, up to the end of the Cold War era, for most of the right-of-center journalists, Americans were "fools" when it came to foreign affairs and, at the same time, were so convinced of their worldwide "mission" that they were likely (to quote Luigi Barzini) to embark "on risky adventures which jeopardize international peace." Other right-wingers wondered whether Americans waited so long before entering two world wars "which they could have nipped in the bud," because they wanted a Europe so enfeebled as to be forced "to entrust its survival to U.S. protection."

Even some of the most traditionally pro-U.S. business groups and the media they controlled attacked American protectionism, an approach which reflected their emphasis on exports as the main engine of the Italian economy, and the sharpening differences between the U.S. and the EU on trade matters.

Anti-American propaganda has gained a wider audience and has had a greater impact since the U.S. armed intervention in Southeast

Asia. Watergate provided additional encouragement and ammunition to all those bent on portraying America as a decadent and bumbling imperial power—one that was racist, corrupt, racked by domestic crises, and increasingly unable to face up to its adversaries and reward its allies in the international arena, but still seeking greedily to promote its selfish interests at the expense of friends and foes. In the mid 1970s, carried away by all-out solidarity with the most militant "movement of liberation" in the Third World, leftist newspapers vented their basic anti-American bias.

There were other factors that increased the anti-American bias during the 1960s and 1970s. Control of *Corriere della Sera* passed into the hands of people who apparently regarded the retention of the paper's traditional line of bourgeois moderation as both unrewarding and unfashionable. The thrust of many other dailies and magazines shifted in the same general direction, whether by decision of the publisher, pressure from unionized printers, and/or journalists, or such other factors as accommodating financial backers and big advertisers. A leading role was played by some weeklies, notably *Espresso* (published by a group including some Agnelli relatives and several radicals and Left wingers). Mondadori teamed up with the *Espresso* group to publish a new daily, *La Repubblica*, which at once moved into the forefront of the anti-American campaign.

In the late 1960s, as most traditional standards, from religion and family to long-entrenched social and moral codes, seemed to be engulfed by an unprecedented and apparently irresistible surge of protest and permissiveness, especially among the young, media operators began to feel that in Italy, too, they could and should play not only an independent but an aggressive role in national affairs. They did it by openly challenging the established authorities and by boldly resorting to investigative journalism. Like other sectors of Italian society, however, quite a few newsmen and publishers lacked a deeply rooted democratic tradition; nor did they have the cultural background required for a mature and balanced approach to their new role. Toward the end of the 1970s, the Italian press became less stuffy and much more enterprising. There began a long overdue debunking of stale ideas and antiquated institutions; graft, abuses, and other illegal activities in high places were exposed. But independence has quickly degenerated into arrogance; boldness into irresponsibility; "investigative" reporting into sensationalism, scandal-mongering and a search for scoops unrestrained by respect for facts and the rights of those involved. In an obsessive competition to uncover "plots," excessive space and consideration have ceded, in widely circulated and (formerly) authoritative papers, to "purple tales."

Most of the Italian newspapers concentrated their fire on the "American Party" in Italy. That is, the groups that were singled out for attack were ones that were perceived as bent on furthering, by hook or by crook, the influence and wicked designs of America, as well as their own selfish interests and privileges. For example, a determined and sustained effort was made to associate the United States (and more specifically, the CIA) with the kidnapping and murder of former premier and *DC* leader Aldo Moro. In the same breath, however, they have used much more violent terms to denounce again the bombings, massacres, and corruption that in their opinion must be blamed on the Americans in Vietnam, Latin America, the Middle East, Greece, and elsewhere. Some radicals and Left-wingers in Italy have admitted, more or less grudgingly, that some of their "evaluations and prophecies" about the nature and behavior of communist regimes have turned out to be wrong. The anti-American slant was certainly more sustained and persistent in newspapers identified officially with political parties, especially *L'Unità*, the daily of the old Communist Party.

This anti-American bias was generally the fruit of a higher political education of the people. For example, in a series of articles appearing in 1979 in *Corriere della Sera*, the Italian writer Goffredo Parise could not be accused of mincing words in his critical assessment of American society. His invective was filled with such characterizations as: "The American people . . . have very little dignity and often no dignity at all. . . . The average American has undergone a sort of historical and political lobotomization and is not aware of his political identity, of the tremendous social and racial differentiations and discriminations that exists in the country. . . . Poverty in the U.S. is the blackest in the world."

In the 1960s and 1970s many of the same media and other leftist journalists and "experts" sought to sell the idea that Italy has been and still is a province, a most compliant and exploited province, of the "American empire." Film reviewers missed no opportunity to blame the troubles of the Italian movie industry on American colonization of the Italian market, and movie directors did likewise when their works received a bad reception. The same media displayed a marked bias in favor of Arab leftists. It should be stressed, however, that this kind of mass-media practice took place in a country where the great majority of the population has a deep respect and admiration for the U.S., as we have seen in chapter IV.

In the 1980s there was a changing trend. Some of the most militantly anti-American contributors left, while others trimmed their sails to the new trade winds and the press reflected more closely the sentiments of the Italian people toward America.

The Italian press has shortcomings even when it tries to report assessments of national conditions. One of its editorial shortcoming as a whole, including *La Repubblica* and *Corriere della sera*, is that it has little tradition of the kind of fearless investigative reporting common in Britain and America. Papers are stronger on polemic or on mere news digest than on fully researched factual exposés when controversy is in the air. There are two underlying factors: first, Italians are generally more concerned with ideas and style than with facts; second, Italians are deferent toward not only the government but most power establishments as well. In this centralized and close-knit society, most journalists rely for their news sources on their personal links with people in positions of influence—be they ministers, civil servants, business tycoons, trade-union leaders, or leading politicians—and they are reluctant to prejudice these sources by making embarrassing revelations. Exceptions were rare until the fall of the First Republic and the national embarrassment caused by the *Tangentopoli* mega-scandal. Still, prudence is the watchword. The fact is that the press relies on millions of dollars worth of assorted annual state aid in the form of newsprint subsidies.

The problem is also one of journalistic tradition and resources, or lack of them. As compared with the quality press in Britain or America, few Italian editors put the same insistence on factual accuracy or balanced judgments, or instill these virtues in their staff. Even on supposedly serious papers, reporting and subediting can be remarkably casual. Take, for example, the coverage of purely foreign stories, where Italian interests are not involved and thus there is no threat from the pressures described above; here the reporting tends to be cavalier, taking refuge in easy clichés, *a priori* judgments, or irrelevant picturesque details, rather than trying to assess the real situation. The higher Italian journalism tries to combine two ingredients that often do not mix well: the brio of ideas and the substance of events; commentary and reporting; evaluation of themes and statement of facts. Moreover, it seems that the deductive methods of teaching used in Italy, whereby all schoolchildren are trained first to enunciate a thesis, then to parade facts to support it, are in no small part a cause of the way Italian journalists' minds work and even of their mixing of news and comment. They lack humility in the empiric pursuit of truth. It is the reverse of the inductive Anglo-Saxon tradition, which likewise spills over from its education into its journalism. Therefore, the Italian system, whatever its intellectual merits, is not the ally of objective inquiry.

Magazines: A Popular Commodity

The low readership in dailies has been balanced, to an extent, by the rise of the weekly news magazines which have become national publications. In a society that is becoming faster-paced, electronic news quickly makes printed news obsolete, and people are today less ready to find the time for reading a morning paper; so they want news-digest and feature material on the weekends. Consequently, news magazines have developed remarkably. Originally borrowing their formula from such publications as the American *Life* and *Look*, Italian weeklies have now become far more glossy than these, with thick shiny pages full of color ads; their content is much more newsy. By European standards their circulations are modest; nevertheless, these are prosperous owing to their high cover price (3,000 to 5,000 lire) and copious advertisements.

While the daily press remained stagnant, the weeklies went from 12.6 million sold each week in 1952 to 21 million in 1972. Published mostly by Egidio Rusconi and Arnoldo Mondadori, the weekly magazines are designed to appeal to everyone. One group follows the lines of the American *Time* magazine. The best known of these are *Panorama*, *L'Espresso*, and *Europeo*. They consist of articles on a wide range of subjects from politics to finance to cultural events. They are more accessible than newspapers on a number of counts: their language is simpler; their abundant use of photographs provide fast imagery reading to those with limited reading skills; the content—stories about private lives of Hollywood stars—are sensationalized. In fact, their specialty is research in depth, usually on sensational subjects dealt with in a serious way: drugs, homosexuality, where the Italians make love, and so forth. But they also deal with recurrent national problems: the crises in justice, housing, the health service, the economy. In summer, nudes appear on their covers to represent research into subjects such as "Torrid Summer: Causes, Effects, and Remedies," "Topless," "On Holiday with Eros." Inside there is little or no suggestive material. After all, the cover may be a way of selling more copies, but at the same time these are subjects that are interesting in themselves. However, the abundant advertisements are very often quite suggestive, or they present products such as prophylactics with the same candidness as goods for a homey kitchen. These magazines have been astute to give particular coverage to lifestyle matters, such as fashion and health. There is no doubt that major changes are taking place within the existing newspapers and magazines because of the growth of a female readership.

Because Italian is not a world language like English, the Italian magazines do not sell internationally and therefore have a limited number of their own foreign correspondents—unlike *Time* and *Newsweek*. Although they are topical and are more concerned with research projects and comment, they get their news items secondhand and are not always completely up to date.

There are more family-oriented magazines that are widely read; two of these are *Oggi* and *Domenica del Corriere*, and both illustrate an important characteristic of the Italian press in general: the fact that they do not write for specific social groups but attempt in one publication to satisfy readers of every kind. There seems to be no differentiation between lowbrow and highbrow—perhaps because most Italians are not aware of this distinction themselves. In either of these magazines one may get advice on *stitichezza* (constipation) in the same edition as an interview with the Italian Prime Minister, or a serious analysis of the iniquities of the taxation system, along with a correspondence page, a horoscope, and two or three opinion pages on topical issues, whether the Mafia or the examination system.

In addition to illustrated magazines, Italy also has high levels of consumption of comics (*fumetti*). *Topolino*, a magazine for children has a wide youth readership and has reached its 2000th edition.

On the whole, then, the Italian press deals with any subject. It is conservative in that it has nothing sensational like *People*, has no tabloids, and displays on the whole a stolid format. It is written more in a literary style than a journalistic one, is rarely vulgar, and illustrates the general absence of divisions of class or of "intellectualism." It gives good coverage to foreign news. Much of the press is local, but it is rarely provincial. Despite, or perhaps for these reasons, it is not so widely read.

Media Geography System

Although the growth of television, especially through the private sector, represents an essential part of the "unification" of North and

South on the language level, it has also created an increasingly polarized and uneven market for cultural goods. The structure of the information system is uneven between North and South. If we look at the written information we will notice a persistent gap: the South has 34% of the total population but publishes only 400 out of 12,000 book titles a year, prints only 16 out of 87 daily papers (not one of which sells more than 100,000 copies in a country where there is no real national press), and buys only 10% of daily papers and 17% of periodicals. Moreover, whereas the bigger papers of the North are sold all over Italy and abroad, those in the South do not have the structure to make this possible. As so often, it is the northerners' points of view that predominate, and this applies particularly abroad, where only the papers from the North are well-known.

If we examine the figures for television we see that there is virtually no consumption gap between North and South: 95% of the southern population owns a television set against a national average of 97%. There is, however, a production gap: most of the programs broadcast that are produced in Italy come from the North or the Center. Southern culture has no outlet. The role of the South in this sector is that of consumer, a market for goods made elsewhere.

Although Italy displays a form of polycentrism in its media industry organization, there are no centers in the South. Rome, Florence, and Turin are home of some important book publishing houses, but their combined national impact is smaller than that of Milan. The publishing industry (above all book and magazine publishing) has Milan as its capital. Milan is the headquarters not only of some major book publishers (Mondadori, Rizzoli, and Garzanti) and distribution agencies, but of almost all of the major periodicals. Because of its central role in publishing, Milan became also the national capital of advertising. However, Milan's pivotal role in the publishing sector is countered by a weakness in the other form of mass communication. Until the advent of private television, Milan had a marginal role in film production.

Film production also began polycentrically, but it subsequently centered increasingly in Rome. With the creation first of the Istituto LUCE (1925) and then Cinecittà (1937), Rome became the capital of film production. The cinema industry was the first national cultural industry to have its production capital in the political capital. With the advent of television broadcasting through RAI, Rome became also the principal geographic area for TV production. This situation changed in a significant way after the arrival, well into the 1980s, of private television stations that made their home in Milan.

It is clear that Italy's cultural and communications industries are firmly rooted in central and northern Italy, in particular on the Rome-Milan axis. However, we cannot underplay the role of Naples in the South as a cultural center, for its important publishing houses, great opera house, prestigious university, and the vital role in the field of popular mass culture. As a national center of live variety theater, it has a tradition of theater in dialect with no equals in the nation, while as the national center of popular music, for many years it boasted the festival of popular music that enjoyed more popular interest than the one in the standard language in San Remo.[12] Until recently, its dialect enjoyed such a popularity that it had national appeal. With the exception of Florentine, it was the only dialect that could safely be assumed to be understood from one end of the peninsula to the other. "It could be said, without forcing the analogy too much, that for a long time Naples was to Italian popular culture what the New Orleans-Nashville axis is to US mass culture."[13] The iconography of the city—Vesuvius, the bay of Naples, the funicular—was an important part of a largely reinvented local tradition. The rise of more modern cultural forms and patterns of consumption associated with the North and Center, most notably television, brought about the decline in the 1950s of Neapolitan song, and of Naples as a center of popular culture in Italy. The popularity of transnational music, the growth of interest in rock music, and the strong emergence of youth culture made regional culture less appealing.

In terms of the distribution of cultural power, then, the postindustrial era in Italy seems to be shaping up to look as bad as the industrial era. There may be a greater range of cultural goods on the market, and a greater variety in the means of distributing them. New audiences may have opened up and they may be responding to an increased supply of television in new ways. But access to the new media technologies and to the full range of cultural goods still depends on a very uneven spread of earnings and dispositions. Traditional inequalities between classes and regions are reinforced. Finally, the patterns of concentrated ownership that became established in the sixties and seventies show few signs of breaking up, and the major cultural industries are as far from any kind of democratic accountability and control as ever.

Material Wealth and Mass Media

The advent of TV as a mass consumer medium coincided with the arrival of mass material wealth in Italy, and so it would be simplistic to say that a total "massification" of culture was brought about exclusively by TV. General material wealth created massification of culture and at same time distinctions in the creation and attraction to form cultures, as distinctions are created by dispositions and competences. People's cultural choices are shaped by many economic and ideological determinants—for instance the amount of disposable income they have, what sort of area they live in, and social pressures to conform. In addition, certainly, the level of education and family both play a crucial role in defining particular cultural dispositions.

Change in attitudes in goods consumption goes hand in hand with change in work attitudes and leisure patterns. Many of these are, of course, the result of rising living standards, for in the postwar period all social categories shared in the general rise in prosperity. In Italy, as in other Western countries, many consumer durables such as cars, which were luxury items owned by the privileged few before the war, became generalized to the mass of the population. Television sets, and more recently, freezers, dishwashers, video-recorders, and cellular phones are all items that began as expensive luxuries and are now widely owned.

Therefore, what is relevant is not so much what people buy, but the different patterns of spending. Considerable differences have emerged over the past generation. Most striking is the fall in the percentage of income spent on food and on clothes. Conversely, the amount spent on transport (including car purchases), on housing, and on health care have all risen significantly. Obviously this does not mean that Italians are eating less well or are less well dressed. What it certainly indicates is that they have surplus income to devote to new kinds of spending.

As consumption patterns change, the traditional socioeconomic categories are crossed by other forms of stratification such as age and gender—groups like old people, young people, and women have significantly different consumption habits. Although many of the elderly today are affluent, they tend not to own cars, they spend less than other age groups on clothes, but they expend more on their domestic interior. The entry of women into the workforce has led to a market increase in spending on restaurant meals in families where women work, while women now spend an astonishing 30% more on clothes than men in a context where overall spending on clothes has declined as a proportion of income. Young people are also a distinct consumer category. Young males, for example, spend up to 35% of their income on transportation—essentially on the purchase of a car and its maintenance—and as they are for the most part single, a great deal on eating out. Similarly, children have been identified both as significant consumers in their own right as major influences on household spending decisions.

Perhaps the greatest change in the way people live is in the expansion of leisure and the growth of leisure industries, especially the domestic leisure industries. At least in theory, Italians today have much more free time than their compatriots of the previous generations. This is partly a result of the enactment of legislation limiting hours of work, providing statutory paid holidays and earlier retirements. With more free time, people take more and/or longer vacations, if they can afford to do so, go away for the weekend, visit museums and sites of historical interest or natural beauty.[14] Not least important is the upsurge of interest in sports on the part of both practitioners and spectators.

By contrast, the expansion of the domestic leisure industries has affected virtually all Italian households; *la casa è diventata la principale sala di spettacolo* (home has become the most important entertainment center). Besides television, most homes own VCRs that are used both to record programs and to watch rented tapes; the same is true of music centers or other means of listening to and recording music. The mass media and the domestic leisure industries have created both a degree of homogenization and different forms of stratification that have more to do with age than class, even though the category of the professional may stand apart for the amount it spends on culture.

However, the state supports culture and leisure activities in inverse proportion to their popularity, giving lots of money to the opera or the theater. Performances there are seen by few people compared to other forms of popular culture. There are attempts to decentralize cultural spending both by supporting and creating museums in smaller towns and encouraging local initiatives and workplace efforts. The regions have engaged in a political struggle with the central government that has been reluctant to relinquish its powers. The central government failed to match the decentralization of administrative functions with the decentralization of funding. Although the regions immediately understood the strong potential of cultural policy in enhancing their political identity, the development of regional cultural policies has indeed progressively slowed down since the late 1970s by a reduction in central government transfer of funds.[15] Instead municipalities understood the need for cultural policies and used them to achieve a variety of strategic objectives. "In an attempt to counteract trends toward social atomization and home-based cultural consumption, one of the aims of cultural policies was to reassert the function of the city center as a catalyst for civic identity and public sociability."[16] Open-air festivals and annual summer programs of cultural events were organized with the intent of pulling together people of different ages, sexes, social classes, and lifestyles.

Probably more than the public institutions but completely in a different way, stars played a role in the way popular culture evolved. The creation and serial production of star personalities for presentation and consumption of merchandise is clearly a feature of a social system whose economy is geared to mass production. The low level of national integration has meant that in place of formal institutions and official traditions, sports and entertainment have often been the principal sources of a shared set of national cultural symbols; thus stars within fields such as popular music, film, cycling, and soccer have been called upon to perform a function in terms of national mobilization. Since stars generally are of lower-class origin, they tend to be embraced by the average person, and hence their images are often used by cultural industries for advertising. Ever since the development of a consumer market of mass dimensions, this function has widened, and entertainment and sports stars have been involved in an ever-greater range of promotion of food, drinks, cars, and household goods. They have become the leaders and illustrators of cultural trends, offering advice on all manner of topics, including beauty, diet, home furnishings, wedding rituals, voting choices, and fashion.

The link with fashion is particularly important because it became Italy's most successful industry in the 1980s. Young Italian women of aristocratic background and many foreign black models modeled their clothes. However, there has been a certain diffidence in Italian fashion circles toward domestic stars. Well-known designers such as Armani, Valentino, Ferragamo, Krizia, and Fendi court Hollywood stars and compete to dress them on occasions such as Oscar night. In the 1980s the designers themselves became international stars and within Italy they also assumed something of the status of gurus on social and economic matters as well as questions of style and fashion.

The emphasis on appearance, combined with the wider importance of the media in social and economic relations, inevitably conditioned politics. Since the 1970s politicians have tended to present themselves as stars to some degree by paying attention to image and dress, and putting family and aspects of their personal lives on display. In the world of visual mass communication, politics and politicians do not escape the laws established by mass cultural consumption.

Therefore, in assessing cultural changes and their causes, one should consider an integrated cultural assessment that not only includes history of ideas and ideologies, sociology of culture (studies of audiences, markets, etc.), mass media research, analysis of cultural objects, study of the circuit production-distribution-consumption, but that also takes into account modes of living. In fact, for a more complete understanding of cultural changes, it is essential that one tries to see the sociocultural space as a whole; one cannot exclude many of the wider anthropological dimensions of culture, such as clothing styles, eating habits, social rituals, and mentalities. The view that "total" cultural change— including the assessment of the forms and sites of socialization and the consumption of particular kinds of goods, such as clothing, food, and drink—encouraged by the development of the mass media, brought about a re-evaluation of the function of the intellectual. The view that intellectuals are producers of culture, and that cultural history is a history of intellectuals, was rejected.

Intellectuals sensed this phenomenon early on. By the end of the sixties, therefore, the Gramscian historical paradigm—the desire to connect intellectual history (history of culture) with material history (political and economic)—was undermined by three modes of critical thought: structuralism-semiotics, media studies, and studies of popular culture. Structuralism produced a new attention to the intrinsic qualities of the cultural artifact as a system of signification. Media studies brought, for the first time, mass cultural products within the purview of academic study. The field of cultural inquiry certainly widened and included areas that were not even included in the assessment of popular culture, in its rare cases of critical attention. The new critical interest in popular culture, like everything else, had a political coloring. The new work on popular culture (ethnography, ethnomusicology, dialectology) was frequently informed by a political commitment to reclaiming the culture of the subaltern social groups against the dominant culture reproduced by the education system. At the same time, the Hegelian theoretical basis upon which the old historicism had rested was challenged by counter-currents in philosophy: neopositivist, neo-Kantian, phenomenological, structuralist.[17]

The early seventies, therefore, were certainly years rich in fermentation, but the challenges to traditional historicism did not come together to produce a new synthesis of cultural studies. Those who favored structuralism tended not just to be antihistoricist but to veer away from history altogether in an attempt to restore the intrinsic specificity of signification of cultural forms.[18] Media studies research was trying to establish its status as an autonomous discipline; in any case, it tended to be fiercely contemporary rather than historical in scope. Popular cultural studies, involving the recording or retrieval of increasingly marginalized traditional cultures, were generally conceived in polemical antithesis not only to the dominant elite culture, but also to mass culture.

These rapid cultural changes suffered a setback toward the end of the 1970s because of the terroristic activities that caused a drastic involution of the Left. The shift that took place away from the Left at the end of the 1970s was more than a temporary downturn; it was a swing of the electoral pendulum. What began to be undermined was the whole cultural legitimacy of the Left itself. Marxism had been throughout the 1950s, 1960s, and 1970s an unquestioned point of reference for most democratic intellectuals but began to go distinctly out of fashion at the end of the 1970s. It would be an exaggeration to talk of a Right cultural hegemony emerging at this point. Nothing as coherent as this seems to have arisen. But there is little doubt that the Left had entered a serious crisis of cultural power since this moment.

By the end of the 1970s, a widespread deradicalization of intellectuals and students was setting in. There was a "return to study" in the universities, perhaps partly brought about by anxiety about employment prospects, but also probably caused by this general change of cultural mood.

In the process of modernization of Italy, not only the urban landscape has changed; the mentality of the inhabitants has changed even more. One can detect an overlaying of three mentalities: traditional (Catholic), consumer culture, and ideology of the Left.

Notes

1. In its initial years, tolerance of free discussion was not permitted, and frequently there was suppression of anti-government views in broadcasts or measures against hostile staff journalists. In those years, news material was edited to show the government in a positive light, while almost any program on a social or economic subject had to be censored in advance by the relevant ministry.

2. See Giorgio Grossi, *Rappresentanza e rappresentazione. Percorsi di analisi dell'interazione tra mass media e sistema politico in Italia* (Milan: Franco Angeli, 1985).

3. In several European countries, especially in Italy, the concept of broadcasting as a public service wholly or mainly financed by licence-fee revenues and regulated by the state started to change in the seventies. Italy, in fact, has gone furthest of all in liberalizing from state control and the tacit approval of wildcat private broadcasting.

4. Franco Rositi, "Sistema politico, soggetti politici e sistema delle comunicazioni di massa," *Problemi del Socialismo* 22, no. 22 (1981): 88.

5. J.-F. Lyotard, *La condizione postmoderna* (Milan: Feltrinelli, 1982), 6-7.

6. Marigrazia Bruzzone, "Come la pubblicità ha influenzato l'evoluzione delle TV private," *Problemi dell'Informazione*, 6, n. 4 (1981): 598-89.

7. Antonio Gramsci, *Selections from Cultural Writings*, eds. David Forgacs and Goffrey Nowell-Smith (London: Lawrence and Wishart, 1985), 209.

8. Stefano Mauri, *Il libro in Italia. Geografia, produzione, consumo* (Milan: Hoepli, 1987), 75.

9. Whereas the ratio was one paper per 6.6 inhabitants in the North, it stood at one per 7.4 in the Center and at one per 16 in the South. M. Olmi, *Il giornalismo in Italia* (Rome: Bulzoni, 1992), 96.

10. A. Papuzzi, *Manuale del giornalista* (Rome: Bulzoni, 1993).

11. Robert Lumley, *Italian Journalism: A Critical Anthology* (Manchester: Manchester U.P., 1996).

12. The Festival of Piedigrotta, held annually in Naples on September 8, became the focus of a massive popularization of the Neapolitan song both in Italy and abroad which had reached its peak in the first half of the twentieth century.

13. Peppino Ortoleva, "Geography of the Media since 1945," in David Forgacs and Robert Lumley, eds., *Italian Cultural Studies* (Oxford: Oxford U.P., 1996), 185-97.

14. Italians have much artistic treasure at their disposal. According to UNESCO, 50% of the world artistic heritage sites are located in Italy. In 1990 there were in Italy 710 state museums, galleries, historic monuments, and archaeological sites, and about 2,300 museums owned by municipalities, foundations, the Church, and private individuals. This number is larger than in other European countries.

15. It was urban local authorities, the municipalities, rather than the regions, which developed high-profile cultural policies in response to interrelated processes of social, political, and cultural changes. *Comuni* understood much more clearly than the central government the need to respond to the growing, more differentiated, and sophisticated demand for cultural needs.

16. F. Bianchini, M. Torrigiani and R. Cere, "Cultural Policy," in D. Forgacs and R. Lumley, eds., *Italian Cultural Studies* (Oxford: Oxford U. P., 1996), 296.

17. For these challenges, see Lucio Colletti, *Il marxismo e Hegel* and *Ideologia e società*, both Bari: Laterza, 1969; Roberto Guiducci, *Marx dopo Marx*, (Milan: Mondadori, 1971).

18. See Filippo Bettini, "Il problema dello strutturalismo in Italia," in *Marxismo e strutturalismo nella critica letteraria italiana* (Rome: La Nuova Sinistra, 1974).

XVI

Conclusion:
A Country in Search of Equilibrium

The Elusive Citizen

Throughout this book I have demonstrated that Italy is alive, well, and thriving; that the Italian democratic system ultimately is one of the most stable in the world, despite its political map; the Italian society is as lively as ever, paradoxically, because problems very often are not solved frontally, and Italians have an innate ability to "manage" in all kinds of situations.

We have agreed with Robert N. Putnam that one of Italy's major problems is the low sense of civic community; indeed, Italy's problems are the more serious in the least civic regions, for they lack the horizontal bonds of collective reciprocity that work more efficiently in the civic regions. In the absence of solidarity and self-discipline, there is a horizontally fractured community that produces daily justification for feelings of exploitation, dependency, frustration, and, consequently, cynicism and alienation. In the less-civic regions nearly everyone expects everyone else to violate the rules; everyone expects everyone else to cheat. (The Italian term for such behavior is *fesso*, which also means cuckolded.) So you cheat, too, and in the end everyone's dolorous, cynical expectations are confirmed.[1]

Therefore, while in most regions in the North citizens are engaged by public issues instead of by personalistic or patron-client politics and value solidarity, civic engagement, and cooperation, in the less-civic regions of the South life is marked by hierarchy and exploitation, not by share-and-share-alike.

However, there is a cynical attitude toward the government that is equally strong in both the South and the North. Indeed, it is charged with both heartfelt hate and unconscious civic irresponsibility. To have an idea of what we mean, let's take a look at how the Italians deal with the many "crises," real and fictitious, that afflict the country. The average Italian is accustomed to associate with a crisis any problem that he encounters in his daily activities. Very often minor or accidental problems are equated to national or regional or local crises. In such a labyrinth, real crises cannot be disentangled from imagined ones, and the country appears to be constantly at the brink of chaos.

The average Italian faults the *classe politica* and *classe dirigente* for such a nightmarish atmosphere. In fact, the political and the ruling classes are the culprits for anything that goes wrong. Here, too, it is difficult to identify what is real or who these classes really are. They are like an accordion; they can be expanded or contracted, depending on the nature of the crisis, who "sees" it, whether one is talking about a city or province or the whole nation, and so on. The *classe politica* is "they," those people, those incompetents and mischief-makers. Certainly not "we" or "I" or any close friend. It is not even uncommon to hear a "prominente," a member of Italy's ruling class excoriate the *classe politica* as if he or she were in no way responsible for the political, fiscal, social *crisi* of the country. There is much unintended irony and self-deception in all of this. One may argue that the Italian situation is nothing uncommon, that everyone likes to blame a scapegoat at one time or another, that we all tend to look elsewhere for the cause of those aspects of society, and of our own lives within it, that we find unpalatable.

But Italy does appear different, not only in the frequency of hostile references or attacks on the *classe politica*, but also in the vehemence with which each condemnation is expressed. The criticism is so ritualized, so well integrated into the citizens' role, so much part of Italian play-acting that it is difficult to tell how much of it is deeply felt. Moreover, what is important is the fact that there is no persuasive evidence that these hostile attitudes have negative or corrosive consequences on the Italian democracy; on the contrary, it seems that Italian democracy thrives on hostile criticism. Criticism calls for constant reassessment of situations, conditions, and prominent individuals.

Notwithstanding the self-criticism that at times is picked up also by the foreign press, in less than three decades Italy has become an advanced industrial country, where the number of persons who work in agriculture has been drastically reduced, and where, as in many other democracies, the so-called tertiary employment sector is in rapid expansion. Modern, well-off Italy got where it is because of the ideas, imagination, and hard work of its people. The progress arrived not by chance or "miracle" but because, the *classe politica* concocted political and economic formulas that the people accepted and, when applied, worked. The *classe politica* has demonstrated how primary political rights and democratic processes can be used to improve the material and the moral condition of the citizens. The Italians created a capitalism as a peculiar phenomenon that does not fit any "ideal type" or rigid preconceived framework. It is rational, of course, and at the same time highly traditional, and while following universal rules it has never abandoned its firm original family base. It is a mixture, a cocktail of different attitudes and contradictory value-orientations. Being called "dynastic capitalism," it is recognized as a masterpiece of adaptation of traditional virtues and traits to modern functional requisites. For Italian capitalism the conventional concept of profit is too narrow, just as the current concept of productivity is too one-sided. Productivity and profit are not conceived only in terms of an individual productive unit. They are measured and assessed in terms of social stability and satisfactory performance of the system as a whole.

It would be wrong to overlook the social dimensions of Italian capitalism. It is less efficient but has less conspicuous waste; it allows for more individual self-expression and permits more conviviality. That is not necessarily bad; human beings desire and probably crave change but they also want and need stability. They might desire competition to vent their aggressiveness, but they also need cooperation, security, and the feeling of working together toward a reasonable goal.

In its leap into industrial prosperity, Italy has escaped the "flatness," the existential monotony that characterizes other industrial countries. In such societies, life is dynamic, but it tends to be tedious and tasteless; things and people become gradually homogenized and interchangeable. Things are still different in Italy. The tempo of life can be irritatingly slow, especially in the South. Italians still prefer to do things leisurely. There seems always to be time for everything. Time is not regarded in Italy as a scarce raw material. One may find hurry and confusion at times, especially in a *piazza* or at a social function, but it is not a purposeful hurry.

Thus, people are usually late for their appointments. In Rome to be half an hour late for *un appuntamento* is not considered serious. It is commonly accepted. South of Rome, arriving on time may be regarded as an almost offensive behavior. Punctuality on the part of one person is viewed as a lack of trust toward others and a clear symptom of petty-mindedness. In some respects Italians' attitudes to leisure still differ from the Anglo-Saxons', notably the way they like their free time divided up; that is, since World War II they have shown a preference for longer annual vacations rather than shorter daily working hours. The Italians are among those in Europe who take the longest vacations. Today, the strains of daily city life incite many people to take off for the country on the weekend, and most likely they will go neither to a hotel nor to relative's but to their own country cottage or villa, *la seconda casa*. Italians can boast about holding the first place among Europeans in owning a second house. The race to the countryside has to be tied with the new trends of ecological back-to-nature and the either hedonistic or spiritual search for privacy. If weekends are now more important, lunches are less so. The leisurely two-hour family lunch, weekdays included, is one Italian tradition that is in decline because of suburban commuting and economic change. This had habitually been the main meal of the day, with children coming home from school and husbands from work—and so it still is, in many small town and rural areas. But the cities have seen big changes.

The Art of *Arrangiarsi*

The Italians have a way to "manage" their lives and their institutions in a manner that surprises even the most open-minded political science experts or the most informed sociologists. The area of politics is very revealing in this regard. Italy has one of the most active and participating electorates. The picture is very positive indeed, if one assesses the strength of its democracy on the basis of public participation in the election process. Even the high percentage of votes for the communists was something positive because the strong opposition to government provided a high level of checks and balances in the democratic process. Contrary to the general American belief that a vote for the Communist Party by Catholics was a sign of political pathology, the Italian vote was highly calibrated to keep a democratic system from falling under the control of groups with extreme ideologies. Now that the heat and the smoke of the Cold War have settled, it is easy to assess the political behavior of the Italians in those years. The fall of communism has brought about a shift of political adherence from the communists but also from the christian democrats—their traditional political enemies—to other political forces, creating a new political landscape which brings an end to *immobilismo*.

The political behavior cannot be understood by the American mind that prefers everything in black and white. Matter-of-factness, which is usually and somewhat pompously referred to as "scientific habit of mind," has not trickled down to permeate mass mentality. Facts per se have no value; there is only interpretation of facts in Italian life. Everything is debatable. The activities in any Italian *caffè* reflects such Italian behavior. Pirandello and his relativistic view of life are the product of a general Italian conception of existence. The Italian mind is still poetic, anthropomorphic, and unpredictable. This is why when the American tourists, who are fond of empirical details and ask questions such as "how tall is the Colosseum" or "how wide is Piazza San Pietro," the average Italian looks up surprised and a little amused at such questioning.

Foreigners are amazed by such a way of thinking and behavior. The question is always, why? Centuries of foreign domination have, according to Eduardo De Filippo, a postwar Italian actor and playwright, created a mind that subconsciously represses truth. In a hostile environment, truth was a luxury that few people could afford; invention at the individual level, a keen sense of life as a permanent theater, a profound and irreducible diversity, and a living challenge to the rules of logic became the normal behavior. Regardless of how tough a situation may be, Italians have learned to face life always with dignity and elegance. Needless to say, the end result of such efforts is the supreme value given to *bella figura*. *Bella figura*, which may mean roughly giving a good impression, is more than simple make-shift or bombastic rhetoric. It has to do with an aesthetic ideal, and at the same time, with a question of survival.

Italians want it to be known that they are present; the fact that Italians are noisy and that Italy is a noisy country can be traced to this particular attitude. Noise can be nervewracking and, in terms of efficiency, time-consuming, but Italians seem to like noise. They regard it as a therapy against solitude. Noise is life, message, exchange, presence, *socialità*. And being sociable has remained a major Italian trait. With the advent of *progresso*, many social manifestations have not changed or become part of a rational notion of society, that is, of a functional society. In a functional society every major activity is planned toward a definite goal and is to be accounted for and evaluated in terms of costs-benefits analysis. In industrialized Italy, ceremonies are still done for purely ceremonial purpose because people still have a love for ceremony.

Measuring Success

Today Italy presents a confusing picture, for society appears to have evolved in certain respects but not in others. Personal attitudes and lifestyles have evolved rather more than the formal or official structures that dominate public life. These still tend to be impeded: by the survival of many out-of-date laws, regulations, and routine practices, and by the "stratified society" with its strong vested interests right across the board. Society is still too corporatist and compartmentalized, with each body protecting itself from its rivals.

Moreover, Italian society is still segmented and individualistic because loyalties are usually restricted to small groups held together by strong personal ties. The family is the most important of these, but it is followed closely by the patron-client relationship, which is very strong and is by no means restricted to the South. Italians join associations with fellow-members of their own trade or social group, but it is done more for mutual self-defense than out of altruistic sentiment or civic duty.

This book has also attempted to trace the positive changes in attitudes and human relations—greater freedom for women and young people, the rise of social informality, the freer climate in education and in working life, and a small sign of a new cooperative spirit of self-help. All this might have led, one would suppose, to a waning of the old Italian traits built around mutual mistrust and to the rise of a less divided and, therefore, more civic-minded society. And in some ways it has. But there are some failures. Some can be found in any capitalist society; some are merely part of the wider human condition—other nations too, including Britain and the U.S., have their own full share of vested interests, corruption, and clumsy bureaucrats.

Italians have now modernized their country, or most of it, and have managed to adjust successfully without losing their essential Italianness. Anyone who travels around Italy today will find a country that is very modern, but in its own way, a blend of the new and the traditional, the native and the imported. Of course a highway or a skyscraper is much the same in any land, but the Italians add stylish innovative touches of their own. Inevitably the new Italy has lost some of the old's quaint picturesqueness, yet the Italians today show a flair for giving a Phoe-nix-like rebirth to the picturesque.

The Italians are showing less success at reinventing the novel, the play, or the great painting. For some years now, Italian creative cul-ture has remained at a low ebb. Intellectual life is dazzle and frenzy more than substance; the theater turns to brilliant gimmicks; and Italy still awaits the arrival of outstanding new talent among novelists, play-wrights, painters, even film-makers. But is this vacuum any deeper in Italy than elsewhere in Western Europe? The Italian cultural staleness is part of the staleness of the West in this age of technology and mass media. This is a time that favors individual creativity less than it does the disseminating of culture to new audiences; and here Italy is full of an impressive activity, notably in the world of museums.

It seems that in today's anxious world, the Italians have been turn-ing in search of security, of personal fulfillment, of what can loosely be termed "quality of life." This could lead them as individuals to be-come more passive and self-absorbed, more anti-social in a civic sense. Certainly there has been a new stress on personal initiative, ambition, and material success, especially among young people. This is cer-tainly not a sign of passivity, but it is somewhat egotistical rather than civic-oriented.

The issue is whether the Italians can harness their abundant ener-gies to work together for new social goals, or whether their old indi-vidualism will lead them down new entrepreneurial paths, or whether as individuals they will relapse into the shuttered, mistrustful isolation that is one strong facet of their nature.

The Ills of Prosperity

In the last few decades, Italians have gone through experiences that have a strong American flavor. In the early 1960s, most Italians be-lieved that prosperity would create the ultimate good society. As in the U.S. of the 1950s and 1960s, in the Italy of the 1960s and 1970s there was a general, fervent belief in the power of prosperity. Soon after the economic recovery, the Italians increasingly became accus-tomed to believing that they were entitled to a great deal: more oppor-tunities, job security, better housing, better education, earlier retire-ment, rising living standards, a clean environment, and more. While family income grew rapidly, the quality of life improved in countless ways. In the process, their expensive notion of entitlement grew increasingly unrealistic.

When the fiscal and political crisis swept the country at the beginning of the 1990s, Italians felt a need to reassess their wants, needs, and moral attitudes. They started to answer some very basic questions: is upward mobility a birthright? Can the state continue to provide a high level of social and public assistance? Is prosperity going to continue? It seems that they started to learn from what the Americans had painfully learned, that prosperity can never satisfy all our expectations. Prosperity is not quite the social stabilizer that we thought it to be. Faith in prosperity is an infatuation, and like all infatuations, one is seduced by its pleasures and blinded to its shortcomings. Economic growth—the creation of new industries and technologies—can be disruptive: it may spawn excesses, overinvestment, speculation, too much borrowing, and recession. Moreover, not only are some social problems beyond prosperity's power to cure, some social ills are the creation of prosperity.

Many Italians have been questioning the worth of such progress. In a book published in 1989, *Non siamo più povera gente* (We Are No Longer Poor People), Cesare Marchi lamented the cost of economic success. It was the follow-up to another book of his, *Quando eravamo povera gente* (When We Were Poor People), in which he had called to mind the Italy of poverty, while underlining the solid moral values of that society.[2] Is Marchi's lamentation symptomatic of a real situation or is it part of the general Italian behavior to be critical of everything?

However, most Italians still remain prey to the economy's euphoric expansions and dispiriting declines; they should realize that prosperity cannot be created at will and that is the most important term in the equation of the high achievements of a country. They must finally realize that even great amounts of prosperity won't solve all their social problems and that prosperity could bring moral decay. In fact, the prospect of the harmonious society is disfigured by huge blemishes—high unemployment, tension between South and North, staggering budget deficits, an uncontrollable Mafia, unprecedented corruption among public officials, and the breakdown of moral values—which cannot continue to be overlooked.

As the country moves toward the twenty-first century, past progress has to be reconsidered. The sophisticated constitution has to be attuned to new political realities; the responsibilities of the state to the citizens and those of the citizens to the state have to be revalued. The "Italian behavior," while keeping its valuable traits, has to start to conform to that of a united Europe and of a shrinking world. With its unique cultural patrimony, artistic tradition, and creative strength—from Dante to Michelangelo, Giotto to Botticelli, Vivaldi to Verdi, Machiavelli to Gramsci, Volta to Fermi—it is unlikely that Italy will fail to contribute greatly to a Europe that may well be on the threshold of a radical new era. Italians have always known how to pair technical expertise with artistic genius, a tradition dating back at least as far as the Renaissance, when painters were also sculptors, architects, scientists, and men of letters. Italian design—the "made in Italy" trademark—has contributed to this tradition of uniting beauty with usefulness. The real challenge to Italy for the next century is how she is going to weld her two cultures, the Western European and the Mediterranean.

How can we conclude and generalize about a people who in our own time have produced types as different as Mussolini and Pope John XXIII? Ever since they began to emerge as a nation, the Italians presented contrasting facets. Which is more typical of the national genius: Dante on his austere quest for truth and perfection or Boccaccio bubbling over with laughter at the human scene? Saint Francis with his love for nature and humankind or Machiavelli with his cynicism and "scientific art"? Which is the real Italy, the country that rose to a major economic power without natural resources, or the nation struggling for fiscal responsibility? Both exist, both are real, and as things go, they are probably both eternal.

No other people over so long a history have shown a greater knack for survival and adaptability than the Italians and in a manner that is full of paradoxes. The national art of "arrangement"—dodging taxes, double-dealing, working only as hard as one must—is counteracted by Italian inventive genius, gusto for life, fierce individuality, and deep family ties, as well as animosity and a marvelously hedonistic sophistication. The Italians are highly resilient, resourceful, and practical people and will keep a balance between work and leisure. Perhaps more than any other nation in Europe, the Italians bring a vast heritage of wisdom, taste, and humanism to the difficult task of preserving the best of the past in order to marry it with the future. They will do it by preserving a *gusto* for life.

Notes

1. Robert N. Putnam, *Making Democracy Work*, 111.

2. Cesare Marchi, *Non siamo più povera gente* (Milan: Rizzoli, 1989) and *Quando eravamo povera gente* (Milan: Rizzoli, 1989).

Bibliography

General

Barzini, Giuseppe. *The Italians: A Full-Lenght Featuring Their Manners and Morals.* New York: Atheneum, 1964.

Braun, Michael. *L'Italia da Andreotti a Berlusconi. Rivolgimenti e prospettive politiche in un paese a rischio.* Milan: Feltrinelli, 1995.

Chubb, Judith. *Patronage, Power and Poverty in Southern Italy.* Cambridge: Cambridge UP, 1982

Di Scala, Spencer M. *Italy. From Revolution to Republic.* Oxford: Westview Press, 1995.

Forgacs, David and Lumley, Robert. *Italian Cultural Studies: An Introduction.* Oxford: Oxford University Press, 1996.

Ginsborg, Paul. *A History of Contemporary Italy: Society and Politics 1943-1988.* New York: Penguin Books, 1990.

————— ed. *Stato dell'Italia.* Milan: Il Saggiatore Mondadori, 1994.

Gramsci, Antonio. *Selections from the Prison Notebooks,* edited by Q. Hoare and Nowell-Smith. London: Lawrence and Wishart, 1971.

Gribaudi, A. *Mondo operaio, mito operaio.* Turin: Einaudi, 1987.

Haycraft, John. *Italian Labyrinth: Italy in the 1980s.* London: Secker & Warburg, 1985.

Mammarella, Giuseppe. *Italy After Fascism: A Political History.* Notre Dame: Notre Dame UP, 1966.

Murray, William. *The Last Italian: Portrait of a People.* New York: Prentice Hall Press, 1991.

Pescosolido, Carl and Gleason, Pamela. *The Proud Italians*. Portland: Graphic Arts Center Pub., 1991.

Rusconi, Gian Enrico and Scamuzzi, Sergio. *Italy Today: An Eccentric Society*. London: Sage, 1981.

Sassoon, Donald. *Contemporary Italy: Politics, Economy & Society Since 1945*. New York: Longman Inc., 1986.

Politics

Bull, Martin J. and Martin, Rhodes, eds. *Transition and Crisis in Italian Politics*. London: Cass, 1996.

D'Alberti, Marco and Finocchi, Renato, eds. *Corruzione e sistema istituzionale*. Bologna: Il Mulino, 1994.

Della Porta, Donatella and Vannucci, Alberto. *Corruzione politica e amministrazione pubblica. Risorse, meccanismi, attori*. Bologna: Il Mulino, 1994.

Di Palma, Giuseppe. *Surviving Without Governing: The Italian Parties in Parliament*. Berkeley: University of California Press, 1977.

Galli, Giorgio and Prandi, Alfonso. *Patterns of Political Participation in Italy*. New Haven: Yale University Press, 1970.

Gozzini, Giovanni and Anderlini, Luigi, eds. *I partiti e lo stato*. Bari: De Donato, 1982.

Guidorossi, Giovanna. *Gli italiani e la politica*. Milan: Franco Angeli, 1984.

Kogan, Norman. *A Political History of Italy: The Postwar Years*. New York: Praeger Special Studies, 1983.

La Palombara, Joseph. *Democracy Italian Style*. New Haven: Yale University Press, 1987.

Mannheimer, Renato and Sani, Giacomo. *La rivoluzione elettorale. L'Italia tra la prima e la seconda repubblica*. Milan: Anabasi, 1994.

Pasquino, Gianfranco. *The End of Post-War Politics in Italy*. Boulder: Westview Press, 1993.

Spotts, Frederic and Wieser, Theodor. *Italy: A Difficult Democracy*. Cambridge: Cambridge University Press, 1986.

Treu, Tiziano, ed. *L'uso politico dello statuto dei lavoratori*. Bologna: Il Mulino, 1975.

Vacca, Giuseppe. *Quale democrazia?* Bari: De Donato, 1977.

Wollemborg, Leo J. *Stars, Stripes, and Italian Tricolor*. New York: Praeger, 1990.

Government

Amato, Giuliano. *Una politica riformare*. Bologna: Il Mulino, 1980.

Brosio, G. *Equilibri instabili*. Turin: Boringhieri, 1994.

Calandra, Piero. *Il governo della repubblica*. Bologna: Il Mulino, 1986.

Cassese, Sabino. *Esiste un governo in Italia?* Rome: Officina, 1988.

———— and Franchini, C. , eds. L'amministrazione pubblica italiana. Un profilo. Bologna: Il Mulino, 1994

Cazzola, Giuliano. Lo stato sociale tra crisi e riforme: il caso Italia. Bologna: Il Mulino, 1994.

Certoma, G. L. *The Italian Legal System*. London: Butterworth, 1985.

Di Palma, Giuseppe. *Surviving Without Governing: the Italian Parties in Parliament*. Berkeley: University of California Press, 1977.

Ferrera, Maurizio. *Modelli di solidarietà: politica e riforme sociali nelle democrazie*. Bologna: Il Mulino, 1993.

Furlong, Paul. *Modern Italy. Representation and Reform*. London: Routledge, 1994.

Guarnieri, Carlo. *L'indipendenza della magistratura*. Padua: Cedam, 1981.

Leonardi, Robert and Nanetti, Raffaella Y. *The Regions and European Integration. The Case of Emilia-Romagna*. London: Pinter, 1991.

Rotelli, E. *Il martello e l'incudine*. Bologna: Il Mulino, 1991.

Sales, O. *Leghisti e sudisti*. Roma-Bari: Laterza, 1993

SVIMEZ, *Rapporto sulla distribuzione Nord-Sud della spesa pubblica*. Bologna: Il Mulino, 1993.

Travaglio, Sergio, ed. *Come funziona l'Italia*. Milan: Sperling and Kupfer, 1994.

Zannotti, F. La magistratura. *Un gruppo di pressione istituzionale*. Padua, Cedam, 1989.

Economy And Industry

Accornero, Aris. *La parabola del sindacato. Ascesa e declino di una cultura*. Bologna: Il Mulino, 1992.

Amato, Giuliano. *Economia, politica e istituzioni in Italia*. Bologna: Il Mulino, 1976.

Blim, Michael. *Made in Italy: Small Scale Industrialization and Its Consequences*. New York: Praeger, 1990.

Blum, Anna, et al. eds. *From Peasant to Entrepreneur*. Providence, RI: Berg, 1993.

Bruni, Michele and De Luca, Loretta. *Unemployment and Labor Market Flexibility*. Bologna: Il Mulino, 1994.

Cento Bull, Anna and Corner, P. *From Peasant to Entrepreneur. The Survival of the Family Economy in Italy*. Oxford: Oxford University Press, 1993.

Daneo, Camillo. *Breve storia dell'agricoltura italiana 1860-1970*. Milan: Mondadori, 1980.

D'Antonio, Mariano. *Sviluppo e crisi del capitalismo italiano 1951-1972*. Bari: De Donato, 1973.

Goodman, Edward and Bamford, Julia, eds. *Small Firms and Industrial Districts in Italy*. London: Routledge, 1991.

Holmstrom, Mark. *Industrial Democracy in Italy: Workers' Co-ops and the Self-Management Debate*. Aldershot: ·Averbury, 1989.

Lange, P. and Tarrow, S., eds. *Italy in Transition: Conflict and Consensus*. London: Frank Cass, 1980.

Lash, Scott and Urry, John. *The End of Organized Capitalism*. Cambridge: Polity, 1987.

Lazerson, Mark H. "Organizational Growth of Small Firms: An Outcome of Markets and Hierarchies?" *American Sociological Review*, 53 (June 1988).

Mershon, Carol. *The Micropolitics of Union Action: Industrial Conflict in Italian Factories*, Ph.D. diss., Yale University, 1986.

Nannetti, Raffaella Y. *Growth and Territorial Policies: The Italian Model of Social Capitalism*. New York: Pinter, 1988.

———— and Leonardi, Robert, eds., *The Regions and European Integration: The Case of Emilia-Romagna*. New York: Pinter, 1990.

Trentin, Bruno. *Da sfruttati a produttori*. Bari: De Donato, 1977.

Triglia, Carlo. *Sviluppo senza autonomia*. Bologna: Il Mulino, 1992.

Reu, Tiziano, ed. *L'uso politico dello statuto dei alvoratori*. Bologna: Il Mulino, 1975.

Sapelli, Giulio. *Sul capitalismo italiano. Trasformazione e declino*. Milan: Feltrinelli, 1993.

Valli, Vittorio. *L'economia e la politica economica italiana*. Milan: Etas Libri, 1979.

————. *Politica economica: I modelli, gli strumenti, l'economia italiana*. Rome: La Nuova Italia Scientifica, 1992.

Villari, L., ed. *Il capitalismo italiano del Novecento*. Bari: Laterza, 1975.

Weiss, Linda. *Creating Capitalism: the State and Small Business since 1945*. Oxford: Blackwell, 1988.

Society

Altan, Carlo Tullio. *L'altra Italia*. Milan: Feltrinelli, 1985.

Balbo, Laura. *Stato di famiglia*. Milan: 1976.

————. *Women's Studies in Italy*. Old Westbury, N.Y.: Feminist Press, 1982.

Arlacchi, Pino. *Mafia Business*. New York: Verso, 1987.

Ascoli, U. and Catanzaro, R. *La società italiana degli anni ottanta*. Bari: Laterza, 1987.

Banfield, Edward. *The Moral Basis of a Backward Society*. Glencoe, Ill.: The Free Press, 1958.

Baranski, Zygmunt G. and Vinall, Shirley W., eds. *Women and Italy: Essays on Gender, Culture and History*. New York: St. Martin's Press, 1991.

Birnbaum, Lucia Chiavola. *Liberazione della donna: A Cultural History of the Contemporary Italian Women's Movement*. Middletown: Wesleyan UP, 1985.

Bono, Paola and Kemp, Sandra, eds. *Italian Feminist Thought: A Reader*. Oxford: Basil Blackwell, 1991.

Caldwell, Lesley. *Italian Family Matters*. London: Macmillan, 1991.

CENSIS. *Italy Today: Social Picture and Trends, 1985*. Milan: Franco Angeli, 1986.

Ceolin, Carlo, ed. *Università, cultura, terrorismo*. Milan: Franco Angeli, 1984.

Della Porta, Donatella, ed. *Terrorismi in Italia*. Bologna: Il Mulino, 1984.

Forgacs, David and Lumley, Robert, eds. *Introduction to Italian Cultural Studies*. Oxford: Oxford University Press, 1995.

Fraser, R. *1968: A Student Generation in Revolt*. New York: Pantheon Books, 1988.

Graziano, Luigi and Tarrow, Sidney, eds. *La crisi italiana*. Turin: Einaudi, 1979.

Gribaudi, A. *Mondo operaio, mito operaio*. Turin: Einaudi, 1987.

Hofmann, Paul. *That Fine Italian Hand*. New York: Henry Holt & Co., 1990.

Jeffries, Giovanna M., ed. *Feminine Feminists: Cultural Practices in Italy.* Minneapolis: University of Minnesota Press, 1994.

Kemp, Sandra and Bono, Paola. *The Lonely Mirror: Italian Perspectives on Feminist Theory.* London: Routledge, 1993.

Kertzer, David. *Sacrificed for Honor.* Boston: Beacon Press, 1993.

Labini, Paolo Sylos. *Le classi sociali negli anni '80.* Bari: Laterza, 1986.

Lumley, Robert. *States of Emergency: Cultures of Revolt in Italy from 1968 to 1978.* London, New York: Verso, 1990.

Lumley, Robert and Baranski, Zygmund G. *Culture and Conflict in Postwar Italy: Essays on Mass and Popular Culture.* London: Macmillan, 1990.

Lupri, E. ed. *The Changing Position of Women and Society: A Cross-National Comparison.* The Netherlands: Leiden-E. J. Brill, 1983.

Meyer, Donald. *Sex and Power: The Rise of Women in America, Russia, Sweden, and Italy.* Middletown: Wesleyan UP, 1987: 119-156, 445-491.

Pantaleone, Michele. *The Mafia and Politics.* London: Chatto and Windus, 1966.

Parks, Tim. *Italian Neighbors.* New York: Grove Weidenfield, 1992.

Pivato, S. *Movimento operaio e istruzione popolare nell'Italia liberale.* Milan: Franco Angeli, 1986.

Richards, Charles. *The New Italians.* London: Penguin, 1995.

Turato, G. and Sasso, C. *I saccheggiatori.* Milan: Sperling and Kupfer, 1992.

Vertone, Saverio, ed. *La cultura degli italiani.* Bologna: Il Mulino, 1994

Watson, James. *The Mafia and Clientelism: Roads to Rome in Post-War Calabria.* New York: Routledge, 1986.

Zuccotti, Susan. *The Italians and the Holocaust.* New York: Basic, 1987.

Arts, Intellectuals, Culture

Baranski, Zygmunt G. and Lumley, Robert. *Culture and Conflict in Postwar Italy.* London: Macmillan, 1990.

Bondanella, Peter. *Italian Cinema. From Neorealism to the Present.* New York: Frederick Ungar, 1983.

Cortellazo, M. and Cardinale, V. *Dizionario di parole nuove: 1964-1984.* Turin: Einaudi, 1985.

De Mauro, Tullio. *Storia linguistica dell'Italia unita*. Bari: Laterza, 1976.

Forgacs, David. *Italian Culture in the Industrial Era 1880-1980*. Manchester, UK: Manchester UP, 1990.

Grossi, Giorgio. *Rappresentanza e rappresentazione. Percorsi di analisi dell'interazione tra mass media e sistema politico in Italia*. Milan: Franco Angeli, 1985.

Inglehart, Ronald. *Culture Shift in Advanced Industrial Society*. Princeton: Princeton UP, 1990.

Jewell, Keala. *The Poiesis of History: Experimenting with Genre in Postwar Italy*. Ithaca: Cornell U.P., 1992.

Kerr, Paul, ed. *The Hollywood Film Industry: A Reader*. London: Routledge and Kegan Paul, 1986.

Lanaro, Silvio. *L'Italia nuova. Identità e sviluppo 1861-1988*. Turin: Einaudi, 1988.

Mancini, Paolo. *Videopolitics: Telegiornali in Italia e in USA*. Turin: ERI, 1985.

Marletti, Carlo. *Media e politica*. Milan: Franco Agnelli, 1984.

Mauri, Stefano. *Il libro in Italia. Geografia, produzione, consumo*. Milan: Hoepli, 1987.

Michalczyk, John J. *The Italian Political Filmmakers*. Cranbury: Associated University Press, 1986.

Misler, Nicoletta. *La vita italiana al realismo. La politica culturale artistica del PCI dal 1944 al 1956*. Milan: Mazzotta, 1973.

Mondello, Elisabetta. *Gli anni delle riviste: Le riviste letterarie dal 1945 agli anni ottanta*. Lecce: Edizioni Milella, 1985.

Pansa, Gianpaolo. *Comprati e venduti: I giornali e il potere negli anni '70*. Milan: Bompiani, 1978.

———. *Carte false*. Milan: Rizzoli, 1986.

Pasolini, Pier Paolo. *Scritti corsari*. Milan: Garzanti, 1975.

———. *Letture luterane*. Turin: Einaudi, 1977.

Pinto, Francesco. *Intellettuali e tv negli anni '50*. Rome: Savelli, 1977.

Porter, William E. *The Italian Journalist*. Ann Arbor: University of Michigan Press, 1983.

Vacca, Giuseppe. *L'informazione negli anni ottanta*. Rome: Riuniti, 1984.

Appendix

Table 1. Communes, territorial area, agricultural and forestry area and population density on 31.12.1995 (areas in Km²)

REGIONI / REGION	Comuni numero / No. communes	SUPERFICIE TERRITORIALE / TERRITORIAL AREA		SUPERFICIE AGRARIA E FORESTALE (a) / AGRICULTURAL AND FORESTRY AREA (a)		Densità (abit. per Km²) (b) / Density (inhabitants per Km²) (b)
		Totale / Total	%	Totale / Total	% su superficie territoriale / % of territorial area	
Piemonte	1.209	25.398,94	8,4	21.678,50	85,4	169
Valle d'Aosta	74	3.263,47	1,1	2.144,62	65,7	36
Lombardia	1.546	23.860,62	7,9	18.713,57	78,4	373
Trentino-Alto Adige	339	13.607,30	4,5	11.455,95	84,1	67
Bolzano-Bozen	116	7.400,43	2,4	6.169,07	83,4	61
Trento	223	6.206,87	2,1	5.286,88	85,0	74
Veneto	580	18.379,01	6,1	14.732,80	80,2	241
Friuli-Venezia Giulia	219	7.844,13	2,6	6.225,56	79,4	152
Liguria	235	5.420,82	1,8	4.754,75	87,8	307
Emilia-Romagna	341	22.123,42	7,4	19.100,97	86,3	177
Toscana	287	22.992,65	7,7	20.614,44	89,7	153
Umbria	92	8.456,04	2,8	7.734,94	91,5	97
Marche	246	9.693,50	3,2	8.829,32	91,1	149
Lazio	377	17.207,35	5,7	14.687,98	85,4	301
Abruzzo	305	10.795,34	3,6	9.779,05	90,6	117
Molise	136	4.437,61	1,5	4.096,61	92,3	75
Campania	551	13.595,33	4,5	11.829,81	87,0	423
Puglia	258	19.363,05	6,4	17.605,02	91,0	210
Basilicata	131	9.992,27	3,3	9.255,73	92,6	61
Calabria	409	15.080,32	5,0	13.466,60	89,3	138
Sicilia	390	25.707,07	8,5	23.091,58	89,8	198
Sardegna	376	24.089,89	8,0	22.230,92	92,3	69
ITALIA	**8.101**	**301.308,13**	**100,0**	**262.028,72**	**87,0**	**190**
NORD-CENTRO	**5.545**	**178.247,25**	**59,2**	**150.673,40**	**84,5**	**204**
MEZZOGIORNO	**2.556**	**123.060,88**	**40,8**	**111.355,32**	**90,5**	**169**

(a) Anno 1990. - (b) Anno 1994. - *(a) Year 1990. - (b) Year 1994.*

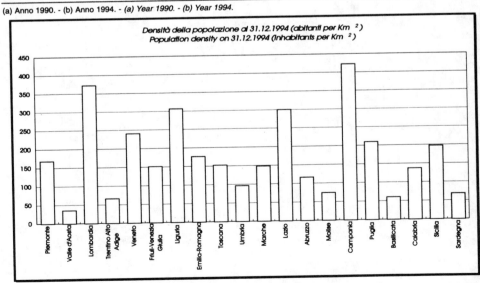

Densità della popolazione al 31.12.1994 (abitanti per Km²)
Population density on 31.12.1994 (Inhabitants per Km²)

Table 2. Resident population in the provinces and provincial capitals at 31.12.1994

| | POPOLAZIONE - *POPULATION* | | |
PROVINCE E REGIONI *PROVINCE AND REGION*	Comuni capoluogo *Commune of provincial capital*	Altri Comuni *Other Communes*	Totale *Total*
Torino	934.732	1.293.436	2.228.168
Vercelli	48.893	324.864	373.757
Novara	102.505	397.872	500.377
Cuneo	55.103	495.431	550.534
Asti	73.847	136.223	210.070
Alessandria	89.731	345.352	435.083
Piemonte	**1.304.811**	**2.993.178**	**4.297.989**
Valle d'Aosta	**35.492**	**82.964**	**118.456**
Varese	85.061	720.259	805.320
Como	85.731	722.393	808.124
Sondrio	22.225	154.790	177.015
Milano	1.321.555	2.593.013	3.914.568
Bergamo	117.140	836.317	953.457
Brescia	190.942	869.039	1.059.981
Pavia	75.602	417.213	492.815
Cremona	72.926	257.480	330.406
Mantova	50.816	317.949	368.765
Lombardia	**2.021.998**	**6.888.453**	**8.910.451**
Bolzano-Bozen	*97.548*	*351.507*	*449.055*
Trento	*103.153*	*356.459*	*459.612*
Trentino-Alto Adige	**200.701**	**707.966**	**908.667**
Verona	254.915	543.618	798.533
Vicenza	107.944	653.072	761.016
Belluno	35.528	176.450	211.978
Treviso	81.213	672.945	754.158
Venezia	301.115	517.737	818.852
Padova	212.904	618.757	831.661
Rovigo	51.462	194.630	246.092
Veneto	**1.045.081**	**3.377.209**	**4.422.290**
Udine	49.351	226.772	276.123
Gorizia	96.090	424.432	520.522
Trieste	38.056	100.030	138.086
Pordenone	225.538	30.979	256.517
Friuli-Venezia Giulia	**409.035**	**782.213**	**1.191.248**
Imperia	41.068	176.583	217.651
Savona	65.463	218.677	284.140
Genova	661.827	273.905	935.732
La Spezia	99.437	126.736	226.173
Liguria	**867.795**	**795.901**	**1.663.696**
Piacenza	101.078	166.615	267.693
Parma	168.387	223.430	391.817
Reggio nell'Emilia	134.980	292.471	427.451
Modena	174.676	433.261	607.937
Bologna	390.434	515.820	906.254
Ferrara	136.215	220.786	357.001
Ravenna	136.987	213.259	350.246
Forlì	108.488	505.717	614.205
Emilia-Romagna	**1.351.245**	**2.571.359**	**3.922.604**
Massa Carrara	66.886	133.580	200.466
Lucca	85.883	290.289	376.172
Pistoia	86.577	178.925	265.502
Firenze	388.304	787.949	1.176.253
Livorno	165.682	171.736	337.418
Pisa	95.448	289.499	384.947
Arezzo	91.077	225.356	316.433
Siena	55.718	195.475	251.193
Grosseto	71.770	145.877	217.647
Toscana	**1.107.345**	**2.418.686**	**3.526.031**
Perugia	148.297	450.105	598.402
Terni	108.928	115.150	224.078
Umbria	**257.225**	**565.255**	**822.480**

Table 2. Continued

PROVINCE E REGIONI *PROVINCE AND REGION*	POPOLAZIONE - *POPULATION*		
	Comuni capoluogo *Commune of provincial capital*	Altri Comuni *Other Communes*	Totale *Total*
Pesaro-Urbino	87.703	250.561	338.264
Ancona	100.058	339.702	439.760
Macerata	42.824	254.996	297.820
Ascoli Piceno	52.852	312.335	365.187
Marche	**283.437**	**1.157.594**	**1.441.031**
Viterbo	60.159	227.635	287.794
Rieti	45.530	104.285	149.815
Roma	2.667.052	1.105.480	3.772.532
Latina	109.681	384.405	494.086
Frosinone	46.343	442.663	489.006
Lazio	**2.928.765**	**2.264.468**	**5.193.233**
L'Aquila	68.289	234.637	302.926
Teramo	52.119	233.046	285.165
Pescara	119.668	172.630	292.298
Chieti	56.444	330.861	387.305
Abruzzo	**296.520**	**971.174**	**1.267.694**
Isernia	21.106	71.220	92.326
Campobasso	51.926	187.903	239.829
Molise	**73.032**	**259.123**	**332.155**
Caserta	71.281	764.750	836.031
Benevento	63.640	232.404	296.044
Napoli	1.062.208	2.027.828	3.090.036
Avellino	55.921	385.580	441.501
Salerno	144.956	937.193	1.082.149
Campania	**1.398.006**	**4.347.755**	**5.745.761**
Foggia	155.641	543.766	699.407
Bari	337.435	1.216.743	1.554.178
Taranto	213.353	378.953	592.306
Brindisi	95.370	318.207	413.577
Lecce	100.698	715.636	816.334
Puglia	**902.497**	**3.173.305**	**4.075.802**
Potenza	65.860	336.258	402.118
Matera	55.777	152.804	208.581
Basilicata	**121.637**	**489.062**	**610.699**
Cosenza	78.858	674.399	753.257
Catanzaro	96.991	647.067	744.058
Reggio di Calabria	179.103	399.710	578.813
Calabria	**354.952**	**1.721.176**	**2.076.128**
Trapani	69.854	362.252	432.106
Palermo	693.387	547.733	1.241.120
Messina	263.982	420.139	684.121
Agrigento	55.713	421.163	476.876
Caltanissetta	62.385	219.849	282.234
Enna	28.332	158.421	186.753
Catania	337.332	738.974	1.076.306
Ragusa	68.772	227.504	296.276
Siracusa	127.588	279.317	406.905
Sicilia	**1.707.345**	**3.375.352**	**5.082.697**
Sassari	121.889	337.374	459.263
Nuoro	37.929	235.217	273.146
Cagliari	31.677	126.059	157.736
Oristano	176.236	593.085	769.321
Sardegna	**367.731**	**1.291.735**	**1.659.466**
ITALIA	**17.034.650**	**40.233.928**	**57.268.578**
NORD-CENTRO	**11.812.930**	**24.605.246**	**36.418.176**
MEZZOGIORNO	**5.221.720**	**15.628.682**	**20.850.402**

Table 3. Natural changes in the population present—Year 1994

REGIONI *REGION*	MATRIMONI *MARRIAGES* Numero *Number*	Per 1.000 ab. (b) *Per 1,000 inhabitants (b)*	NATI VIVI (a) *LIVE BIRTHS (a)* Numero *Number*	Per 1.000 ab. (b) *Per 1,000 inhabitants (b)*	MORTI (a) *DEATHS (a)* Numero *Number*	Per 1.000 ab. (b) *Per 1,000 inhabitants (b)*	Saldo movimento naturale (a) *Balance of natural changes (a)*
Piemonte	20.678	4,8	31.880	7,4	49.651	11,5	-17.771
Valle d'Aosta	585	4,9	964	8,1	1.228	10,4	-264
Lombardia	43.044	4,8	74.883	8,4	80.573	9,0	-5.690
Trentino-Alto Adige	4.658	5,1	9.588	10,6	8.170	9,0	1.418
Bolzano-Bozen	*2.334*	*5,2*	*5.125*	*11,4*	*3.668*	*8,2*	*1.457*
Trento	*2.324*	*5,1*	*4.463*	*9,7*	*4.502*	*9,8*	*-39*
Veneto	22.777	5,2	36.273	8,2	41.172	9,3	-4.899
Friuli-Venezia Giulia	5.445	4,6	8.544	7,2	14.874	12,5	-6.330
Liguria	7.666	4,6	10.776	6,5	22.802	13,7	-12.026
Emilia-Romagna	17.283	4,4	28.023	7,1	45.039	11,5	-17.016
Toscana	16.550	4,7	24.986	7,1	41.229	11,7	-16.243
Umbria	4.152	5,1	6.504	7,9	9.128	11,1	-2.624
Marche	6.735	4,7	11.475	8,0	14.816	10,3	-3.341
Lazio	24.883	4,8	48.409	9,3	46.120	8,9	2.289
Abruzzo	5.868	4,6	11.250	8,9	12.618	10,0	-1.368
Molise	1.566	4,7	2.919	8,8	3.318	10,0	-399
Campania	35.650	6,2	73.216	12,8	44.814	7,8	28.402
Puglia	23.773	5,8	45.659	11,2	31.527	7,7	14.132
Basilicata	3.033	5,0	5.612	9,2	5.136	8,4	476
Calabria	10.782	5,2	21.681	10,4	16.962	8,2	4.719
Sicilia	28.202	5,6	60.119	11,9	45.384	9,0	14.735
Sardegna	8.277	5,0	14.645	8,8	13.520	8,2	1.125
ITALIA	**291.607**	**5,1**	**527.406**	**9,2**	**548.081**	**9,6**	**-20.675**
NORD-CENTRO	**174.456**	**4,8**	**292.305**	**8,0**	**374.802**	**10,3**	**-82.497**
MEZZOGIORNO	**117.151**	**5,6**	**235.101**	**11,3**	**173.279**	**8,3**	**61.822**

(a) Dati provvisori ottenuti sulla base di modelli riepilogativi del Movimento naturale della popolazione presente mensile. - (b) Rispetto all'ammontare medio annuo della popolazione residente anagrafica. - *(a) Provisional data obtained based on summary models of monthly natural changes in the population present. - (b) Compared to the total average annual resident population registered.*

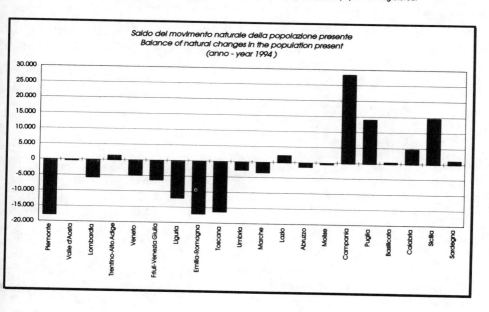

Saldo del movimento naturale della popolazione presente
Balance of natural changes in the population present
(anno - year 1994)

Table 4. Marriages, legal separations and divorces—Year 1994

REGIONI REGION	MATRIMONI MARRIAGES		SEPARAZIONI LEGALI LEGAL SEPARATIONS		DIVORZI DIVORCES		
	Totale Total	Rito religioso sul totale % % with religious ceremony	Totale Total	per 100.000 ab. per 100,000 inhabitants	Totale Total	per 100.000 ab. per 100,000 inhabitants	Per cessazione degli effetti civili % sul totale (a) % of total by cessation of civil effects (a)
Piemonte	20.678	77,7	5.029	116,9	2.882	67,0	85,3
Valle d'Aosta	585	72,3	158	133,5	68	57,5	79,4
Lombardia	43.044	79,6	8.857	99,5	5.515	61,9	80,0
Trentino-Alto Adige	4.658	67,6	960	105,9	610	67,3	75,6
Bolzano-Bozen	2.334	57,7	524	117,0	308	68,8	74,0
Trento	2.324	77,4	436	95,1	302	65,9	77,2
Veneto	22.777	80,6	3.857	87,3	1.594	36,1	79,1
Friuli-Venezia Giulia	5.445	65,3	1.357	113,8	610	51,2	73,4
Liguria	7.666	71,2	2.642	158,9	1.664	100,0	78,8
Emilia-Romagna	17.283	73,8	4.590	117,0	2.764	70,4	79,2
Toscana	16.550	74,7	3.806	107,9	2.028	57,5	75,1
Umbria	4.152	82,7	706	86,0	330	40,2	89,7
Marche	6.735	85,3	926	64,3	474	32,9	83,5
Lazio	24.883	74,8	6.664	128,4	3.552	68,4	78,5
Abruzzo	5.868	87,5	651	51,4	293	23,2	85,7
Molise	1.566	91,4	134	40,4	43	12,9	86,0
Campania	35.650	84,3	3.133	54,7	1.438	25,1	72,6
Puglia	23.773	91,3	2.281	56,0	1.100	27,0	91,5
Basilicata	3.033	93,4	177	29,0	87	14,2	92,6
Calabria	10.782	91,5	854	41,1	415	20,0	87,7
Sicilia	28.202	86,7	3.356	66,4	1.580	31,3	87,0
Sardegna	8.277	76,4	1.307	78,8	463	27,9	83,8
ITALIA	**291.607**	**80,9**	**51.445**	**90,0**	**27.510**	**48,1**	**80,5**
NORD-CENTRO	**174.456**	**76,9**	**39.552**	**108,7**	**22.091**	**60,7**	**79,7**
MEZZOGIORNO	**117.151**	**86,8**	**11.893**	**57,3**	**5.419**	**26,1**	**83,9**

(a) Trattasi di scioglimenti relativi a matrimoni celebrati con il rito concordatario. - *(a) By mutual consent.*

Table 5. Voluntary induced abortions—Year 1994

		QUOZIENTI - *RATES*	
REGIONI	Dati assoluti	Per 1.000 nati vivi	Per 1.000 donne (15-49 anni)
REGION	*Absolute data*	*Per 1,000 live births*	*Per 1,000 women (aged 15-49)*
Piemonte	11.256	345,1	10,8
Valle d'Aosta	287	281,6	9,9
Lombardia	17.081	221,5	7,5
Trentino-Alto Adige	1.570	161,0	6,9
Bolzano-Bozen	*413*	*80,8*	*3,6*
Trento	*1.157*	*249,0*	*10,2*
Veneto	5.405	129,8	4,8
Friuli-Venezia Giulia	2.434	274,6	8,4
Liguria	4.018	373,7	10,5
Emilia-Romagna	11.041	380,2	11,8
Toscana	9.601	373,9	11,3
Umbria	2.614	395,9	13,6
Marche	2.541	217,7	7,4
Lazio	12.581	255,2	9,3
Abruzzo	2.905	254,0	9,5
Molise	1.133	396,8	14,4
Campania	10.331	136,6	6,9
Puglia	16.099	347,0	15,1
Basilicata	818	141,4	5,4
Calabria	2.706	124,5	5,2
Sicilia	7.829	130,9	6,1
Sardegna	2.084	141,2	4,7
ITALIA	**124.334**	**231,7**	**8,6**
NORD-CENTRO	**88.429**	**275,9**	**8,9**
MEZZOGIORNO	**43.905**	**185,0**	**8,2**

(a) I dati relativi all'anno 1994 sono provvisori. - *(a) Data relating to year 1994 are provisional.*

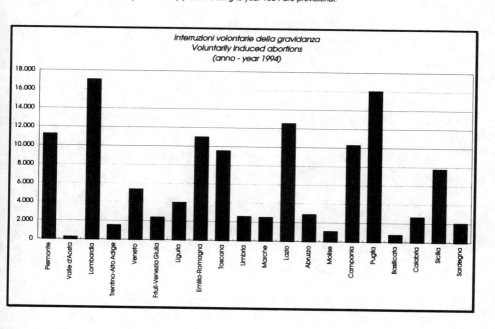

Table 6. Newspapers and other periodicals by region in which published—Year 1994

REGIONI *REGION*	Quotidiani *Dailies*	Settimanali *Weeklies*	Altra periodicità *Other frequency*	Totale *Total*
Piemonte	7	87	1.050	1.144
Valle d'Aosta	-	5	10	15
Lombardia	23	136	1.878	2.037
Trentino-Alto Adige	4	20	573	597
Bolzano-Bozen	*3*	*13*	*236*	*252*
Trento	*1*	*7*	*337*	*345*
Veneto	13	44	843	900
Friuli-Venezia Giulia	6	24	370	400
Liguria	4	15	241	260
Emilia-Romagna	9	68	1.314	1.391
Toscana	6	43	912	961
Umbria	2	5	56	63
Marche	1	11	235	247
Lazio	29	73	1.210	1.312
Abruzzo	1	6	94	101
Molise	-	3	23	26
Campania	4	15	217	236
Puglia	5	14	136	155
Basilicata	-	8	29	37
Calabria	1	11	44	56
Sicilia	3	24	216	243
Sardegna	2	9	64	75
ITALIA	**120**	**621**	**9.515**	**10.256**
NORD	**66**	**399**	**6.279**	**6.744**
CENTRO	**38**	**132**	**2.413**	**2.583**
MEZZOGIORNO	**16**	**90**	**823**	**929**

Table 7. Private expenditure for public performances, sporting events and other entertainment (a)—Year 1994 (overall expenditure in millions of lira, per inhabitant in lira)

REGIONI REGION	SPESA DEL PUBBLICO PRIVATE EXPENDITURE		COMPOSIZIONE PERCENTUALE PERCENTAGE COMPOSITION				
	Totale	Per abitante (b)	Teatro di prosa e dialettale	Lirica e balletti, concerti di musica classica	Operetta, rivista e commedia musicale	Concerti e spettacoli di musica leggera	Burattini e marionette, saggi culturali
	Total	Per inhabitant (b)	Theatres	Opera, ballet and classical music concerts	Light opera, reviews, musical comedy	Popular music concerts and performances	Puppets, marionettes, cultural events
Piemonte	376.667	87.638	3,8	3,9	0,6	3,2	0,2
Valle d'Aosta	12.516	105.658	2,2	0,5	0,2	1,3	-
Lombardia	838.971	94.156	4,9	5,3	1,1	3,5	0,2
Trentino-Alto Adige	74.856	82.380	5,4	2,5	0,5	5,1	0,2
Bolzano-Bozen	40.285	89.711	6,0	3,2	0,5	7,0	0,2
Trento	34.571	75.218	4,8	1,6	0,5	2,8	0,2
Veneto	459.257	103.850	3,7	9,2	0,3	1,5	0,1
Friuli-Venezia Giulia	96.444	80.960	5,3	4,1	0,7	4,6	0,2
Liguria	169.439	101.845	6,1	5,4	0,9	2,9	0,1
Emilia-Romagna	646.088	164.709	3,5	2,6	0,5	2,2	0,1
Toscana	389.149	110.364	4,1	3,2	0,6	1,9	0,1
Umbria	66.699	81.095	5,1	4,6	0,4	1,2	0,3
Marche	122.100	84.731	3,6	3,9	0,5	1,9	0,2
Lazio	408.534	78.667	7,8	4,6	2,3	3,4	0,1
Abruzzo	77.071	60.796	3,4	1,4	0,2	1,8	0,1
Molise	8.856	26.663	3,7	1,2	0,3	1,6	0,1
Campania	210.446	36.626	7,4	3,4	1,0	4,3	0,3
Puglia	146.228	35.877	3,9	1,5	0,6	2,7	0,1
Basilicata	15.628	25.590	4,5	1,5	0,3	2,1	..
Calabria	58.124	27.996	3,0	1,3	0,1	2,0	0,3
Sicilia	198.270	39.009	8,1	3,5	1,0	2,9	0,2
Sardegna	100.617	60.632	2,1	1,8	0,4	2,2	0,2
ITALIA	**4.475.959**	**78.157**	**4,8**	**4,3**	**0,8**	**2,8**	**0,1**
NORD	**2.674.237**	**105.138**	**4,3**	**5,0**	**0,7**	**2,8**	**0,1**
CENTRO	**986.482**	**89.821**	**5,6**	**4,0**	**1,3**	**2,5**	**0,1**
MEZZOGIORNO	**815.239**	**39.099**	**5,5**	**2,5**	**0,7**	**2,9**	**0,2**

(a) Fonte SIAE-Società Italiana Autori ed Editori: Annuario "Lo spettacolo in Italia" - Anno 1994. - (b) Dati calcolati sulla popolazione residente al 31 dicembre 1994. - (a) Source SIAE- Italian Authors and Publishers Society: Yearbook "Public Performances in Italy" - Year 1994. - (b) Data calculated using the resident population on December 31, 1994.

Spesa del pubblico per spettacoli, manifestazioni
sportive e trattenimenti vari
Private expenditure for public performances, sporting
events and other entertainment

(anno - year 1994)

A Teatro di prosa e dialettale
Theatres

B Lirica e balletti, concerti di musica classica
Opera, ballet and classical music

C Operetta, rivista e commedia musicale
Light opera, reviews, musical comedy

D Concerti e spettacoli di musica leggera
Popular music concerts and performances

E Burattini e marionette saggi culturali
Puppets, marionettes and cultural events

F Cinematografo
Cinema

G Calcio (Div. Naz.serie A B)
Football (1st and 2nd division)

H Altre manifestazioni sportive
Other sporting events

I Ballo e concertini
Dance halls, other musical events

J App. da divertim., biliardi, juke-boxes
Entertainment equip., billiards, juke-boxes

K Altri
Other

Table 7. Continued

SEGUE: COMPOSIZIONE PERCENTUALE - *CONTINUED: PERCENTAGE COMPOSITION*

REGIONI / *REGION*	Cinema-tografo / *Cinema*	Calcio (Div. Naz. serie A B) / *Football (1st and 2nd divisions)*	Altre mani-festazioni sportive / *Other sporting events*	Ballo e concertini / *Dance halls, other musical events*	Apparecchi da divertimento, biliardi, juke-boxes / *Entertainment equipment, billiards, juke-boxes*	Al... / *Oth...*
Piemonte	19,6	8,9	3,7	32,0	10,2	13
Valle d'Aosta	11,8	-	4,5	52,5	13,5	13
Lombardia	19,5	11,3	5,6	26,6	10,0	12
Trentino-Alto Adige	12,9	-	9,1	36,9	15,1	12
Bolzano-Bozen	*9,8*	-	*12,9*	*36,0*	*11,1*	*13*
Trento	*16,5*	-	*4,8*	*38,0*	*19,8*	*11*
Veneto	13,1	4,1	4,2	24,8	11,4	27
Friuli-Venezia Giulia	17,8	10,2	7,5	20,0	12,1	17
Liguria	21,0	13,9	2,3	21,7	11,9	13
Emilia-Romagna	15,9	7,4	9,2	31,2	9,5	17
Toscana	19,9	6,3	9,6	30,2	11,9	12
Umbria	16,0	4,1	10,7	29,3	13,5	14
Marche	17,6	4,4	9,0	31,0	16,5	11
Lazio	26,9	15,0	5,1	11,3	10,8	12
Abruzzo	15,0	3,8	7,9	24,5	21,4	20
Molise	9,4	-	5,9	14,1	33,9	29
Campania	18,2	11,8	7,6	11,2	16,6	18
Puglia	17,6	15,8	3,9	14,4	20,1	19
Basilicata	13,8	-	13,4	10,6	33,8	20
Calabria	13,3	4,0	9,8	12,7	25,0	28
Sicilia	20,7	5,3	4,9	16,4	19,1	17
Sardegna	12,1	9,8	5,3	23,5	14,8	27
ITALIA	**18,4**	**8,8**	**6,4**	**24,6**	**12,5**	**16**
NORD	**17,4**	**8,6**	**5,9**	**28,0**	**10,5**	**16**
CENTRO	**22,3**	**9,5**	**7,7**	**22,4**	**12,1**	**12**
MEZZOGIORNO	**17,1**	**9,0**	**6,3**	**16,0**	**19,2**	**20**

(a) Cfr. corrispondente nota a pagina precedente. - *(a) See note on previous page.*

Table 8. Population by sex and condition (a)—Year 1995—Average of the four surveys (absolute data in thousands)

REGIONI / REGION	FORZE DI LAVORO - LABOUR FORCE		NON FORZE DI LAVORO - NON-LABOUR FORCE IN ETÀ LAVORATIVA OF WORKING AGE			Totale / Total	% sulle forze di lavoro (b) / % of the labour force (b)
	Totale / Total	% sulla popolazione / % of population	Totale / Total	di cui: disposte a lavorare / of whom: willing to work	In età non lavorativa / of non-working age		
FEMMINE - FEMALES							
Piemonte	743	38,6	918	23	517	1.435	193,1
Valle d'Aosta	23	42,3	22	0	14	36	156,5
Lombardia	1.538	38,6	1.908	42	1.093	3.001	195,1
Trentino-Alto Adige	157	40,6	179	2	121	300	191,1
Bolzano-Bozen	81	43,1	83	0	61	144	177,8
Trento	76	38,2	96	2	60	156	205,3
Veneto	726	37,3	966	20	545	1.511	208,1
Friuli-Venezia Giulia	202	36,6	253	5	159	412	204,0
Liguria	252	32,5	379	10	233	611	242,5
Emilia-Romagna	752	41,8	746	16	505	1.252	166,5
Toscana	607	37,8	727	30	474	1.201	197,9
Umbria	126	34,4	183	9	109	292	231,7
Marche	243	38,0	296	13	195	491	202,1
Lazio	760	33,5	1.264	53	618	1.883	247,8
Abruzzo	178	32,8	293	16	172	465	261,2
Molise	48	33,1	73	6	47	120	250,0
Campania	677	29,2	1.390	103	829	2.219	327,8
Puglia	434	25,7	1.073	55	563	1.636	377,0
Basilicata	74	29,8	149	17	83	232	313,5
Calabria	257	30,6	482	47	299	781	303,9
Sicilia	487	23,3	1.361	87	724	2.085	428,1
Sardegna	207	29,8	420	19	207	627	302,9
ITALIA	**8.490**	**34,2**	**13.083**	**572**	**7.508**	**20.591**	**242,5**
NORD-CENTRO	**6.128**	**37,6**	**7.842**	**223**	**4.583**	**12.425**	**202,8**
MEZZOGIORNO	**2.362**	**27,6**	**5.241**	**349**	**2.925**	**8.166**	**345,7**
MASCHI E FEMMINE - MALES AND FEMALES							
Piemonte	1.839	49,4	1.448	36	956	2.404	130,7
Valle d'Aosta	54	52,9	36	0	26	62	114,8
Lombardia	3.904	51,1	2.953	62	1.964	4.917	125,9
Trentino-Alto Adige	402	53,5	271	3	223	493	122,6
Bolzano-Bozen	205	56,2	124	0	114	237	115,6
Trento	197	51,0	147	2	109	256	129,9
Veneto	1.910	50,7	1.457	28	997	2.454	128,5
Friuli-Venezia Giulia	499	47,9	400	8	277	678	135,9
Liguria	650	44,0	592	15	403	995	152,8
Emilia-Romagna	1.780	51,5	1.190	22	915	2.105	118,3
Toscana	1.488	48,4	1.144	43	857	2.001	134,5
Umbria	329	46,5	284	12	202	486	147,7
Marche	602	48,8	466	19	361	827	137,1
Lazio	2.063	47,3	1.885	93	1.176	3.061	148,3
Abruzzo	488	46,3	443	24	326	769	157,3
Molise	127	46,0	112	9	90	202	160,3
Campania	2.011	44,6	2.088	211	1.607	3.695	183,8
Puglia	1.378	42,4	1.566	98	1.090	2.656	192,6
Basilicata	212	43,3	228	29	164	392	184,0
Calabria	716	43,8	749	86	578	1.327	185,3
Sicilia	1.663	41,3	1.954	164	1.405	3.359	201,9
Sardegna	618	45,4	620	33	404	1.024	165,4
ITALIA	**22.734**	**47,4**	**19.886**	**995**	**14.021**	**33.906**	**149,1**
NORD-CENTRO	**15.522**	**49,5**	**12.126**	**340**	**8.358**	**20.483**	**132,0**
MEZZOGIORNO	**7.212**	**43,4**	**7.760**	**654**	**5.663**	**13.422**	**186,0**

(a), (b) Cfr. corrispondenti note a pagina precedente. - (a), (b) See corresponding notes from previous page.

Table 8. Continued

REGIONI / REGION	FORZE DI LAVORO - *LABOUR FORCE*		NON FORZE DI LAVORO - *NON-LABOUR FORCE* IN ETÀ LAVORATIVA *OF WORKING AGE*					
	Totale / Total	% / % of population	Totale sulla popolazione / Total	di cui: disposte a lavorare / of whom: willing to work	In età non lavo- rativa / non-working age	Totale / Total	% sulle forze di lavoro (b) / % of the labour force (b)	
MASCHI - *MALES*								
Piemonte	1.096	60,9	529	12	439	969	88,4	
Valle d'Aosta	32	64,0	14	0	12	26	81,3	
Lombardia	2.366	64,4	1.045	20	871	1.916	81,0	
Trentino-Alto Adige	245	67,3	92	1	102	193	78,8	
Bolzano-Bozen	*124*	*70,1*	*41*	*0*	*52*	*93*	*75,0*	
Trento	*121*	*64,7*	*51*	*1*	*49*	*100*	*82,6*	
Veneto	1.184	65,1	492	8	451	943	79,6	
Friuli-Venezia Giulia	297	60,5	147	3	118	265	89,2	
Liguria	398	57,1	213	6	170	384	96,5	
Emilia-Romagna	1.029	61,9	443	6	410	853	82,9	
Toscana	881	60,0	417	13	383	800	90,8	
Umbria	203	59,4	100	3	93	194	95,6	
Marche	359	60,4	170	6	166	336	93,6	
Lazio	1.303	62,3	621	40	558	1.179	90,5	
Abruzzo	309	60,7	149	8	154	304	98,4	
Molise	78	59,9	39	4	43	82	105,1	
Campania	1.334	60,8	698	108	778	1.476	110,6	
Puglia	944	60,5	493	43	527	1.020	108,1	
Basilicata	138	57,5	80	12	80	160	115,9	
Calabria	459	57,7	267	39	279	546	119,0	
Sicilia	1.176	60,6	592	77	681	1.274	108,3	
Sardegna	412	61,8	200	14	197	396	96,1	
ITALIA	**14.244**	**61,7**	**6.803**	**423**	**6.512**	**13.315**	**93,5**	
NORD-CENTRO	**9.394**	**62,4**	**4.284**	**117**	**3.775**	**8.058**	**85,8**	
MEZZOGIORNO	**4.850**	**60,3**	**2.519**	**306**	**2.738**	**5.256**	**108,4**	

(a) Risultati delle indagini sulle forze di lavoro effettuate trimestralmente dall'ISTAT su un campione di famiglie. Per le definizioni e le classificazioni: cfr."Collana d'informazione - Rilevazione delle forze di lavoro" (risultati trimestrali e media annua). - (b) La percentuale esprime il numero medio di persone non attive su 100 persone attive. Poichè gli arrotondamenti sono stati effettuati direttamente dal computer, uno stesso aggregato puo' presentare cifre diverse (qualche unità di migliaia o qualche decimo di punto di percentuale in piu o in meno) da tavola a tavola: inoltre,nell'ambito di ciascuna tavola, non sempre si trova realizzata la quadratura orizzontale o verticale.
(a) Results from the labour force surveys performed quarterly by ISTAT covering a sample of households. For the definitions and classifications see "Information series - Labour force survey" (quarterly results and annual average). - (b) The percentage indicates the average number of non-active persons per 100 active persons. As rounding has been carried out directly by computer, the same aggregate may be indicated by a different figure (sometimes a few thousands or decimal points more or less) in the various tables furthermore, column and line totals do not necessarily balance in each of the separate tables.

Table 9. Employment by sector of economic activity and professional position (a)—Year 1995 Average of the four surveys (absolute data in thousands)

REGIONI / REGION	SETTORI DI ATTIVITÀ ECONOMICA / SECTOR OF ECONOMIC ACTIVITY				POSIZIONI NELLA PROFESSIONE / PROFESSIONAL POSITION	
	Totale / Total	Agricoltura / Agriculture	Industria / Industry	Altre Attività / Other activity	Indipendenti / Self-employed	Dipendenti / Employees
MASCHI - MALES						
Piemonte	1.037	54	505	478	325	712
Valle d'Aosta	30	3	10	17	11	20
Lombardia	2.266	80	1.118	1.068	678	1.588
Trentino-Alto Adige	237	26	87	124	76	161
Bolzano-Bozen	121	17	43	60	40	81
Trento	117	9	44	63	36	80
Veneto	1.142	73	512	557	377	765
Friuli-Venezia Giulia	284	15	115	154	84	200
Liguria	362	15	119	228	115	248
Emilia-Romagna	993	91	414	488	382	611
Toscana	835	39	343	454	289	547
Umbria	191	14	75	102	58	132
Marche	343	27	142	174	121	222
Lazio	1.176	52	312	812	327	848
Abruzzo	291	22	110	158	96	195
Molise	69	9	25	35	25	45
Campania	1.058	87	305	666	324	734
Puglia	820	98	249	473	248	571
Basilicata	120	15	47	58	37	83
Calabria	375	49	95	230	110	265
Sicilia	957	135	238	583	303	653
Sardegna	347	51	113	183	118	229
ITALIA	**12.933**	**956**	**4.934**	**7.043**	**4.104**	**8.829**
NORD-CENTRO	**8.897**	**489**	**3.752**	**4.656**	**2.843**	**6.054**
MEZZOGIORNO	**4.036**	**467**	**1.183**	**2.387**	**1.261**	**2.775**
FEMMINE - FEMALES						
Piemonte	647	34	183	430	155	492
Valle d'Aosta	21	1	2	18	6	14
Lombardia	1.397	40	441	916	274	1.123
Trentino-Alto Adige	147	10	20	118	33	114
Bolzano-Bozen	78	7	10	61	19	59
Trento	69	3	9	57	15	55
Veneto	661	33	216	411	142	518
Friuli-Venezia Giulia	178	9	37	132	38	140
Liguria	212	10	25	177	60	152
Emilia-Romagna	679	52	173	455	170	509
Toscana	526	22	132	371	150	376
Umbria	106	7	23	77	28	79
Marche	219	17	71	131	59	160
Lazio	624	29	64	532	133	491
Abruzzo	151	15	31	104	50	101
Molise	36	9	3	24	16	21
Campania	445	83	55	307	115	330
Puglia	327	63	45	220	73	254
Basilicata	54	14	6	34	18	36
Calabria	174	43	7	123	38	136
Sicilia	331	33	15	282	73	258
Sardegna	141	12	10	119	36	105
ITALIA	**7.077**	**534**	**1.560**	**4.982**	**1.667**	**5.409**
NORD-CENTRO	**5.417**	**262**	**1.387**	**3.769**	**1.249**	**4.168**
MEZZOGIORNO	**1.660**	**273**	**173**	**1.213**	**418**	**1.241**

Table 9. Continued

REGIONI REGION	SETTORI DI ATTIVITÀ ECONOMICA *SECTOR OF ECONOMIC ACTIVITY*			POSIZIONI NELLA PROFESSIONE *PROFESSIONAL POSITION*		
	Totale *Total*	Agricoltura *Agriculture*	Industria *Industry*	Altre Attività *Other activity*	Indipendenti *Self-employed*	Dipendenti *Employees*
MASCHI E FEMMINE - *MALES AND FEMALES*						
Piemonte	1.684	88	688	908	480	1.204
Valle d'Aosta	51	4	12	35	17	34
Lombardia	3.663	120	1.559	1.984	952	2.711
Trentino-Alto Adige	385	36	107	242	109	275
Bolzano-Bozen	*199*	*24*	*53*	*122*	*58*	*141*
Trento	*186*	*12*	*54*	*121*	*51*	*135*
Veneto	1.802	106	728	968	520	1.283
Friuli-Venezia Giulia	462	24	152	286	122	340
Liguria	574	24	145	405	174	400
Emilia-Romagna	1.672	142	587	943	552	1.120
Toscana	1.361	61	475	825	438	923
Umbria	297	21	97	179	86	211
Marche	562	43	213	306	180	382
Lazio	1.800	81	376	1.344	461	1.339
Abruzzo	442	37	142	263	146	296
Molise	106	18	29	59	41	65
Campania	1.503	170	361	973	439	1.064
Puglia	1.147	161	293	693	321	826
Basilicata	174	29	53	91	55	119
Calabria	548	92	102	354	147	401
Sicilia	1.288	169	253	866	376	911
Sardegna	488	63	123	302	154	334
ITALIA	**20.010**	**1.490**	**6.494**	**12.025**	**5.771**	**14.239**
NORD-CENTRO	**14.314**	**751**	**5.138**	**8.425**	**4.092**	**10.222**
MEZZOGIORNO	**5.696**	**739**	**1.356**	**3.600**	**1.679**	**4.017**

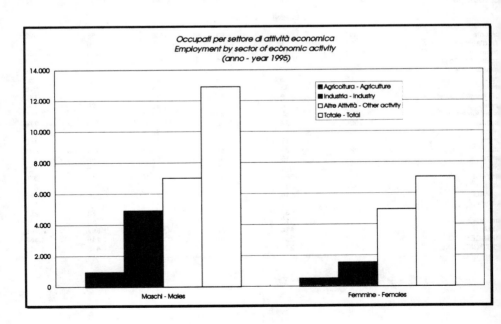

Occupati per settore di attività economica
Employment by sector of economic activity
(anno - year 1995)

Table 9. Continued

REGIONI *REGION*	SETTORI DI ATTIVITÀ ECONOMICA *SECTOR OF ECONOMIC ACTIVITY*			POSIZIONI NELLA PROFESSIONE *PROFESSIONAL POSITION*		
	Totale *Total*	Agricoltura *Agriculture*	Industria *Industry*	Altre Attività *Other activity*	Indipendenti *Self-employed*	Dipendenti *Employees*
MASCHI - *MALES*						
Piemonte	100,0	5,2	48,6	46,2	31,3	68,7
Valle d'Aosta	100,0	10,0	33,2	56,8	36,7	63,3
Lombardia	100,0	3,5	49,3	47,2	29,9	70,1
Trentino-Alto Adige	100,0	11,0	36,7	52,3	31,9	68,1
Bolzano-Bozen	*100,0*	*14,3*	*35,5*	*50,2*	*33,1*	*66,9*
Trento	*100,0*	*8,0*	*37,5*	*54,5*	*31,0*	*69,0*
Veneto	100,0	6,4	44,8	48,8	33,0	67,0
Friuli-Venezia Giulia	100,0	5,3	40,5	54,2	29,6	70,4
Liguria	100,0	4,1	32,9	63,0	31,8	68,2
Emilia-Romagna	100,0	9,2	41,7	49,1	38,5	61,5
Toscana	100,0	4,7	41,1	54,2	34,6	65,4
Umbria	100,0	7,3	39,3	53,4	30,4	69,6
Marche	100,0	7,9	41,4	50,7	35,3	64,7
Lazio	100,0	4,4	26,5	69,1	27,8	72,2
Abruzzo	100,0	7,6	37,8	54,6	33,0	67,0
Molise	100,0	13,0	36,2	50,8	36,2	63,8
Campania	100,0	8,2	28,9	62,9	30,6	69,4
Puglia	100,0	12,0	30,4	57,6	30,2	69,8
Basilicata	100,0	12,5	39,2	48,3	30,8	69,2
Calabria	100,0	13,1	25,3	61,6	29,3	70,7
Sicilia	100,0	14,1	24,9	61,0	31,7	68,3
Sardegna	100,0	14,7	32,8	52,5	34,0	66,0
ITALIA	**100,0**	**7,4**	**38,2**	**54,4**	**31,7**	**68,3**
NORD-CENTRO	**100,0**	**5,5**	**42,2**	**52,3**	**32,0**	**68,0**
MEZZOGIORNO	**100,0**	**11,6**	**29,3**	**59,1**	**31,2**	**68,8**

Table 9. Continued

REGIONI REGION	SETTORI DI ATTIVITÀ ECONOMICA SECTOR OF ECONOMIC ACTIVITY			POSIZIONI NELLA PROFESSIONE PROFESSIONAL POSITION		
	Totale Total	Agricoltura Agriculture	Industria Industry	Altre Attività Other activity	Indipendenti Self-employed	Dipendenti Employees
FEMMINE - *FEMALES*						
Piemonte	100,0	5.3	28,3	66,4	24,0	76,0
Valle d'Aosta	100,0	4,8	9,5	85,7	28,6	71,4
Lombardia	100,0	2,9	31,6	65,5	19,6	80,4
Trentino-Alto Adige	100,0	6,8	13,5	79,7	22,4	77,6
Bolzano-Bozen	*100,0*	*9,0*	*12,8*	*78,2*	*23,1*	*76,9*
Trento	*100,0*	*4,3*	*14,4*	*81,3*	*21,7*	*78,3*
Veneto	100,0	5,0	32,7	62,3	21,7	78,3
Friuli-Venezia Giulia	100,0	5,1	20,8	74,1	21,3	78,7
Liguria	100,0	4,2	12,2	83,6	27,8	72,2
Emilia-Romagna	100,0	7,5	25,5	67,0	25,0	75,0
Toscana	100,0	4,2	25,1	70,7	28,3	71,7
Umbria	100,0	6,6	20,8	72,6	26,4	73,6
Marche	100,0	7,3	32,4	60,3	26,9	73,1
Lazio	100,0	4,6	10,3	85,1	21,5	78,5
Abruzzo	100,0	9,9	21,2	68,9	33,1	66,9
Molise	100,0	24,2	10,8	65,0	43,2	56,8
Campania	100,0	18,7	12,5	68,8	25,8	74,2
Puglia	100,0	19,3	13,5	67,2	22,3	77,7
Basilicata	100,0	26,3	11,6	62,1	33,3	66,7
Calabria	100,0	24,9	4,0	71,1	21,3	78,7
Sicilia	100,0	10,3	4,5	85,2	22,1	77,9
Sardegna	100,0	8,4	7,2	84,4	25,5	74,5
ITALIA	**100,0**	**7,5**	**22,0**	**70,5**	**23,6**	**76,4**
NORD-CENTRO	**100,0**	**4,8**	**25,6**	**69,6**	**23,1**	**76,9**
MEZZOGIORNO	**100,0**	**16,4**	**10,4**	**73,2**	**25,2**	**74,8**
MASCHI E FEMMINE - *MALES AND FEMALES*						
Piemonte	100,0	5,2	40,9	53,9	28,5	71,5
Valle d'Aosta	100,0	7,8	23,6	68,6	33,3	66,7
Lombardia	100,0	3,3	42,6	54,1	26,0	74,0
Trentino-Alto Adige	100,0	9,4	27,8	62,8	28,3	71,7
Bolzano-Bozen	*100,0*	*12,0*	*26,5*	*61,5*	*29,0*	*71,0*
Trento	*100,0*	*6,7*	*29,2*	*64,1*	*27,5*	*72,5*
Veneto	100,0	5,9	40,4	53,7	28,9	71,1
Friuli-Venezia Giulia	100,0	5,2	32,9	61,9	26,4	73,6
Liguria	100,0	4,2	25,3	70,5	30,3	69,7
Emilia-Romagna	100,0	8,5	35,1	56,4	33,0	67,0
Toscana	100,0	4,5	34,9	60,6	32,2	67,8
Umbria	100,0	7,1	32,7	60,2	29,0	71,0
Marche	100,0	7,7	37,9	54,4	32,0	68,0
Lazio	100,0	4,5	20,9	74,6	25,6	74,4
Abruzzo	100,0	8,4	32,1	59,5	33,0	67,0
Molise	100,0	17,0	27,4	55,6	38,7	61,3
Campania	100,0	11,3	24,0	64,7	29,2	70,8
Puglia	100,0	14,0	25,5	60,5	28,0	72,0
Basilicata	100,0	16,7	30,7	52,6	31,6	68,4
Calabria	100,0	16,8	18,6	64,6	26,8	73,2
Sicilia	100,0	13,1	19,6	67,3	29,2	70,8
Sardegna	100,0	12,9	25,4	61,7	31,6	68,4
ITALIA	**100,0**	**7,4**	**32,5**	**60,1**	**28,8**	**71,2**
NORD-CENTRO	**100,0**	**5,2**	**35,9**	**58,9**	**28,6**	**71,4**
MEZZOGIORNO	**100,0**	**13,0**	**23,8**	**63,2**	**29,5**	**70,5**

Table 10. Persons seeking employment by sex and condition—Year 1995—Average of the four surveys (absolute data in thousands)

REGIONI / REGION	Maschi / Males	Femmine / Females	N. / Number	% sulle forze di lavoro / % of labour force	Disoccupati / Unemployed	Persone in cerca di 1° occupazione / Persons seeking first job	Altre persone in cerca di lavoro / Other persons seeking employment
Piemonte	59	96	155	8,4	67	54	35
Valle d'Aosta	1	2	3	5,6	2	1	1
Lombardia	100	141	241	6,2	103	81	58
Trentino-Alto Adige	8	9	17	4,2	6	2	9
Bolzano-Bozen	3	3	6	2,9	2	1	3
Trento	5	7	11	5,6	4	1	6
Veneto	42	65	107	5,6	49	30	29
Friuli-Venezia Giulia	13	24	37	7,4	17	10	10
Liguria	35	40	76	11,7	31	32	13
Emilia-Romagna	36	72	108	6,1	60	24	25
Toscana	46	81	127	8,5	55	42	30
Umbria	12	20	32	9,7	13	12	7
Marche	16	24	40	6,6	17	14	9
Lazio	128	135	263	12,7	87	123	53
Abruzzo	19	27	46	9,4	17	18	11
Molise	9	12	21	16,5	6	9	6
Campania	276	231	508	25,3	120	289	99
Puglia	124	107	231	16,8	81	106	94
Basilicata	19	20	38	17,9	19	14	5
Calabria	84	83	167	23,3	56	73	39
Sicilia	219	157	376	21,5	143	172	61
Sardegna	65	66	130	21,0	56	47	27
ITALIA	**1.311**	**1.414**	**2.725**	**12,0**	**1005**	**1.150**	**570**
NORD-CENTRO	**497**	**711**	**1.208**	**7,8**	**506**	**423**	**279**
MEZZOGIORNO	**814**	**702**	**1.517**	**21,0**	**449**	**727**	**291**

Column group headers: SESSO - SEX / MASCHI E FEMMINE / MALES AND FEMALES (covering Maschi, Femmine, N., % columns); CONDIZIONI - CONDITION (covering Disoccupati, Persone in cerca di 1° occupazione, Altre persone in cerca di lavoro).

Table 11. Value of household consumption (a)—Year 1994

REGIONI *REGION*	Consumi alimentari *Foodstuffs consumption*	Consumi non alimentari *Non-foodstuffs consumption*	Totale *Tota*
MEDIA ANNUALE PER FAMIGLIA - Lire - *ANNUAL AVERAGE PER HOUSEHOLD*			
Piemonte	7.782.576	31.048.431	38.831.007
Valle d'Aosta	7.649.015	28.054.390	35.703.405
Lombardia	8.294.757	36.108.068	44.402.825
Trentino-Alto Adige	7.615.513	31.090.683	38.706.196
Bolzano-Bozen	*7.646.029*	*30.918.970*	*38.564.999*
Trento	*7.589.034*	*31.239.678*	*38.828.712*
Veneto	8.431.706	35.398.469	43.830.174
Friuli-Venezia Giulia	7.749.443	29.445.844	37.195.287
Liguria	8.133.587	27.024.049	35.157.636
Emilia-Romagna	8.031.938	33.843.523	41.875.461
Toscana	8.354.799	31.215.843	39.570.642
Umbria	8.258.341	29.585.929	37.844.270
Marche	8.407.256	28.894.267	37.301.523
Lazio	7.833.313	29.332.619	37.165.931
Abruzzo	7.264.442	23.108.765	30.373.207
Molise	8.188.895	24.338.190	32.527.085
Campania	8.045.715	20.873.938	28.919.652
Puglia	8.373.875	23.653.209	32.027.084
Basilicata	6.285.976	19.832.295	26.118.271
Calabria	7.603.689	20.973.334	28.577.023
Sicilia	7.468.345	20.955.847	28.424.191
Sardegna	8.239.804	22.695.330	30.935.134
ITALIA	**8.021.688**	**28.953.625**	**36.975.314**
NORD-CENTRO	**8.115.542**	**32.492.335**	**40.607.877**
MEZZOGIORNO	**7.830.956**	**21.762.161**	**29.593.117**

(a) Cfr. corrispondente nota a pagina 79. - *(a) See note on page 79.*

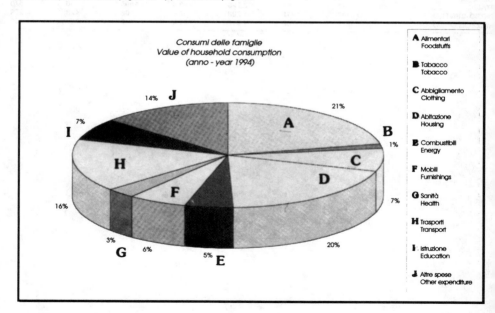

Consumi delle famiglie
Value of household consumption
(anno - year 1994)

14% **J**   21%
7%   **I**   **A**   **B**   1%
H   **C**
F   **D**   7%
16%   3%   **G**   6%   5% **E**   20%

A Alimentari
   Foodstuffs

B Tabacco
   Tobacco

C Abbigliamento
   Clothing

D Abitazione
   Housing

E Combustibili
   Energy

F Mobili
   Furnishings

G Sanità
   Health

H Trasporti
   Transport

I Istruzione
   Education

J Altre spese
   Other expenditure

Table 11. Continued

REGIONI REGION	Alimentari Foodstuffs	Tabacchi Tobacco	Abbigliamento Clothing	Abitazione Housing	Combustibili Energy	Mobili Furnishings	Sanità Health	Trasporti Transport	Istruzione Education	Altre spese Other expenditure
	COMPOSIZIONE PERCENTUALE - *PERCENTAGE COMPOSITION*									
Piemonte	20,0	1,1	6,5	18,6	5,9	6,5	3,0	17,7	7,0	13,5
Valle d'Aosta	21,4	1,1	6,3	17,3	6,0	7,0	3,2	16,0	7,4	14,4
Lombardia	18,7	1,1	6,9	20,0	4,8	6,2	3,2	17,3	6,7	15,2
Trentino-Alto Adige	19,7	0,9	7,6	17,8	5,1	6,8	3,0	16,3	7,9	14,8
Bolzano-Bozen	19,8	0,9	8,3	19,7	3,9	6,9	2,8	14,5	7,9	15,3
Trento	19,5	0,9	7,0	16,3	6,2	6,7	3,1	17,9	8,0	14,3
Veneto	19,2	0,8	7,1	17,6	5,8	7,4	3,4	16,9	7,0	14,7
Friuli-Venezia Giulia	20,8	1,0	6,5	17,7	5,2	5,3	3,9	16,0	7,7	15,8
Liguria	23,1	1,3	6,0	21,3	4,2	6,0	3,8	13,1	7,6	13,6
Emilia-Romagna	19,2	1,1	6,8	19,5	4,9	6,1	3,1	17,0	6,9	15,3
Toscana	21,1	1,1	6,8	19,5	4,8	6,3	3,6	16,3	6,8	13,5
Umbria	21,8	1,2	7,4	19,5	5,1	5,6	2,4	18,2	6,1	12,5
Marche	22,5	1,2	8,1	15,4	5,7	5,7	2,6	16,0	7,0	15,8
Lazio	21,1	1,5	6,6	22,9	4,4	5,9	2,6	15,4	6,6	13,0
Abruzzo	23,9	1,5	7,7	19,7	5,4	5,7	2,5	14,3	5,6	13,7
Molise	25,2	1,5	8,3	17,2	4,7	7,2	2,2	15,4	5,8	12,5
Campania	27,8	1,8	6,5	21,8	4,3	5,1	2,8	14,1	5,3	10,5
Puglia	26,1	1,4	8,3	17,9	4,2	6,8	2,1	14,6	5,6	12,9
Basilicata	24,1	1,9	7,9	18,0	5,3	5,2	2,1	17,3	5,5	12,7
Calabria	26,6	1,3	7,8	15,1	4,5	6,1	2,9	17,6	6,1	12,1
Sicilia	26,3	1,9	7,5	20,3	3,5	6,3	2,6	14,5	5,4	11,7
Sardegna	26,6	1,4	6,9	18,8	4,3	6,5	2,3	16,0	5,8	11,4
ITALIA	**21,7**	**1,3**	**7,0**	**19,5**	**4,8**	**6,2**	**3,0**	**16,2**	**6,5**	**13,7**
NORD-CENTRO	**20,0**	**1,1**	**6,8**	**19,6**	**5,1**	**6,3**	**3,2**	**16,7**	**6,9**	**14,4**
MEZZOGIORNO	**26,5**	**1,6**	**7,4**	**19,4**	**4,2**	**6,1**	**2,5**	**14,9**	**5,5**	**11,8**

(a) I dati riportati nel presente fascicolo rappresentano taluni risultati delle rilevazioni mensili sui consumi delle famiglie effettuate dall'Istituto Nazionale di Statistica nell'anno 1994. Risultati piu' analitici sono reperibili nella Collana d'informazione: "I consumi delle famiglie - Anno 1994". La raccolta delle informazioni avviene sia attraverso un "libretto" sul quale le famiglie-campione annotano le spese alimentari e quelle non alimentari a carattere corrente per un periodo di 10 giorni in ciascun mese di riferimento, sia attraverso un "riepilogo" nel quale per intervista vengono riportate le spese per beni e servizi di particolare entità, sostenute nell'intero mese. Nel corso del 1994 all'indagine hanno effettivamente partecipato circa 36.000 famiglie previste nel campione teorico. - *a) The data shown in the current table represent the results of several monthly surveys of household consumption done by the National Statistical Institute in 1994. The more analytical results are found in the information Series: "Household consumption - 1994". Collection of information is carried out both through a "booklet", in which the sample households record food and non-food expenditures for a period of 10 days for each reference month, and through a "summary" interview, in which expenditures for goods and services of a particular amount during the whole month are recorded. During the 1994 survey 36,000 families actually participated.*

Table 12. Imports and exports—Year 1994 (values in millions of lire) (a)

RIPARTIZIONI E REGIONI *DIVISION AND REGION*	IMPORTAZIONI *IMPORTS*			ESPORTAZIONI *EXPORTS*		
	Valore *Value*	% *%*		Valore *Value*	% *%*	Saldo *Balance*
Piemonte	29.130.118	10,69		40.138.343	13,03	+11.008.225
Valle d'Aosta	335.299	0,12		437.267	0,14	+101.968
Lombardia	102.134.663	37,50		93.362.027	30,31	-8.772.636
Liguria	6.048.070	2,22		5.794.127	1,88	-253.943
Trentino- Alto Adige	4.520.297	1,66		5.616.483	1,82	+1.096.186
Bolzano-Bozen	*2.972.010*	*1,09*		*3.171.130*	*1,03*	*+199.12(*
Trento	*1.548.290*	*0,57*		*2.445.354*	*0,79*	*+897.06(*
Veneto	30.019.448	11,02		42.358.751	13,75	+12.339.303
Friuli - Venezia Giulia	4.810.830	1,77		10.055.287	3,26	+5.244.457
Emilia - Romagna	17.735.101	6,51		34.120.860	11,08	+16.385.759
Toscana	16.792.807	6,17		25.852.106	8,39	+9.059.299
Umbria	1.604.512	0,59		2.530.723	0,82	+926.21
Marche	3.309.651	1,22		8.848.803	2,87	+5.539.15:
Lazio	22.226.551	8,16		11.771.795	3,82	-10.454.75(
Abruzzo	2.994.487	1,10		4.091.559	1,33	+1.097.07:
Molise	320.675	0,12		474.169	0,15	+153.49
Campania	8.389.543	3,08		7.979.930	2,59	-409.61:
Puglia	5.358.936	1,97		6.747.692	2,19	+1.388.75(
Basilicata	343.157	0,13		550.192	0,18	+207,03(
Calabria	553.889	0,20		308.935	0,10	-244.95
Sicilia	9.812.725	3,60		4.284.607	1,39	-5.528.11.
Sardegna	4.385.105	1,61		2.380.867	0,77	-2.004.23
PROVINCE DIVERSE NON SPECIFICATE - *VARIOUS UNSPECIFIED MOVEMENTS*	1.555.789	0,57		341.104	0,11	-1.214.68
ITALIA	**272.381.647**	**100,00**		**308.045.632**	**100,00**	**+35.663.98**
NORD-CENTRO	**238.667.347**	**87,62**		**280.886.575**	**91,18**	**+42.219.22**
MEZZOGIORNO	**32.158.513**	**11,81**		**26.817.950**	**8,71**	**-5.340.56**

(a) Gli arrotondamenti delle cifre sono effettuati direttamente dal computer, pertanto non sempre si trova realizzata la quadratura verticale
(a) The figures were rounded directly by computer so that vertical quadratures are not always found.

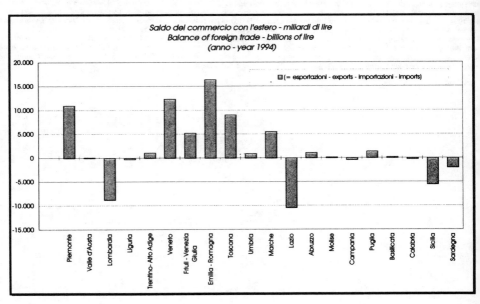

Saldo del commercio con l'estero - miliardi di lire
Balance of foreign trade - billions of lire
(anno - *year* 1994)

Table 13. Censed population from 1861 to 1991 by sex (a) (absolute data in thousand)

CENSIMENTI / CENSUS	POPOLAZIONE RESIDENTE CONFINI ATTUALI / RESIDENT POPULATION WITHIN CURRENT NATIONAL TERRITORY				Popolazione presente / Population present
	Maschi / Males	Femmine / Females	Totale / Total	Incremento medio annuo per 1.000 (a) / Average annual increment per 1,000 (a)	
31.12.1861	13.399	12.929	26.328	-	25.756
31.12.1871	14.316	13.835	28.151	6,7	27.578
31.12.1881	15.134	14.657	29.791	5,7	29.278
10.02.1901	16.990	16.788	33.778	6,6	33.370
10.06.1911	18.608	18.313	36.921	8,6	35.695
1.12.1921	18.814	19.042	37.856	2,4	37.404
21.04.1931	20.181	20.862	41.043	8,6	40.582
21.04.1936	20.826	21.573	42.399	6,5	42.303
4.11.1951	23.259	24.257	47.516	7,4	47.159
15.10.1961	24.784	25.840	50.624	6,4	49.904
24.10.1971	26.476	27.661	54.137	6,7	53.745
25.10.1981	27.506	29.051	56.557	4,4	56.336
20.10.1991	27.558	29.220	56.778	0,4	56.765

(a) Il tasso di incremento è calcolato in base alla formula dell'interesse composto, prendendo come intervallo di tempo quello intercorrente tra le date dei vari censimenti. - *(a) The rate of increase was calculated using the compound interest formula and taking the time interval as that between dates of the various censuses.*

Table 14. Average annual consumption per inhabitant of certain foodstuffs (a) (quantities in kil unless stated otherwise)

ANNI YEAR	Frumento Wheat	CEREALI CEREALS		Patate Potatoes	PRODOTTI ORTOFRUTTICOLI FRUIT & VEGETABLES			CARNI MEAT			Latte Milk	ALTRI OTHER		
		Granoturco Maize	Risone Rice		Pomodori Tomatoes	Frutta fresca Fresh fruit	Agrumi Citrus fruit	Bovina Beef	Suina Pork	Altra Other		Olio di oliva Olive oil	Zucchero Sugar	Vino (litri Win (litres
1901-10	146,9	32,8	13,3	34,0	18,1	25,2	11,2	5,7	4,4	4,5	34,0	5,4	3,3	119,
1911-20	154,9	27,9	15,1	25,7	20,6	30,6	14,2	7,7	5,4	5,2	32,5	4,5	4,6	112,
1921-30	180,3	31,4	10,4	30,1	20,8	30,8	9,8	9,8	5,3	5,6	35,5	6,6	7,9	112,
1931-40	165,4	31,2	12,2	38,1	15,9	26,4	10,2	9,0	5,3	6,1	38,1	5,9	7,5	88,
1941-50	139,1	19,7	10,9	34,3	17,6	30,5	9,5	5,3	3,4	4,9	36,2	3,9	7,7	74,
1951-60	159,3	9,4	9,0	38,3	20,1	52,5	11,4	9,7	5,8	6,8	54,2	6,1	16,7	99,
1961	159,6	8,2	8,0	46,4	26,8	76,3	14,0	14,0	6,4	10,3	61,6	9,0	22,3	108,
1962	161,3	8,0	7,8	41,6	27,9	79,5	14,7	15,6	6,8	11,4	60,5	9,8	22,8	108,
1963	162,5	6,6	8,1	47,9	30,2	88,0	16,8	17,8	6,6	12,3	61,1	9,9	24,0	107,
1964	163,6	5,2	7,9	47,7	25,2	89,9	19,0	17,3	7,7	13,4	61,2	10,1	24,9	103,
1965	164,7	5,0	7,8	42,3	37,1	87,2	20,1	17,3	7,8	15,3	63,4	9,7	24,5	110,
1966	165,8	4,9	7,5	42,5	40,4	91,6	22,7	20,4	7,7	16,1	67,7	9,4	25,0	110,
1967	168,0	4,8	7,0	43,0	37,5	90,9	25,8	22,5	8,6	16,1	68,3	8,9	25,7	111,
1968	171,0	4,8	6,4	44,7	39,4	89,6	29,6	22,5	9,4	16,2	67,6	9,1	25,7	116,
1969	172,0	4,9	6,0	46,1	48,9	84,7	32,1	23,5	9,3	17,5	65,8	9,6	27,1	114,
1970	173,3	4,9	5,9	45,1	47,2	87,5	32,5	24,8	10,7	18,7	66,8	10,6	27,6	113,
1971	174,2	4,9	6,0	41,4	41,8	85,1	34,2	25,2	11,9	19,8	69,5	11,2	27,6	112,
1972	176,3	4,9	6,0	37,7	31,5	75,9	32,1	24,3	12,4	21,0	72,6	11,8	29,6	110,
1973	178,4	5,1	6,2	37,0	41,6	73,6	33,3	26,0	13,4	22,7	72,7	12,2	31,4	109,
1974	179,1	5,1	6,2	41,0	37,7	74,4	37,0	24,5	14,7	23,6	72,9	12,2	32,1	109,
1975	174,1	4,5	6,2	43,1	46,7	73,2	37,5	22,4	15,5	24,4	73,3	11,5	26,1	104,
1976	172,5	4,1	6,1	42,0	46,1	74,3	34,0	23,0	16,1	25,2	75,1	11,0	29,0	98,
1977	171,6	3,5	6,0	43,8	48,9	73,7	35,2	23,1	16,8	25,7	78,1	10,1	28,2	94,
1978	171,0	3,5	6,5	41,6	48,7	76,6	34,5	24,1	18,7	26,6	80,8	10,1	29,0	94,
1979	169,3	3,4	7,2	44,6	48,1	77,2	34,6	24,5	19,5	27,2	82,2	10,0	30,2	93,
1980	170,7	3,4	6,8	43,7	52,7	79,7	35,6	25,5	21,1	28,0	82,7	10,4	31,0	90,
1981	168,7	-	6,8	43,4	49,8	74,9	35,8	25,2	21,2	27,7	83,5	10,6	30,9	86,
1982	166,1	-	6,9	43,3	50,6	77,4	36,8	25,1	21,1	28,1	84,5	10,4	28,4	81,
1983	165,0	-	7,0	43,8	52,4	80,6	37,3	25,4	22,6	28,4	84,5	10,5	27,5	82,
1984	163,3	-	6,6	41,3	55,0	78,4	37,4	25,2	23,7	28,2	84,6	10,8	26,6	80,
1985	163,3	-	6,3	41,3	57,8	75,4	38,2	25,1	23,7	28,2	84,6	11,3	24,8	74,
1986	163,5	-	6,2	42,8	58,3	82,3	39,0	25,5	24,1	29,5	84,4	11,6	25,2	68,
1987	163,0	-	6,3	42,2	57,5	81,4	37,1	26,2	25,1	28,8	84,6	11,8	25,2	64,
1988	162,2	-	6,4	42,3	58,6	83,9	39,2	26,3	25,5	29,7	83,5	11,8	25,5	62
1989	160,6	-	6,8	42,7	61,2	87,8	41,3	26,9	26,3	29,9	81,6	11,9	26,2	62,
1990	162,0	-	7,5	42,3	63,4	86,5	42,9	26,6	27,0	30,1	81,2	11,9	26,5	61,
1991	162,8	-	7,1	42,0	65,1	87,7	45,1	26,4	27,4	30,5	82,2	12,1	26,7	61,
1992	160,1	-	8,0	45,2	57,6	107,2	50,8	25,9	28,8	31,0	82,5	11,2	26,9	60,
1993	155,8	-	8,3	42,9	57,1	157,7	55,0	22,1	27,4	29,3	79,9	12,6	26,7	57,

(a) I dati della presente tavola, elaborati sulla base dei Bilanci alimentari che esprimono i consumi complessivi della popolazion riguardano i soli "consumi domestici" rilevati attraverso l'indagine campionaria dei bilanci di famiglia. - *(a) Data in this table are based o overall consumption of the population as opposed to the "domestic consumption" referred to in the sampling survey of household budget*

Table 15. Area, population, natural population changes—Average life expectancy at birth—Year 1993, unless otherwise indicated (areas in thousands of Km², population in thousands of inhabitants)

PAESI	Superficie	Popola- zione (c)	Densità abit. km²	MOVIMENTO NATURALE DELLA POPOLAZIONE (a) NATURAL POPULATION CHANGES (a)			Mortalità infantile (d)	VITA MEDIA ALLA NASCITA IN ANNI (b) AVERAGE LIFE XPECTANCY AT BIRTH (b)		COUNTRIES
				Nati vivi	Morti	Saldo tra nati vivi e morti		M	F	
	Area	Popula- tion (c)	Popula- tion density per Km²	Live births	Deaths	Balance between live births and deaths	Infant mortality (d)	M	F	COUNTRIES
				UE - EEC						
Danimarca	43	5.189	120	13,0	12,1	0,9	5,7	72,2	77,7	Denmark
Irlanda	70	3.563	51	14,0	8,6	5,4	6,0	71,0	76,7	Ireland
Regno Unito	244	58.191	238	13,5	10,9	2,6	6,6	(e) 73,5	(e) 79,1	Great Britain
Paesi Bassi	41	15.298	375	12,8	9,0	3,8	6,3	74,2	80,2	Netherlands
Belgio	31	10.010	328	12,1	10,8	1,3	8,0	72,4	79,1	Belgium
Lussemburgo	3	380	147	13,2	9,7	3,5	8,5	70,6	77,9	Luxembourg
Germania	357	81.187	228	9,7	11,0	-1,3	6,2	71,8	78,4	Germany
Francia	552	57.379	104	12,3	9,2	3,1	7,3	72,9	81,1	France
Italia	301	57.049	190	9,4	9,5	-0,1	7,4	73,8	80,4	Italy
Grecia	132	10.305	78	10,0	9,4	0,6	8,5	72,1	76,4	Greece
Spagna	506	39.141	77	9,9	8,7	1,2	7,6	73,4	80,5	Spain
Portogallo	92	9.864	107	11,5	10,8	0,7	8,7	70,1	77,2	Portugal
				ALTRI PAESI - OTHER COUNTRIES						
Austria	84	7.988	95	11,8	10,3	1,5	6,5	72,9	79,4	Austria
Bulgaria	111	8.472	76	10,0	12,9	-2,9	15,5	68,1	74,8	Bulgaria
Repubblica Ceca	79	10.328	131	11,7	11,5	0,2	8,5	67,2	75,8	Czech Republic
Finlandia	338	5.067	15	12,8	10,1	2,7	4,4	70,9	78,9	Finland
Jugoslavia	102	10.485	103	13,4	10,0	3,4	18,4	69,5	74,5	Yugoslavia
Norvegia	324	4.312	13	13,7	10,7	3,0	6,2	74,2	80,3	Norway
Polonia	323	38.505	119	12,8	10,2	2,6	13,4	66,1	75,3	Poland
Romania	238	22.755	95	10,9	11,6	-0,7	23,4	66,6	73,2	Rumania
Svezia	450	8.712	19	13,5	10,9	2,6	4,8	75,4	80,8	Sweden
Svizzera	41	6.938	168	12,1	9,1	3,0	6,2	74,3	81,2	Switzerland
Ungheria	93	10.294	111	11,3	14,4	-3,1	13,3	64,6	73,7	Hungary
Australia	7.713	17.661	2	15,1	7,1	8,0	7,0	74,5	80,4	Australia
Canada	9.971	28.755	3	13,8	7,0	6,8	6,8	73,0	79,8	Canada
Giappone	378	123.653	327	9,7	6,9	2,8	4,5	76,1	82,2	Japan
Federaz. Russa	17.075	147.760	9	10,7	12,2	-1,5	18,4	62,0	73,8	Russian Federation
USA	9.364	258.233	28	15,9	8,5	7,4	8,5	72,0	78,9	USA

(a) Quozienti per 1.000 abitanti. - (b) La vita media alla nascita indica il numero di anni di vita che spettano mediamente ad un nato vivo. I dati si riferiscono ad anni compresi tra il 1980 e il 1993, tranne nel caso della Romania in cui il periodo di riferimento è il 1976-78. - (c) Stime a metà anno. - (d) Morti nel primo anno di vita per 1.000 nati vivi. Alcuni Paesi nel determinare il quoziente di mortalità infantile escludono dal calcolo i bambini nati vivi ma morti prima della registrazione, riducendo in tal modo sensibilmente il valore del quoziente. - (e) Inghilterra e Galles. - *(a) Rate per 1,000 inhabitants. - (b) Average life expectancy at birth indicates the average number of years of life that can be expected for a live born infant. Data refer to years between 1980 and 1993 except for the case of Rumania where the reference period is 1976-1978. - (c) Mid-year estimates. - (d) Deaths in the first year of life per 1,000 live births. Certain countries determine the rate of infant mortality excluding from the calculation infants born alive which die before being registered, this significantly reduces the rate. - (e) England and Wales.*

Index

Studies in Modern European History

The monographs in this series focus upon aspects of the political, social, economic, cultural, and religious history of Europe from the Renaissance to the present. Emphasis is placed on the states of Western Europe, especially Great Britain, France, Italy, and Germany. While some of the volumes treat internal developments, others deal with movements such as liberalism, socialism, and industrialization, which transcend a particular country.

The series editor is:

Frank J. Coppa
Director, Doctor of Arts Program
in Modern World History
Department of History
St. John's University
Jamaica, New York 11439